KIRÁLY ZSOLT

BLACKBIRD

ELŐKÉSZÍTŐ TANFOLYAM
A „C" TÍPUSÚ
KÖZÉPFOKÚ ANGOL NYELVVIZSGÁRA

For Brian with
my deepest gratitude

from
Zsolt

Budapest,
6 August 1998

KIRÁLY ZSOLT

BLACK-BIRD

ELŐKÉSZÍTŐ TANFOLYAM A „C" TÍPUSÚ KÖZÉPFOKÚ ANGOL NYELVVIZSGÁRA

1828

AKADÉMIAI KIADÓ

1998

Lektorálta: Christopher Ryan és Róna Annamária
Illusztráció: Szűcs Édua
Szerkesztő: Horváth Balázs

Hangfelvétel: Posta Pál
Kazettasokszorosítás: MC&CD Hangfelvétel Sokszorosító Kft.

ISSN 1418-0405
ISBN 963 05 5727 2
Kiadja az Akadémiai Kiadó Rt.
1117 Budapest, Prielle Kornélia u. 19–35.

Első kiadás: 1998

Printed in Hungary

Thanks

First of all, I'd like to say how grateful I am to:

the proofreaders, CHRISTOPHER RYAN and BRIAN MAGUIRE, for their patience, support, continual advice and encouragement throughout my work on the book.

Thanks very much also to:

SZŰCS ÉDUA for lending her genius to a project like this;

RÓNA ANNAMÁRIA for her help with the bilingual aspects of the book;

FEKETE HAJNAL, Chief Examiner at "Rigó utca", for her kind help with exam-related issues;

my students at the EURÓPAI NYELVEK STÚDIÓJA LANGUAGE SCHOOL in Budapest for their enthusiastic cooperation in the development of the materials which form this book;

RÁKI VIVIEN for planting the idea of the project in my mind;

HUDÁK ILONA for her help with my first steps in getting the thing off the ground;

LÁDONYI JÁNOS for the photos he took for me in the US;

all the teachers who used the pilot editions of the book with their classes and contributed detailed comments on them;

CAROLINE BODÓCZKY, ROBERT DAWSON, PETER DOHERTY, MARION MERRICK, CHRISTOPHER RYAN, ELIZABETH SZÁSZ, and KIM WILLCOCKS for lending their voices to the audio recording;

the staff at Akadémiai Kiadó, and especially VINCZE KATALIN and HORVÁTH BALÁZS for their thorough and considerate management of the project;

and last, but by no means least, ILDIKÓ, BALÁZS and BÁLINT for putting up with it all.

For my students, present and past.

THE MAP OF THE BOOK

UNIT	TITLE	TOPIC AREAS	GRAMMAR FOCUS	FUNCTIONS	WRITING TASK
Introduction	**Personal Particulars**	personal particulars, personal history			
1.	**Family Background**	family life, appearance	the Articles	introduction, asking for permission, suggesting, expressing surprise, saying you don't know	composition
2.	**Education**	schools, subjects and lessons, teachers and students, higher education	the Present and the Past	offering help, asking for information, hesitating, giving advice, thanking	informal letter
3.	**Making a Living**	employment, payment, working conditions, trades, professions, unemployment	the Perfect Tenses	asking for opinion, saying you can't do sg, saying you like an idea, thanking, responding to thanks	formal letter
4.	**A Place to Live**	villages, towns, cities, houses and flats, neighbourhood, furnishings	talking about the future	asking for advice, giving advice, expressing surprise, reminding	formal letter
Revision	**Test 1**	revision of topics in Units 1–4	revision of Units 1–4 and additional structures		
5.	**Daily Life**	daily routine, managing the household, chores	Auxiliaries 1	asking sy to do a favour, responding to ~, suggesting, refusing a suggestion, thanking, responding to ~	formal letter
6.	**Leisure and Pleasure**	reading, radio, television, cinema, theatre, music	Auxiliaries 2, Conditionals, I wish …	complaining, saying you are not satisfied, finding the problem, apologising, responding to an apology	formal letter
7.	**Sport and Hobbies**	sporting activities, sports and games, events and participants, hobbies	Auxiliaries 3	greetings, asking how sy is, saying how you are, asking if anything is wrong, suggesting, saying goodbye	composition
8.	**Weather and Clothes**	weather and clothing	Reported Speech, the Sequence of Tenses	greetings, expressing anger, saying you made a mistake, offering sg, accepting sg, complimenting	informal letter
Revision	**Test 2**	revision of topics in Units 5–8	revision of Units 5–8 and additional structures		
9.	**Shops and Goods**	shopping for food, foodstuffs, healthy eating, shopping for other articles	Relative Clauses	asking sy to do a favour, responding to ~, asking for details, giving information, thanking	composition
10.	**A Picture of Health**	parts of the body, symptoms, diseases, treatment, health service	the Gerund	giving information, asking for advice, giving advice, asking about price	composition
11.	**Transport and Travelling**	cars, public transport, trains, coaches, air travel, holidays, going abroad, accommodation	the Infinitive	saying what you want, saying you don't like an idea, persuading, giving reasons, suggesting	formal letter
12.	**The World We Live In**	crime, environment, social problems, politics, religion	the Gerund or the Infinitive?, the Participles	requesting, asking sy to do sg, offering to do sg, apologising, refusing an offer	composition
Revision	**Test 3**	revision of topics in Units 9–12	revision of Units 9–12 and additional structures		
Mock Exam	**Oral Exam Written Exam**	home, neighbourhood, transport	miscellaneous	saying what you want, protesting, suggesting, explaining, complaining	informal letter and composition
First Aid Kit 1	**Letter Writing**				
First Aid Kit 2	**Functions**				
First Aid Kit 3	**Link Words**				
First Aid Kit 4	**Pronunciation Dictionary**				

Bevezető

A galambtól eltekintve aligha van Magyarországon még egy olyan madár, amelyet annyit és úgy emlegetnek mint a rigót, ráadásul többnyire igazságtalanul, mert – szemben a galambbal – a RIGÓ-val kapcsolatos kínos meglepetések jó hatásfokkal elkerülhetők.

Mindenekelőtt: ez az esemény nem váratlanul éri az embert, viszonylag pontosan lehet tudni, hogy mikor mire lehet számítani; másrészt: itt az is számít, hogy ki mennyire felkészült. A RIGÓ csak akkor okoz kellemetlenségeket, ha madárnak nézik.

A Blackbird célja az, hogy a középfokú állami nyelvvizsga minden lehetséges buktatójára felkészítse a nyelvtanulót. Természetesen ez elsősorban az alapos nyelvi felkészítést jelenti, de semmiképpen nem csak azt; szükség van magára a vizsgára való felkészítésre is.

Ami a nyelvi felkészítést illeti: a nyelvtudásban benne foglaltatik a nyelv ismerete (szókincs, szituációs kifejezések, nyelvi kötőelemek, nyelvtan, kiejtés, kulturális vonatkozások), valamint a nyelv használatához szükséges készségekben (aktív kommunikációs [beszéd- és írás-] készség, olvasási készség, hallott szöveg megértésének készsége, fordítási készség, a nyelvhasználattal összefüggő társadalmi/kulturális tudatosság) való jártasság is. Sokan buktak meg már azért, mert a felsoroltaknak csak egyes elemeit tudták – mondjuk csak kommunikálni vagy csak a nyelvtant –, márpedig a vizsga a nyelvtudás egészét vizsgálja. Ez egy ilyen vizsga. Nyilvánvaló, hogy a felkészülés során ezekre az összetevőkre mind figyelmet kell fordítani.

Ennek a sokféle ismeretnek és készségnek a mérése megbízhatóan csak sok különböző feladattal oldható meg. A nyelvvizsga állandó feladattípusait (kilenc ilyen van) érdemes külön is gyakorolni, mert az általános nyelvi készségeken kívül itt speciális, csak az adott feladatra jellemző készségekre is szükség lehet. Sokan buktak már meg azért, mert megbíztak a bizonyos szituációkban jól működő angoltudásukban, és arra nem gondoltak, hogy mondjuk a fordításhoz vagy az olvasott szöveg értéséhez egészen más jellegű készségekre is szükség van. Ez egy ilyen vizsga.

Kicsit olyan ez az egész, mint amikor autót vezetni tanul az ember: meg kell ismerni az autó kezelésének elemeit, meg kell tanulni a forgalomban mozogni, és nem árt külön gyakorolni a vizsgán szokásos „rutin" feladatokat sem. Aki mondjuk elég jól elautózgatott vagy elautózgatna a széles és gyér forgalmú utakon Amerikában valahol vidéken, az komoly bajban lehet a budapesti forgalomban, pláne ha a Rigó utcába szeretne eljutni.

A Blackbird szigorú felépítésű könyv, tizenkét nagyjából azonos összetételű Unit-ból áll. Minden Unit egy-egy, a nyelvvizsgán gyakran előforduló témakörre épül, annak nyelvi hátterét dolgozza fel a vizsgán szokásos feladatokhoz hasonló feladatokon keresztül. Fokozatosság jellemzi, a vizsgafeladatokra jellemző összes nyelvi, nyelvhasználati és feladatismereti követelmény a maga teljességében csak a könyv vége felé jelenik meg, egységes, igazi vizsga-formában pedig csak a könyv végén található „próbavizsgában".

Minden Unit négy Lesson-ből áll. Mivel a könyv valamiféle átmenet a hagyományos tankönyv és a munkafüzet között, minden Lesson-höz házi feladat is tartozik.

Egy-egy Unit felépítése többé-kevésbé a túloldalon látható táblázatban megjelenített sémát követi. (A *-gal jelölt feladatok vagy feladatrészek a könyv utolsó harmadában már nem szerepelnek. Minden negyedik Unit után teszt következik, amely az előző négy Unit szókincsére, nyelvtanára, valamint a Unit-okban nem kiemelt egyéb nyelvtani kérdésekre épül.)

LESSON 1

A FELADAT NEVE	A FELADAT JELLEGE
Vocabulary: survival kit	➜ A témakör szókincse, otthoni, szótárral való feldolgozásra.
Speaking: conversation	➜ Beszélgetés a témakörrel kapcsolatban, a legalapvetőbb szókincs felhasználásával.
Speaking: pictures - a-c	➜ A témakörhöz kapcsolódó képek; a feladat lépésenkénti gyakorlása*.
Functions: role-play - a-c	➜ Szituációs szerepjáték feladat; szituációs kifejezések*.
Pronunciation*: sounds & word stress	➜ Magnós gyakorló feladatok: hangok és szóhangsúly.
<u>Homework:</u>	
Vocabulary: survival kit - study task	➜ A témakör szókincsének megtanulása. Gyakorló/ellenőrző feladatok
Grammar focus: preview	➜ A *Unit* kiemelt nyelvtani kérdésének rövid összefoglalása.

LESSON 2

A FELADAT NEVE	A FELADAT JELLEGE
Vocabulary: survival kit - checkpoint a-d	➜ A témakör szókincsének gyakorlása/ellenőrzése kötött írásbeli-szóbeli feladatokkal.
Grammar focus: translation into English	➜ A *Unit* kiemelt nyelvtani kérdésének gyakorlása magyar mondatok fordításával.
Listening	➜ Magnós szövegértési feladat globális és részletes értést vizsgáló feladatokkal.
<u>Homework:</u>	
Translation: English into Hungarian	➜ Egyre hosszabb és igényesebb angol szövegek otthoni fordításra; tanácsok*.

LESSON 3

A FELADAT NEVE	A FELADAT JELLEGE
Translation: English into Hungarian – checkpoint	➜ A HF fordítás közös ellenőrzése feladatok segítségével.
Reading & vocabulary: article(s) - a-c	➜ A témával összefüggő újságcikk(ek), a szókincs és a tartalom szóbeli és írásbeli feldolgozása.
Pronunciation*: stress, rhytm & intonation	➜ Magnós gyakorló feladatok: mondathangsúly és hanglejtés.
Link words*	➜ A folyamatos beszéd/írás kötőelemeit gyakoroltató feladat.
<u>Homework:</u>	
Vocabulary: article(s) - stíudy tasks	➜ A cikk szókincsének megtanulása. Gyakorló/ellenőrző feladat és szempontok az újságcikk tartalmi összefoglalásának gyakorlásához.
Writing: composition	➜ Fogalmazási vagy levélírási feladat egyre kevesebb nyelvi és tartalmi segítséggel.

LESSON 4

A FELADAT NEVE	A FELADAT JELLEGE
Vocabulary: article - checkpoint a-c	➜ A házi feladat ellenőrzése; angol–magyar mondatfordítás a cikk szókincsének gyakorlására/ellenőrzésére; a cikk tartalmának elmondása
Grammar focus: mini test	➜ A *Unit* fő nyelvtani problémájának gyakorlása és elsajátításának ellenőrzése teszttel.
Speaking: discussion a-d	➜ A témakör szókincsének gyakorlása vita-jellegű feladatokon keresztül
<u>Homework:</u>	
Vocabulary: survival kit - preview	➜ A következő *Unit* szókincs-gyűjteményének otthoni feldolgozása
Exam tips	➜ Tanácsok/tájékoztatás a vizsga egyes feladataival kapcsolatban.

A könyv végén található First Aid Kit (függelék) a szituációs kifejezések és a nyelvi kötőelemek összefoglalását tartalmazza, valamint formai és tartalmi segítséget kínál a levélíráshoz. Az összes feladat megoldása és a kazetták szövegkönyve megtalálható a Tanári Kézikönyvben, amely a részletes módszertani útmutatás mellett további tippeket is ad az anyag tanításához.

Ellentétben a nyelvvizsgával, amely számos feladatban a magyar nyelvet használja közvetítő nyelvként (magyar nyelvű válaszok a szövegértési feladatokra, magyar nyelvű instrukciók a szerepjátékhoz), a Blackbird szinte végig az angolt részesíti előnyben, részben mert – akármilyen hihetetlen – ez megkönnyíti a felkészülést, részben pedig azért, hogy több lehetőség legyen az angol nyelv használatára az órákon. Természetesen ez nem vonatkozik a kifejezetten fordítási feladatokra vagy olyan esetekre, ahol valamilyen szempontból előnyösebb lehet a magyar nyelv használata (például az újságcikkek szókincsével kapcsolatosan a könyv első kétharmadában).

Fontos tudni, hogy ezt a könyvet csak mintegy 400–500 órányi angoltanulás (általában a tankönyvsorozatok harmadik kötetének vége) után ajánlatos elkezdeni. Mindenképpen érdemes megcsinálni a Tanári Kézikönyv függelékében található Entry Quicktest-et, amelynek segítségével megállapíthatjuk, hogy tudásszintünk eléri-e a szükséges minimumot.

Aki ezt a könyvet választotta, annak biztos, hogy nagyon sokat kell tanulnia (véletlenül se higgyék el senkinek, hogy lehet Magyarországon komolyan angolt tanulni máshogy is, mint sok tanulással!), de remélem ez a tanulás szórakoztató és élvezetes lesz. Nem beszélve persze a majdani sikeres RIGÓ-vadászatról: állítom, hogy aki ezt a könyvet tisztességesen végigtanulja, annak át kell mennie a vizsgán!

Good luck!
Budapest, 1998. március

KIRÁLY ZSOLT

A KÖVETKEZŐ OLDALAKON LÁTHATÓ KÉT TÁBLÁZAT
A KÖZÉPFOKÚ NYELVVIZSGA ÉS A KÖNYV ÖSSZEFÜGGÉSÉT MUTATJA BE

SZÓBELI VIZSGA

VIZSGAFELADAT	NYELVI TARTALOM	FELKÉSZÍTÉS MÓDJA
irányított interjú (beszélgetés) megadott témakörök alapján	szókincs, nyelvhelyesség, kiejtés, beszédértés, kommunikációs készség, kötőelemek, szituációs kifejezések	*a legfontosabb témakörök áttekintése: Unit-onként egy-két témakör szókincsének feldolgozása, gyakorlása, a szavak elsajátításának ellenőrzése, kommunikatív feladatok; minden negyedik Unit után szókincsellenőrző teszt; kötőelemek áttekintése, begyakorlása, feladatok a kiejtés gyakorlására*
önálló témakifejtés kép(ek) alapján, a témakörökkel összefüggésben	szókincs, nyelvhelyesség, kiejtés, kötőelemek	*a (témakörrel összefüggő) feladat fázisainak fokozatos bevezetése, gyakorlása (képleírás, tippelés, asszociáció egy-egy adott témakörre, saját vélemény, élmény stb.); később a komplex feladat gyakorlása*
szituációs párbeszéd a vizsgáztatóval magyar nyelvű szituációs kártya alapján	szituációs kifejezések, kötőelemek, kiejtés, kommunikációs készség	*a szituációs kifejezések áttekintése, gyakorlása; (a témakörrel összefüggő) szituációk gyakorlása (szerepjáték)*
hallás utáni megértési feladat: magyar nyelvű kérdésekre magyar nyelvű válasz; a feladatlapot az első lejátszás után osztják ki, majd a párbeszédet még kétszer lejátsszák.	beszédértés, szókincs	*(témakörrel összefüggő) hanganyag meghallgatása; első hallgatás után globális értést vizsgáló, második hallgatás után alaposabb megértést igénylő, angol nyelvű kérdésekkel*

A szóbeli vizsga kb. 15 percig tart, felkészülési idő nincs. A magnós feladat megoldása külön, Budapesten fejhallgatóval történik.

ÍRÁSBELI VIZSGA

<table>
<tr><th>VIZSGAFELADAT</th><th>NYELVI TARTALOM</th><th>FELKÉSZÍTÉS MÓDJA</th></tr>
<tr><td>50 feladatból álló, feleletválasztós teszt</td><td>nyelvhelyesség (45 feladat), szókincs (5 feladat)</td><td rowspan="2">a legproblematikusabb nyelvtani kérdések áttekintése (Unit-onként egy kiemelt terület): Unit-onként a témához kapcsolódó tíz feladatos miniteszt és példamondatok fordítása, angol nyelvű nyelvtani összefoglaló; minden negyedik Unit után 40 feladatos teszt ismétlő és az egyes Unit-okban nem érintett nyelvtani kérdéseket tartalmazó feladatokkal</td></tr>
<tr><td>magyarról angolra fordítás</td><td>nyelvhelyesség (nyelvtan)</td></tr>
<tr><td>fogalmazás/levél magyar nyelvű irányító kérdések alapján a témakörökkel összefüggésben</td><td>íráskészség, kifejezőkészség, nyelvhelyesség, kötőelemek, helyesírás</td><td>a fogalmazás lépéseinek áttekintése; a levélírás formai követelményeinek áttekintése; levélben használatos nyelvi fordulatok gyakorlása; egyre komplexebb, a témakörhöz kapcsolódó feladatok, angol, majd a könyv legvégén magyar nyelvű irányító kérdésekkel (házi feladat), valamint fokozatosan egyre kevesebb tartalmi és nyelvi támogatással</td></tr>
<tr><td>angolról magyarra fordítás</td><td>szókincs, olvasás- és fordításkészség</td><td>egyre igényesebb fordítási feladatok (házi feladat), közös ellenőrzés; kapcsolódó feladatok</td></tr>
<tr><td>olvasott szöveg értését ellenőrző feladat: újságcikk(ek)re magyar nyelvű kérdések, magyar nyelvű válaszokkal</td><td>olvasáskészség, szókincs</td><td>(egyre hosszabb és nehezebb) újságcikkek feldolgozása: első olvasás után globális értést ellenőrző, majd alaposabb megértést vizsgáló, angol nyelvű kérdések/ feladatok; kapcsolódó szókinccsel összefüggő feladatok (az új szavak visszakeresése a szövegben, eleinte magyar, majd angol nyelvű definíciók segítségével); a szókincs elsajátításának ellenőrzése; a cikkek szóbeli tartalmi összefoglalása

gyakorlati tanácsok az egyes feladattípusokhoz minden Unit-ban

a könyv végén egy teljes próbavizsga</td></tr>
</table>

A tesztre 30 perc áll rendelkezésre, a többi feladatra összesen 3 óra. A teszt kivételével szótár használható.

INTRODUCTION
Personal particulars

SPEAKING
conversation

Working in pairs, find out about each other's background, habits, plans, likes and dislikes. Take notes to make sure you remember your partner's personal particulars, as it will be your job to introduce her/him to the rest of the class.

First name: ______

Family name: ______

Age: ______

Immediate family: ______

Address: ______

School/Profession/Job: ______

Qualifications: ______

Special/Leisure interests: ______

Other languages: ______

Previous English studies: ______

Plans for the near/distant future: ______

Good/Bad habits (if any):

HOMEWORK

VOCABULARY
survival kit
study task

Use the following guidelines (and a dictionary if necessary) to prepare for a fluent oral presentation about yourself (a kind of an informal CV) which includes the information you shared with the rest of the class last lesson.

CURRICULUM VITAE/RESUME (AmE)

I was born on 17 May 1960. (Read: *on the seventeenth of May, 1960)*
I was born on May 17, 1960. (Read: *on May the seventeenth, 1960)*
I grew up in …
*I was brought up/raised by …**
As my mother went out to work I went to a crèche/day nursery\nursery school.
I had a wonderful\terrible\interesting\exciting childhood.
I started school in …
I went to the X Street primary school.
I left primary school in …
*I went on to the … secondary school/high school [AmE].***
I left\I am leaving secondary school in …/I graduated\I am graduating from high school in … [AmE]
I applied\I'd like to apply for admission to the university\college of …
I was admitted to …
I study\I'd like to study …/I read\I'd like to read … [BrE]/I am majoring in …\I majored in … [AmE]
I graduated from university\college in …
I got a degree in …
I did two years national/military service.
I started learning English in …
I took up a job as a …
I started working for …
I work for … as a …
I make/earn a living as a …/
by …-ing.
I got married\divorced in …
I am married\single\divorced.
I have two kids, …

I live in a small town in the west of Hungary, in Kőszeg, in the county of Vas.
I live at 10 Baross utca, in the eighth district of Budapest.
I live with my parents\I live in digs\I share a flat with ...\I rent a flat.
In my free time I like ...-ing/What I really like is ...-ing/What I like most in life is ...-ing.

---

* The symbol / means *synonyms* or *variants*, and the symbol \ refers to *alternatives* in this book.
**This book focuses on British English *[BrE]*, but it also mentions the American English equivalent *[AmE]* when there is a very important difference between the British and American usage.

VOCABULARY survival kit preview

Read through the new vocabulary list on page 17-18, and consult a dictionary if you come across something that is unfamiliar or unclear to you.

UNIT 1
Family background

LESSON 1

SPEAKING
conversation

In small groups of three or four, take turns to talk about your personal history.

VOCABULARY
survival kit

Names
first/Christian\family\full\maiden name, nickname

Relatives
(natural) parents, a step\foster mother\father close\distant relatives/relations on our mother's\ father's side
an only child, brothers and sisters, a twin\step sister, grandparents, cousin, aunt, uncle, nephew, niece, God-mother, the in-laws

Marital status
single, unmarried, married (to sy), divorced, separated, bachelor, widow\widower
to go out with sy, to live/co-habit with sy, co-habitation, to split up

Marriage
a girl\boyfriend, a fiancée, a fiancé, a spouse, a/an (ex\future) husband/hubby or wife
wedding, bride, (bride)groom, honeymoon
to marry\divorce sy, to get engaged\married\divorced, to separate from sy
a broken home/marriage, one/single-parent family

Kids
to be pregnant, pregnancy, to be on maternity leave, to bring up/raise/rear children, to be childless

Age
child, baby, toddler, kid, adolescent / teenager, young person\lady\man, adult/grown-up, middle-aged\elderly person\lady\man,

pensioner, in your early\mid\late teens\twenties\30s

Appearance

to have fair\pale\dark\good complexion, suntan

blond/fair\brown\red\black\grey\short\long\straight\wavy\curly\dyed\thick\thinning hair, in a ponytail\bun, combed back\to the side, bald(ing), beard, moustache

a round\long\oval face; a high\low forehead; ordinary\big\snub nose; thin\thick lips

to have a good figure, broad shoulders, short/small tall/big, medium/average height, thin, skinny, fat, chubby, plump, strong, well-built, pretty, good-looking, handsome, (rather) plain, ordinary-looking, well/smartly\ shabbily dressed, to wear glasses, elegant\casual clothes

Making ends meet

to live/get by on 20,000 a month\unemployment benefit\our salary

family budget, income: basic earnings + extras, outgoings: bills, mortgage, installments

to get/receive child benefit/family allowance, the three-year child care allowance system

to get/receive alimony, maintenance *[BrE]*/child support *[AmE]*

SPEAKING conversation

Use the following guidelines to tell your partner about yourself.

parents → (brothers\sisters) → grandparents → (wife\husband) → (kids) → future plans [family]

Agree with your partner which one of you has picture A and B, and then cover up your partner's picture in your book.

SPEAKING pictures

a Make sure you know what the following adverbials and prepositions mean, and then discuss with the class what other vocabulary you might need to describe your picture.

in the picture, in picture A, in the foreground\background, in the middle, on the right (hand side of the picture), at the top\bottom, in the top\bottom left hand corner, near, next to, beside, above, under(neath), behind, in front of, opposite, across from, (in) between, along

Verbs:	Nouns:	Adjectives:

b Working silently, use the following structures to practise describing your picture.

This picture/drawing/cartoon shows a …
In this picture/drawing/cartoon …
This is a picture/drawing/cartoon of …
There's\There're …
I can see …
The … is\are …-ing.

c Working with a partner, take turns to describe your pictures so that you can find the differences.

1. ....
2. ....
3. ....
4. ....
5. ....
6. ....
7. ....

8. ....

9. ....

10. ....

11. ....

FUNCTIONS
role-play

a Read both role-cards, and agree with your partner who's A and who's B.

A The person sitting next to you looks a bit familiar to you, but you have no idea where you saw her/him.

- Turn to the person, introduce yourself, and tell him/her that s/he looks a bit familiar to you, and ask her/him if s/he thinks you have ever met.
- Ask her/him if she wants to find out.
- Give realistic answers to her/his questions.
  Ask her/him if s/he ...
  - does any of your out-of-school/work activities (sporting activities, clubs, discos, church, holidays, etc.).
  - regularly travels on the same buses/trams/ etc. as you do.
  - went to the same primary school as you did.
  - goes/went to the same secondary school as you do/did.
- If you are classmates or colleagues, express your surprise, and just remark that your partner has changed a lot since you last saw her/him.
  If it still seems unlikely that you have ever met, just agree with your partner that this may only be a typical case of déjà vu. Ask her/him if s/he has ever experienced the feeling before.

B The person sitting next to you turns to you, introduces her/himself, and tells you that you look familiar to her/him.

- ♣ Introduce yourself, and tell her/him that s/he looks slightly familiar to you as well, but you have no idea where you might have met.
- ♣ Give true answers to the person's questions. Ask her/her …
  - if s/he does any of your out-of-school/work activities (sporting activities, clubs, discos, church, holidays, etc.).
  - if s/he lives somewhere close to you.
  - what s/he does and where s/he works.
- ♣ If you are classmates or colleagues, show how surprised you are, and just remark that your partner has changed a lot since you last saw her/him.
  If it still seems unlikely that you have ever met, just agree with your partner that this may only be a typical case of déjà vu.

b Agree with the rest of your class how you could use the following phrases in this situation; complete the phrases and answer the questions.* If you think it is necessary, you can also consult the First Aid Kit on functions at the end of the book.

A: ***Excuse me.***

A: ***May I introduce myself: … // Let me introduce myself: … // Hello, I'm …***

B: *How do you do? My name's … // I am … // Hello. My name's …*

A: ***I hope you don't mind my asking // Excuse my asking // Forgive me for asking, but … ?***

B: *Well, actually/as a matter of fact/in fact … // Well, to tell you the truth …*

A: ***Why don't we … ? // Do you think it would be an idea to … ? // Let's … , shall we?***

X: Did/do you … , by any chance? // Didn't you …?

X: No/Yes, actually I … // No, I am afraid I didn't, I … // Practically never. // Very rarely. // Hardly ever. // Occasionally. // Every now and then. // Sometimes. // Once in a blue moon. // Yes, I do/did/am! // Yes, quite often!

X: Really? // What? // Never! // Oh, no! // You must be joking/kidding! // Are you serious? // That is/What a surprise! // Good heavens! // My goodness! // Good Lord! // No, I don't believe it! // Well, I'm blowed/damned! // Well, that's unbelievable/extraordinary!

X: Well, I have no idea … // I haven't got the faintest idea … // Well, as it seems …, // Well, it seems quite unlikely that …

A: ***I wonder if you have ever …?***

*** X means *both* A & B. The symbol / means *synonyms*, and the symbol // means *alternatives* in the given situation.**

c Rehearse the situation with your partner. Read the cards again before starting but try and rely only on the notes below while practising.

introduction ➜ question ➜ the present (school/work/travel/address/activities) ➜ the past (nursery, schools) ➜ surprise/déjà vu

PRONUNCIATION 1

sounds & word stress

Sounds

☞ The English [ɪ], [e], [ʊ], [ʌ] and [ə] sounds are all problematic for Hungarian speakers. To improve your pronunciation, pay attention to the following:

[ɪ] is a very short sound somewhere between the Hungarian *i* and *é* sounds. Give your [ɪ]-s a little *é* flavour.
[e] is a very short sound somewhere between the Hungarian *e* and *é* sounds. Give your [e]-s a little *é* flavour.
[ʊ] is a very short sound somewhere between the Hungarian *u* and *o* sounds. Give your [ʊ]-s a very little *o* flavour.
[ʌ] is like an extremely short Hungarian *á* sound.
[ə] *(schwa)* is the most frequent sound in the English language. It occurs in unstressed syllables of words and in weak forms. It's similar to a Hungarian *ö* sound, but it's much shorter, weaker and it's not rounded.

Listen and repeat.

[ɪ]	[e]	[ʊ]	[ʌ]	[ə]
kiss	bed	foot	bus	sister
lift	pen	book	front	better
pick	best	good	come	cooker
fit	bury	would	done	butter
sit	head	put	son	letter
six	says	wool	won	ever

Word stress

☞ Normally there is one stressed syllable in a word, and the other syllables have a weak pronunciation; the vowel sounds in them lose their clear quality, they become a [ə] (except for unstressed [ɪ] sounds, which can remain an [ɪ]), and they may even disappear completely.

Listen and repeat.

■□	■□□	□■	□■□	□■□□
letter	accident	hotel	November	impossible
travel	usually	address	important	advertisement
certain	gentleman	abroad	policeman	original
backward	bachelor	event	exactly	particular

HOMEWORK

VOCABULARY
survival kit
study task

Study the word list on page 17-18, and memorise the words and phrases that you think are important and relevant to you and your family background. When you have finished, put the following words in their correct places in the passage below to check your knowledge. (You might try and do the task without using the box.)

benefits, budget, wife, child care allowance system, breadwinner, crèche, married, get married, one-parent, bring up, wedding, make ends meet, housewife, get divorced, co-habit

A few decades ago the stereotypical Hungarian family consisted of husband and .... and at least three children. The father was the .... and the head of the family, the mother was a .... and brought up the children. This stereotypical family pattern is dramatically changing now because there are more and more .... families; a lot of people .... and live on their own, and .... their children on their own. In addition, nowadays most women want to go out to work, and even if they have small children they just send them to a .... and go back to work as soon as possible.
Also, people tend to .... later than they used to; more and more people .... for years before the .... It also means that they have their first child later in their .... life. This is one of the reasons why there are fewer and fewer kids in the average family, the other reason, of course, is of a financial nature. Most families have to .... on miserable salaries, and as the three-year .... is collapsing and .... are worth less and less, the family .... simply doesn't allow more children.

GRAMMAR FOCUS
p r e v i e w

The Articles

when speaking about the noun in general

Unlike in Hungarian, **there's no definite article (the)** before
plural countable nouns.
➢ *I like horses.*
uncountable nouns.
➢ *I like milk.*
names of languages.
➢ *I like English, but I like the English language.*
names of colours.
➢ *I like black.*
names of meals, days of the week, months, seasons, holidays and feasts.
➢ *I like spring.*

However, we use the definite article with specific things.
➢ *I like the green in this sweater. The horses in the stable … The water in this bottle …*

In addition, there is no definite article before
the names of streets, squares, parks.
➢ *I live in Albion Street, near Hyde Park.*
before names of sports and school subjects.
➢ *I like football but I hate chemistry.*
before certain institutions: *prison, church, (primary/secondary) school, market, hospital,*
except when we talk about them as buildings or places of employment; + *bed, work, home.*
➢ *She is in hospital again. My grandma goes to market every day. Where do you go to school?* But: *Everything was quiet, there was nobody else in the church but me. I'll be waiting for you outside the school.*
before *last, next, this* in time phrases.
➢ *I saw him last week.*
before names of lakes, peaks.
➢ *I've seen Mount Kilimanjaro, but I've never seen Lake Balaton.*
in the phrase *on TV.*
➢ *What's on TV tonight?*

On the other hand, **there is a definite article** with
morning, afternoon, evening.
➢ *I never watch TV in the morning.*
musical instruments when we (learn how to) play them.
➢ *Can you play the oboe?*
cinema, theatre, opera.
➢ *Why don't we go to the cinema tonight?*
family names when we refer to the whole family.
➢ *The Ewings are wonderful people.*
adjectives as plural nouns.
➢ *The French drink a lot of wine. The rich are becoming richer, and the poor are becoming poorer.*
in the east\west\north\south, on the right\left.

➢ *There will be some rain in the south. Who's this lady on the right?*

to look sy in the eye, to be paid by the hour, on\over the phone, in the country, on the radio.

➢ *I couldn't look him in the eye afterwards, knowing that I had caused a lot of trouble.*

Unlike in Hungarian, **there is no indefinite article (a/an)**

with *information, advice, news, luggage, furniture, work, homework, damage, equipment.*

➢ *Looking after kids is hard work. Let me give you a piece of advice.*

plural nouns like *jeans, trousers, shoes, trainers, glasses, damages.*

➢ *She was wearing blue jeans. We had to pay damages of 2000 forints. I must buy a new pair of glasses.*

However, we **use the indefinite article**

with a person's job or situation, like *a teacher, a pensioner, a widow.*

➢ *My mother's a psychologist.*

before any indefinite countable noun.

➢ *She was wearing a skirt.*

in the structure *What\Such a* + countable noun.

➢ *What a great teacher!*

in *once an hour\year\etc., to be in a hurry, to make a noise, to take a seat, to go for a walk.*

➢ *I do aerobics once a week. Are you in a hurry?*

LESSON 2

VOCABULARY
survival kit
checkpoint

a **Check the fill-in-the-blank homework task with the rest of the class.**

b **What are the "opposites" of the following words and phrases?**

- natural parents
- married
- family name
- tall
- curly
- well-dressed
- income
- close relatives
- a family with two parents
- chubby
- handsome
- dark complexion

c What money is provided to the people in the following situations?

- a divorced person with two kids
- families with children
- an unemployed person
- someone who is too old to work
- a mother who stays home with a baby

d Complete the definitions.

- If you stop going out with someone, you .... with them.
- If you haven't got any children, you are ....
- If the money you earn is not enough for you to pay for the things you need, you can't ....
- If you live together with someone from the opposite sex and you are not married, the two of you ....
- If you are 22, you are in your ....
- If you look after kids until they become grown-ups, you .... them.

e Working in pairs, take turns to describe the different "reincarnations" of the actor in the advertisement.

GRAMMAR FOCUS
translation into English

Translate the following sentences into English, discussing each section with the rest of the class as you progress.

1 A papám orvos. Okos fiú\kislány vagyok. Ez tény.

2 Szereted az állatokat? Úgy sajnálom az állatokat az állatkertben. *(to feel sorry for)*

3 A víz alapvető fontosságú az élethez. *(essential)* A víz a Dunában nagyon szennyezett. *(polluted, Danube)* Nem szeretem a whiskyt. Megkóstoltad már a whiskyt? *(to try)*

4 A szerelem mindennél fontosabb nekem. Nem érdekel a divat, engem a minőség érdekel. Mi az új divat? Csodálatos időnk van ma.

5 A fiam börtönben\kórházban\iskolában\templomban van. Már megint botrány van az iskolában. *(another scandal)*

6 A kedvenc színem a kék. A kék különösen szép ebben a pulóverben. A német nehezebb mint az angol. A magyar nyelv még nehezebb. Alig értem azt az angolt, amit ő beszél. *(hardly)*

7 A tavasz a legvidámabb évszak. *(cheerful)* Soha nem fogom elfelejteni azt a nyarat, amelyet Veled töltöttem. A hétfő a legnehezebb napom. Az ebéd fél kettőkor van.

8 A legtöbb ember szereti a fagyit. A legszebb ünnep a Karácsony. Utálom a kémiát (is).

9 A Filmpalota Budapest legújabb mozija. Az Astória Szállodában laknak. *(to stay at)* A legdrágább üzletek a Váci utcában vannak.

10 A Balaton már drágább mint az Adria. *(Lake Balaton, Adriatic Sea)* A Kékes a Mátra legmagasabb csúcsa. *(Mátra Mountains, peak)*

LISTENING

SOS

An interview with a family counsellor

a Read the question and try to answer it after you have listened to the recording once. Discuss your answer with your partner.

- What background information is there about the members of the family the counsellor talks about?

b Answer the following questions as you listen to the tape for the second time. Discuss your answers with the rest of the class.

- What were the symptoms the little boy's parents and teachers were so worried about?
- How did the little girl behave during the first session?
- What sort of changes did the counsellor make when the family went to see him for the second time?
- What difference did these changes make?
- What was the cause of the boy's problems according to the counsellor?

HOMEWORK

TRANSLATION
English into Hungarian

Use a dictionary to read the following article, and translate the *highlighted* part of the text into Hungarian in writing.

☞ Before you look up a word in the dictionary, decide if the item is a verb (marked *v, vt, vi* or *phr v* in the dictionary), a noun *(n)*, an adjective *(a* or *adj)*, an adverb *(adv)*, etc., because that will help you find a suitable meaning in the context of the text more quickly (e.g. mass, ties in this text).

☞ Be particularly careful with the words and phrases that are underlined in the text below, even more so if you use the *Országh* dictionary. If necessary (and it is almost always necessary), change or modify the Hungarian words so that they really fit into the context of the article. Make sure that the Hungarian text really sounds Hungarian (e.g. promote, intended, around).

70,000 in Moon's Mass Wedding

Days before his wedding, Hana Lee still had not met his future wife. Like hundreds of thousands married today in simultaneous mass ceremonies around the world, he has put his faith in divine guidance.

"I told my bride it was a match intended by God, and that I was so happy," said Lee, 26, who is in the US studying advertising. The matchmaker is the Rev Sun Myong Moon, head of the Unification* Church, which preaches that arranged marriages promote family ties and global peace.

For his 13th mass wedding, Moon and his wife will bless 35,000 couples in a stadium in Seoul, South Korea, surpassing his record of 20,000 in 1992. A satellite link will permit simultaneous ceremonies at 545 sites in more than 100 countries. Altogether, 720,000 people will be involved, although two-thirds will be renewing vows.

Some are paying dearly for the privilege of being married by Moon – £18,000 for Japanese couples to £1,250 for Americans. Protestant organisations called the wedding a huge swindle designed to make Moon rich and claim the church has collected more than £800 million over the years.

The Mail on Sunday

**Egyesítő*

LESSON 3

TRANSLATION
English into Hungarian
checkpoint

70,000 in Moon's Mass Wedding

a What kind of translations have the different people in the class come up with for the following words and phrases in the context of the passage?

- simultaneous mass ceremonies
- around the world
- put faith in divine guidance
- … and that I was so happy
- the Rev Sun Myong Moon
- the Unification Church
- arranged marriages
- promote family ties

b Compare and discuss the possible translations for each and every sentence of shaded part of the text with the whole class.

c Choose three new words or phrases from the text that you think are worth remembering.

READING & VOCABULARY
article

a Read through the article and try to answer the following questions without using a dictionary. When you have finished, discuss your answers in pairs.

- Where and when did the event take place?
- Who are the people involved?
- What do we know about the marital history of the two people?

b **Now try and find the English for the following words and phrases in the text, and make guesses about the possible derivatives (i.e. other words that are related to the one in the article, for example *láz ⇒ lázas*). When you have finished, discuss them with the rest of the class.**

RECIPE

Los Angeles (AP) – Movie star John Travolta knows the recipe for a successful wedding proposal: begin with a vacation in Switzerland, add a big diamond ring, wait until midnight on New Year's Eve.

Travolta popped the question to actress Kelly Preston on New Year's Eve during a romantic holiday in Gstaad, Switzerland, said publicist Paul Bloch. She accepted, Bloch said.

Travolta, 36, who starred in such blockbuster movies as "Grease", "Saturday Night Fever" and "Urban Cowboy", has never been married. It will be the second marriage for the 28-year-old actress.

városi ⇒ elővárosi ⇒ előváros

hozzáadni ⇒ összeadás ⇒ további, újabb

láz ⇒ lázas

zsiradék ⇒ zsíros ⇒ zsírosság

elfogadni ⇒ elfogadható ⇒ elfogadhatatlan

recept

újságíró ⇒ nyilvános ⇒ nyilvánosság/hírverés ⇒ kiadvány ⇒ megjelentetni ⇒ kiadó

leánykérés ⇒ ajánlat, javaslat ⇒ indítványozni

bombasiker*

megkérni a kezét valakinek (!)

**Words printed in small letters do not belong to the basic vocabulary that you need at intermediate level.*

c Now read the following questions and answer them in writing after reading the article again. When you have finished, discuss the answers with the rest of the class.

What is the recipe for a successful proposal according to the article?

....

....

What do we know about the couple?

....

....

PRONUNCIATION 2

stress, rhythm & intonation

Stress & rhythm

☞ Generally speaking, ***content words*** (nouns, verbs, adjectives, adverbs *[quite, only, etc.]*, interrogative pronouns *[who, what, etc.]*, demonstratives *[this, that, etc.]*), which carry the meaning of the phrase or sentence, are ***stressed***, and ***form words*** (prepositions, auxiliaries *[can, is, have, etc.]*, conjunctions *[and, but, etc.]*, pronouns *[he, they, us, etc.]*), which have a grammatical function, are usually ***unstressed***. In form words, quite like in the unstressed syllables of content words, vowel sounds lose their clear quality in an unstressed position in the phrase or sentence ***(weak forms)***.

Listen and repeat.

a **cup** of **tea**
bread and **but**ter
on the **table**
we are **poor**

there's **wine** in the **bottle**
I am a**fraid** she is **ill**
it is a **quar**ter to **five**
Peter can **help** you

as **green** as **grass**
older than I **thought**
some **mon**ey
far from **home**

☞ *Unlike in Hungarian*, the length of time between stressed syllables is always about the same in English, and if there are several unstressed syllables, they must be said more quickly. The strongest stress of all is normally on the *last stressed syllable* in the sentence.

Listen and repeat.

She is **read**ing a ↘**book**.
I have **asked** him if he ↘**likes** it.
My **car** must be **fixed** as **soon** as ↘**pos**sible.

Your **friend** must have been ↘**kid**ding.
My **sis**ter would have ↘**liked** it.
I should have **kept** my **mouth** ↘**shut**.

Intonation

☞ *Unlike in Hungarian*, the tune of English Wh-questions, quite like in the case of statements, *falls* on the *last stressed syllable*. This is the strongest stress in the sentence.

Listen and repeat.

Where do you ↘**live**?
What are you ↘**do**ing ?
Why are you ↘**smil**ing?
When can I **see** your ↘**sis**ter?
When did it ↘**hap**pen?
How did you **spend** your ↘**ho**liday?
When was she ↘**born**?
What did she ↘**do**?

LINK WORDS

Make sure you know what the following link words mean, and working in pairs, decide how you could use them to make the text below sound more natural and dynamic. When you have found a suitable place for all seven of them, take turns to read out the new text. If you think it is necessary, you can also consult the First Aid Kit on link words at the end of the book.

(1) interestingly/funnily/strangely (enough) (2) as far as I remember/if I am not mistaken (3) as for (4) second(ly) (5) whereas/while (6) first of all/first and foremost/first/firstly/to begin with (7) unfortunately/sadly

My family:

……………………, something about my parents: my mother is a teacher; she is 40, whereas my father is an economist, and is 50.

……………………, a few words about my brothers and my sister: my brother Clyde is 20, and he is doing his military service now. My sister Bonnie is in primary school, she is 13, …………………… my brother Archibald is only 3.

…………………… my grandparents, the ones on my mother's side got divorced last year. Grandma, who is 80, lives with us, and, ……………………, grandpa, who is 75, married a 20-year-old girl earlier this year. My grandma on my father's side is 90 years old, and, believe it or not, she still likes rock music. ……………………, grandpa died long ago, …………………… he died in 1970.

HOMEWORK

VOCABULARY
article
study tasks

Recipe

a Read the article again and memorise any vocabulary items that are new to you. When you have finished, use the words in the box to fill in the gaps in the passage below. Change the form of the words if necessary.

No wonder Peter Spaghetti's new movie, '*If your hair is ...., wash it sometimes*' has got so much .... recently. It is a great film and a real ....: millions of people have seen it in the past few weeks. The action takes place in Hungary and it is the sad story of a bus driver who thinks he knows the .... for a successful .... On a hot July day he takes his girlfriend on an outing to Kőbánya, waits until midnight, buys her a hamburger, and then he .... the question to the surprised girl, who ...., on condition that the bus driver buys her an .... hamburger. I won't tell you more about the story, just go and see it for yourselves, it is really worth it.

wedding
to accept
greasy
additional
blockbuster
to pop
publicity
recipe

b Use the following guidelines to prepare for a short oral summary of the article about Travolta's proposal.

The "recipe" ➜ Where and when ➜ The couple

WRITING
composition

What advice would you give to the people who said the following things? Choose at least two statements and react to them in a few sentences in writing using the guidelines below.

- "We do not want more than one child."
- "Although we are just 17, we love each other and want to get married."
- "It is true that he is 65 and I am just 18, but I love him and I want to marry him."
- "We are planning to change the two flats for a big one and live together with my parents."
- "We do not want to get married because our relationship does not need any 'official' or formal reinforcement, and we are not interested in a piece of paper."

Step one	Step two	Step three
Make up your mind whether you want to argue for or against the statement.	Brainstorming: Think of some important ideas, points for or against the statement.	Sum up your opinion in the form of some advice.
Write a first sentence that contains your judgement.	List your points in order of importance, start with the most powerful one. Link your sentences.	Write a last sentence (or two) containing your advice, which should sound quite a logical conclusion in the light of your argument.
Well, to tell you the truth // quite honestly // as a matter of fact. *As I see it, ... // In my view/opinion, ... // Personally, I feel ... // The way I see it, ...* *(I'm afraid) I entirely disagree with ... // I can't say that I share your view ... // I see things rather differently myself.* *I agree entirely with ... // I am of exactly the same opinion.* *There's a lot in what you say, but ... // I agree with much of what you say, but ...*	*Another way of looking at it would be that ... // Think of it this way, ... // Look at it like this, ... // I wonder if you have taken everything into account. For example, ...* *I wonder if you would agree ... // Don't you think ...?* *First of all ... // secondly // and finally // last but not least, ...* *And there's one more thing ... // Don't forget that ... // Have you thought of ...?*	*If I were you, I'd ... // You'd better ... // Take my advice and ... // The way I see it, you should ... // If you follow my advice, you will ... // If I were you, I would/might ...* *I'd think twice about/before ... // I would be extremely careful to\not to ... if I were you.*

☞ When you have finished, don't forget to check your work for grammatical mistakes.

LESSON 4

VOCABULARY
article
checkpoint

Recipe

a **Compare your solutions to the fill-in-gap homework task with the rest of the class.**

b **Discuss with the rest of the class what you think the English would be for the following Hungarian sentences.**

Ez egy teljesen elfogadhatatlan javaslat.

....

Kedvelem őt, de a kezét nem fogom megkérni.

....

Van valakinek hozzátennivalója ehhez a javaslathoz?

....

Óriási hírverés volt az esküvő körül.

....

A legtöbb kiadványuk szakácskönyv.

....

Utálom a zsíros kaját.

....

Nincs általánosan elfogadott recept a boldogságra.

....

c **Working in pairs, give a brief summary of the article we read last lesson.**

GRAMMAR FOCUS

m i n i t e s t

The Articles

Do the following test and check it with the rest of the class.

1. … most young people aren't really fond of … classical music.

A — // the
B The // —
C — // —
D The // the

2. I like … blue anyway, but … blue in your eyes simply drives me crazy.

A — // the
B the // —
C — // —
D the // the

3. When I was in London, I stayed at … Hilton Hotel near … Trafalgar Square.

A — // the
B the // —
C — // —
D the // the

4. Why don't we go to … cinema instead? There's a very good film on at … Globe.

A — // the
B the // the
C the // —
D a // —

5. I'm not sure if … spelling of this word is correct. … spelling has always been my weak point.

A — // —
B — // the
C the // the
D the // —

6. … Danube flows into … Black Sea.

A — // —
B The // the
C The // —
D — // the

7. I love … dogs, but what … dogs in this neighbourhood are doing in the street is just terrible.

A the // the
B the // —
C — // the
D — // —

8. The forecast says … weather is going to be hot today and I don't like … hot weather at all.

A the // —
B — // the
C the // the
D — // —

9. My father is … doctor and he is in … hospital now with … broken arm. He is in … hospital where he works, and his own colleagues are treating him.

A — // — // a // the
B a // — // — // the
C a // the // a // the
D a // — // a // the

10. … unemployment is a very serious problem in this country; the number of … unemployed people is growing year by year.

A The // the
B — // —
C The // —
D — // the

SPEAKING
discussion

a What's your opinion about the following statements? Think of some reasons to support your view and then compare your ideas with your partner's.

1. The old family pattern of husband as breadwinner and wife as housewife was a lot better than the present pattern.
2. There is nothing wrong with the custom of polygamy (having more than one wife at the same time) and polyandry (having more than one husband).
3. It is pretty risky to marry anyone without co-habiting with them for some time before.
4. "Opposites attract each other." In other words men and women whose appearence is quite different (e.g. fair hair – dark hair) are often attracted to each other.

b Discuss the pros and cons of the following issues in small groups, and come up with a written list of the possible advantages and disadvantages. (Choose a secretary.) When you have finished, compare your ideas with the other groups.

- Being an only child.
- Having a family where three or four generations live together.
- Getting married at a very early age. (For example, immediately after leaving secondary school.)
- Being taller than average.

HOMEWORK

VOCABULARY
survival kit
preview

Read through the vocabulary list on page 41-42, and consult a dictionary if you come across something that is unfamiliar or unclear to you.

EXAM TIPS

Dictionaries

☞ When doing your translations, it is extremely important that you should use the right dictionary. First of all, forget the *Országh* Pocket Dictionary, it is only for tourists. The Comprehensive *Országh* Dictionary (*"nagyszótár"*) isn't a very good idea either, because it contains too many words and definitions, so it takes ages to find anything there. The best idea is still the Concise *Országh* Dictionary (*"középszótár"*), but ...

If you only rely on the *Országh* dictionary when doing your translations, you could get into serious trouble. First of all, particularly in the old additions of the dictionary, you simply will not find a lot of modern words and phrases, and, on the other hand, you may well find misleading translations, which don't fit into the context of your passage. It's time you obtained and got accustomed to using a good *monolingual* dictionary! Ideally, in addition to the latest addition of the *Országh* Concise Dictionary, you will have one of the following publications (as they have specifically been written for foreign students of English):

- *Collins Cobuild English Language Dictionary*
- *Longman Dictionary of English Language and Culture*
- *Longman Dictionary of Contemporary English*
- *Oxford Advanced Learner's Dictionary of Current English (New, 5th edition!)*
- *The Cambridge International Dictionary of English*

UNIT 2
Education

LESSON 1

VOCABULARY
survival kit

Schools

day-nursery/crèche, nursery school/kindergarten
(at) primary, secondary/(in) high *[AmE]* school
grammar \ vocational \ trade \ comprehensive ~
public/private/fee-paying ~, boarding ~
(lower \ upper) sixth form college, sixth-former
tuition fee, language school, one-to-one teaching

to start school, to leave school
to go to school/to attend a school, to be a first year student, to be in one's first year
to play truant, to skip a lesson, to be absent
to go to evening classes \ private lessons
to take/do \ enrol in/join a course (on \ in …)

Subjects & lessons

the humanities \ sciences, arts & science subjects
optional & compulsory subjects
curriculum, syllabus, timetable, (in a) lesson
requirements, standard(s), form, class
school year, term, course, lesson, break
school report, mark/grade, straight As
textbook/coursebook, teaching methods

to do/study a subject
to do well at school \ in a subject
to be good \ bad at … \ weak in …
to get good/high \ low marks in …
to do a test, to answer questions
to do/study a subject
to specialise in a subject, specialised class

Teachers & students

staff, form \ head teacher/master \ mistress
strict, lenient, just, fair, unfair
a native \ non-native English teacher
gifted/talented \ weak/hopeless (at/in), bright/ quick on the uptake, hardworking, lazy
discipline problems

to make sy interested in …
to fail sy, to pass sy
to give a test in a subject
to have a gift for …
to coach sy (in a subject, for an exam)
to keep discipline

Higher education

to take one's school leaving/final exams
General Certificate of Secondary Education (GCSE) *[BrE]*, A-levels *[BrE]*, school leaver
to go on to university/college
to apply (for admission) to ~,
to get a place at/to be admitted to ~
to be rejected, to get a grant\scholarship
to study/do/read … *[BrE]*/to major in … *[AmE]*
lecture, seminar, semester, thesis
to prepare/(to cram/to swot) for an exam
to take/sit/sit for an entrance\oral\written\intermediate\advanced level exam in …
to pass\fail\scrape through an exam
to graduate from university
to qualify as a (doctor)
to take a degree in (medicine)
(under\post)graduate (course)
MA, MSc, PhD

SPEAKING
conversation

Use the following guidelines to tell your partner about yourself.

I started\left primary school in …
I went on to the …
I am in the … year now.
In our school, educational standards\requirements are …
I go\went to a class specialised in …
*I am\was quite good at …, I am\was not particularly good at …**
As for languages, I do\did …
I have already passed // I am preparing for the intermediate\advanced level exam in …
*After my school leaving exams, I would like to apply for admission to … // I applied to …***
If I am not admitted, …
After graduation from college\university, …

*

History
Geography
Biology
Art/Arts *[AmE]*
History of Art
Maths/Math *[AmE]*/Mathematics
Sciences, Physics, Chemistry
Hungarian Language and Literature
Foreign Languages
Philosophy
Singing/Music *[AmE]*
Religious Education/RE
Physical Education/PE
Computer Science
Technology

**

Eötvös Loránd University
Faculty of Humanities\Sciences\Law
University of Economics
Medical School/University of Medicine
Academy of Music\Fine Arts
Technical University, College of Technology
University of Horticulture\Forestry
University of Agronomics/Agriculture
Academy of Dramatic and Cinematographic Art
College of Finance and Accountancy\Foreign Trade
College of Trade, Tourism and Catering
School of Veterinary Sciences
Teacher Training College
Training College for Kindergarten Teachers
University of Physical Education

A

SPEAKING pictures

B

a Discuss with the class what vocabulary you need to describe the pictures.

Verbs:	Nouns:	Adjectives:

b Agree with your partner which one of you has picture A and B, and take turns to describe what you can see in them.

In the foreground: ➜ In the background: ➜ On the left: ➜ On the right:

c Still in pairs, make intelligent guesses about the situation in your pictures. (Your teacher has all the information about the true circumstances in which the pictures were taken.) Focus your attention on the following things:

Where (and when) do you think the picture was taken? What are the clues?
Who do you think the person/people in the picture is/are? Any clues?
What do you think might be happening? Any clues?

You may find the following phrases useful here: *In this picture ... ➜ This photo shows a ... ➜ This is a photo of ... ➜ I think they are/may be (...-ing). ➜ I'm not sure // I can't say for sure/certain, but it may be .../it could be .../it might be ... ➜ I can see a ..., so it must be ... ➜ I can/can't see a ..., so it can't be ... ➜ I think this photo was taken ... ➜ This photo must have been taken ... ➜ It looks (very much) like a ... ➜ I'm absolutely sure/certain ... // I have/There's no doubt that ... // There can't be any doubt that ...*

FUNCTIONS
role-play

a Read both role-cards, and agree with your partner who's A and who's B.

A You want to inquire about advanced level courses at the reception of a language school in Oxford.

- Go up to the receptionist and tell her/him what you are interested in.
- Tell the receptionist that you would like information about the following things:
  - the different types of courses (number of lessons a day/week, length of course, when it begins).
  - group sizes.
  - qualification of teachers.
  - prices.
- Tell the receptionist that you are not looking for a course for yourself, but for your spouse, who speaks quite good English but is not very confident about her/his knowledge.
- Tell the receptionist that you want both courses for your spouse. Explain that you are a Hungarian teacher, so money does not matter at all, and anyway you want a lot of free time in Oxford.

B You are a receptionist at an Oxford language school and a person walks up to your desk.

- Greet her/him, and ask him what s/he is interested in.
- Give her/him the necessary information about your advanced level courses.

ADVANCED LEVEL COURSES

a maximum of 10 students per class; qualified teachers of English

COURSE 1	***COURSE 2***
3 WEEK INTENSIVE	**6 WEEK INTENSIVE**
16 June – 5 July	*16 June – 26 July*
three 45-minute lessons in the morning	two 45-minute lessons in the afternoon
£150	*£200*

- ♣ Tell the person that you don't really think an advanced level course would be suitable for her/him, and s/he should choose a beginner's course instead.
- ♣ Ask the person which course s/he wants.

b **Agree with the rest of your class how you could use the following phrases in this situation; complete the phrases and answer the questions. If you think it is necessary, you can also consult the First Aid Kit on functions at the end of the book.**

B: *What can I do for you? // Can I help you?*

A: ***I'd like to inquire about … // Could you tell me …, please? // I'd like to know …***

B: *What exactly …?*

B: *Well, let me see.*

A: ***And there's another/one more thing I'd like to know … // And how about … ?***

B: *The way I see it, you should …// If you follow my advice, you'll …// Take my advice, and …*

A: ***As a matter of fact, … // Actually, … // In fact, …***

A: ***Thanks for …***

c Rehearse the situation in pairs. Read the cards again before starting but try and rely only on the notes below while practising.

greeting → the courses → beginner's course → decision → leave-taking

PRONUNCIATION 1

sounds & word stress

Sounds

☞ The English [ɒ], [ɑː], and [æ] sounds are also quite problematic for Hungarian speakers. The following tips might help you pronounce them correctly.
[ɒ] is a short sound somewhere between the Hungarian *o* and *a* sounds. Give your [ɒ]-s a little *a* flavour.
[ɑː] is a long sound somewhere between the Hungarian *a* and *á* sounds. It's like a long *a*, but it is not rounded.
[æ] is a fairly long sound somewhere between the Hungarian *e* and *á* sounds. Give your [æ]-s a little *á* flavour.

Listen and repeat.

[ɒ]	[ɑː]	[æ]
job	bar	bad
box	car	sad
want	staff	bag
gone	can't	match
what	heart	jam
watch	clerk	man

☞ Note that the [æ] sound is always written with a single *a*. However, an *a* can be pronounced in a number of different ways; in the case of *any*, *many*, *ate*, and *Thames* it is an [e].

Word stress

☞ In a lot of words and word combinations there are two stresses. The second stress is the main stress.

Listen and repeat.

▪■	▪□■	▪■□	▪□■□	▪□■□□
fifteen	afternoon	uncertain	education	understandable
unknown	understand	condition	mathematics	nationality

HOMEWORK

VOCABULARY
survival kit
study task

Study the word list on page 41-42, and memorise the words and phrases that you think are important and relevant to you and your educational background. When you have finished, put the following words in their correct places in the passage below to check your knowledge. (You might try and do the task without using the box.)

school leaving exams, degree, apply, subjects, did, nursery, higher, primary, went, leaving, secondary, admitted, graduated, specialised, requirements, attend, education, gift

My educational history is a pretty ordinary story. As my mother didn't go out to work and I didn't have to .... either day nursery or .... school, I started my formal .... at the age of six in a small school where there were only lower .... classes. I can remember my first day at school quite clearly; I enjoyed that first day just as much as the rest of those four years there. At the age of ten I had to change schools, and I .... on to the "big" school, which wasn't quite as much fun as the old one, but I survived. After .... primary school I went on to a .... grammar school where I attended a ....English class. Educational standards and .... were pretty high and there were wonderful people in our huge (49 boys and girls) class. Although I wasn't particularly good at the science ...., I think it was clear that I had a .... for languages, so after my .... I decided to .... for admission to the Faculty of Humanities at ELTE. I was ...., and I started the most enjoyable part of my education, (well, except perhaps for the first four years at lower primary). It was a great change after secondary school, I enjoyed the freedom, and I .... a lot better than earlier. In fact I was one of the best students in my year. I .... from university in 1979, and I got a .... in English Literature and Linguistics. I have been working as a teacher both in secondary and .... education ever since.

GRAMMAR FOCUS
preview

The Present and the Past

Use the Present Simple

to talk about routines, habits, customs [typical adverbs: *always*, *usually*, *often*, *normally*, *regularly*, *sometimes*, *every day*, *never*, *generally*].
➢ *I normally wear jeans. It never rains in Southern California.*
to talk about states and facts.
➢ *I go to school. Plastic doesn't rust.*
to talk about things that are happening now with verbs on the Black List*.
➢ *I love you. It seems OK.*

Use the Present Continuous

to talk about things that are happening at the moment [typical adverbs: *now*, *at the moment*, *at present*, *right now*, *just now*, *this minute*].
➢ *It's raining (at the moment).*
to talk about a routine or situation that we see as temporary.
➢ *We are building a house.*
to criticise sy or sg when an action is repeated [typical adverbs: *always*, *continually*, *forever*, *constantly*].
➢ *You're always complaining. You're forever leaving your things around.*

Use the Past Simple

to talk about a finished action at a known time *[last night, last year, three years ago, when I was young, from ... to, in 1995]*.
➢ *I sold my car yesterday.*
to talk about a past habit.
➢ *When I was a kid, I played football every day.*
to talk about several past events which happened one after another.
➢ *He got into the car, started the engine and pulled away.*
with verbs on the Black List.
➢ *I didn't recognise him.*

Use the Past Continuous

to talk about sg that was happening at a specific time in the past.
➢ *I was doing the test at this time yesterday.*
to talk about sg that was happening when another event (Simple Past) happened.
➢ *I was watching the match on TV when suddenly the screen went black and I heard this nasty sound.*
to talk about two events which were happening at the same time in the past *[while, when, just as, at the same time as]*.
➢ *My wife was watching the match while I was doing the washing up.*
to talk about "alibis" or "excuses" for not doing sg else in the past.

➢ *"Why didn't you come to the party?" "I was preparing for my exams, you know."*
to describe an action in the past that continued over a length of time (this is more emphatic than the Past Simple) *[all afternoon, for three hours, from 3 to 6, etc.].*
➢ *I was studying all yesterday evening!*
to describe the background scene for a story in the past (the Past Simple for actions and events!).
➢ *I was standing at the bus stop the other day when this beautiful girl came up to me and ...*

*The Black List (verbs that are not used in the Continuous tenses)

verbs of the senses: *to see, to hear, to smell, to taste, to feel* (with the fingers)
verbs of feeling: *to like, to love, to hate, to dislike* (you can use both Simple and Continuous with *to feel)*
verbs of thinking: *to believe, to know, to think* (to believe) [when it means "to use your mind" however, it is not a Black List verb], *to mean, to doubt, to fear, to want, to suppose, to wish, to recognise, to realise, to remember, to forget, to prefer, to mind, to see* (understand) [when it means "to visit", it is not a Black List verb], *to understand*
+ *to be*, except when used to describe temporary, unusual behaviour
➢ *You are being silly.*
+ *to have* (to possess/to own), except in special phrases
➢ *We were having breakfast when ...*
+ *to appear, to belong to, to depend on, to concern, to include, to sound, to cost, to need, to weigh, to deserve, to owe, to own, to possess, to seem, to resemble*

LESSON 2

VOCABULARY
survival kit
checkpoint

a Check the fill-in-the-blank homework task with the rest of the class.

b What are the "opposites" of the following words and phrases?

- compulsory subjects
- science subjects
- to start school
- to pass an exam
- written exam
- to be rejected
- final exams
- weak, hopeless

c What kind of school are these people likely to go to?

- a two-year-old toddler
- a fifteen-year-old in a rich British family
- an adult who wants to learn languages
- an adolescent who wants to learn a trade
- a four-year-old kid
- a sixteen-year-old in the US
- someone who wants to study economics at secondary level in Hungary
- the average sixteen-year-old in Britain
- someone who wants to become a teacher
- someone who wants be a lawyer

d Complete the definitions.

- When people complete their studies at university or college, they ....
- .... is a situation when people do what they are told to and their behaviour is controlled.
- People who are .... are not very strict when they have to punish or supervise others.
- When you prepare people for a particular exam, you .... them for it.
- The level between the first level and the advanced level is the .... level.
- A person whose mother tongue is English is a .... speaker of the language.

GRAMMAR FOCUS

translation into English

The Present and the Past

Translate the following sentences into English, discussing each section with the rest of the class as you progress.

1. Általában farmert hord, de ma szoknyában van. *(to wear)*

2. Bocs, hogy nem hívtalak fel tegnap, de egész nap értekezleteken ültem. *(to have a meeting)*

3. Nem értem, miért nézel így rám. Nem tetszik a ruha, ami rajtam van?

4. Éppen a hajamat mostam, amikor elzárták a vizet. *(to turn off, water supply)*

5. Állandóan tisztességtelen ajánlatokat tesz. *(to make a proposal, indecent)*

6. Bár egy csomó problémám van, most nagyon jól érzem magam itt Acapulcóban.

7. Úgy látszik, nem érted, amit mondok neked; most nincs pénzem, mert Mercedesre spórolok. *(to save up)*

8.
– Fantasztikusan nézel ki!
– Á, csak udvariaskodsz! *(to be polite)*
– Nem, komolyan gondolom. *(to mean it)*
– Szerintem csak viccelsz.
– Soha nem szoktam viccelni.

9.
– Kik laknak a harmadik emeleten?
– Fogalmam sincs, soha nem találkozom velük.

10. Amíg ők a focimeccset nézték, mi a másik szobában a bélyeggyűjteményt tanulmányoztuk. Eközben ellopták az összes kabátot az előszobából. *(hall)*

LISTENING

Public school life

Interview with an ex-Harrow student

a Read the question and try to answer it after you have listened to the recording once. Discuss your answer with your partner.

- What important biographical dates and events does Peter mention?

b Answer the following questions as you listen to the tape for the second time. Discuss your answers with the rest of the class.

- How did Peter get to Britain?
- How was it possible for him to attend a public school?
- Why was the new school a dramatic change for him?
- What particular rules and regulations does he mention?
- What does he say about beating at Harrow?
- How well did he do at school?
- Why didn't he go on to Oxford or Cambridge?
- What does he do now?
- What does he say about his Hungarian?

HOMEWORK

TRANSLATION

English into Hungarian

Use a dictionary to read the following article, and translate the *highlighted* part of the text into Hungarian in writing.

☞ Be very careful with the underlined words in the text; you will find all of them in the dictionary, but it won't be easy to come up with a Hungarian translation which is suitable in the context of the article. What you should do is the following:

1. Look up the word, and see what the dictionary has to offer, e.g.: complete:
Országh: **II.** *vt* **1.** befejez **2.** betetőz [boldogságot] **3.** kiegészít **4.** kitölt [űrlapot]
Longman: v [T] 1 to finish doing something especially when it has taken a long time *The students have just completed their course*. …

2. Now that you have some idea of the possible meaning, take a good look at the context in which the word appears in the text: obviously it refers to the word task, and it could be done with the help of the textbook, so the question is: What do you do with a task with the help of a textbook? (Not "befejezni"!)

☞ There is a slightly different problem with such words as now, able or small hours. Surely, these words are not new to you, but they may not make good sense in the context of this text. Do not be satisfied with a meaningless word-for-word translation, turn to the dictionary or use your imagination.

☞ used to take is problematic because of its grammatical role in the sentence. If you are not familiar with this structure (you should, but anyway you will before you *complete* this book), you could try the dictionary (in this particular case it will help), you could consult a grammar book, or you could just use your imagination again.

Homework Can Have Harmful Effects

Homework can have harmful effects: it may be the real reason behind lateness and absenteeism. But how has this situation arisen?

The nature of homework has changed. It used to take the form of manageable, short tasks, which had to be completed with the help of textbooks. Now homework consists of a number of different assignments, which require an awful lot of hard work, and, consequently, a great deal of time.

Even the most conscientious and able suffer under an ever-increasing workload, which forces them to work into the small hours and to curtail extra-curricular activities.

Homework is also being set at an earlier age. If the current trend continues, five-year-olds will be leaving the nursery class with rucksacks heavy with homework, with no time left in the day to play because they have to do their tasks.

All work and no play makes Jack and Jill dull people. If we don't want this generation on sedatives before they've reached 18, we must fight this crazy attitude to homework. Someone should organise a National No Homework Day. I'm sure the sun would come up the next morning.

Jeremy Davies, The Independent

LESSON 3

TRANSLATION
English into Hungarian
checkpoint

Homework Can Have Harmful Effects

a What kind of translations have the different people in the class come up with for the following words and phrases in the context of the passage?

- How has this situation arisen?
- used to take the form of short tasks
- had to be completed
- now
- consequently
- able
- they suffer under an ever-increasing workload
- into the small hours
- to curtail extra-curricular activities

b Compare and discuss the possible translations for each and every sentence with the whole class.

c Choose three new words or phrases from the text that you think are worth remembering.

READING & VOCABULARY
article

a Read through the article and try to answer the following questions without using a dictionary. When you have finished, discuss your answers in pairs.

- How many students have been hurt?
- What do the students want?
- When were police called in?
- What do students say about education in west Bangladesh?
- How many students have got into trouble so far?

b Now try and find the English for the following words and phrases in the text, and make guesses about the possible derivatives. When you have finished, discuss them with the rest of the class.

esélye van valamire

....

rohamrendőrség ⇒ lázadni (!)

....

követelni ⇒ követelés

....

állítani valamit ⇒ állítás

....

csalni/puskázni

....

....

kizárni valakit ⇒ kizárás

....

....

felügyelő ⇒ felügyelni ⇒ felügyelet

....

....

tömegtüntetés ⇒ tüntetni

....

....

jog valamihez

....

....

színvonal

....

....

megsebesülni ⇒ sebesülés

....

....

felvételi teszt

....

verekedni/küzdeni

....

CHEATING

Dhaka, Bangladesh (AFP) — More than thirty students have been injured fighting with police following a mass demonstration. The students were demanding the "right to cheat" in their university entry tests, and when exam supervisors refused, police riot squads were called in. Students in west Bangladesh claim that poor education standards mean that they must cheat to stand any chance of passing their tests. In the first exam week alone, over 4,000 students have been expelled for cheating.

c **Now read the following questions and answer them in writing after reading the article again. When you have finished, discuss the answers with the rest of the class.**

What did students in Bangladesh demand and why?

....

....

How did the thirty students get injured?

....

....

How do we know that this is a very serious problem in Bangladesh?

....

....

PRONUNCIATION 2

stress, rhythm & intonation

Stress, rhythm and intonation

☞ In certain positions in the sentence, normally unstressed form words will carry some stress. *Have/has, is/are/am, do/does/did, can, could, would, etc.* will be stressed at the beginning and at the end of the sentence ***(strong forms)***. However, the main stress will remain on the last stressed syllable in the sentence.

☞ The tune of Yes-or-No-questions falls and then *rises on the last stressed syllable* of the sentence.

Listen and repeat.

Did you ↗**like** it?
Are you ↗**ha**ppy?
Can you ↗**read** it?
Is this ↗**yours**?
Have you **been** to A↗**me**rica?
Shall I ↗**help** you?
Would you ↗**stop** it please?
Could you **say** it a↗**gain** please?
Did you ↗**see** her?
Would you **like** some ↗**wine**?
Was it ex↗**pen**sive?
Oh **yes**, I **can**.
Of **course**, she **would**.
Yes, I **am**.

☞ The negative forms of auxiliaries are also always stressed *(strong forms)*. However, the main stress is on the main verb.

Listen and repeat.

- I **did**n't **like** it at **all**.
- She **is**n't a **good teach**er.
- You **can't leave** her.
- You **must**n't **read** it.
- I am **not** a **great sing**er.
- I **did**n't under**stand** a **word**.
- I **haven't seen** her for **ages**.
- We **need**n't have **bought** it.
- You **should**n't have **lied** to me.
- It **would**n't have **been good**.

LINK WORDS

Make sure you know what the following link words mean, and working in pairs, decide how you could use them to make the text below sound more natural and dynamic. When you have found a suitable place for all ten of them, take turns to read out the new text. (If you think it is necessary, you can also consult the First Aid Kit on link words at the end of the book.)

(1) all in all/all things considered (2) second(ly) (3) another problem is that . . . (4) unfortunately (5) as for . . . (6) on the other hand (7) and last but not least (8) above all/most important of all (9) third(ly) (10) for example/instance

My school:

On the one hand, there are a number of things I really like about my school, but, ..., there are certain things that I can't say I'm particularly happy about.

First let's look at the strong points: ...., it's not far from where I live; ...., it has got some extremely good teachers; ...., there are specialised maths classes, then there's a very good drama society, ..., there are very nice people in my class.

.... the weak points or disadvantages: ...., it isn't very well equipped, (......................, there is no shower in the gym, there aren't enough computers). .... teachers are far too strict.

......................, I don't think this school was a bad choice; I've certainly heard of worse schools.

HOMEWORK

VOCABULARY

article study tasks

Cheating

a Read the article again and memorise any vocabulary items that are new to you. When you have finished, use the words in the box to fill in the gaps in the passage below. Change the form of the words if necessary.

right
to call in
standard
to be injured
to demand
to claim
demonstration

At a huge .... yesterday, thousands of people .... that the government should immediately do something about the low .... of medical services in this country. Demonstrators .... that in the present situation ordinary people couldn't even exercise their .... to the most basic treatment. The demonstration was peaceful, the police were not ...., and no one was ....

b Use the following guidelines to prepare for a short oral summary of the article about cheating students.

Students' demands → Their reasons → The demonstration → Expulsion

WRITING
letter

Use the following guidelines to write to an old primary school friend about whether you think it was a good idea to choose the secondary school you go/went to.

Step One	Step two	Step three
General outline: Plan the general structure of the composition.	Brainstorming: Think of as many ideas, points and examples as possible.	Work out a more detailed paragraph structure.
Introduction	greeting, reference to the time that has passed, introducing topic.	*Dear …* *Sorry for not writing to you for so long, but I have …* *In your last letter you asked me to write you about …* *Now I'll summarise the most important things in a few sentences …*
Points in favour	(nice old building, good reputation, high requirements, etc.)	Introductory sentence (short summary) *On the one hand, …* *First of all, …* *Secondly, …* *And finally, …* *On the other hand, …* *However, …*
Points against	(too far away, too strict, small gym, etc.)	
Conclusion	balance of pros and cons, closing the letter	*In conclusion, …* *Well, I hope I have remembered everything, but if I haven't, please write again and ask any questions you've got.* *Write soon.* *Yours/Love, …*

If you need more help or more information about letter writing, consult the First Aid Kit at the end of the book.

☞ When you have finished, don't forget to check your work for grammatical mistakes.

LESSON 4

VOCABULARY
a r t i c l e
checkpoint

Cheating

a Compare your solutions to the fill-in-the-gap homework task with the rest of the class.

b Discuss with the rest of the class what you think the English would be for the following Hungarian sentences.

Két ember súlyosan megsérült a balesetben.

....

....

Egyáltalán nem vagyok elégedett a szolgáltatás színvonalával ebben a szállodában.

....

....

A követeléseid teljesen elfogadhatatlanok.

....

....

Semmi esélyem nincs arra, hogy megnyerjem a versenyt.

....

....

Harcolunk a jogért, hogy békében élhessünk.

....

....

c Working in pairs, give a brief summary of the article we read last lesson.

GRAMMAR FOCUS
mini test
The Present and the Past

Do the following test and check it with the rest of the class.

1. You can't talk to the manager now. He ... a meeting.
A still is having
B still has
C is still having
D has still had

2. I haven't spoken to her since she ... for the United States.
A has left
B left
C has been left
D had left

3. We ... badminton in the garden when it ... to rain.
A played, was beginning
B have been playing, began
C were playing, has begun
D were playing, began

4. I am really sorry Peter, but I don't believe you. You ... excuses.
A always are making
B have always been made
C are always making
D make always

5. Who ... that fantastic American film three days ago?
A saw
B was seeing
C did see
D has seen

6. Air pollution ... the natural environment in large areas in Europe.
A have destroyed
B was destroyed
C destroy
D is destroying

7. What ... think that they are any better than us?
A is making you
B makes you
C does make you
D make you

8. Now, tell me who ... .
A did kiss you
B you were kissed
C kissed you
D are you kissed

9. As soon as she ... me, she began to smile.
A saw
B was seeing
C had been seen
D has seen

10. "I ... to university from 1974 until 1979." "So you ... for 5 long years."
A was going // studied
B went // studied
C have gone // have studied
D went // have studied

SPEAKING
discussion

a What's your opinion about the following statements? Think of some reasons to support your views and then compare your ideas with your partner's.

1. In the last two years of secondary school students should be allowed to choose the subjects they want to study. No subjects should be compulsory.
2. Instead of two compulsory foreign languages we should only have one, but it should be taught very intensively.
3. Learning (and teaching) classical languages is a waste of time.

b Read the newspaper article, and discuss the questions in pairs.

What do you think are or could be the advantages and disadvantages for this little boy of being such a genius?
Would you like your own son/daughter to be such an exceptionally talented child?
Why (not)?

> ### University at seven
>
> **AUCKLAND:** At the age of seven, maths genius Michael Tan is about to become the world's youngest undergraduate. He has passed entrance examinations and is expected to enrol in March at Canterbury University in Christchurch, New Zealand.
>
> Michael, whose elder brother David completed a degree course at the age of 16, began lessons with his mother when he was four. His father, Choon, a teacher, gave him extra tuition.
>
> Until now, the world's youngest undergraduate is believed to have been the mathematician Lord Kelvin, who enrolled at Glasgow University aged ten in 1834.

c Discuss the following issues in small groups. When you have finished, compare your ideas with the other groups.

1. The following boxes contain a possible list of "good" and "bad" features of schools. Choose the three most acceptable features from the "good news" list, and the three least acceptable features from the "bad news" list according to your personal taste, and then discuss your choice with the other people in your group. When you have finished, choose the most and least acceptable "horizontal" combinations. (As if each line were a particular school.)

"Good news"	**"Bad news"(?)**
1. offers first-class computer education	**1.** its teachers are extremely strict
2. has small class sizes	**2.** is a boarding school
3. has a long tradition of high-quality education	**3.** there is a high tuition fee
4. offers a wide variety of after-school activities	**4.** doesn't offer English as a foreign language
5. offers top-quality foreign language education	**5.** is 40 kilometres away from where you live
6. has a friendly and relaxed atmosphere	**6.** there is no computer education offered
7. has a highly qualified staff	**7.** is very poorly equipped
8. is modern and well-equipped	**8.** has practically no social life
9. has a varied and exciting social life	**9.** is a new school without any tradition

2. What do you think should happen to school students who …

a) repeatedly do not do their homework?
Should they be given a "one"? Should they be given extra homework? Should they be asked oral questions about the subject? Anything else?

b) are caught cheating during a test?
Should they be given a "one"? Should the test be taken from them immediately and marked on the basis of what they have written so far? Should they be given one mark less? Should they be given a new test but not a "one"? Anything else?

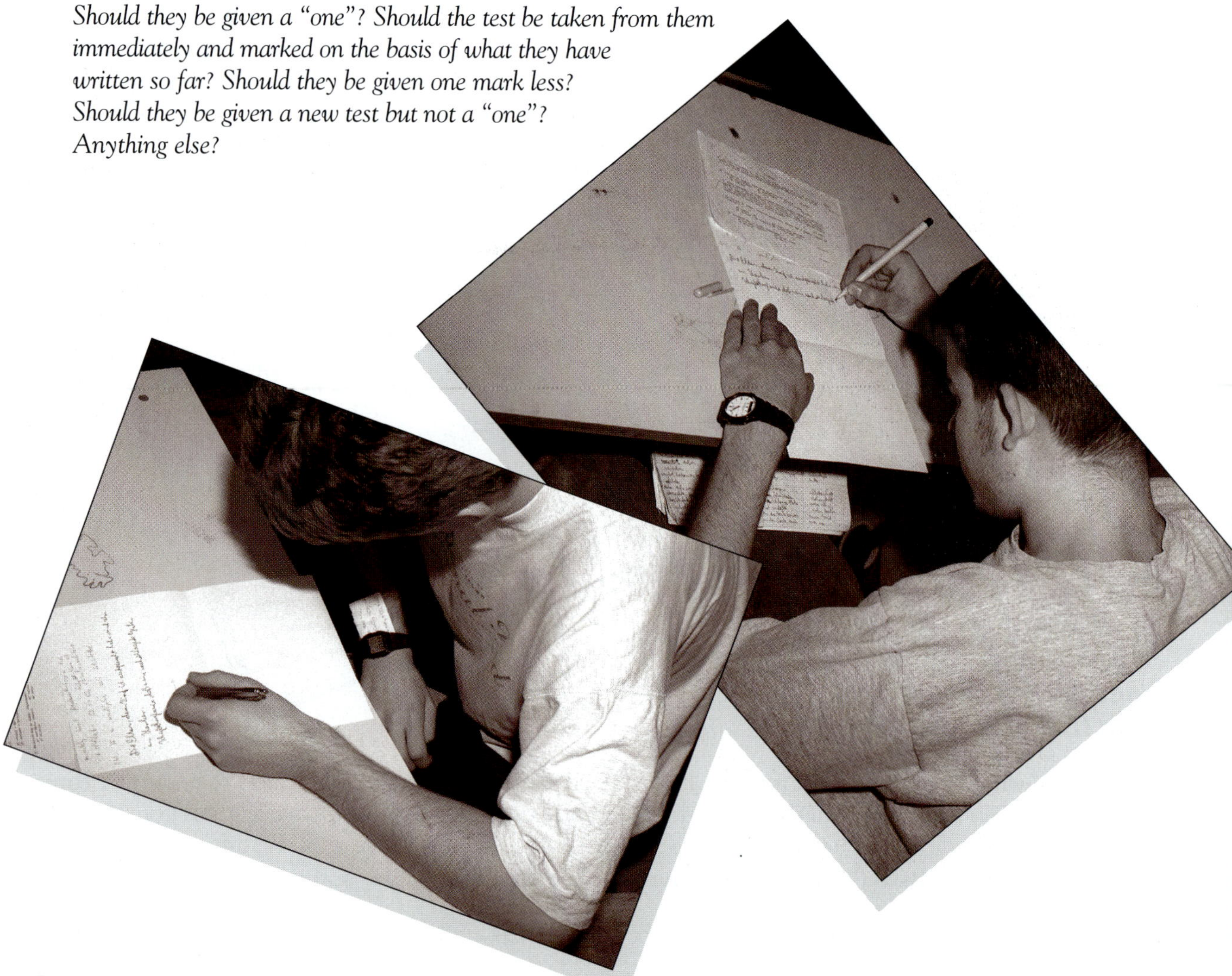

HOMEWORK

VOCABULARY survival kit preview

Read through the new vocabulary list on page 65-66, and consult a dictionary if you come across something that is unfamiliar or unclear to you.

EXAM TIPS

The English into Hungarian translation task

☞ This is the most demanding/difficult/dangerous component of the exam – most people who fail the exam suffer damaging losses in points in this particular task. There are a number of reasons for this:

The texts in this task are sometimes really difficult and they probably require a better command of English than other components of the exam.

Translation is a very complex skill: it requires a lot of things that go far beyond mere foreign language proficiency; a good translator is intelligent, educated, well-read and, last but by no means least, a very competent user of her/his mother tongue. Although the examiners are mainly interested in whether you have really understood the text, and you are not expected to be a professional translator, these factors still play an important role here.

A lot of people think that translations are all about dictionaries, but this is *not true at all.* Of course, a good dictionary is a must (see the exam tips in Unit 1), but it also takes an intelligent and experienced person to find the correct meaning in the given context and its suitable Hungarian equivalent even in the best dictionary. In addition to this, you have to "decode" the *structure* in which the word occurs as well, which might prove to be an even more difficult task, and dictionaries aren't much help here unfortunately.

☞ So, what's the best way to go about translating an English text?

Always read the whole text before you set about the actual translation so that you have at least a vague idea of what it is all about; this will make your life a lot easier when it comes to looking up words and selecting the appropriate meaning in the dictionary.

When you have found a meaning for a word that makes good sense in the context, think of a suitable Hungarian equivalent, (not necessarily listed in the English–Hungarian dictionary!) and that's it. If you haven't, it does not mean that the text is meaningless; it's only that you haven't been careful enough or that your dictionary is *not* good enough – unfortunately, no dictionary is good enough for everything. In this case, you will have to make an intelligent guess. Proper names are always problematic; check the *Országh* dictionary for conventional translations (it's very good at those!), if you can't find anything there, it's up to you to decide whether it is necessary to translate it at all. Ask yourself the question: "If a friend of mine read my translation, could s/he make sense of this?"

"Decode" the structure: if it is something that you have never seen before, and you have no idea what the "message" might be, just rely on pure logic and try to deduct the possible meaning from the context (the previous or the next sentence or paragraph may be very helpful). You should rely on your logic even if you think you are familiar with the structure, if it doesn't make good sense, it cannot be correct, so give it another try! *Do not leave out whole sentences, and do not give alternative solutions;* a brave attempt may turn out to be a lucky guess, and you have nothing to lose, anyway.

If you get completely stuck on one sentence, move on to the next part and come back to the problem later.

When you have finished the translation, read the text as a whole. Make sure it sounds fluent and Hungarian. Don't hesitate to change anything that sounds strange in the given context; remember that you are not translating isolated words or sentences and it is the "message" that really matters.

Translation is very time-consuming, so hurry up!

UNIT 3 Making a living

LESSON 1

VOCABULARY survival kit

Line of work
qualifications, occupation, job, work, trade, profession, professional people, vocation, post, career, all/every walk(s) of life, white\blue collar worker, management, manager, boss, employee, department, manual work/job, menial work, skilled\unskilled worker, factory hand, to be self-employed, to be a freelance …, entrepreneur, to run sy's own business, capital, funds, to set up a business enterprise, private\public sector

Employment
job advertisement, vacancy, job interview, to take sy on/to employ sy, to be employed, permanent\temporary job, to get\find\apply for\do\lose\quit\change a job, to retrain

Payment
to work/make a living as a …, What do you do for a living?, to earn/make money, a well\badly-paid job, to be underpaid, towards\at the lower\upper end of the wage range, high\low\reasonable\insufficient pay\wages\salary, starting salary, fringe benefits/perks, (pay) rise, bonus, income, net\gross

Working conditions
job satisfaction, (flexible, regular, irregular) working hours, to work flexitime, annual holiday, job description, to be promoted, promotion, to work for a company, to be on holiday, to have a day off, to be on day\night shift, full\part-time job, to do overtime, to have a second job

Out of a job
to be dismissed/fired, to be given the sack, to be made redundant, to retire, to be unemployed, to be on the dole *[BrE]*, to be out of work, job centre, redundancy, unemployment, unemployment benefit/dole money, retirement, pension, (old age) pensioner, school-leaver

Some trades and professions
(car) mechanic, electrician, hairdresser/hair stylist, plumber, waiter\waitress, shop assistant, painter and decorator, cook, bus\taxi driver, turner, carpenter, joiner, policeman, postman, dustman, nurse, secretary, road sweeper, farmer, security officer, guard, hotel manager, child minder, cleaner, clerk, tailor\dressmaker, photographer, travel\estate agent, social worker

doctor, school\kindergarten teacher, university lecturer, scientist, research worker, librarian, mechanical\electrical\civil\production engineer, economist, accountant, specialist in finance, architect, interior decorator, artist, dancer, pilot, broker, solicitor/lawyer, builder, vet, priest, psychologist, police inspector, advertising executive, computer programmer\operator

SPEAKING
conversation

Use the following guidelines to tell your partner about yourself (if you have some kind of a job) or your mother\father. In either case, talk about your own future plans, too.

qualifications → occupation → employed or self-employed → position → job description → salary → working conditions\colleagues\boss → satisfaction → (part-time activities) → future plans

SPEAKING
pictures

A

B

a Discuss with the class what vocabulary you need to describe the pictures.

Verbs:	Nouns:	Adjectives:

b Agree with your partner which one of you has picture(s) A and B, and take turns to describe what you can see in them.

In the foreground: ➜ In the background: ➜ On the left: ➜ On the right:

c Still in pairs, make intelligent guesses about the situation in your pictures. (Your teacher has all the information about the true circumstances in which the pictures were taken.) Focus your attention on the following things:

- Where do you think the picture was taken? What are the clues?
- Who do you think the people in the picture are? Any clues? (Be careful with picture A!)
- What do you think could have happened before photo B/2 was taken?
- What do you think might be happening? Any clues?

You may find the following phrases useful here:

This photo shows a ... ➾ This is a photo of ... ➾ In this picture ... ➾ I think they are/may be (...-ing). Perhaps .../Maybe ... ➾ I'm not sure // I can't say for sure/certain, but it may be .../it could be .../it might be ... ➾ He/They may/might/could have (done) ... ➾ He/They must have (done) ... ➾ I can see a ..., so it must be ... ➾ I can/can't see a ..., so it can't be ... ➾ I think this photo was taken ... ➾ This photo must have been taken ... ➾ It seems ... ➾ It looks (very much) like a ... ➾ I'm absolutely sure/certain ... // I have/There's no doubt that ... // There can't be any doubt that ...

FUNCTIONS
role-play

a Read both role-cards and agree with your partner who's A and who's B.

A You are a counsellor at a job centre, and a person has come to see you about her/his problem.

- Greet her/him and ask her/him what the problem is.
- Ask the person if s/he is interested in ballet dancing.
- Ask her/him if s/he wants to be a nurse.
- Ask him if s/he wants to be a pilot.
- Ask him/her if s/he is interested in a job at the Hungarian Embassy in London.

B You are an English teacher and you have been made redundant. You have been unemployed for six months and now you are at the job centre to ask for help.

- Tell the counsellor about your situation, and tell her/him that you would like to find a job.
- Tell her/him that you can't dance, and anyway you wear size 46 shoes.
- Tell her/him that you faint when you see blood, and anyway you are not satisfied with the wages there.
- Tell her/him that you have a fear of heights.
- Tell the counsellor that you like the idea, because you could practise your English there.

b Agree with the rest of your class how you could use the following phrases in this situation; complete the phrases and answer the questions.

***A:* What can I do for you? // Can I help you?**

B: *I'd like to inquire about …*

***A:* Well let me see…**

***A:* What/How about …? // What would you say to …-ing …?**

***A:* Do you think you could …? // Do you have any experience of …? // Do you feel capable of …?**

A: *As a matter of fact, … // Actually, … // In fact, … // I'm not sure I am capable of … // I don't feel I could // There's no way I could … // I must admit I'm no good/hopeless at … // I have no experience of … // I'm afraid I couldn't cope with …*

B: *That sounds quite … // I find … very interesting/exciting.*

B: *Thank you very much (indeed) for … // Many thanks for …*

***A:* I'm glad to have been of some service/help.**

c Rehearse the cards in pairs. Read the cards again before starting but try and rely only on the notes below while practising.

the situation ➜ ballet dancer ➜ nurse ➜ pilot ➜ embassy job ➜ leave-taking

PRONUNCIATION 1

sounds & word stress

Sounds

☞ The English [ɔː], [uː], and [ɜː] sounds are also quite different from the nearest Hungarian sounds. The following tip might help you pronounce them correctly: *decrease the rounding* of the corresponding Hungarian sounds.

Listen and repeat.

[ɔː]	[uː]	[ɜː]
law	food	girl
walk	rude	firm
talk	soup	learn
all	two	shirt
bought	tune	flirt
thought	few	word

Word stress

☞ In real compound words the main stress is *on the first element*, though the second element doesn't normally lose its original sounds.

Listen and repeat.

'**black**bird	'**co**pyright	'**birth**day	'**nick**name
'**rail**way	'**mo**torbike	'**sub**way	'**sun**light
'**post**card	'**week**day	'**foot**ball	'**sun**tan
'**ev**erything	'**pass**port	'**some**times	'**Main** Street

☞ In relatively new compound words, however, the main stress remains *on the second (or last) element* of the combination, while the first element has secondary stress. All abbreviations are like this.

Listen and repeat.

,inner '**city**	,half '**price**	,CD '**ROM**	,world '**fa**mous
,front '**door**	the ,BB'**C**	,Central '**Eu**rope	,first '**floor**
,back '**seat**	Euro,pean '**U**nion	the ,AB'**C**	,good '**bye**
,full '**time**	,London '**Road**	Tra,falgar '**Square**	U,nited '**King**dom

HOMEWORK

VOCABULARY
survival kit
study task

Study the word list on page 65-66, and memorise the words and phrases. When you have finished, put the following words in their correct places in the passage below to check your knowledge. (You might try and do the task without using the box.)

> *retire, unemployment, wages, wage, dole, occupation, unemployed, work, range, retrained, shifts, underpaid, working for, permanent, conditions, redundant, benefit, job, fringe benefits*

Frankly, I hate work. Of course I could say with equal truth that I love work: that it is an extremely interesting activity; that it is often fascinating; that I wish I didn't have to do it; that I wish I had a .... at which I could earn a decent .... That makes six subjective statements about .... and all of them are true of me.

I can tell you about my experiences of being a miner, for mining is the work I've mostly done. I have been .... this mine for over 20 years now and I can't say it's been easy. I work ...., I either get up very early or I get to bed late at night, in any case I spend eight hours a day down the pit. I don't have to tell you much about the working ...., everybody knows about the lack of sunlight, the dirt, the hazards, not to mention the monotony. Even worse, ... are truly miserable, miners are sliding towards the lower end of the wage .... As for ...., we get some free coal in winter, and we can .... a few years earlier than others, but that's about it. Still, we can be happy we are not ....: dozens of mines have been closed down and thousands of miners have been made .... in the past five years. .... is becoming a very serious problem in this town, most of my neighbours have been on the .... for months. It's true, I am ...., but it is still better than having to make ends meet on unemployment .... And, anyway, what new .... can a miner be .... for? A nurse or a banker? So I think I should be very thankful for the lesser evil of having a .... job. But even that doesn't mean I have to pretend to like work.

GRAMMAR FOCUS
p r e v i e w

The Perfect Tenses

1. Use the **Perfect Tenses**

to talk about actions and events that
have already happened *[already, before, yet* (in questions)].
➢ *I have already told you.*
have not happened yet *[yet, before].*
➢ *I haven't eaten anything yet.*
have been happening for some time *[for two minutes, how long?, etc.].*
➢ *They've been going out together for two years.*
have been happening since a particular time or event *[since 1995, since I saw him, etc.].*
➢ *The've been quarreling since I came home.*
have just happened *[just]* (could be Past Tense with *just now* at the end).
➢ *He has just arrived. He arrived just now.*
have happened in a period of time that links to the present moment *[today, ever, never, this century, all my life, recently, lately, so far, up to now, as yet, this lesson, etc.].*
➢ *We've had a lot of problems recently.*
have happened *for the first\second\last\only time.*
➢ *It's the first time I have driven a Mercedes, and I really like it.*

to report that an event has happened. (No adverbs of finished time are allowed here!)
➢ *My car has been stolen. I've lost my keys. Peter and Mary have got married.*

by a particular time.

2. Whether the sentence is in the **Present, Past** or **Future Perfect** will be determined by ***this particular time:***

If the action/event is related to the present, it will be a **Present Perfect** sentence.
➢ *We've been married for ten years. It's the first time I've been here. I haven't been feeling very well recently. How long have you been sitting here? I've broken my arm.*
If it is related to a particular time (or action/event in the Past Simple) in the past, it will be a **Past Perfect** sentence. *[after, before, as soon as, when, because, by the time, by 6 o'clock, until, no sooner ... than, hardly/scarcely ... when].*
➢ *We'd known each other for three years when we got married. It was the second time he'd been in trouble. I didn't say anything until he'd finished. I had no sooner/No sooner had I put the phone down than somebody started to knock on the door. The match had hardly/Hardly had the match begun when it started to rain. I went back to the garage, because I'd forgotten to switch off the light.*
Similarly, if we are already talking about the past, we use the Past Perfect to talk about an earlier event.
➢ *I was sure I had seen her before. The key wasn't there; I'd left it in the car.*

The Past Perfect is common in reported speech.

➢ *He said he hadn't eaten anything for three days. Snow White wondered who had slept in her bed.*

We also use the Past Perfect to talk about an unrealised hope, plan, wish.

➢ *I had hoped that we would meet in London, but they were in the States at the time.*

If it is related to a future time (or action/event in the Present Simple), it will be a **Future Perfect** sentence *[by 6 o'clock, by the time, before]*.

➢ *We'll have been married for ten years (by) next June. By the time we get there, the film will have already started.*

3. Use the **Continuous Perfect Tenses**

if the continuous nature of the activity or event is obvious.

➢ *I'd been standing at the stop for 30 minutes when at last the bus arrived.*

to refer to an activity with a result at a particular time.

➢ *Her eyes are red because she's been crying. He was hot because he'd been running.*

if you want to emphasise the length of time (optional).

➢ *I have been working/I have worked here for ten years.*

LESSON 2

VOCABULARY survival kit checkpoint

a **Check the fill-in-the-blank homework task with the rest of the class.**

b **What are the "opposites" of the following words and phrases?**

- a full-time job
- a temporary job
- a white-collar worker
- to take someone on
- a reasonable salary
- net
- a well-paid job
- day shift
- the public sector
- to be employed

c **Identify the occupation by the "tools of the trade".**

- chalk, white-board
- sauce-pan, wooden spoon
- syringe, scalpel
- scissors, comb
- camera, telephoto lenses
- brush, glue
- prayer-book, cross
- plane, saw
- drawing-board, ruler
- spanner, hydraulic jack

d **Working together in pairs, try to identify the jobs the different Lego bricks portray.**

e Complete the definitions.

- Additional services or other advantages given with a job besides your salary are called ....
- If you work ...., you work a fixed number of hours, but you can choose the times at which you start and finish each day.
- Money given by the (British) government to people who are unemployed is informally called ....
- .... work is boring, needs no skill, may be looked upon as unimportant, and is often looked down on by other people.
- When you stop working because you have reached the age when you can get a pension, you ....

GRAMMAR FOCUS

translation into English

The Perfect Tenses

Translate the following sentences into English, discussing each section with the rest of the class as you progress.

1. Már megcsináltam a matek házi feladatomat, de még el sem kezdtem az angolt.
Már két éve járnak, de még meg sem csókolta őt. *(to go out)*

....

....

2. – Mióta ismeritek egymást?
– Karácsony óta, azaz tíz hónapja. *(that is)*

– Mióta szerencsétlenkedsz ezzel a pár mondattal? *(to tinker with, few)*
– Mióta hazajöttem.

....

....

....

3. – Milyen jegyeket kaptál angolból ebben a félévben?
– Kaptam egy kettest, egy hármast, egy négyest és egy ötöst, de egyest eddig még nem kaptam. Tulajdonképpen még soha nem kaptam egyest. *(to be given)*
Idén háromszor emelték a benzin árát, de még nem érte el az arany árát. *(to raise, petrol)*

....

....

....

....

....

❹ – Bocs, de elfelejtettem.
– De hát éppen most mondtam!

....

....

❺ – Ezt most hallom először. – Ez nem igaz! Említettem neked a problémát a múlt héten, az volt az első alkalom, hogy hallottál az ügyről.

....

....

....

❻ Felemelték a benzin árát? Ellopták az autómat. Levágattad a hajad? *(to have sg done)* Igazgatónak nevezték ki. *(to appoint sy something)*

....

....

❼ Már öt éve ismertük egymást, amikor végül összeházasodtunk.
Azonnal egyest adott, mikor rájött, hogy nem készültem.
Mesélt nekem a barátairól, akiket már gyerekkora óta ismert. *(tell sy about)*
Amikor felébredtem, ő már órák óta dolgozott.
Mire hazaértem, a galádok mind felfalták a gombócot. *(bastard, eat up, dumpling)*

....

....

....

....

....

....

❽ Januárban lesz húsz éve, hogy megvan a Kispolszkim.
Mire a busz Párizsba ér, tizenöt órája lesz, hogy utazni fogunk.

....

....

LISTENING

A difficult job

Interview with Mrs Audrey Scottney, a library property recovery officer

a Read the question and try to answer it after you have listened to the recording once. Discuss your answer with your partner.

- What exactly is the woman's job?

b Answer the following questions as you listen to the tape for the second time. Discuss your answers with the rest of the class.

- What kind of jobs did Audrey have in her "previous life"?
- What typical excuses do people have when Audrey turns up to collect the missing items?
- How does she react when she knows "punters" are lying?
- What did the unpleasant guy, the "borrower from hell" do to get rid of Audrey?
- What was embarrassing about the recovery of the picture?
- What story does she tell the interviewer to illustrate the "dangerous" nature of her job?

HOMEWORK

TRANSLATION

English into Hungarian

Use a dictionary to translate the following article into Hungarian. Pay special attention to the underlined words and phrases.

☞ Be particularly careful with pronouns; in certain cases there's no need to translate them at all because the Hungarian verb "contains" them (e.g. but he got his ...), in other cases (e.g. impersonal subjects) the Hungarian equivalent will not be a word-for-word translation of the original (e.g. you might think ...).

☞ Geographical names may be problematic, particularly when they have an English "translation". If you are suspicious about such a name, it's a good idea to check it in the *Országh* dictionary (e.g. Viennese).

☞ "International" words (usually words of Latin origin) may be easy to understand but not very easy to translate. In most cases it is better to find a "real" Hungarian word (if it is possible at all) instead of the foreign word (e.g. inspiration).

☞ It might happen that you can't find an item in the form it occurs in the text even in a good monolingual dictionary. In this case, you will have to try and work out the meaning from the different components of the item (e.g. distraction-free).

Genius at Work

You might think that great artists, writers and musicians would need distraction-free surroundings to create their best work. Not so.

Mozart is said to have done a good part of his composing while playing billiards. Christoph Gluck could compose only when sitting in a field. Johann Strauss wrote one of his most famous waltzes on the back of a menu in a Viennese restaurant. Noel Coward composed "I'll See You in My Dreams" in a taxi while caught in a traffic jam. And Richard Wagner did his best work while dressed in flamboyant costumes.

Bed was the place where Mark Twain, Marcel Proust and Edith Whartton liked to write. Enrico Caruso rehearsed in the bathtub.

The poet Friedrich von Schiller worked at his desk, but he got his inspiration from a bowl of rotten apples that he kept nearby. It seems the smell stimulated him.

Judith Chase Churchill, Woman's Day

LESSON 3

TRANSLATION
English into Hungarian
checkpoint

Genius at Work

a What kind of translations have the different people in the class come up with for the following words and phrases in the context of the passage?

- genius at work
- you might think
- distraction-free surroundings
- Mozart is said to have done …
- Viennese
- while caught in a traffic jam
- Wagner did his best work in flamboyant costumes
- he got his inspiration
- the smell stimulated him

b Compare and discuss the possible translations for each and every sentence with the whole class.

c Choose three new words or phrases from the text that you think are worth remembering.

READING & VOCABULARY
article

a Read through the article and try to answer the following questions without using a dictionary. When you have finished, discuss your answers in pairs.

- What is the aim of this action?
- How effective is it?

Scarecop

Copenhagen (UPI) — A life-size cardboard policeman positioned at street corners has turned out to be an efficient weapon against speeding motorists in a Copenhagen suburb.

Real-life colleagues of the so-called scarecop, who requires no salary, vacation or lunch breaks, say speeding drops 30 per cent when the cardboard figure is on duty in Taarnby.

"After some time most motorists recognise the cardboard cop," police said. "Then he has to be replaced with real police officers if we are to maintain the effect."

b Now try and find the English for the following words and phrases in the text, and make guesses about the possible derivatives. When you have finished, discuss them with the rest of the class.

fenntartani ⇒ fenntartás, karbantartás

....

....

helyettesíteni ⇒ pótlás ⇒ pótolhatatlan

....

....

hatékony ⇒ eredményesség, hatásfok, hatékonyság, termelékenység

....

....

szolgálatban lenni ⇒ szolgálaton kívül lenni

....

....

gyorshajtó ⇒ sebességkorlátozás

....

....

hatás ⇒ hatásos, eredményes ⇒ hatásosság

....

....

....

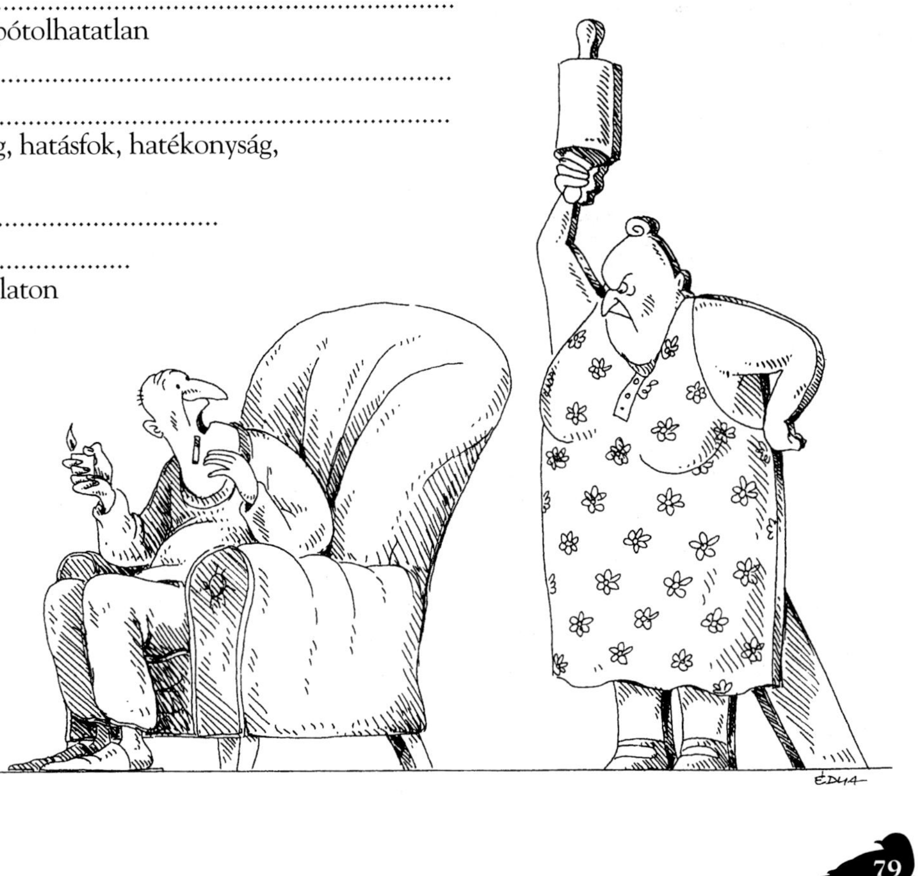

százalék ⇒ százalékarány

....

csökkenni/leesni ⇒ csepp

....

fegyver

....

felismerni ⇒ felismerhetetlen

....

bizonyulni

....

ha (ezt és ezt) akarjuk

....

karton

....

autós ⇒ autózás

....

megijeszteni (!)

....

zsaru

....

madárijesztő (!!)

....

c Now read the following questions and answer them in writing after reading the article again. When you have finished, discuss the answers with the rest of the class.

What new weapon have the Copenhagen police introduced in Taarnby?

....

What are the advantages of this new weapon?

....

What is its drawback and how can the problem be solved?

....

PRONUNCIATION 2

stress, rhythm & intonation

Stress & rhythm

☞ Weaks forms: *am* [əm or m], *are* [ə or ər], *you're* [jə or jər], *have* [əv], *there is* [ðəz], *there are* [ðərə or ðərər], *there is a* [ðəzə], *there + vowel* [ðər], *Is there a* [ɪzðərə], *Are there any* [ɑːðərenɪ], *their* [ðə or ðər], *your* [jə or jər], *her* [hə or hər], *our* [ɑː or ɑːr], *us* [əs], *them* [ðəm], *him* [ɪm], *her* [ə or ər]. The [r] appears at the end when the next word begins with a vowel sound: compare *her brother* [hə'brɒðə] with *her aunt* [hə'rɑːnt].

Listen and repeat.

- I'm O.K.
- Two and two are four.
- The girls are pretty.
- What are you doing?
- You're beautiful.
- You're funny.
- I've got money.
- You've got style.
- There's money in it.
- There's nothing here.
- There're problems with him.
- There're girls in there.
- There's a problem here.
- There's a mistake in it.
- There aren't any people here.
- There isn't any trouble.
- Is there a solution here?
- Are there any good films on TV?
- Here's their phone number.
- It's your husband.
- All her kids.
- This is our house.
- He bought us chocolate.
- I gave them everything.
- I told him to go home.
- I told her my name.

Intonation

☞ In compound sentences, there is very often a *rising tune* before the new clause.

Listen and repeat.

- As I'd left all my money at ↗home, I was left with no choice but to drink water.
- If it weren't so ↗late, we could climb that hill, too.
- It's not only ex↗pensive, but rather ugly as well.
- When he finally a↗rrived, we opened the bottle and drank to his health.

LINK WORDS

Make sure you know what the following link words mean, and working in pairs, use as many as you can to make the text below sound more natural and dynamic. When you have found a suitable place for all of them, take turns to read out the new text.

(1) not to mention (2) in a/one word/briefly/in brief/(to put it) in a nutshell (3) in addition/besides (4) needless to say (5) I think/guess/believe/reckon (6) in other words (7) in fact/actually/as a matter of fact

My job:

I am an economist and I work for a multinational foreign trade company. I'm in management, ..., I am the head of the sales department. This job is a real challenge to me; it takes a lot of responsibility, and, ..., it is exciting, too. As for my working hours, I work flexitime; I usually start at 9 a.m. and I very rarely leave for home before 6 p.m. Compared to other jobs, ... both the working conditions and the salary are extremely good, ... the considerable fringe benefits that I enjoy. ...., I can say am definitely towards the upper end of the Hungarian wage range, which is fantastic. ...., I haven't got any part-time jobs. ...., I'm really satisfied with everything.

HOMEWORK

VOCABULARY
article
study tasks

Scarecop

a Read the article again and memorise any vocabulary items that are new to you. When you have finished, use the words in the box to fill in the gaps in the passage below. Change the form of the words if necessary.

weapon
per cent
to replace
to be on duty
to turn out
to drop
cardboard
to maintain

Budapest (FTC) — A life-size .... teacher positioned in exam rooms has .... to be an efficient .... against cheating students in a Budapest school.

Real-life colleagues of the so-called scareprof, who – quite like themselves – requires hardly any salary, say cheating .... 100 .... when the cardboard figure is on ....

"After some time most students recognise the cardboard prof" a headmaster said. "Then he has to be .... with real teachers if we are to .... the effect."

b Use the following guidelines to prepare for a short oral summary of the article about the "scarecop" in a few sentences.

The new weapon (what? where? what for?) → Efficiency → The advantages → The problem

WRITING
letter

Use the guidelines to reply to the following job advertisement:

You are a qualified and experienced nursery teacher and you are interested in the job.

Brainchild Pre-School is seeking qualified & experienced kindergarten and nursery teachers. Contact Jill Cosby, Budapest, XII., Hegy u. 1.

Write a letter to Ms Cosby to enquire about the job.

Step One	Step two	Step three
General outline: Plan the general structure of the composition.	Brainstorming: Think of as many questions about the job as possible.	Work out a more detailed paragraph structure.
Introduction	greeting, reference to advertisement, introducing yourself.	*Dear Ms …* *Referring to/I read your advertisement in last Tuesday's issue of* The Budapest Sun *… // I am writing to you in connection with …* *I would like to get/Iwould be very grateful if you would send me some information about …\full details of …*
Questions	language (level of English? Hungarian?), kids (age, nationality), working hours, salary, fringe benefits, etc.	*First and foremost, // Most important of all …* *I'd also like to know … // I should be interested to know …* *Another important issue/question is … //As regards … // As for … // With regard to …* *I wonder if …,*
Conclusion	closing the letter	*I thank you in advance for your reply \kind help.* *I am looking/I look forward to hearing from you soon; I would greatly appreciate an early reply.* *I enclose my CV.* *Yours sincerely(,)*

☞ When you have finished, don't forget to check your work for grammatical mistakes.

LESSON 4

VOCABULARY
article
checkpoint

Scarecop

a **Compare your solutions to the fill-in-the-gap homework task with the rest of the class.**

b **Discuss with the rest of the class what you think the English would be for the following Hungarian sentences.**

A hír igaznak bizonyult.

....

Senki sem pótolhatatlan.

....

Teljesen felismerhetetlen vagy ezen a fotón.

....

A nyilvánosság hatékony fegyver a korrupció ellen.

....

Halálra ijesztettél!

....

Ha el akarjuk érni a vonatot, jobb lesz ha sietünk.

....

Egy Rolls Royce gyakorlatilag semmilyen karbantartást nem igényel.

....

c **Working in pairs, give a brief summary of the article we read last lesson.**

GRAMMAR FOCUS
m i n i t e s t
The Perfect Tenses

Do the following test and check it with the rest of the class.

1. I … hard since dawn and I'm really tired now.
- **A** was working
- **B** worked
- **C** have been working
- **D** am working

2. I was tired because I …. for several hours.
- **A** have been travelling
- **B** had been travelled
- **C** have travelled
- **D** had been travelling

3. Look! Clyde … all the dishes for us.
- **A** had washed up
- **B** has washed up
- **C** washes up
- **D** washed up

4. It was the first time I … a cigarette, and I was quite sick.
- **A** had smoked
- **B** was smoking
- **C** had been smoking
- **D** smoked

5. The police … the case for six months when the first arrests … .
- **A** were investigating // had been made
- **B** have been investigating // were made
- **C** had been investigating // were made
- **D** were investigating // has been made

6. If I get lucky, I … all my exams by the end of this month.
- **A** have passed
- **B** will have been passing
- **C** will pass
- **D** will have passed

7. I … as a teacher since I … from university.
- **A** worked // graduated
- **B** have worked // graduated
- **C** has worked // have graduated
- **D** worked // have graduated

8. The lecture was so boring that students began to leave early. By the end most of them … .
- **A** have already left
- **B** already left
- **C** had already left
- **D** had already been left

9. No sooner … to sleep than the phone … to ring.
- **A** did I go // had begun
- **B** had I gone // began
- **C** had I gone // had begun
- **D** did I go // has begun

10. By this time tomorrow they … in London.
- **A** have arrived
- **B** had arrived
- **C** will have been arriving
- **D** will have arrived

SPEAKING
discussion

a **If you are a student, put the following aspects of work in order of importance for you. If you already have a job, decide which aspects are relevant and which ones are less characteristic or missing in your work. When you have finished, compare your results with those of your partner.**

- salary
- social status
- (intellectual) challenge
- variety
- working conditions
- exercising power
- responsibility
- independence
- meeting people through work
- business travel
- the respect of colleagues \ customers \ clients
- helping other people

b **Discuss with your partner whether you would be interested in a career in the following jobs. (Forget entrance exams.) State your opinion and give reasons.**

- a physician
- the owner/manager of a restaurant
- an actor/actress
- a stewardess/steward
- a teacher
- a model
- a politician
- a detective

c **Suppose all jobs were paid by the hour. Imagine that your group is a committee whose task is to determine the hourly pay for the different occupations. Make your decisions about the following jobs, and when you have finished, compare them with the other groups. Let's have 100 units for driving a bus as a basis for comparison.**

- a dentist
- a banker
- a hospital nurse
- a university professor
- an actor
- a policeman
- a pilot
- a sports coach
- a teacher
- a pop singer
- a greengrocer
- a diplomat

d **According to a recent survey in Britain, the most disliked occupations are the following: *politician, journalist, lawyer, used car dealer, traffic warden.* Working in small groups, try to give an explanation for these findings. Make a list of the possible reasons in each case.**

What do you think would be the results of a similar survey in Hungary?

e **If you were made redundant or just couldn't find a suitable job in your line of business, what would you do to earn some money to survive on? Discuss the possible strategies in pairs, and then share your ideas with the rest of the class.**

HOMEWORK

VOCABULARY
survival kit
preview

Read through the new vocabulary list on page 89-90, and consult a dictionary if you come across something that is unfamiliar or unclear to you.

EXAM TIPS

The role-play task

☞ While doing the role-play task, it is very important that you should try and behave as naturally as possible, even if you do not find the situation itself particularly natural. The following tips might help you achieve this aim.

There's no need to follow the instructions on the card word by word (there is no preparation time during the exam, anyway). Rather than do this, read the card very carefully once, try to memorise the three or four most important *points* about it, and concentrate on the situation itself. While doing the task, however, make sure you do touch upon these main points, or else you will lose points. Don't worry, you are allowed to peep into the card during the role-play.

As this is a dialogue, you should be an active partner in the conversation, e.g. ask questions if you think it is appropriate, avoid simple *yes or no* answers, etc.

Instead of asking direct questions and giving very straight answers, try and introduce them with polite phrases, link words, fillers, or, in one word, dummies. When, for example, the task says "*Ask a stranger for directions*", instead of just saying "*Can you tell me ...*" you should say something like this: "*Excuse me, I wonder if you can help me. You know I'm a stranger in this town, and I don't exactly know ...*". If you reply to this stranger, you should not just say "*Go down this street, turn left ...*" but something like this: "*Certainly. Well, let me see. OK, I suppose it's quite simple. The best thing to do is ...*"

UNIT 4
A place to live

LESSON 1

VOCABULARY
survival kit

Villages, towns, cities
in the west\east\north\south of Hungary, 50 kilometers south of the capital, Transdanubia, the Great Hungarian Plain, county, industrial\agricultural area, the countryside, has a population of ..., is famous/known for ..., tourist attraction, the sights, cathedral, statue, monument, museum

the Castle Hill, the Castle District, the Danube bank, Matthias Church, the Royal Palace, the Fishermen's Bastion, Chain Bridge, Elizabeth Bridge, Margaret Island, the Parliament Building, the Citadel and the Liberty Monument, the Museum of Fine Arts, the Art Gallery, the National Museum, Heroes' Square, the Millenary Monument, the Tunnel, the City Park, the baths, the Buda Hills, the Danube Bend, Lake Balaton

Houses and flats
semi(detached house), bungalow, cottage, terraced house, a block of flats *[BrE]*, apartment block/high-rise block *[AmE]*, condo(minium) *[AmE]*, bed-sitter, on the first floor, stairs

A place to live
property, freehold\council housing, lodgings/digs, dorm, to rent, rented accomodation/housing/flat/house, rent, tenant, building society, bank loan, mortgage, a roof over one's head, squatter, squatting, to evict, eviction, homeless(ness), housing shortage

The neighbourhood
situated/located ..., just off ..., in the city centre/centre of the city/inner city, downtown *[AmE]*, district, on the outskirts, greenbelt, on a housing estate, handy for the shops, within easy reach of ..., with good public transport connections, with every amenity\the basic amenities

Buildings and rooms
a three-storey building, on the third floor, a three-bedroom flat, a 3 by 4 room, square meter, to overlook/look onto ... , to face south, upstairs, downstairs, bed-sitting room, sitting/living room/lounge, bedroom, kitchen, lavatory/loo *[BrE]*, bathroom/john *[AmE]*, larder/pantry, dining room, study, hall, balcony, patio, garden *[BrE]*/yard *[AmE]*

Furnishings

Fixtures and fittings

with all mod(ern) con(venience)s, central\gas heating, tile stove, bath, tap *[BrE]*/faucet *[AmE]*, shower, wash basin, towel rack, fitted kitchen, sink, cooker, (microwave) oven, dustbin, (wall-)paper, (wall-to-wall) carpet, rug, curtain *[BrE]*/drapes *[AmE]*

Furniture

three-piece suite, armchairs, settee/sofa, chest of drawers, wall units, coffee table, book-case, shelf, flower stand, double bed, bedside table, wardrobe *[BrE]*, closet *[AmE]*, cupboard, cabinet, desk, standing\reading\bedside lamp, light, TV-set, stereo, cassette\CD player, VCR, vase, candlestick, poster

Home improvements

to furnish, to modernise, to refurbish/to do up, to decorate, to make improvements, to convert, to move house, to have something repaired/fixed\installed/fitted/etc., D(o)-I(t)-Y(ourself)

SPEAKING
conversation

Use the following guidelines to tell your partner about where you live.

address → town/sights → neighbourhood → building → inside → your room → things you particularly like about the place → things you don't like → your dream house

SPEAKING
pictures

A

B

a **Discuss with the class what vocabulary you need to describe the pictures.**

Verbs:	Nouns:	Adjectives:

b **Agree with your partner which one of you has picture A and B, and take turns to describe what you can see in them.**

In the foreground: → In the background: → On the left: → On the right:

c **Still in pairs, make intelligent guesses about the situation in your pictures. (Your teacher has all the information about the true circumstances in which the pictures were taken.) Focus your attention on the following things:**

Where do you think the picture was taken? What are the clues?
Who do you think the people in the picture are?
What do you think could have happened before photo A was taken?

You may find the following phrases useful here: *This photo shows a … ⊸ This is a photo of … ⊸ In this photo … ⊸ I would say … ⊸ I think they are/may be (…-ing). Perhaps …/Maybe … ⊸ I'm not sure // I can't say for sure/certain, but it may be …/it could be …/it might be … ⊸ It may/might/could have … ⊸ It must have … ⊸ I can see a …, so it must be … ⊸ I can/can't see a …, so it can't be … ⊸ I think this photo was taken … ⊸ This photo must have been taken … ⊸ I can't see very much of … ⊸ It's difficult to make it out because … ⊸ It looks as if/though they are … ⊸ It looks (very much) like a … ⊸ I'm absolutely sure/certain … // I have/There's no doubt that … // There can't be any doubt that …*

FUNCTIONS
role-play

a **Read both role-cards, and agree with your partner who's A and who's B.**

A You have just bought a new flat on a housing estate. You have certain ideas about the interior design, but you want your friend's advice because you are not quite sure about certain details. Ask your friend if s/he thinks it would be a good idea to …

- paint the walls pink.
- have a nice fireplace in the living room.
- put up huge Mickey Mouse and Donald Duck posters in her/his bedroom.
- have an artificial palm tree in the hall.
- having garden gnomes on the balcony.

B Your friend has just bought a new flat on a housing estate and s/he wants your advice on her/his ideas about the interior design of the flat.

- Tell her/him that you think cream-coloured or white walls would be better.
- Tell her/him you don't think it is a good idea in a small housing estate flat.
- Remind her/him that s/he is 28 years old.
- Tell her/him a real one would be a lot better.
- Remark that you think they look nicer in gardens.

b Try and agree with the rest of your class how you could use the following phrases in this situation; complete the phrases and answer the questions.

A: ***I'd like your advice on/about ... // Can/Could you give me some advice on/about ... // What do you reckon I should do? // What would you do if you were me/in my shoes?***

A: ***Do you think I should ...? // Would you advise me to ...? // Reckon I should ...? // Do you think it would be a good idea to ...? // What would you recommend ..? // What would you say to ...?***

B: *As a matter of fact, ... // Actually, ... // Quite frankly/honestly, ...*

B: *I think ... // The way I see it, ... // If you ask me, ... // What I reckon is ... // I'd say ... // If I were you ... // As I see it, ... // In my opinion ... // In my view ... // To my mind ... // Personally, I feel ...*

B: *But don't you think ... // Do you really think ... // Surely you don't think ... // Are you kidding? // You must be joking. // You don't really think ...*

B: *You're forgetting ... // Please don't forget ... // I'd like to remind you ... // After all ...*

B: *Take my advice, and ... // If you follow my advice, you'll ...*

c Rehearse the situation in pairs. Read the situation again before starting but try and rely only on the notes below while practising.

asking for advice → walls → fireplace → posters → palm → gnomes → thanking

PRONUNCIATION 1

sounds & word stress

Sounds

☞ There is usually no difficulty in pronouncing diphthongs; the real problem is that it is so tempting to be lazy and shorten them … . Please don't.

Listen and repeat.

[eɪ]	[aɪ]	[əʊ]	[aʊ]	[ɔɪ]	[eə]	[ɪə]	[ʊə]
pay	time	low	cow	boy	hair	here	poor
day	ice	old	house	toy	pair	near	moor
great	find	both	loud	voice	wear	clear	sure
take	eye	most	town	point	pear	beer	tour
break	buy	road	down	coin	bear	real	cure
able	height	told	now	joy	mayor	cheers	Europe

Word stress

☞ In some word combinations the main stress can be either on the first or the second element. If we pronounce such a word on its own, or if there's no stressed word immediately after it, the stress will be *on the second element*; if there is a stressed word after it, the stress will be *on the first element*.

Listen and repeat.

- Why don't we go down'**stairs**?
- He is extremely good-'**look**ing.
- She is not more than six'**teen**.
- I haven't been to New '**York**.

- The '**down**stairs part of the house.
- He is a very '**good**-looking guy.
- A nice '**six**teen-year-old Trabant.
- He's got a strong '**New** York accent.

HOMEWORK

VOCABULARY

survival kit

study task

Study the word list on page 89-90, and memorise the words and phrases that you think are important and relevant to you and your living conditions. When you have finished, put the following words in their correct places in the passage below to check your knowledge. (You might try and do the task without using the box.)

squatters, societies, evict, shortage, mod cons, place, property, council, roof, rent, homeless, furnish, squatting, rented

.... of housing has always been a serious problem in Hungary but today, with the vast majority of the population reduced to poverty, the situation has become truly desperate. Actually, if you have a .... to live, you can consider yourself very lucky: .... housing and building .... (cheap bank loans) are practically non-existent, the private .... sector is far too expensive, so you should either inherit something or marry the right person.

We hurry past a growing number of .... people in the streets every day. These miserable people are hopeless victims of unemployment and divorce, or both, and there are more and more young people among them.

It's small wonder ...., in other words taking someone else's .... and using it without paying a ...., is becoming increasingly widespread. .... move into properties that are empty and in a terrible condition. They repair them, ... them and, although they are still not luxury homes equipped with all ...., at least they can avoid having to sleep in the street until, sooner or later, the police .... them.

Some people say this is stealing, others say this is just sheer self-defence. The moral dilemma is this: Can you blame these people for doing something illegal if there are no other realistic chances for them to have a .... over their heads? What would you do if you were in a situation like this?

GRAMMAR FOCUS
p r e v i e w

Talking about the future

There are a number of different ways of talking about the future:

Use the Simple Future Tense
when you decide to do sg at the time of speaking *[OK/all right/I think …]*.
➢ *OK, I'll buy it.*
for threats, promises and offers.
➢ *I'll tell mum if you don't stop immediately.*
for predictions about the future *[probably, I'm sure, I think, I expect…]*.
➢ *You'll probably like her. I expect they'll be a bit late.*

Use the *to be going* to structure
when you talk about sg you have already decided to do (an intention).
➢ *I'm going to marry her.*
when you talk about a prediction based on present "symptoms".
➢ *He is not hardworking enough; he is going to fail the exam. Look at those clouds; it's going to snow.*
(or the Simple Future) to say what we think will happen in the future (predictions).
➢ *It is going to be expensive.* (Just look at those diamonds in it!) *It will be expensive.* (Such things are usually expensive.)

Use the Present Continuous Tense
to talk about sg you have arranged to do.
➢ *I'm going to the cinema this evening.*

Use the Future Continuous Tense
to talk about sg that will be happening at a particular time in the future.
➢ *I'll be walking down Oxford Street this time tomorrow.*
to talk about sg that will be happening when another event (Present Simple!) happens in the future.
➢ *We'll be still doing the test when they finish.*
to talk about two events that will be happening at the same time in the future. (The part introduced by *while* is in the Present Continuous!)
➢ *While we're doing the test they'll be lying in the sun.*
to describe an action that will be continuing for a length of time in the future (often as an "alibi" or excuse).
➢ *I'll be working all evening.*
to politely ask somebody about their plans, especially when we want something.
➢ *Will you be using your bike on Sunday?*
(or the Present Continuous Tense) to talk about sg you have already planned, decided or arranged to do.
➢ *We're seeing/we'll be seeing my parents at the weekend.*

Use the Simple Present
to talk about timetables and programmes.
➢ *Our train leaves at 5.30. The film starts at 9.*
to talk about the future after *when, as, before, after, as soon as , until, while, if, who/which, that.*
➢ *Students who cheat will be expelled. If you have any news, can you let me know? You'll be quite as pretty when you're 40. I'll let you know as soon as they arrive.*

Use *to be to*

to talk about plans and arrangements for the future. (*úgy van, hogy …, az a szándéka, hogy …, a tervek szerint*)

➢ *Joan and Peter are to get married in the near future. The British Prime Minister is to visit Hungary in May.*

Use *to be about to*

to say that sg is going to happen very soon, in the very near future

➢ *Sit down, the lecture is about to start.*

LESSON 2

VOCABULARY
survival kit
checkpoint

a **Check the fill-in-the-blank homework task with the rest of the class.**

b **What kind of housing would you expect the following people to have in Hungary?**

- a farmer with a family of three
- a city doctor with wife and one kid
- a tramp
- a rather poor student who goes to college in a different town than his home
- a middle aged divorced secretary
- a rich business executive and his family
- a factory worker with wife and two kids
- a young married couple, both teachers
- a successful actor in his 60s with his wife

c **Study the picture and name as many different pieces of furniture as you can.**

d **Complete the definitions.**

- An apartment in a building with several apartments, each of which is owned by the people living in it, and also the building itself is called a .... in American English.
- A kitchen that has fixed cupboards that fit exactly into a particular space is called a ....
- .... are things, for example shops, restaurants, parks, sports facilities, etc. that make it easier and nicer to live somewhere.
- The money you pay for the use of someone else's room/flat/house is the ....
- A large piece of furniture that is used for hanging clothes in is called a ....

GRAMMAR FOCUS

translation into English

Talking about the future

Translate the following sentences into English, discussing each section with the rest of the class as you progress.

❶ – Mit csinálsz szombat este?
– Színházba megyek.

....

....

❷ A nővérem augusztusra várja a kisbabáját. *(to have a baby)*

....

....

❸ A film 8-kor kezdődik, és 9.30-kor fejeződik be.
A vonat 10-kor indul, és 12-kor érkezik.

....

....

....

❹ – Hallom, örököltél egy csomó pénzt. Mit fogsz vele csinálni? *(I hear, to inherit)*
– Veszek egy új Trabantot.
– És mit csinálsz a régivel?
– Eladom.

....

....

....

5 Archibald reménytelen eset, meg fog bukni a vizsgán.
Ez le fog törni, már lötyög. *(to be loose)*

....

....

....

6 – Túl fáradt vagyok ahhoz, hogy gyalog menjek haza. Azt hiszem, fogok egy taxit.

....

....

7 – Elmondok neked egy titkot, ha megígéred, hogy nem mondod el senkinek.
– Nem mondom el senkinek, ígérem.

....

....

8 Jövő ilyenkor Angliában leszek.
Valószínűleg egy kicsit késni fogok.
Azt hiszem, megveszem.

....

....

....

9 Holnap ilyenkor az angol tesztet fogom írni.
Meg fogsz ismerni, egy piros öltöny lesz rajtam.
– Használod az autót ma este? Ha nem, elviszem.

....

....

....

10 Írok, mihelyt válaszolsz a levelemre.
Amikor a vizsgáknak vége, síelni megyünk.
Mire hazajönnek, kész lesz a vacsora.
Ha túl drága lesz, nem veszem meg.

....

....

....

LISTENING

Housing problems in Hungary

**Interview with Mr Rupert Johnson,
partner in Benson & Johnson Real Estates International, Budapest**

a Read the question and try to answer it when you have listened to the recording once. Discuss your answer with your partner.

- What does Mr Johnson say is the main cause of the housing problem in Hungary?

b Answer the following questions as you listen to the tape for the second time. Discuss your answers with the rest of the class.

- What does Mr Johnson say about the prices on the Hungarian property market?
- What does he say about average wages?
- Where does he say a real shortage exists?
- How long does he say the average citizen would have to save up to buy a cheap place of his own?
- What does he say about the private rented sector?
- How can real estate agencies survive on this market?
- What are the most important features of the home Mr Johnson describes?
- How much is it?

HOMEWORK

TRANSLATION

English into Hungarian

Use a dictionary to read the following article, and translate the *highlighted* part of the text into Hungarian in writing.

☞ In any text there may be words and phrases where you have no particular difficulty in understanding the meaning, but a word-for-word or even a close translation seems to be – or really is – impossible. These are the cases when you are free to do whatever you want; the important thing is that the "message" should come through, and that your sentence should sound Hungarian (e.g. apartment complexes, housing structures, scarred).

Cellars In the Sky

My old home was the suburbs of Washington D.C. Now my home is in the Budapest suburbs. There are a lot of differences.

The biggest one is that Washington is much bigger. On the one hand, the city boasts three international airports, a beltway and other major thruways, making transportation in, out and around the city easy. On the other hand, public transportation there is very expensive and not very effective compared to Budapest.

Another "bigness" factor is the height of the city's buildings. Most American cities are tall; there are tall, shiny glass or marble covered office buildings or sleek apartment complexes everywhere. They stand in sharp contrast to the "socialist" housing structures here, which are the only buildings to reach for the heavens, although in a very ugly way. "Cellars in the sky", I've heard them called.

There is also an age difference between the two cities. Budapest is marked by the ages, distinguished, graceful, yet scarred. Washington, although a babe in comparison, has outgrown its limits, turning last year's suburbs into little metropolises.

Joseph K. Balintfy, Daily News

LESSON 3

TRANSLATION
English into Hungarian
checkpoint

Cellars in the Sky

a **What kind of translations have the different people in the class come up with for the following words and phrases in the context of the passage?**

- another "bigness" factor
- sleek
- apartment complexes
- housing structures
- in a very ugly way
- I've heard them called
- Budapest is marked by the ages
- scarred
- a babe in comparison
- turning

b **Compare and discuss the possible translations for each and every sentence with the whole class.**

c **Choose three new words or phrases from the text that you think are worth remembering.**

READING & VOCABULARY
article

a **Read through the article and try to answer the following questions without using a dictionary. When you have finished, discuss your answers in pairs.**

- What was the crime Gordon Walker committed?
- How long did he stay in the house?
- What did he do there?

BREAKING and ENTERTAINING

Darlington, England. — "I couldn't help myself" said burglar Gordon Walker, "I just admired the house."

Walker, 30, broke into a luxury bungalow while the occupants were on holiday but when he discovered that the home was empty, he settled in and stayed for three days.

During the prolonged break-in the thief took the opportunity to wash and iron all his clothes, and cook himself a few meals from the family larder.

Before passing sentence the Teeside Crown Court judge told Walker: "Despite the comforts you enjoyed you did not wash a single dish. I have also noted police reports which say you left the bathroom in a mess, too."

Newcastle Evening Chronicle

b **Now try and find the English for the following words and phrases in the text, and make guesses about the possible derivatives. When you have finished, discuss them with the rest of the class.**

bíróság

....

kihasználni az alkalmat

....

valami ellenére

....

csodálni ⇒ csodálat ⇒ csodáló

....

edény ⇒ mosogatógép ⇒ mosogatóvíz/lé

....

lakó ⇒ lakni, elfoglalni

....

luxus ⇒ luxus minőségű

....

hosszas/hosszantartó

....

rendetlenség ⇒ rendetlenséget csinálni ⇒ elfuserálni/elrontani/eltolni valamit

....

tolvaj ⇒ lopás

....

betörő ⇒ betörni ⇒ betörés ⇒ lakás riasztó

....

ítéletet hozni ⇒ életfogytiglanra ítélni ⇒ halálra ítélni ⇒ halálos ítélet

....

berendezkedni/betelepedni

....

bíró ⇒ megítélni ⇒ ítélet

....

jólét/kényelem

....

nem tudtam ellenállni

....

szórakozás (!) ⇒ szórakoztató

....

zárfeltörés és behatolás (!!)

....

c **Now read the following questions and answer them in writing after reading the article again. When you have finished, discuss the answers with the rest of the class.**

What was unusual about the crime Gordon Walker committed?

....

Why did he say he had done that?

....

What are the things that he did not do, which might make things worse for him?

....

PRONUNCIATION 2

stress, rhythm & intonation

Stress & rhythm

☞ Weak forms: *do* [dʊ or də or d], *does* [dəz], *can* [kən or kn], *could* [kəd], *had* [həd or əd or d], *must* [məst], *shall* [ʃəl or ʃl], *should* [ʃəd], *was* [wəz], *were* [wə or wər], *will* [l], *would* [wəd or əd or d]

Listen and repeat.

- Do I have to tell you?
- Do you like it?
- Do you speak German?
- Where does he work?
- How does it feel?
- You can ask him.
- I can help you.
- I could do it.
- She could have bought it.
- Had you ever been there before?
- I thought I'd lost it.
- She said she'd eaten it.
- I must go now.
- You must tell him immediately.
- I shall wait for you.
- Shall I open it?
- We should have bought it.
- It should be cheap.
- It was terrible.
- She was wonderful.
- We were really disappointed.
- You were great.
- What'll you do now?
- It'll be expensive.
- I'd like to marry you.
- She said she'd give it to me.

Intonation

☞ If there's something we couldn't quite understand or believe, we ask a question to clarify the message. In this case there is a strong stress on the *wh*-word, and the tune starts *rising* from the next word.

Listen and repeat.

I was born in 1848. ↗**When** were you born???

She married her English teacher. ↗**Who** did she marry???

They eat cat meat. ↗**What** do they eat???

You should have your hair cut. ↗**What** should I do???

LINK WORDS

Make sure you know what the following link words mean, and working in pairs, use as many as you can to make the text below sound more natural and dynamic. When you have found a suitable place for all of them, take turns to read out the new text.

(1) preferably (2) after all (3) as for/regards (4) at least (5) by the way/incidentally (6) talking of (7) to begin with/first and foremost (8) it is essential that

My dream house:

......................., the house should be situated in a quiet neighbourhood, ... in one which is within easy reach of the city centre. My wife and kids don't drive, so .... the place should have good public transport connections. In addition, it should be handy for the shops, too.

.... the house itself, it should have a huge living room, four bedrooms, ... three bathrooms, a study, a playroom, a large balcony, and, above all, a garden, because I want to keep a lot of dogs and cats.

.... garden, I also want a huge heated swimming pool and, needless to say, a nice patio as well, where I'd have breakfast after swimming.

......................., I'd also need a large garage, ..., I must keep my Mercedeses, Jaguars and BMWs somewhere, mustn't I?

HOMEWORK

VOCABULARY

article

study tasks

Breaking and Entertaining

a Read the article again and memorise any vocabulary items that are new to you. When you have finished, use the words in the box to fill in the gaps in the passage below. Change the form of the words if necessary.

occupant
comforts
dish
mess
burglar
to help
admiration
judge
luxury
to break
to settle
larder
prolonged
bungalow
opportunity

Hi there. My name's Gordon and I'm a .... by trade. I was hanging about in this fancy neighbourhood the other day when I caught sight of this beauty. Quite frankly, it was about the most terrific .... I'd ever seen, a ginormous garden, a pool, four bedrooms, anything you can possibly imagine. I've always felt a deep .... for .... places, and this one was in complete darkness with a couple of milk bottles on the doorstep meaning that the .... were away. No wonder I couldn't .... myself and took the .... to break into the house and .... in for a .... stay to enjoy its .... I cooked wonderful meals from the things I'd found in the ...., I had a nice bath every day; in short, I had a great time there. Now this .... is telling me that I should have washed up the .... and that I shouldn't have left the bathroom in a .... The old guy doesn't seem to see the point: I .... into the place because I'd had enough of doing the housework at home.

b **Use the following guidelines to prepare for a short oral summary of the article about the burgler in a few sentences.**

What the guy did → Why he did it → What he should have done

WRITING
letter

Use the guidelines to reply to the following advertisement:

You have won a scholarship to study philosophy at Oxford, so you won't be around for a couple of years;

> **English businessman requires fully furnished house or flat in nice area for a reasonable price for long-term lease.**
> **Please send offers to Sun Personals, Budapest, Bp. 114 Pf. 99, 1525 Hungary**

letting your house\flat seems to be a good way to earn some extra money.

Step One	Step two	Step three
General outline: Plan the general structure of the composition.	Brainstorming: Think of the most important things the future tenant may be interested in.	Work out a more detailed paragraph structure.
Introduction	greeting, reference to advertisement, introducing yourself, the situation	*Dear Sir …, Referring to/I read your advertisement in last Monday's issue of* The Budapest Sun *… // I am writing to you in connection with …*
Description of house\flat	address, public transport, neighbourhood, building, size, rooms, furniture, state of repair, heating, phone, TV channels, orientation, etc., price	*There is/are …; As regards … // As for … // With regards to …; By the way, …; In addition (to)*
Conclusion	closing the letter	*I am looking/I look forward to hearing from you soon; I would greatly appreciate an early reply; Yours faithfully*

☞ When you have finished, don't forget to check your work for grammatical mistakes.

LESSON 4

VOCABULARY
a r t i c l e
checkpoint

Breaking and Entertaining

a **Compare your solutions to the fill-in-the-gap homework task with the rest of the class.**

b **Discuss with the rest of the class what you think the English would be for the following Hungarian sentences.**

Az egész lakásban szörnyű rendetlenség volt.

....

....

A bíró három évre ítélte a férfit betöréses lopásért.

....

....

Szeretném kihasználni az alkalmat, hogy elmondjam Önnek, hogy mennyire csodálom.

....

....

Az autólopások száma megduplázódott az elmúlt három évben.

....

....

Mindenki szeretné egy Mercedes kényelmét élvezni, de csak kevesen engedhetik meg maguknak ezt a luxust.

....

....

c **Working in pairs, give a brief summary of the article we read last lesson.**

GRAMMAR FOCUS
mini test

Talking about the future

Do the following test and check it with the rest of the class.

1. Unless the government … something about unemployment, there will be serious problems.
A will do **C** doesn't do
B won't do **D** does

2. This time tomorrow I … on a train bound for Lake Balaton.
A am sitting **C** will sit
B will be sitting **D** will have been sitting

3. I feel quite awful. I think I … down with the flu.
A will come **C** will be coming
B am going to come **D** come

4. When … know whether you … the exam or not?
A are you going to // have passed **C** will you // passed
B will you // will pass **D** will you // have passed

5. "What would you like to drink, coffee or tea?" "I … coffee, please."
A will have **C** am having
B have **D** going to have

6. "Why are you putting on those old jeans?" "I … the car."
A am washing **C** will wash
B will be washing **D** am going to wash

7. I … my school leaving exam in June.
A am taking **C** take
B will be take **D** going to take

8. … anything this weekend? You know, we … a party on Saturday. Would you like to come?
A Will you be doing // are having **C** Do you do // are having
B Do you do // will have **D** Will you do // have

9. According to the weatherman it … again tomorrow.
A is snowing **C** will snow
B will be snow **D** snows

10. I think they … the elections. I will be very surprised if they … .
A are winning // won't **C** win // don't
B will win // don't **D** will win // won't

SPEAKING

discussion

a **Suppose you and your partner have a room exactly like the one you are in at the moment. You can carry out any improvements you wish, the aim is that this room should be converted into a nice sitting room or bedroom for two people. Use a separate piece of paper to draw the plan of the redecorated and refurnished room. When most pairs have finished, put all the plans on the wall and compare your finished products.**

b **What's your opinion about the following statements? Think of some reasons to support your view and then compare your ideas with your partner's.**

1. "You are what your house/flat/room is like". Just by looking at someone's place you can pass a pretty good judgement on the occupant's personality.
2. "You are where you live." Just by looking at someone's address you can size up the person's social standing and living standards.

c **Answer the following questions in pairs.**

- Would you ever have the walls of your sitting room painted a) dark brown, b) pink?
- Would you rather live in digs or a dorm if you were studying at university in another town?
- Do/Did you have to share a room with a brother or a sister?
- Would you be ready to live in digs during the first few years of your marriage?
- What Budapest tourist attractions would you advise a foreigner to visit if s/he had only one day for sightseeing?

d **Choose the interior that most appeals to you, and then describe it to your partner so that s/he can identify it. When you have finished, find out about the most popular interiors in the class.**

HOMEWORK

VOCABULARY
survival kit
preview

Read through the new vocabulary list on page 117-118, and consult a dictionary if you come across something that is unfamiliar or unclear to you.

EXAM TIPS

The reading comprehension task

☞ When doing the reading comprehension task (the article), you must get used to the idea that you simply cannot afford to look up *all* the words you don't know, or else you will run out of time. These texts are usually rather tough, and dictionary work is very time-consuming. Don't forget that time-constraints are your worst enemy at the written exam.

What you should do instead is start *with the* (Hungarian language) *questions*, because **a)** they will give you the general idea about the whole story, **b)** they will focus your attention on the aspects that are really important from the point of view of the exam. When you have read the questions, read the article once but *do not look up any words* at that point yet. By now you should have at least a vague idea of what the whole thing is all about. Go back to the questions for a second time (you might be able to answer a few of them now) and let them lead you as you read the article again, looking up the necessary words this time. Avoid *yes* or *no* answers, and do not use the same information to answer two different questions. (Your answers should be in Hungarian, too.) Make sure you've found *all* the relevant pieces of information to answer the question (most questions refer to the article as a whole, so the relevant pieces of information might come from different parts of the article).

REVISION Test 1

A

Do the following multiple choice test, and when you have finished, discuss it with the rest of the class.

1. Small wonder … English language has become a lingua franca; … English speaking countries are world powers and … English is relatively easy, too.

A — // — // the
B the // — // —
C the // — // the
D — // the // —

2. I like pizza and …

A so my kids do.
B so do my kids.
C my kids do so.
D my kids so do.

3. I am sorry it … so long to reply to your letter but I … rather busy recently, you know, I … for my school-leaving exams in June.

A has taken // have been // am preparing
B took // was // have been preparing
C took // have been // prepare
D is taking // was // was preparing

4. Each of the girls …

A have an own room.
B has an own room.
C have own rooms.
D has a room of her own.

5. At this time tomorrow I … the last chapter of the book, and hopefully I … the whole thing by ten o'clock.

A will write // finish
B am writing // will be finishing
C am going to write // will finish
D will be writing // will have finished

6. We must go now; … is quite late and … is no public transport after eleven.

A it // there
B it // it
C there// it
D there // there

7. "Can I borrow your bike on Saturday, please?" "Oh, I am afraid I … it. You know, we … on a day excursion to Blackpool."

A am going to use // go
B will use // will be going
C will be using // are going
D am using // will go

8. This test is … the one we did last week.

A almost so difficult like
B even more easy as
C not quite as easy as
D a bit less difficult as

9. Darwin's theory of evolution … hotly disputed ever since his famous book The Origin of Species … first published.

A was // had been
B has been // had been
C has been // was
D was // has been

10. Time seems to fly … when you are having fun.

A more fast
B much more fastly
C much faster
D a lot fastlier

11. Can you hear that? Peter and Mary … again. They … , and it … worse and worse.

A are arguing // are always arguing // is getting
B have been arguing // always argue // has got
C have argued // always argue // gets
D argue // are always arguing // will get

12. As nobody speaks Russian in our family, we had to ask a friend of my … to help us with the translation.

A parents
B parent's
C parents'
D parents's

13. I don't think … girls will be very keen on the idea. In my experience, … girls don't particularly like … football matches.

A the // the // the
B the // — // —
C — // the // —
D — // — // the

14. Inflation is a vicious circle; the more wages go up, …

A the better the prices.
B the more prices do.
C prices do even better.
D so do prices.

15. We … about the problem for some time now, but we … able to find any solution so far.

A have thought // aren't
B have been thought // haven't been
C have been thinking // have not been
D think // are not

16. Both my mother … left-handed.

A and my father is
B and my father are
C both my father are
D and both my father is

17. We decided to go to … cinema, so we went to … Odeon in … Leicester Square.

A a // — // —
B the // the // —
C a // the // the
D the // — // —

18. Peter is growing very fast; I have to buy him … every other month.

A a new shoes
B a new piece of shoes
C a new pair of shoes
D a new shoe

19. After five hours of deliberation the jury … to a decision. They … up their minds to declare the man guilty.

A came // had made
B had come // have made
C came // have made
D has come // made

20. I didn't remember his address and … my wife.

A so did
B neither did
C also didn't
D so didn't

21. Normally I … work at five o'clock, but I … at nine this week. You know, we are very busy just now.

A am finishing // will finish
B finish // going to finish
C finish // am finishing
D finish // finish

22. He's devoted his whole life to helping …

A poors.
B the poor.
C the poors.
D poor.

23. Look, there isn't a single cloud in the sky. It … be another hot day. I think I .. to the beach.

A will // am going
B is going to // go
C will // go
D is going to // will go

24. It won't be easy to sell a … Trabant, I'm afraid.

A such old
B fifteen years old
C so old
D fifteen year old

25. … literature is my favourite subject. I am particularly interested in … contemporary literature, especially … literature of Eastern European peoples.

A — // — // the
B the // the // —
C the // — // —
D — // the // the

26. … of the American states has its own system of public education.

A All
B Most
C Each
D Every

27. Someone … the gate open. I'm sure my father … when he … out.

A left // has done // went
B has left // did // went
C left // did // had gone
D had left // did // had gone

28. They said my English wasn't … for that job.

A enough good
B quite good
C too good
D good enough

29. As soon as I … any news I … you know immediately.

A hear // let
B will hear // will let
C hear // will let
D will hear // let

30. "Are coaches any cheaper than trains?" "…"

A I think so.
B I think it.
C I think.
D I think yes.

31. Peter ... an accident. He ... down the motorway when a tyre ... flat and he crashed into another car.

A has had // was driving // went
B had // drove // went
C had // had been driving // had gone
D had // was driving // had gone

32. What kind of ... do you think I should buy for the sitting room?

A pieces of furnitures
B furnitures
C furniture
D a furniture

33. "... American films are awful." "Well, that's a generalisation. You shouldn't form an opinion on the basis of ... American films you can see on ... TV."

A the // the // the
B the // — // the
C — // — // —
D — // the // —

34. Such plans have ... reality in the present economic situation.

A not
B a few
C little
D few

35. The judge ... a word until he ... to both parties.

A had not said // listened
B did not say // had listened
C had not said // had not listened
D wasn't saying // had not listened

36. I had to do an awful lot of translation ... I was at secondary school.

A during
B in the meantime
C meanwhile
D while

37. "Just take a look at Judy's eyes, I'm sure she ... ." "You are right, they ... a loud argument when I ... them a few minutes ago."

A has cried // had // saw
B was crying // had // have seen
C has been crying // were having // saw
D cried // were having // was seeing

38. He is ... intelligent guy, I'm sure he'll be admitted to university.

A such
B so
C so an
D such an

39. "What ... on Saturday afternoon?" "I ... football with my friends. I ... football on Saturdays."

A are you going to do// am playing//always play
B do you do//am going to play//play always
C will you do//play//am always playing
D are you doing//will play//play always

40. John's got ... man friends, but he doesn't go out with any girls.

A plenty of
B a lots of
C a great deal of
D a lot

B

Read the definitions and supply the appropriate words or phrases.

1. Your .... is the person you are married to. This is a rather formal word.

2. A .... is a person who lives in an unused building without having the legal right to do so and without paying any rent.

3. A .... is a person or a company that arranges the writing, production and sale of books, papers, etc.

4. An .... is a businessman who uses his money to set up business deals in order to make a profit.

5. If you .... , you stay away from school when you should be there.

6. If you have been made ...., you have been made unemployed because the employer you worked for no longer has a job for you.

7. An .... is damage or harm done to the body caused by an accident or an attack.

8. A .... is a small area of a town where people live.

9. If you .... something that has been carefully made, done or planned, you spoil or ruin it.

10. If you .... university, you fill in a form asking to be allowed to do your studies there.

11. .... are extra things you get from your employer in addition to your salary.

12. When teachers are ...., they are not as strict as teachers are supposed to be.

13. A .... is a bank loan you get from a financial institution in order to buy a flat or a house.

14. .... is the quality of being able to do a task successfully without wasting time and energy.

15. The .... is (used to be?) the fantastic Hungarian system that allows a mother to spend three years away from work when she has a baby.

16. A .... is a book containing facts, information and practice material that we regularly use during lessons on a particular subject.

17. If something is .... it is so special that it cannot be replaced if it is lost or destroyed.

18. If you have a .... house or flat, you have complete ownership of it.

19. If you ...., you are able to manage financially because you have just enough money for your needs.

20. If you say that something is ...., you mean that you are strongly against it and you feel that you cannot allow it to continue.

C

Translate the following text into English. (Use a dictionary if necessary.)

✓ Te jó ég, mi történt az autóddal?

✓ A piros lámpánál várakoztam a Moszkva térnél tegnap délután, amikor egy idióta hátulról belémjött.

✓ Na de miért nem állt meg ő is?

✓ Azt mondja a pasas, hogy meg akart ő állni, csak már nem volt elég ideje.

✓ De a biztosító ki fogja fizetni a kárt, nem?

✓ Hála Istennek, legalább ez úgy tűnik rendben van. Lesz elég tennivalóm amúgy is.

✓ Hát, mi tagadás, elég csúnyán néz ki. Most mit fogsz csinálni?

✓ A biztosítónál már voltam, most elviszem a kocsit egy szerelőhöz.

✓ El fog tartani egy darabig, amíg megjavítják.

✓ Hát éppen ez a probléma! Most nem lesz kocsim egy pár napig, pedig a hétvégén a Balatonra megyünk. A szerelők állandóan panaszkodnak, hogy nincs elég munka, és akkor napokba telik amíg megjavítanak egy kocsit. Azért remélem, péntekre megjavítják.

UNIT 5 Daily life

LESSON 1

VOCABULARY
survival kit

Getting ready
daily routine, to get up, to wake up, to oversleep, a late\early riser, to wash oneself, to have a shower\bath, to brush one's teeth, to have a shave, to get dressed, to have breakfast, to leave home, to leave for school\work

Getting there
to walk to the bus stop, to take/catch a number 7 bus, to go as far as ..., to get off, to change to ..., to take\drive the kids to ..., to get to work\school (at\by), to be late for school\work

Back to work
to have an early morning lesson, to have a snack in the school\office canteen, to have lunch in the school dining-room\at a restaurant, to miss lunch, to finish school\work, to leave for home

At home
to get home, to collect the kids from ..., to drop/ doze off, to have a snooze/to take a nap, to go to/to have a training session, to have a private lesson, to do the homework, to have dinner/tea/ supper, to go to bed, to go to sleep/to fall asleep, to put the kids to bed

Freetime
on weekdays, at weekends/at the weekend, in sy's spare time, leisure (time), leisure/spare time activity, to have a rest, to stay in, to go out

Managing the household
to do the housework, to do\split/share the (household\daily) chores, to keep the house clean/tidy, to tidy up/clean the flat/to do the cleaning, to do the hoovering *[BrE]*/vacuum cleaning, to dust the furniture, to clean the windows, to sweep\scrub the floor, to empty the rubbish/bin, to make the bed, to air the room, to water the flowers, to do the cooking,

to prepare a meal, to do the washing-up, to dry up the dishes, to wash the clothes, to hang out the clothes to dry, to iron the clothes, to sew, to mend/repair/fix *[AmE]* things, to clean the car, to do the shopping and buy ..., to buy the daily groceries, to do (some) gardening, to mow the lawn, child rearing, to look after \ to take care of the kids, to keep the kids clean

Labour-saving devices

household gadgets/appliances, automatic washing machine, detergent, washing powder, broom, hoover *[BrE]*/vacuum cleaner, duster, dishwasher, washing-up liquid, henpecked husband, cleaning lady/charwoman

SPEAKING conversation

Use the following guidelines to tell your partner about a typical weekday in your life, say today, and then about the way housework is split in your family.

getting ready in the morning → going to school\work → lunch → the afternoon → the evening, going to bed → who does what? → your regular chores and your attitude towards them

SPEAKING pictures

A

B

SPEAKING
pictures

a Discuss with the class what vocabulary you need to describe the pictures.

Verbs:	Nouns:	Adjectives:

b Agree with your partner which one of you has pictures A and B, take turns to describe what you can see in them, and make guesses about the situation.

c Looking at all the pictures now, discuss what you think is relevant of the following questions in pairs (It is your personal experience/judgement/opinion/etc. that is important here!):

- Have you ever been in a situation like this?
- What is it (What do you think it could be) like to be in a situation like this?
- What do you do if you are (What would you do if you were) in a situation like this?
- What do you think of what you can see and/or what is happening in the picture?

You may find the following phrases useful here: I (can still) remember ...-ing ... ➺ I've already been in a situation like this. ➺ That reminds me of ... ➺ If I were in a situation like this ... // If such a thing happened to me ..., I would ... ➺ I think/guess ... ➺ In my opinion/view ... ➺ As far as I'm concerned ... ➺ The way I see it ... ➺ From my point of view ... ➺ It seems to me that ... ➺ I'd say ... ➺ If you ask me ... ➺ To my mind ...

FUNCTIONS

role-play

a Read both role-cards and agree with your partner who's A and who's B.

A The person sitting next to you asks you to help her/him catch up with the rest of the class as s/he has missed the past three lessons because s/he's been in bed with the flu. You would need at least two hours for this.

- ♣ Agree to get together to sit down and look at the material s/he has missed.
- ♣ Use your own (real) schedule for the next few days, and try to find a slot which is convenient for both of you. Let's suppose that today is not suitable for you, and you don't want to sacrifice your evenings (i.e. after 7 p.m.).

B You have missed the past three lessons because you have been in bed with the flu. You ask the person sitting next to you to help you catch up with the rest of the class.

- ♦ Go up to the person and tell her/him about your problem.
- ♦ Tell her/him that you would like to get together as soon as possible, but certainly before the next lesson.
- ♦ Use your own (real) schedule for the next few days, and try to find a slot which is convenient for both of you. Let's suppose that today is not suitable for you, and you don't want to sacrifice your evenings (i.e. after 7 p.m.).

b **Try and agree with the rest of your class how you could use the following phrases in this situation; complete the phrases and answer the questions.**

B: *Can I ask a favour of you? // I wonder if you could do me a favour.*

A: ***By all means. // It'd be a pleasure. // Yes, of course. // Sure.***

A: ***What's it all about? // What's the problem? // What is it? // What's up?***

B: *Well, the thing is that … // Well, the situation is that …*

B: *Do you think you could …? // Would you …? // I wonder if you could/would mind …-ing/ would you be kind enough to …*

X: Why don't we ...? // How about ...-ing ...? // What would you say to ...?

X: I'm afraid ... // I'm (very) sorry but ... // That's no good.

X: That seems to be ...

B: *Thanks a lot. // Thanks a million. // Cheers. // Great.*

A: ***It's a pleasure. // My pleasure. // That's OK/all right. // Any time.***

c **Rehearse the situation in pairs. Read the cards again before starting but try and rely only on the notes below while practising.**

explaining the situation/asking for help ➜ finding a slot ➜ thanking

PRONUNCIATION 1

sounds & word stress

Sounds

☞ [θ] is produced like a Hungarian *sz*, except that the tongue is put to the upper front teeth (if any).

[ð] is produced like a Hungarian *d*, except that the tongue is put to the upper front teeth (if any).

[w] is produced like a Hungarian *u*. Start forming a Hungarian *u* but do not actually pronounce it; immediately go over to the next sound.

[ŋ] is like a Hungarian *ng*, except that the *g* is not actually pronounced.

[r] is like a Hungarian *r*, but it's not rolled.

[ɫ] *(dark l)* is produced with a flat tongue.

[p], [t], and [k] are pronounced with a strong [h]-like sound at the beginning of stressed syllables.

Listen and repeat.

[θ]	[ð]	[w]	[ŋ]	[r]	[ɫ]	[p] [t] [k]
three	though	walk	ring	rain	cool	park
thick	mother	wash	sing	right	well	two
thin	brother	what	wrong	ring	meal	cool
bath	either	require	song	roll	milk	pain
birth	other	queen	king	spring	girl	tennis
nothing	with	persuade	Hungary [ŋg]	very	table	coffee

☞ N. B.
In *BrE*, the [r] is only pronounced if there is a vowel sound after it. The Americans pronounce all *r*-s.
The *l* will always be dark at the end of words and before consonants.
Double letters do not mean longer sounds.

Word stress

☞ There are a number of words where grammatical function determines the stress. In these cases it is the noun that is stressed at the front.

Listen and repeat.

noun	verb	noun	verb	noun	verb
'addict	a'ddict	'insult	in'sult	'record	re'cord
'decrease	de'crease	'object	ob'ject	'reject	re'ject
'desert	de'sert	'permit	per'mit	'subject	sub'ject
'escort	es'cort	'present	pre'sent	'survey	sur'vey
'export	ex'port	'produce	pro'duce	'suspect	sus'pect
'import	im'port	'progress	pro'gress	'transport	trans'port
'increase	in'crease	'rebel	re'bel	'upset	up'set

HOMEWORK

VOCABULARY
survival kit
study task

Study the word list on page 117-118, and memorise the words and phrases that you think are important and relevant to your circumstances. When you have finished, put the following words in their correct places in the passage below to check your knowledge. (You might try and do the task without using the box.)

put to bed, doing the shopping, driving, chores, cleaning lady, wash, housework, prepare, henpecked, household, kept, riser, take care, kept clean, meal, keep the house clean, groceries, watering, collects, emptying, split, finishes work

I'm not saying that I divorced my first husband only because I'd had enough of him taking me for a cheap .... and expecting me to do all the ...., but I have no doubt in my mind that his old-fashioned attitude to male and female roles played a pretty important part in my decision. Small wonder I was a lot more careful the next time; I can tell you I have no such problems with my present husband. You might think he is the stereotypical .... husband, but that's not the case at all, it's only that he has been properly trained.

Managing the .... is really a joint responsibility in our family, and we .... all the........................ and any other duties between the two of us fairly evenly. As my husband is an early ...., and I'm completely useless in the morning, it is usually his job to .... the breakfast and .... of the children, including .... them to school on his way to work. On the other hand, however, as he .... a lot later than me, it is normally me who .... the kids from school in the afternoon. I also prepare some kind of a hot .... in the evening, and we both take part in the struggle to make sure they eat properly, they are ...., the toys are picked up after them and put away, and finally that they are .... at the right time. It is usually my husband's duty to .... and to keep track of our doctor and dentist appointments. I am responsible for keeping the clothes clean, and for buying the daily .... Otherwise we either do most other things together or we take turns depending on which one of us has the time to do them. In this way we routinely share chores like ironing, washing up, ... the plants, ... the rubbish, planning menus, and .... at the weekend.

There's one thing however, that my husband will never do; and that's taking care of bills and money affairs in general. As far as I'm concerned, I would never touch the car; if my husband doesn't .... it, it will certainly stay dirty for ever.

GRAMMAR FOCUS
preview

Auxiliaries 1

Obligation *(kell)*, **ability** *(tud)*, and **permission** *(szabad, -hat/het)* can be expressed ***within the standard framework of the tenses of the verb*** (however, without the simple – continuous distinction).

a) with real ***modal auxiliaries***, which are usually rather 'damaged' (i.e. can only be used in particular tenses),

b) and ***modal verb phrases***, which, on the one hand, can be used in all tenses in their own right, and, on the other hand, instead of the real modals in the tenses where they are not available. In tenses where both the real auxiliary and the verb phrase are available, there will be a slight difference in the meaning.

Obligation

- **must** can only be used in the present and the future in questions and positive sentences.
  ➢ *I must go now.*
- **needn't** can only be used in the present and the future (in negative sentences).
  ➢ *You needn't go.*
- **to have to** and **to need to** can be used in all tenses and will replace *must* and *needn't* where they are not available.
  ➢ *I've had to take this medicine for three years. We didn't need to pay a penny.*
- **to have got to** is also common in the present and future tense.
  ➢ *We've got to be there in time.*
- **to be to** (both the active and the passive) can also be used to give orders and instructions.
  ➢ *You're to clean your teeth before you go to bed. This product is to be kept in a cool place.*

In the present and the future, where both the auxiliaries and the phrases are possible, there will be a slight difference in the meaning: *must* suggests that the obligation comes from the speaker, whereas *to have to* suggests that the obligation comes from a third person or an authority.
➢ *I must tell you something. We'll have to ask for permission.*

Ability

- **can, can't (cannot)** can be used in the present and the future.
  ➢ *We can do this tomorrow.*
- **could** can be used in the past to express general ability, but it is not used to talk about a successful act performed in a particular situation (except in the case of *to see, to feel, to hear, to smell, understand, remember)*. There is no such restriction on **couldn't**, however.
  ➢ *I could speak quite good Russian when I was in secondary school.*
- **to be able to** can be used in all tenses.
  ➢ *I haven't been able to do anything useful in the past few days.*
- **managed to** and **succeeded in** (besides *to be able to*, of course) can be used instead of the missing *could* to talk about specific occasions/actions in the past.
  ➢ *I managed/was able to do four out of the five tasks. I succeeded in doing ...*

When both the auxiliary and *to be able to* are possible (particularly in the present), the latter will put more emphasis on temporary physical or mental ability.
➢ *I can't lift this weight. (I am simply not strong enough to do it.) I'm not able to lift this weight now. (I'm not in the condition, mood, etc. now, but otherwise ...)*

Permission

- **can**, **could**, **may**, **might** can all be used in the present and the future to ask for permission. When giving permission, however, we can only use *can* and (the rather formal) *may*.
  ➢ *Can/May/Could/Might I ask you to …? You certainly can. You may, indeed.*
- **can't**, **may not** (formal), can be used to express prohibition.
  ➢ *You can't watch TV unless you do you homework. You may not take these books out of this room.*
- **mustn't** is used to express very strong prohibition.
  ➢ *You mustn't touch these documents.*
- **could** is used for general permission in the past, but not for permission for a particular action.
  ➢ *When I was in management, I could use the company car whenever I wanted to.*
- **to be allowed to** can be used in all tenses, and can replace the missing *could* for specific permission in the past.
  ➢ *I've been allowed to use the family car since I was 18. I was allowed to watch the film last night, although it was quite late.*

LESSON 2

VOCABULARY
survival kit
checkpoint

a **Check the fill-in-the-blank homework task with the rest of the class.**

b **What are the "opposites" of the following words and phrases?**

- to wake up
- to get up
- a late riser
- to get dressed
- to leave home
- to get on a bus
- to take the kids to school
- to have lunch
- on weekdays

c **What should be done to put the following things right?**

- the dishes are dirty
- there's mud on the floor
- the bin's full
- the air is stale in the room
- the dishes are wet
- your clothes are creased
- the plants have wilted
- the furniture is dusty
- the bed's unmade
- the clothes are wet
- your shirt is torn
- the grass has grown too high
- there's something wrong with the light
- there're breadcrumbs on the carpet

d Complete the definitions.

- When you sleep longer than you intended or should, you ....
- The things that people enjoy doing when they are not working or studying are called ....
- When you have a short sleep during the day, you ....
- A woman who cleans offices or houses as her job is a ....
- .... is a liquid or powder that contains soap used for washing clothes or dishes.

GRAMMAR FOCUS

translation into English

Auxiliaries 1

Translate the following sentences into English, discussing each section with the rest of the class as you progress.

1. Mióta kell szemüveget hordanod?

....

2. Bocsánat, de most már tényleg mennem kell.
Mondanom kell neked valamit.
Ez fantasztikus! Ezt meg kell vennem.

....

....

....

3. Nem kell mindent megenned, ha nem vagy éhes.
Mit kell ahhoz tennem, hogy megfeleljek a követelményeknek? *(to meet the ...)*

....

....

4. Azt kell tenned, amit mondok neked.

....

5. Csak az utolsó pillanatban tudtam megállni.
Négyet meg tudtam csinálni az öt feladatból.
A rendőrség nem tudta megállapítani a baleset pontos okát. *(to establish, exact cause)*

....

....

....

6 Mióta tudsz vezetni?

7 Nem fogom tudni megcsinálni a házi feladatot, mert orvoshoz kell mennem.

8 Rettenetes állapotban van, még felülni sem tud segítség nélkül.

9 – Feltehetek Önnek még egy kérdést?
– Nem, sajnálom, nem tehet, lejárt az idő. *(to be over)*

– Használhatom a telefont?
– Hát persze, hogy használhatod.

– Befordulhatok itt jobbra?
– Nem, nem szabad, ez egyirányú utca. *(one-way street)*

10 Szörnyű volt! Meg sem volt szabad szólalnom egész nap. *(to say a word)*
Mióta utazhatnak a magyar állampolgárok vízum nélkül az Egyesült Királyságba? *(citizen, visa)*

L I S T E N I N G

Working nights

Interview with Mr Geoff Michaels, a printer on permanent night-shift

a Read the questions and try to answer them after you have listened to the recording once. Discuss your answers with your partner.

- What does Mr Michaels do?
- How does he feel about working the permanent night shift?

b **Answer the following questions as you listen to the tape for the second time. Discuss your answers with the rest of the class.**

- What does Mr Michaels say is the most important difference between his daily activities and those of people working the day shift?
- What does the morning usually look like for him?
- What does he say about his TV habits?
- How does he usually spend the day until he leaves for work?
- What does he say about travelling?

HOMEWORK

TRANSLATION

English into Hungarian

Use a dictionary to read the following article, and translate the *highlighted* part of the text into Hungarian in writing. Pay particular attention to the underlined words and phrases.

A Life In The Day Of George Brumwell Jameson

I don't feel 102. I know lots of people who are 74 and 75, and I feel much younger than they do. I'm sure age is a state of mind – I think of things in a young way, even more so since I married my second wife Julie, 54, last March.

I'm at my most alert in the morning. Most days I'm awake at 6.30 am, and sitting up in bed drinking tea soon afterwards. Julie brings me my favourite mix – one spoonful of Assam and one of Earl Grey*. We drink the pot dry, talk about what we're going to do that day, and read the papers.

After a shave and shower – I can't risk getting into a bath, I might not be able to get out – I put in my hearing aid and get dressed. Given the chance, I like to swim every morning. In the summer I usually meet my friend, Douglas, at a local pool, and we'll swim a few lengths. In the winter we'll go into town and do some shopping. Often we'll wind up at the Anchor, where I enjoy a bacon sandwich and a scotch; I need several scotches during my day.

After lunch, at about 1.30 I'll have a nap in my special chair which Julie bought me; you push a button and the back reclines and a footrest shoots out. By 3 I'm on top form again. Then people ring up for a chat or drop by for afternoon tea.

We have a light supper about 7pm. I'll have a little scotch and water while we talk. I usually go to bed about 10 and I drop off very easily and contentedly – much more so since I got married.

The Sunday Times

**asszami, Earl Grey - types of quality teas*

LESSON 3

TRANSLATION
English into Hungarian
checkpoint

A Life In The Day Of George Brumwell Jameson

a What kind of translations have the different people in the class come up with for the following words and phrases in the context of the passage?

- a state of mind
- I think of things in a young way
- we drink the pot dry
- given the chance
- at a local pool
- we'll swim a few lengths
- I enjoy a bacon sandwich

b Compare and discuss the possible translations for each and every sentence with the whole class.

c Choose three new words or phrases from the text that you think are worth remembering.

READING & VOCABULARY
articles

a Read through the articles and try to answer the following questions without using a dictionary. When you have finished, discuss your answers in pairs.

- What background information have we got about Mr Mop?
- How much does he charge for his services?
- How successful is his business?
- What does the "burglar" do in the houses he breaks into?
- What does he leave in the houses he "visits"?

The Nude Mr Mop

Manchester, England — There is a chap here who is going round advertising himself as Britain's first Nude Mr Mop. Naturist Richard Stead, who comes from glamorous Batley in Yorkshire, charges housewives £ 15 to turn up with his trusty hoover and feather duster, then he peels off as many clothes as they want before buffing up their ornaments and sweeping their shagpiles. The 6 foot 4 inch bachelor has proved to be a big hit, already completing ten jobs since he set up his service three weeks ago. Last night he admitted: "I've never enjoyed working so much in my life".

The Sun

Clean Getaway

Madrid, Spain — Police are looking for a house-proud housebreaker who sneaks into homes and cleans them from top to bottom. The "burglar" makes the beds, mops the floors, washes and dries up the dishes, cleans the windows, and vacuums before leaving his calling card. The suspect signs his name "Raul", but the press have already dubbed him the "Dustpan Desperado". One officer explained the law in this case: "It may be tough to find him, but surely it will be even harder to find somebody willing to press charges".

Guardian International

b Now try and find the English for the following words and phrases in the text, and make guesses about the possible derivatives. When you have finished, discuss them with the rest of the class.

megbízható/hűséges

....

felmosó

....

lehámozni

....

nudista

....

beindítani/megkezdeni/megalapítani

....

megjelenni/fellépni/szerepelni

....

pucér ⇒ akt

....

tollseprű

....

fickó/fazon

....

bizonyulni

....

siker

....

felszámolni/kérni (pénzt)

....

beismerni ⇒ kétségtelenül

....

porcica/pihe

....

dísztárgy

....

elbűvölő/bűbájos

....

"hirdetgeti" magát

....

kifényesíteni

....

szemeteslapát

....

törvény

....

sajtó

....

névjegy *[AmE]* ⇒ ~ *[BrE]*

....

vádat emelni ⇒ megvádolni

....

aláírni ⇒ aláírás

....

belopódzni/besurranni ⇒ tornacipő *[AmE]*

....

(el)menekülés ⇒ elmenekülni

....

tisztaságszerető/mániás

....

nehéz (ügy)

....

gyanúsított ⇒ gyanús ⇒ gyanúsítani ⇒ gyanakvó

....

hajlandó ⇒ vonakodó

....

elnevezni

....

bandita

....

c **Now read the following questions and answer them in writing after reading the articles again. When you have finished, discuss the answers with the rest of the class.**

What are the common features of the two cases?

....

....

What is special about Mr Mop's service?

....

....

Describe the technique applied by the "Dustpan Desperado"?

....

....

PRONUNCIATION 2

stress, rhythm & intonation

Stress & rhythm

☞ Note the schwa in the following weak forms:
a [ə], *an* [ən], *and* [ənd or ən or n], *as* [əz], *at* [ət], *but* [bət], *for* [fə or fər], *from* [frəm], *nor* [nə or nər], *of* [əv], *or* [ə or ər], *Saint* [sənt], *some* [səm], *than* [ðən], *that* [ðət], *the* [ðə+consonant or ðɪ+ vowel], *to* [tə]

Listen and repeat.

- Is anyone at home?
- Give it to me, please.
- Let's go for a walk.
- Most of us agree.
- Would you like some wine?
- She said that she liked it.
- This is the best CD that I have.
- He is as good as gold.
- She is taller than me.
- Your place or my place?
- I am poor but happy.
- Saint James's Park.

Intonation

☞ The tune of question-tags depends on whether the speaker is really interested in the answer or not. If the speaker doesn't really ask a question, but invites the listener to agree with a statement rather, the tune will be *falling;* if the speaker is not sure of the answer, the tune of the question-tag will be *rising*.

Listen and repeat.

There's no doubt. (I expect you to agree).	I'm not really sure if it's true.
You can speak English, ↘can't you?	You have sold you car, ↗haven't you?
You like ice-cream, ↘don't you.	She goes out with Peter, ↗doesn't she?
You haven't met her, ↘have you?	You are not drinking wine, ↗are you?

LINK WORDS

Make sure you know what the following link words mean, and working in pairs, use as many as you can to make the text below sound more natural and dynamic. When you have found a suitable place for all of them, take turns to read out the new text.

(1) quite understandably (2) naturally/needless to say/of course (3) as a result of this/consequently/as a consequence (4) I was left with/had no choice but (5) on top of everything else (6) to make things worse (7) what's more (8) believe it or not (9) generally speaking

A terrible day:

I've had such a terrible day today, you wouldn't believe it. .... Mondays are fine, but today I overslept because foolishly I'd forgotten to set my alarm clock. ...., I had to hurry. .... the water supply was turned off while I was in the bathroom, so I couldn't clean my teeth, which meant that the rest of the day was ruined for me. .... my bus got stuck in a traffic jam, and .... I was 30 minutes late for work. ...., my boss was very angry with me and gave me an awful lot of work, so I didn't even have time to have lunch. When I got home at 6, I realised there wasn't any bread in the house, so .... to go and get some. Much to my surprise, the corner shop was still open and ...., they even had fresh bread. .... now I'm calling you from a dark room, as the electricity was cut off 10 minutes ago. Thank God, the phone seems to be all right.

HOMEWORK

VOCABULARY
articles
study tasks

The Nude Mr Mop/Clean Getaway

a Read the articles again and memorise any vocabulary items that are new to you. When you have finished, use the words in the box to fill in the gaps in the passage below. Change the form of the words if necessary.

Although I .... my name Richard Stead, my grateful clients have .... me "Mr Mop". I come from a .... little town called Batley in Yorkshire, I am a six foot tall .... and I am a ...., which means I don't like wearing things when they are not absolutely necessary. If you are a .... housewife and you are .... to combine pleasant things with useful things, no doubt you will be interested in my offer: just ring the number on the attached .... and I will .... with my hoover and my .... duster, and I will clean the house from top to bottom. So far so good. But now comes the interesting part: in addition to .... your .... and sweeping and vacuuming your floor, I will also .... as many of the clothes I am wearing as you like. Although I .... my revolutionary service only three weeks ago, I have had 10 jobs so far, and believe me, I have always done the work to the full satisfaction of my clients. And I will only .... a ridiculous £ 15 for all that fun. If you are ...., you will miss out: hurry up, call my number now and ask for the .... Mr Mop!

house-proud
to dub
calling card
willing
to sign
ornament
glamorous
suspicious
to charge
feather
to peel off
bachelor
to turn up
to buff up
to set up
nude
naturist

b Use the following guidelines to prepare for a short oral summary of the articles about the houseproud gentlemen in a few sentences.

The Nude Mr Mop: ➜ his special service ➜ charge
Dustpan Desperado: ➜ what he does and why

WRITING
letter

You have read an article in a magazine which advises readers to change their daily routines to live a healthier and more balanced life. Taking your own present duties and possibilities and into account, write a letter to the editors, telling them how practical you think their advice would be in your particular case.

The article suggests that readers should

a) have a comfortable morning without any hurry, with a substantial breakfast, and a nice swim before school or work.
b) go to school or work on foot every day.
c) take a 60–90 minute nap after lunch.
d) do things in the afternoon/evening that are completely different from the things they have to do at school\work.
e) do some physical exercise/workout every day.
f) go to bed at 9 at the latest.

Step One	Step two	Step three
General outline:	Brainstorming:	Details:
Introduction	greeting, reference to article, your reason for writing	*Dear Sir(s)/Madam; I read your/Referring to your article in the January issue of* Playboy … *I am writing to you to …/because …*
The particular pieces of advice	**a)** early morning lessons; family; can't eat so early; water in pool too cold; etc. **b)** too far away; air pollution; etc. **c)** physics teacher/boss would be angry; etc. **d)** homework; housework; etc. **e)** sounds a good idea: you'll start body building tomorrow; etc. **f)** homework; TV; family; etc.	*Well, to tell you the truth // quite honestly // as a matter of fact …* *In my particular case …; As far as I am concerned …* *As far as … is concerned // I think …* *As for/regards your advice concerning …* *As I see it, // In my view/opinion, // Personally, I feel …// The way I see it, …* *(I'm afraid) I entirely disagree with … // I can't say that I share your views on … // I see things rather differently myself.* *I entirely agree with … // I am of exactly the same opinion.* *There's a lot in what you say, but… // I agree with much of what you say, but …*
Conclusion	summary, closing the letter	*In conclusion, // all in all // all things considered, // briefly // in short // to sum up // in summary,* *Yours faithfully*

☞ When you have finished, don't forget to check your work for grammatical mistakes.

LESSON 4

VOCABULARY
articles
checkpoint

The Nude Mr Mop/Clean Getaway

a **Compare your solutions to the fill-in-the-gap homework task with the rest of the class.**

b **Discuss with the rest of the class what you think the English would be for the following Hungarian sentences.**

Nem kritizálgathatsz mindig mindent.

....

Egy elegáns étteremben akár kétszáz forintot is elkérhetnek egy csésze kávéért.

....

A gyanúsítottak egy lopott autóval menekültek el.

....

Be kell ismernem, hogy hiba volt ennek a vállalkozásnak a beindítása.

....

Ha nem jelennek meg egy órán belül, vádat emelünk ellenük.

....

Kemény munka megpucolni tíz kiló krumplit.

....

c **Working in pairs, give a brief summary of the articles we read last lesson.**

GRAMMAR FOCUS
m i n i t e s t

Auxiliaries 1

Do the following test and check it with the rest of the class.

1. When I was a kid, we ... play football in our street; now the traffic is so heavy that we ... cross it.
- **A** managed to // hardly can
- **B** could // can hardly
- **C** were able to // hardly can
- **D** could // hardly are able to

2. You ... smoke here – there are small children in the room.
- **A** needn't
- **B** don't allowed to
- **C** don't have to
- **D** mustn't

3. When I was in the army, we ... to have a shower only once a week.
- **A** could
- **B** allowed
- **C** able
- **D** were allowed

4. I ... wear glasses since I left primary school.
- **A** must
- **B** have to
- **C** had to
- **D** have had to

5. I don't think I ... go to the airport to see you off this afternoon. I'm very busy.
- **A** won't be able to
- **B** will able to
- **C** can
- **D** will be able

6. Although there was something wrong with the brakes, I ... drive back to the city.
- **A** succeeded to
- **B** could
- **C** was able to
- **D** manage to

7. I ... borrow my father's car last Saturday.
- **A** was allowed to
- **B** could
- **C** allowed to
- **D** might

8. I'll ... work late tomorrow.
- **A** must
- **B** have to
- **C** have got to
- **D** must to

9. I ... eat meat since I visited a slaughterhouse in 1995.
- **A** am not able to
- **B** couldn't
- **C** haven't been able to
- **D** can't

10. "... I ask you a rather personal question?" "Yes, of course you ... ."
- **A** might // may
- **B** must // might
- **C** can // could
- **D** could // could

SPEAKING
discussion

a **Imagine you and your partner share a flat, which means you must share the housework as well. Taking your likes and dislikes into account, try and agree on a fair division of chores. Discuss which one of you should do the following chores:**

- watering the flowers
- doing the bathroom
- cleaning the windows
- doing the hoovering in the communal living room
- dusting the furniture in the living room
- doing the shopping for shared things
- taking out the rubbish
- making coffee in the morning
- doing the cooking for shared meals
- laying and clearing the table
- washing up the dishes
- drying up the dishes

b **What's your opinion about the following statements? Think of some reasons to support your view and then compare your ideas with your partner's.**

1. "If I were really rich and I could afford it, I would have a servant/domestic/maid in the house so that I wouldn't have to do any housework."
2. "I envy the Spanish: they start work at 10 a.m., they take a siesta after lunch, they go back to work until seven or eight, and they go to bed at about one or two. It means that they have a proper morning and a proper evening."

c **Answer the following questions in pairs.**

- Do you think there is anything about your daily routine that you should change?
- How is the housework split in your family? What are your responsibilities (if any)?
- What would you say are the three most important household gadgets? Give reasons.

HOMEWORK

VOCABULARY

survival kit

preview

Read through the new vocabulary list on page 141-142, and consult a dictionary if you come across something that is unfamiliar or unclear to you.

EXAM TIPS

The composition task

☞ You can choose between two composition tasks in the exam, at least one of which is usually a letter. When you make your decision, ask yourself the following questions: *Which one of the two tasks provokes more thoughts in me?* (It *does* matter how logical and intelligent your ideas are.) *Is my active vocabulary richer for either of the two topics?* (Using the dictionary is not only time-consuming, but very dangerous as well.)

Obviously, it is easier to prepare for the letter – actually, you can write the first and last few lines of the letter at home – all you have to do is prepare for a nice beginning and closing part for both formal and personal letters. Remember that these usually contain a number of *clichés*, which means they should be used very precisely; in fact you'd better learn them by heart. (See the First Aid Kit for a collection of such *clichés* and advice on the formal requirements of letter writing.)

Don't forget that you're supposed to follow the guidelines (there are five of them) even if you think you have better ideas about the topic. In fact, your task is to write three or four lines around each guideline between your introduction and conclusion – 17–20 lines in all – making sure there is a smooth transition between them. (Link words!)

Just as in the case of vocabulary, it is also better to rely on what you already know with sentence structures. Rather than experimenting with fancy solutions, you should have structures you can use confidently.

UNIT 6
Leisure and pleasure

LESSON 1

VOCABULARY
survival kit

Spare time
free/leisure time, time off, to have a rest, to relax

Going out
to stay in, outdoor\indoor activities, to go on an outing, to go on an excursion, to go hiking, to go for a walk\ride, to go swimming\fishing\cycling, to do some sporting activity

Reading
The story
the title/name of a book, a book about\on ..., the plot/story line is set in .../the action takes place in ..., message, main\minor characters, hero\heroine
Genres and writers
(non-)fiction, prose, educational book, novel, romance, memoirs, (auto)biography, historical novel, humorous reading, light reading, thriller/crime story/whodunit, horror story, sci-fi, travel book, adventure, war story, fairy tale, philosophy, comic strips, cookbook, guidebook, reference book, technical literature, short story, poetry, poem, drama, play, tragedy, comedy, volume, paperback, author/writer, short story writer, novelist, poet, dramatist, playwright
The press
the mass media, (daily) (news)paper/daily, quality paper, popular paper/tabloid, national\local\evening paper, to cover home\foreign news\events, sports page(s), sensational headlines, small ads, leading article/editorial, magazine, journal, journalist, weekly, women's magazine, radio & TV magazine/guide, a magazine dealing with ... , a children's comic, to publish, to come out, to subscribe to a ...

Radio, TV, etc.
on TV/telly/the box, on the radio, radio station, TV channel, listener, viewer, commercial & satellite TV/stations/channels, to broadcast, feature

film, news feature, sports programme, magazine-style programme, chat show, quiz/game show, general interest programme, current affairs programme, soap (opera), series, serial, blue movie, educational programme, political programme, discussion, documentary, cartoon, commercial, live broadcast, couch potato, CD\record player, a new release, hit, album, single, pop\rock\country\techno\acid house\heavy metal\jazz (music), video, VCR, CD-ROM

Theatres, cinemas, concerts, etc.
to go to the theatre\opera\cinema/movies, moviegoer, theatregoer, to book a seat, box office, stalls, circle, performance, play, musical, operetta, cast, actor, actress, director, production, (leading) role, stage, screen, films with subtitles, dubbed films, war\action\horror films, comedy, audience, fans, orchestra, classical\pop\rock\folk music, a piece, group/band, musician, soloist, conductor, to go dancing, to go to a disco, to go to art galleries & museums

SPEAKING
conversation

Use the following guidelines to tell your partner about a) the kind of books you like to read, b) the papers\magazines you regularly read, c) your favourite TV channels\programmes, d) the kind of films\theatricals\music you are interested in.

what kinds? → how often?
books → papers\magazines → TV channels\programmes → films\theatricals\music

A

SPEAKING
pictures

B

a Discuss with the class what vocabulary you need to describe the pictures.

Verbs:	Nouns:	Adjectives:

b Agree with your partner which one of you has picture A and B, take turns to describe what you can see in them, and make guesses about the situation.

c Looking at both pictures now, discuss what you think is relevant of the following questions in pairs (It is your personal experience/judgement/opinion/ etc. that is important here!):

- Does the photo remind you of anything you have done, experienced or seen?
- What do you think of what you can see and/or what is happening in the picture?

You may find the following phrases useful here:

I (can still) remember ...-ing ... ➾ I've already (been in a situation like this.) ➾ That reminds me of ... ➾ I think/guess ... ➾ In my opinion/view ... ➾ As far as I'm concerned ... ➾ The way I see it ... ➾ From my point of view ... ➾ It seems to me that ... ➾ I'd say ... ➾ If you ask me ... ➾ To my mind ...

FUNCTIONS
role-play

a Read both role-cards and agree with your partner who's A and who's B.

A You are quite angry, because in the past couple of months your paperboy has been delivering *Playgirl* magazine instead of your favourite *Playboy* magazine. You decide to give the guy a good dressing-down.

- ♠ Tell him about the situation.
- ♠ Refuse the explanation, and suggest that he should check the data on the subscribers' list.
- ♠ Protest that your name is not *Christina* Reader, but *Christopher* Reader.
- ♠ Accept the apology, but ask the guy to report the mistake to the newsagent.

B You are a paperboy on your morning round, and an angry subscriber comes up to you to make a complaint. There is something wrong with his magazine.

- ♥ Ask her/him what the problem is.
- ♥ Tell him that you deliver the papers and magazines according to the subscribers' list, and you always check it very carefully before you drop them round, so it's highly unlikely that you have made a mistake.

- Agree to check the list immediately. Point out that there's a *Playgirl* next to Ms Christina Reader, so you haven't made a mistake.
- Explain that the names and magazines must have got mixed up in the computer at the newsagent's, and apologise for the mistake.
- Promise that you will report the mistake to the newsagent as soon as possible.

b Try and agree with the rest of your class how you could use the following phrases in this situation; complete the phrases and answer the questions.

A: ***Excuse me. I'm afraid I have a complaint to make. // I'm afraid I must complain about ... // I've got a complaint about ...***

B: *What seems to be the problem?*

A: ***Well, the problem is that ... // Well, the situation is that ...***

B: *Really? I'm very sorry but …*

A: ***Well, this is most unsatisfactory. // But that's impossible/ridiculous.***

A: ***Look, why don't you ... ? // Would you mind ...-ing ..., please?***

B: *By all means. // Yes, of course. // Sure. // Not at all.*

A: ***Ah! That's funny/strange. // That's where the problem is. // There/Here's the problem.***

B: *I'm really/very/extremely/terribly/awfully sorry. That was entirely our fault.*

A: ***That's OK. // That's all right***

A: ***Do you think you could ... ? // Would you (be kind enough to) ...?***

A: ***Thanks a lot. // Great.***

c Rehearse the situation in pairs. Read the cards again before starting, but try and rely only on the notes below while practising.

complaint ➜ explanation ➜ checking sheet ➜ finding mistake ➜ apology ➜ report

PRONUNCIATION 1

sounds & word stress

Sounds

☞ The pronunciation of the additional *s* at the end of words (and *is/has got* inside the sentence), and the pronunciation of *-ed* depends on the sound before it.
-s, -'s, -s', is, has got
If the last sound is [p, t, k, f], the pronunciation will be [s].
If the last sound is a hissing sound [s, z, ʃ, ʧ, ʤ], it will be [ɪz].
In all other cases it will be [z].
-ed
If the last sound is [p, k, f, s, ʃ, ʧ], the pronunciation will be [t].
If the last sound is [t, d], it will be [ɪd].
In all other cases it will be [d].
☞ Note that in the English language – unlike in Hungarian – the pronunciation of a sound is not influenced by the sound after it.

Listen and repeat.

[z]	[s]	[ɪz]	[d]	[t]	[ɪd]	!!!
boys	cats	nurses	arrived	finished	posted	finished it
Tom's life	it's OK	James's car	killed	stopped	included	John's car
there's one	Pat's time	James is fat	played	laughed	collected	needs time
he's got it	it's got one	this is nice	opened	wished	lifted	she likes us

Word stress

☞ Certain suffixes cause the main stress to fall on the syllable immediately before them. These suffixes (*-ic, -ity/ety, -ion, -ian, -ible, -lity, -ular, -al, -tion)* are called *strong endings*.

Listen and repeat.

'drama → dra'mat*ic*
e'lectric → elec'tric*ity*
'continent → conti'nent*al*
'operate → ope'ra*tion*
'qualify → qualifi'ca*tion*
'music → mu'sic*ian*
'science → scien'tif*ic*
e'xamine → exami'na*tion*
'national → natio'nal*ity*
'Hungary → Hun'gar*ian*
pho'tography → photo'graph*ic*
'origin → o'riginal → origi'nal*ity*

☞ N.B.: *Weak endings (-ing, -ed, -er, -ly, -ful, -ist, -ism, -ize, -less, -ness)* do not affect stress.

HOMEWORK

VOCABULARY survival kit

study task

Study the word list on page 141-142, and memorise the words and phrases that you think are important and relevant to your circumstances. When you have finished, put the following words in their correct places in the passage below to check your knowledge. (You might try and do the task without using the box.)

fiction, magazines, TV/telly, concerts, reference books, productions, subscribe to, going out, volumes, theatregoer, release, soaps, programme, free time, fairy tales, satellite channels, technical literature, thrillers, plays, rock music, theatre

There are a number of good reasons why I've been reading, watching television and .... less and less in the past couple of years. First and foremost, I've simply got much less ....; on the one hand, I must work more if I am to keep up the standard of living we are used to, and on the other hand, looking after and playing with the kids takes up a lot of time. The second reason is that I simply cannot afford to do a lot of things that I used to; for example I used to .... a great number of different papers and .... , and now I can only afford the two most basic ones.

The situation is even worse in the case of books; I've practically stopped buying ...., and I concentrate my financial resources on .... of poetry and ...., mainly .... in my field. Similarly, much as I like ...., I can't afford a CD these days; a new .... costs as much as one-tenth of my salary.

As for watching ...., besides the time constraints, I have serious problems with the .... as well; television has been flooded with stuff I am not particularly keen on: ...., talk shows and third-rate action-packed .... are in abundance. With the exception of Sky News and Eurosport perhaps, easier access to foreign .... hasn't made the situation any better either.

Interestingly enough, as regards going to the ...., cinema or concerts the situation hasn't got much worse, as I didn't use to be much of a cinema/concert/........................ earlier either. We can still scrape together the money for those three or four ...., six or seven films and two or three .... a year, in fact the bigger problem here is finding a babysitter to look after the children while we are out.

There's a particular area however, where our consumption has increased considerably in the past years: we have bought hundreds of .... and kids'magazines, and we must have been the biggest supporters of the Zoo during that time. Also, as you can well imagine, I've had to suffer through much more than my fair share of Walt Disney .... as well.

GRAMMAR FOCUS

preview

Auxiliaries 2

Instead of the well-known framework of the tenses of the verb, these auxiliaries operate on the basis of ***antecedence (előidejűség) and simultaneity (egyidejűség)***. They have only two forms:

- the ***present*** *(auxiliary + infinitive without to)*, which is used instead of the traditional present and future.
  ➢ *You shouldn't eat so much.*
- the ***perfect*** *(auxiliary + perfect infinitive without to)*, which is used instead of the traditional past and the perfect tenses.
  ➢ *You shouldn't have eaten so much.*

However, the simple – continuous distinction is observed here.
  ➢ *He must be lying.*

- **must** (biztosan, bizonyára, feltétlenül)
  ➢ *You must have heard the news. He must be at least 60.*
- **may** (lehet, hogy), **may as well** (akár ... -hetek)
  ➢ *They may have missed the train. You may be right. He may not know anything about it. I may as well go home.*
- **might** (az is lehet/lehetséges, hogy; esetleg ...-né/-[het]ett volna), **might as well** (akár ...-hetnék/-hettem volna), **might well** (nagyon is lehetséges [lett volna], hogy)
  ➢ *She might have forgotten about it all. You might well have died in the accident. She might be at home now. They might not have heard the news yet. I might as well stay here. You might well find that you'll need more money than that.*
- **can? can't** (létezik/lehetséges az, hogy?, az nem lehet/létezik, hogy)
  ➢ *Can they have finished already? It can't be true. They can't have arrived yet.*
- **could** (az is lehet/lehetséges, hogy; tudna/tudott volna), **could as well** (akár ...-hetnék/-hettem volna)

➢ *Could they have finished yet? They couldn't have arrived yet. I couldn't have done it any better, either. I could as well stay have stayed a bit longer.*

- **needn't** (fölösleges, fölöslegesen, nem [lett volna] szükséges)
  ➢ *You needn't have bought a ticket, I could've taken you in. You needn't have bought so much food, there will be only three people there.*
- **should** (kellene, kéne, szabadna, kellett volna, lett volna szabad)
  ➢ *You shouldn't have married him. She should be home by now.*
- **ought to** (kellene, kellett volna), the authority comes from outside the speaker, e.g. rules, laws
  ➢ *This job ought to be finished in two weeks.*
- **would** (-na/-ne/-t volna)
  ➢ *I wouldn't like to be in your shoes. He wouldn't have sold it any cheaper, I'm afraid.*

In these meanings
- you cannot use *must*, *may*, and *might* in questions.
- you cannot use *must* in negative sentenses at all.
- you cannot use *may* and *might* in negative sentenses when you mean *az nem lehet(séges), hogy*. However, when you mean *lehet(séges), hogy nem*, *may not* and *might not* are OK.

The missing forms are substituted by *can?* and *can't* or *could/couldn't*. Note that you cannot use *can* in positive sentences in this meaning.

Conditional (if/suppose/supposing) clauses

Note that three of these auxiliaries have a conditional meaning: *might* ("perhaps [I] would"), *could* ("would be able to"), and, of course, *would*. There are two types of clauses that can go with these auxiliaries:

- the ***unreal present conditional*** clause, often called the second conditional (ha ...-na/ne) formed with the *past simple* (often with *were* [more formal] instead of *was*).
  ➢ *If you really loved me, you wouldn't be so nasty to me. He could help us if he were here. If he were rich enough, I might marry him. Supposing he were rich, would you marry him?*
- the ***unreal past conditional*** clause, often called the third conditional (ha ...-t volna) formed with the past perfect.
  ➢ *If you'd really loved me, you wouldn't have been so nasty to me. He could've helped us if he'd been here. If she'd been rich enough, I might have married her. If you'd prepared for the test, you wouldn't be in trouble now.*
- ***Open future conditional*** clauses (often called the first conditional), and ***general conditionals*** do not require conditional auxiliaries; the first type takes *will*, the second type takes the *simple present tense*.
  ➢ *If you don't put on a pullover, you'll be cold. We'll go to the cinema if it rains.*
  ➢ *If I am in a bad mood, I just listen to some music and I am OK. If she can't buy any new clothes for two days, she feels very depressed.*

Optative (wish/if only) sentences

We use **wish/if only**
- with the past tense to say that we would like something to be different in the present.
  ➢ *I wish I weren't (or wasn't) so fat. If only I could play the sax.*
- with the past perfect to express regret that something happened (or did not happen) in the past.
  ➢ *I wish I had drunk water instead. If only I hadn't married her.*
- with *would* when we want something to stop happening (often complaining about someone's behaviour), or we want something different to happen. We cannot use this structure for the past, and we cannot refer to our own behaviour.
  ➢ *I wish you would stop smiling like that. If only you would tell me what's going on here.*

LESSON 2

VOCABULARY
survival kit
checkpoint

a **Check the fill-in-the-blank homework task with the rest of the class.**

b **What are the "opposites" of the following words and phrases?**

- indoor activities
- main characters
- fiction
- comedy
- popular paper
- national paper
- foreign news
- a dubbed film

c **What is the corresponding word or phrase with a similar meaning?**

free time	→	**l.....-....**
author	→	**w.....**
whodunit	→	**t.......**
play	→	**d....**
the press	→	**the m.... .....**
paper	→	**d....**
tabloid	→	**p...... .....**
editorial	→	**l...... ....**
the box	→	**the t....**
station	→	**c......**
movie	→	**f...**

d **Complete the definitions.**

- If you go on a short journey organised for a group of people to visit a particular place, you go ....
- The most important idea that the author is trying to tell readers about in a book is the .... of the book.
- An .... is an account written by a famous person about her/his life and experiences.
- A person who writes plays is a ....
- A .... film is a full length film that has a story and is acted by professional actors.
- A person who spends an awful lot of time sitting and watching television is a ....
- A story that is broadcast in several separate parts on television is a ....

GRAMMAR FOCUS

translation into English

Auxiliaries 2

Translate the following sentences into English, discussing each section with the rest of the class as you progress.

1. Ez az pasas nagyon intelligensnek látszik; biztosan angoltanár.

   – Á, nem lehet angoltanár; túl jól van öltözve.

   ....

   ....

2. – Létezik az, hogy elfeledkezett a születésnapomról?

   – Az nem létezik, hogy elfeledkezett róla. Biztosan elromlott a telefonja. *(to go wrong)*

   ....

   ....

   ....

3. – Már itt kellene lenniük.

   – Lehet, hogy lekésték a vonatot.

   ....

   ....

4. – Lehet, hogy nincs igazam, de nem lett volna szabad őt meghívni a bulira.

   – Lehetséges, hogy igazad van, de mi mást tehettem volna?

   ....

   ....

   ....

5. – Most persze rosszul vagy. *(of course, to be sick)* Nem kellett volna ennyi sört innod! Ihattál volna Colát vagy narancslevet.

   – Akár vízet is ihattam volna; a probléma az, hogy rossz itt a levegő.

   ....

   ....

   ....

6. Nem kellett volna kabátot venni, nagyon meleg van.

Az adóbevallást március 20-ig kell benyújtani. *(tax return, to submit/file)*

7. Nem volt drága, meg tudtam volna venni, de nem igazán tetszett. Esetleg meg is vettem volna, ha nem lett volna olyan ronda lila. *(nasty)*

8. – Te mit tettél volna ebben a helyzetben, ha ott vagy?

– Nem tudom, talán ugyanazt tettem volna, mint te, de én nagyobbat ütöttem volna. *(harder)*

Ha megtanultad volna a szavakat, most nem kapnál egyest.

Ha nem kellene házi feladatot írnom, most a meccset nézném a tévében.

9. Ők most biztosan alszanak.

Lehet, hogy most éppen rád gondol.

Most tanulnod kellene, kisfiam.

10. Bárcsak már nyár lenne! Bárcsak több időm lenne! Bárcsak tudnék gitározni!

Bárcsak ne lett volna igazam! Bárcsak idejében elindultunk volna!

Bárcsak befognád végre a szád! *(to shut up)* Bárcsak jönne már a busz!

LISTENING

Popular reading

Interview with a journalist about the British popular press

a **Read the question and try to answer it after you have listened to the recording once. Discuss your answer with your partner.**

- What kind of things does the journalist say are different about quality papers and popular magazines/tabloids? (He mentions 8 such differences.)

b **Answer the following questions as you listen to the tape for the second time. Discuss your answers with the rest of the class.**

- How do the circulations of quality papers and popular magazines/tabloids compare?
- What four categories/kinds of topics are favoured by popular magazines and tabloids according to the journalist?
- What does the interviewer say are the two extremes offered by these magazines/tabloids?
- What are the things popular magazines and tabloids are *not* interested in?
- What is the difference between the ways the two kinds of publications treat the news?
- What kind of pictures do popular publications often have on their first pages?
- What's the journalist's favourite headline, and what is the article all about?

HOMEWORK

TRANSLATION

English into Hungarian

Use a dictionary to read the following article, and translate the *highlighted* part of the text into Hungarian in writing. Pay particular attention to the underlined words and phrases.

You can't blame it on the box

"The search for direct 'effects' of television on behaviour is over. Every effort has been made but such effects simply cannot be found."

This is the message of a book of research published this week by the University of Leeds, *Television's influences and effects*. Yet it is almost certain that this conclusion will be ignored by most moralisers and politicians.

Researchers refer to the phenomenon of moral panic and point out that it has happened a number of times before. In Victorian Britain, music halls were believed to cause violence and immorality; so, unbelievably, in the 1890s were bicycles; and who can forget what was said about the terrible effects of rock'n'roll in the Fifties and Sixties?

TV has been made the scapegoat of a society that feels it cannot cope with its frustrating problems like drugs, crime, violence, poverty and unemployment. Blaming TV for these, and claiming that there is a causal link between TV and, say violence is just an easy way of getting rid of this frustration.

It has been proved that young offenders watch the same sort of TV (though much less of it) as young non-offenders. Their favourite programmes are also the same, but individuals do not react in the same ways to the same programmes.

Of course TV has an influence. Like newspapers, movies, novels, parents, friends, work, genes and so on. No one denies that. What researchers do deny, is that – to take the hottest area – acts of violence on TV cause acts of violence in society.

No doubt, politicians will not be particularly happy to hear that.

Melvyn Bragg, The Times

LESSON 3

TRANSLATION
English into Hungarian
checkpoint

You can't blame it on the box

a **What kind of translations have the different people in the class come up with for the following words and phrases in the context of the passage?**

- TV has been made the scapegoat of a society that ...
- frustrating problems
- blaming TV for these
- say violence
- frustration
- it has been proved that ...
- the same sort of TV
- what researchers do deny, is that ...
- to take the hottest area
- no doubt

b **Compare and discuss the possible translations for each and every sentence with the whole class.**

c **Choose three new words or phrases from the text that you think are worth remembering.**

READING & VOCABULARY
articles

a **Read through the articles and try to answer the following questions without using a dictionary. When you have finished, discuss your answers in pairs.**

- What was the topic of the television talk show?
- What was special about it?
- Why are Indian television viewers angry?
- How do some people react to the situation?

Talk show in the NUDE

New Haven, Connecticut (AFP) — Five guests on Sally Jesse Raphael's television talk show, taped here, wore necklaces and watches. They wore nothing else. But Ms Raphael, who said she felt "better with something on," was clothed.

The five, including a married couple and a mother and daughter, appeared naked before the cameras and a studio audience to discuss nudism. "I'd like you all to be undressed, too," guest Sharon McMahon told the studio audience of about 200.

A sixth guest was dressed. Author Dennis Smith appeared to discuss his study of nudists' children, "Growing Up Without Shame."

The hour-long show is to be broadcast by 100 television stations across the US on Feb. 5, but home viewers will only see shots of heads and shoulders.

Ratings drop

Bombay, India — After years of state-controlled television stations, India is experiencing a flood of foreign soap operas. This has caused a reaction from families who are sick of bland US dramas, insipid advertisements and religious zealots using the TV for their own gain. Now the craze of throwing television sets out of windows is gaining momentum, and hundreds of sets are being flung from tower-block windows.

Fed-up viewer Safari Ali Mohammed told reporters: "Ours was a family effort, with all of us pushing it out of the window together. Destroying the television is much sweeter revenge than just changing channels or switching-off."

Times of India

b Now try and find the English for the following words and phrases in the text, and make guesses about the possible derivatives. When you have finished, discuss them with the rest of the class.

fellépni/szerepelni ⇒ fellépés

....

közvetíteni ⇒ közvetítés ⇒ élőben közvetítik ⇒ tévés

....

....

szégyen ⇒ szégyenletes ⇒ arcátlan ⇒ szégyenkezve

....

....

felöltözött ⇒ ruházat ⇒ ruházkodás

....

tanulmány ⇒ tanulmányozni

....

közönség ⇒ nézőtér

....

ruhátlan ⇒ levetkőzni ⇒ levetkőztetni

....

meztelenül

....

beleértve

....

nyaklánc

....

felvenni (magnóra/videóra)

....

kép/felvétel ⇒ felvenni (fényképezőgéppel, kamerával)

....

....

kikapcsolni ⇒ kapcsoló

....

erőfeszítés ⇒ erőfeszítést tenni

....

előny/haszon ⇒ nyer/szerez/kap

....

divatőrület

....

elege van (2!)

....

bosszú ⇒ bosszút állni

....

tapasztalni ⇒ tapasztalat

....

elpusztítani ⇒ pusztítás

....

áradat ⇒ elárasztani

....

nézettségi index

....

unalmas

....

jellegtelen

....

egy megszállott ⇒ fanatikus

....

lendület

....

hajítani/dobni

....

c Now read the following questions and answer them in writing after reading the articles again. When you have finished, discuss the answers with the rest of the class.

How were the different participants dressed on the show?

....

Where, when, and how is the show to be broadcast?

....

Why do Indian viewers throw TV sets out of their windows?

....

Why don't they just switch off or change channels?

....

PRONUNCIATION 2

stress, rhythm & intonation

Stress & rhythm

☞ If we want to emphasise a particular verb, we put a lot of stress *on the auxiliary* instead of the verb itself.

Listen and repeat.

But I ↘**am** studying!
I ↘**do** appreciate your help.
I ↘**have** paid it back!
You ↘**must** marry her, my son.
I ↘**did** tell him in time.
But you ↘**are** beautiful!

☞ In English adverbial structures the adverb carries less stress than the word it refers to.

Listen and repeat.

- terribly ex**pen**sive
- quite **pre**tty
- so **in**teresting
- very **keen** on
- impossible to under**stand**
- always **ti**red
- such a **beau**tiful city
- very **slee**py

Intonation

☞ *, ... shall we/I? and , ... will/won't you?* have a special tune. The tune falls on the last stressed syllable of the main part, and rises sharply on the auxiliary. However, in negative commands, when *, ... will/won't you?* is not a polite request but rather an order or a warning, the tune will be falling.

Listen and repeat.

Let's go to the ↘cinema, ↗shall we?
Let's go ↘home now, ↗shall we?
Let's for↘get it, ↗shall we?

Get me some ↘water, ↗will you?
Turn down the ↘volume, ↗will you?
Stop that ↘noise, ↗will you?

Don't ↗drop it, ↘will you?
Don't be ↗late, ↘will you?
Drive ↗carefully, ↘won't you?

LINK WORDS

Make sure you know what the following link words mean, and working in pairs, use as many as you can to make the text below sound more natural and dynamic. When you have found a suitable place for all of them, take turns to read out the new text.

(1) still (2) thank God/fortunately/to my great relief (3) (quite) on the contrary (4) needless to say/it goes without saying (5) no wonder/small wonder (6) you know/you see (7) although/ though/even though/in spite of the fact/despite the fact that (8) believe it or not/incredible as it sound (9) however

Channel trouble:

.... my wife is completely mad about football matches on TV. The only problem is I'm not interested in football at all. ...., I hate it. .... what I really like is soap operas. .... we often have fights about which channel to watch if there's a match and a soap on at the same time. ...., usually it is she who wins.

The other day we had a very nasty row. .... she knew I was particularly interested in the next broadcast of Neighbours (something very interesting had happened to Apple) but she .... wanted to watch a Champions' League semi-final on Channel 2. This time ...., I put my foot down and told her she could choose between me and the match. ...., she chose me and now I know how Apple solved her problem.

HOMEWORK

VOCABULARY
articles
study tasks

Talk show in the nude/Ratings drop

a Read the articles again and memorise any vocabulary items that are new to you. When you have finished, use the words in the box to fill in the gaps in the passage below. Change the form of the words if necessary.

It may sound strange from someone who has just .... a TV set out of the window, but me and my family are actually very peaceful people. We are not crazy, and we are not religious .... either. It's only that we are absolutely .... of what's going on on TV these days. We've been literally .... with .... soap operas and .... talk shows, which ruin our evenings. Last night, for example, there was this horrible talk show .... by Channel 3, the Sally Raphael Show, and we decided enough was enough and we .... the TV set. Let me tell you about the show very briefly, and I'm sure you will understand our reaction to the whole thing.

Well, five guests on Sally Raphael's talk show wore heavy wintercoats, and were wrapped in thick scarves. But Ms Raphael, who said she felt "better without anything on," was stark .... The guests, ... two pensioners, ... fully .... before television cameras and a studio .... of about 200 naked people to .... the problems of the textile industry. A sixth guest was completely .... Author Dennis Smith appeared to discuss his .... of the children of people working in the textile industry, "Growing Up With ...."

Now, tell me, does that make any sense to you? Is it any wonder .... are dropping and people are getting more and more .... and take .... on the bloody box? I think this is absolutely .... and I am sure broadcasters just do it for their own ....

shameful
tired
gain
naked
zealots
study
to destroy
revenge
ratings
dressed
to discuss
to fling
insipid
to broadcast
audience
to be fed up
bland
to appear
to flood
nude
including
shame

b **Use the following guidelines to prepare for a short oral summary of the articles about the talk show and the new Indian craze in a few sentences.**

The talk show: ➜ the participants ➜ the reason ➜ how it will be broadcast
The Indian story: ➜ the reason ➜ the reaction ➜ the explanation

WRITING
letter

The Vice publishing house wishes to start up a new women's/men's magazine and announces a competition for plans. As usual, they are interested in making a quick and handsome profit, in fact what they really want is to come out with a magazine which is even more popular than the current market leader Mucus/Macho. Write a proposal which contains your suggestions for the most important topic areas, columns and the format\distribution\advertising.

Step One	Step two	Step three
General outline:	Brainstorming:	Details:
Introduction	greeting, reference to competition	*Dear Sir(s)\Madam; I read/Referring to your announcement …* *I am writing to you to …/because …*
Your suggestions	**a)** the main topic areas: articles on celebrities, etc. **b)** ideas for columns: agony column, etc. **c)** recommendations for format, etc.: large colour photos, TV commercials, etc.	*As I see it, // In my view/opinion, // Personally, I feel // The way I see it, …* *I'd like to suggest/propose …* *As far as … is concerned, I think … // As for/regards …* *Besides // In addition to …* *I'm quite/absolutely/fairly sure/certain … // I have no doubt (that, about // I don't think there could be any doubt about // I have very little doubt in my mind (about, as to) // It is quite obvious that …* *We might as well …* *There is a good chance … // I shouldn't be surprised if … // I expect …* *I would choose … in preference to … // Rather than … , I'd prefer to …*
Conclusion	summary, closing the letter	*On balance/On the whole, I consider … to be more attractive/interesting than …* *In conclusion // all in all // all things considered* *I am looking forward to …; Yours faithfully*

☞ When you have finished, don't forget to check your work for grammatical mistakes.

LESSON 4

VOCABULARY
articles
checkpoint

Talk show in the nude/Ratings drop

a Compare your solutions to the fill-in-gap homework task with the rest of the class.

b Discuss with the rest of the class what you think the English would be for the following Hungarian sentences.

Megvan a CD otthon; ha akarod, felvehetem neked (kazettára).

....

Az Evita című film néhány jelenetét Budapesten vették fel. *(scene)*

....

Egyre jobban elegem van ebből az unalmas pasasból.

....

Már vagy tíz filmben szerepelt, de ez az első igazi sikere.

....

Úgy állt bosszút a szomszédon, hogy elpusztította a macskáját.

....

A meccset élőben közvetítette a televízió.

....

A szappanoperák rendkívül népszerűek a nézők körében; nézettségi indexük magasabb mint a talk show-ké. *(popular with)*

....

....

c Working in pairs, give a brief summary of the articles we read last lesson.

GRAMMAR FOCUS
mini test

Auxiliaries 2

Do the following test, and check it with the rest of the class.

1. We ... have brought an umbrella. Look what a lovely day it is.
A mustn't **C** wouldn't
B oughtn't **D** needn't

2. I ... make a phone call, but I'll just drink a cup of coffee first.
A would **C** ought to
B — **D** need

3. In fact, I am not sure that he's lying. He ... have heard anything about the whole thing at all.
A might not **C** should
B mustn't **D** can

4. Come on, you ... have been at the library yesterday! The library is closed on Mondays!
A can't **C** mightn't
B mustn't **D** oughtn't to

5. This car is just wonderful. It ... have cost a fortune.
A can **C** ought
B must **D** would

6. I have a guilty conscience. As a matter of fact, I ... for my exams now.
A must be preparing **C** ought to prepare
B should prepare **D** should be preparing

7. If we ... quite as much at Christmas, we ... any worries about the bills now.
A didn't spend // wouldn't have had **C** hadn't spent // wouldn't had
B hadn't spent // mightn't have **D** didn't spend // couldn't have had

8. If I ... any news, I ... you know immediately.
A hear // will let **C** hear // would let
B will hear // will let **D** heard // would have let

9. I wish I ... somewhere in the greenbelt. I am sick of all this noise and pollution.
A had lived **C** lived
B would live **D** have lived

10. I wish you ... all the time. You are driving me mad.
A haven't complained **C** hadn't complain
B wouldn't complain **D** wouldn't have complained

SPEAKING
discussion

a **Discuss with your partner what you think of the following TV channels, TV programmes, TV shows, magazines, literary genres, film genres, theatricals, etc. Say what you like or dislike about them, and make a list of the things both of you like and dislike. When you have finished, compare your lists with the other pairs, and make a final list of the most and least popular items.**

- operettas
- action-packed thrillers
- comic strips
- the Friderikusz-show
- discos
- the Museum of Modern Art
- classical music concerts
- quiz programmes
- live TV broadcast of the European Figure Skating Championships
- Dallas
- poems
- blue movies
- political discussions
- TV commercials
- cartoons
- Eurosport
- science fiction
- ballet
- horror films
- Kiskegyed

b **What's your opinion about the following statements? Think of some reasons to support your view and then compare your ideas with the rest of the class.**

1. "Violent cartoons (e.g. Tom & Jerry) are harmful for kids."

2. "Books are going out of fashion."

3. "Books, films, TV, newspapers, etc. should be *censored*, i.e. examined to remove anything that is pornographic, morally harmful, or politically dangerous."

c **Answer the following questions in small groups. Make lists, and then compare them with the rest of the class.**

1. What are the pros and cons of watching films at the cinema as opposed to watching them on TV?
2. What are the pros and cons of subtitles as opposed to dubbed films?
3. What do you think would be gained and lost if television disappeared from your life completely? (Say, if your TV set went wrong, and you didn't have the money to have it repaired or to buy a new one? Or, even better, if you threw it out of the window?)

d **Read the newspaper article, and discuss the question in pairs.**

Is there any kind of music that makes you flee in terror when you hear it?

Patwarthan, India – A farmer here is playing Michael Jackson songs over a loudspeaker in his field – because it scares away wild pigs. Anath Patwarthan says he "accidentally" played a Jackson tape in his field one day, and was surprised to see that the wild pigs fled in terror. Now the farmer has invested in an outdoor loudspeaker system to keep the hungry pigs away from his crops.

HOMEWORK

VOCABULARY

survival kit

preview

Read through the new vocabulary list on page 167-168, and consult a dictionary if you come across something that is unfamiliar or unclear to you.

EXAM TIPS

The listening comprehension task

☞ In Budapest, the listening exam is administered in a language lab (with headphones), elsewhere it takes place in a separate room and there are no headphones. The two or three-minute-long recording is played three times, and the task-sheet (containing 4–7 Hungarian language comprehension questions) is handed out after you have listened to the tape once. Your answers should be in Hungarian, too.

Interestingly, from the point of view of exam strategies, the listening comprehension task is quite similar to the reading comprehension task. The two key issues are *understanding the gist* and *focus on the questions*.

When you listen to the recording for the first time, you should just concentrate on one single question: *What is the whole thing all about?* At that stage you should not worry about the details or the things you haven't been able to catch, instead of panicking, just *focus on the gist*. Then *read the questions very carefully* (they will focus your attention on the aspects that are really important). While you are listening to the recording for the second and the third time, do not write anything (except, perhaps, for jotting down numbers or names), concentrate on what you can hear instead – you will be given enough time to do the writing afterwards. Just as in the case of the reading comprehension task, try and avoid *yes* or *no* answers, and do not use the same information to answer two different questions.

UNIT 7 Sport and Hobbies

LESSON 1

VOCABULARY survival kit

Sporting activities

Doing exercise: Do you do any sport/physical exercise?, Well, I don't get much physical exercise these days., to do/take/get (some\any\a lot of\little) exercise, to take part in sport\physical\sporting activities, to do some\any\much\ a lot of\little sport, to be good at sports, to be keen on/to be interested in sport\a game/a sport, to be a sporty person

Taking part in particular sporting activities: to play games (tennis, football, chess, etc.), to do gymnastics and body sports (karate, keep-fit, workout, judo, etc.), to ride a bike\horse, to go swimming\skiing\ jogging\fishing\etc., to take up\to give up a sport

Sports, events & participants

Types of sports: indoor\outdoor games, amateur\pro(fessional)\ spectator\participant\competitive\leisure\one-to-one\team\solitary\technical\extreme\blood sports

Athletes: sportsman/woman, competitor, player, to be a Hungarian international/capped (for Hungary), Olympic\World\ European\ national champion, coach, manager

Events: training (session), competition, game, match, sporting event, championship(s), cup, heat, to qualify for the (semi-)final, cup final, (at) the (1936) Olympics/the Olympic Games, the (football) World Cup, fan/supporter, club

Results: Hungary played\beat/defeated England, Hungary went down to/lost to/against England, to beat/defeat\win\lose/go down by two goals, a draw, to draw (with), to score (a goal), to score/ win\lose a point, score, to take the lead, to hold\break a record (for a sport), to win a gold\silver\bronze (medal) in the ..., to come in first\second\last, sports equipment, stadium

Hobbies

pastime, to collect stamps\coins\napkins\phone cards, keeping pets, knitting, playing computer games, board games, playing musical instruments, singing in a choir, dancing, DIY, taking photographs, gambling, charitable work, doing crosswords, (football) pools, lottery, keep-fit classes

SPEAKING
conversation

Use the following guidelines to tell your partner about a) any sports* you have ever tried your hand at, b) any sporting activities/physical exercise you take part in on a regular basis, c) any sporting events you like attending, d) any sports programmes you like watching on TV, and e) any hobbies you have.

the past ➜ the present ➜ attending sporting events ➜ sports on TV ➜ hobbies

***SPORTS & GAMES**

water sports swimming ⇒ breast\back\butterfly stroke, crawl, freestyle; diving; scuba diving; sailing/yachting ⇒ sail, mast, rowing ⇒ oar; canoeing ⇒ paddle; surfing; windsurfing; water-skiing; water polo; speed boating

athletics*[BrE]*/track and field*[AmE]* long distance\marathon running; sprint; hurdles; relay; walking; high\long\triple jump; shot put; pole vault; hammer\discus\javelin throw; (modern) pentathlon

ball games football/soccer ⇒ player, defender, forward, goalkeeper; referee; penalty; free kick; header; goalpost; football field/pitch\ground; American football; cricket; baseball; golf ⇒ course, club; tennis ⇒ court, racket, net; to play doubles\singles, umpire; squash; rugby (football)/ rugger; polo; hockey; basket\volley\handball; tabletennis/ping-pong ⇒ bat; badminton ⇒ shuttlecock *[BrE]*/birdie *[AmE]*; snooker, billiards, pool ⇒ cue (sports)

combat sports
wrestling ⇒ mat; boxing ⇒ gloves, punch, knockout; martial arts: karate, judo

winter sports
skiing ⇒ downhill ~, cross-country ~, skijump; skating ⇒ ice ~, figure ~, speed ~; ice rink; bobsleighing; snowboarding; ice hockey

other sports
weightlifting; fencing ⇒ sabre, foil, piste; horse riding\racing; mountaineering/mountain climbing; shooting ⇒ rifle; archery ⇒ bow, arrow; cycling; gymnastics ⇒ gym(nasium); flying; parachuting/sky diving; gliding; hang\para gliding; bungee jumping; motor/car\motorbike racing

leisure sports
keep fit (classes); workout ⇒ press-up *[BrE]*/push-up *[AmE]*, trunk bending, hand\headstand, arch; aerobics; body building; jogging; bowling; bowls; darts; roller-skating; rollerblading; skateboarding; boating; chess; cards; sledging/tobogganing; fishing/ angling ⇒ ~ grounds, bait, line, hook, rod; hunting ⇒ ~ grounds; sunbathing ⇒ tan; hiking/walking ⇒ rucksack *[BrE]*/ backpack *[AmE]*; camping ⇒ to set up camp, to put up a tent; caravanning

A

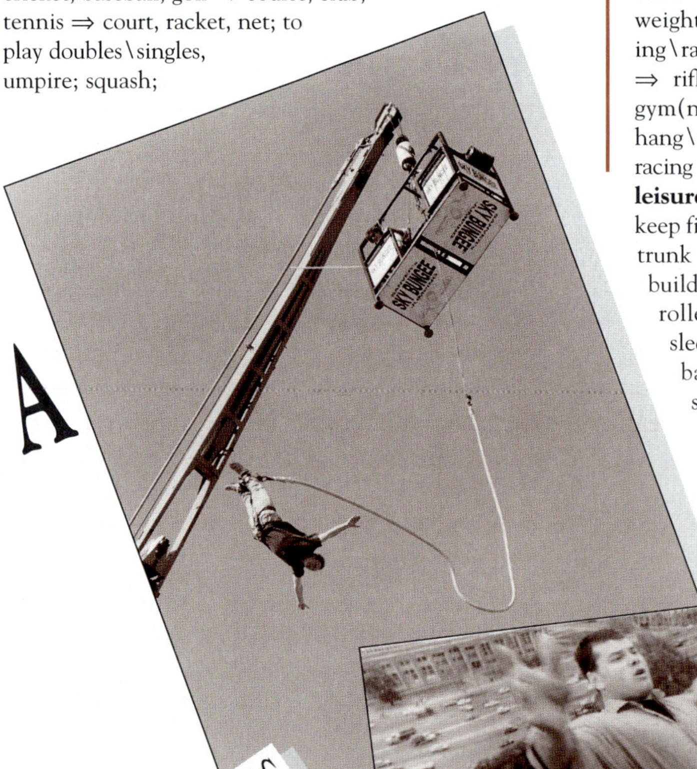

SPEAKING pictures

a **Discuss with the class what vocabulary you need to describe the pictures.**

Verbs:	Nouns:	Adjectives:

b **Agree with your partner which one of you has picture(s) A and B, take turns to describe what you can see in them, and make guesses about the situation.**

c **Looking at all three pictures now, discuss what you think is relevant of the following questions in pairs (It is your personal experience/judgement/opinion/ etc. that is important here!):**

Have you or anybody you know ever been in a situation like this?
What do you think it could be like to be in a situation like this?
Would you like to be in a situation like this?
What do you think of what you can see and/or what is happening in the picture?

You may find the following phrases useful here:

I (can still) remember ...-ing ... ➺ I've already ... ➺ That reminds me of ... ➺ I think/guess ... ➺ In my opinion/view ... ➺ As far as I'm concerned ... ➺ The way I see it ... ➺ From my point of view ... ➺ It seems to me that ... ➺ I'd say ... ➺ If you ask me ... ➺ To my mind ... ➺ Yes, why not? // It'd be great ... ➺ Well, to be honest, I don't think ... // I have no head for heights. ➺ Under/In no circumstances would I ever ... // No way would I ... ➺ I wouldn't do it for anything. // Not likely! ➺ No, thank you, ... is not for me. // ... is not my cup of tea. ➺ I'd rather not (do something). ➺ I don't feel I could ... // I'm not sure I'd be capable of ...-ing.

B

SPEAKING pictures

FUNCTIONS
role-play

a Read both role-cards and agree with your partner who's A and who's B.

A You run into a friend you have not seen for some time. To your astonishment, s/he looks rather run-down, s/he is pale and has big bags around the eyes.

- Tell her/him that you don't really like what you see, and ask her/him what's wrong.
- Tell your friend that the real problem is that s/he sits in the office all day. Suggest that s/he should do some physical exercise.
- Tell her/him that s/he could do some swimming before work in the morning.
- Tell her/him that s/he could do body building after work in the evening.
- Tell her/him that s/he could go jogging either in the morning or the evening.
- Tell her/him that at least s/he should do some workout at home.
- Wish her/him all the best and say goodbye.

B You run into a friend you have not seen for some time, and s/he says that you look pretty awful.

- Reassure you friend that there's nothing wrong with you, it's just that you've been working quite hard recently, and you're a bit tired.
- Admit that you're certainly not on top form, but you must spend most of the day sitting in front of the computer at work, and there's no time for physical exercise.
- Say that you could, but you don't like the cold water in the swimming pool, and anyway you would rather do something in the evening.
- Say that you could, but you don't like the smell in the gym, and anyway it's so expensive.
- Say that you could, but you've heard so much about air pollution, and anyway it's so boring.
- Agree to do some breathing exercise before going to bed at night occasionally.
- Thank your friend for the advice and say goodbye.

b Try and agree with the rest of your class how you could use the following phrases in this situation; complete the phrases and answer the questions.

A: ***Hi/Hello (there, Peter)! Long time no see! // Good to see you again!***

B: *Hello! It's good to see you!*

A: ***How's life?/How are you (keeping)? // How's it going? // How's things?***

B: *Quite well. // So-so. // OK. // Mustn't grumble. // Can't complain. // Not too bad. // Surviving. // Still alive, thanks.*

A: ***Well, to tell you the truth, ... // To be frank, ... // Quite honestly, ... // ..., if you don't mind my saying so.***

What's the trouble/wrong with you? // Is everything all right?

B: *No, really, there's nothing to worry about // I assure you that ... // It's just that ... //*

A: ***Why don't you ... ? // How about ... ? // Don't you think it would be a good idea to ...?***

B: *That's a good idea, but ... // That sounds OK, but ... // The problem/trouble is that ...*

All right/OK, I'll ...

X: Bye then!//Bye-bye!//Bye!/Bye for now!//I'll be seeing you//Cheers! // Take care.//Look after yourself.//Mind how you go, bye!

c Rehearse the situation in pairs. Read the cards again before starting but try and rely only on the notes below while practising.

greeting → what's the trouble? → suggestions: swimming, body building, jogging, exercise → leave-taking

PRONUNCIATION 1
sounds & word stress

Sounds

☞ Be particularly careful with the pronunciation of international words, trademarks, and geographical names.

Listen and repeat.

television	supermarket	satellite	Berlin
telephone	football	cassette	Madrid
computer	cigarette	philosophy	Mercedes
pullover	brandy	kilometre	Porsche
farmer	pizza	Nike	Washington
hotel	police	Levis	Los Angeles
thriller	jam	London	San Francisco

Word stress

☞ Words ending with *-ate* and *-ise/-ize* have their main stress on the third syllable before the end.
☞ Words ending with *two consonants* always have their main stress on the last syllable.

Listen and repeat.

'illustrate	'recognize	in'form
'irritate	'criticize	de'mand
co'mmunicate	'realise	ac'cept
par'ticipate	'advertise	reco'mmend

☞ The stress of *self*-pronouns depends on their function; as *reflexive pronouns* they are *unstressed*; but as *emphatic pronouns* they are *stressed*, and the stress is on the second syllable.

Listen and repeat.

reflexive pronoun	emphatic pronoun
Just look at yourself in the mirror.	She's knitted it her**self.**
I've cut myself again.	The wrapping paper is more expensive than the book it**self.**
You'll hurt yourself!	

HOMEWORK

VOCABULARY survival kit
study task

Study the word list on page 167-168, and memorise the words and phrases that you think are important and relevant to your circumstances. When you have finished, put the following words in their correct places in the passage below to check your knowledge. (You might try and do the task without using the box.)

Teams, skating, formula, competitions, played, racing, sessions, championships, figure, water, Olympic, training, did, do, rink, competitive, coach, sports, games, keen, technical, gliding, country, events, parachuting, climbing, glider, distance, fencing, flying, supported, gave, sporting, playing

When I was a young kid I didn't like sports very much. Most probably it was because I had to .... swimming, which I really hated; I had to get up very early for the training ...., the water was cold, and most important of all, the .... was a very rude elderly lady, who was only interested in potential .... champions, which I was clearly not to be. Except for a little sailing much later, I've been trying to stay as far away from .... sports as possible ever since.

In my very early schooldays, I used to go .... on the natural .... in the school-yard. I think I was very good at it, but unfortunately I grew out of my skates and that was it.

Later at primary school I got really crazy about football. I used to play with my friends in the park after school and we would have regular local "......................" with the other .... in the neighbourhood. We also .... Ferencváros, and we often went to see them when they .... at home. This was the only period of my life when I attended sporting .... on a regular basis.

It was also at that time that I took up ...., foil to be exact, and started the most intensive .... activity I have ever been involved in. I had four or five .... sessions a week, and quite often there were .... at the weekend. I liked everything about it enormously; I enjoyed the company of the other kids, I liked the coach, and I enjoyed the atmosphere of the competitions, too. I .... fencing for seven years and I only .... it up before the entrance exams to university.

In the meantime I tried some more sports and ...., too, although not on a regular basis. I really enjoyed .... tennis, table tennis, and badminton, but I wasn't particularly .... on basketball, running and, interestingly enough, skiing.

There are some sports and games which I've never had the chance to experience, but, at least in theory, I would really like to. Most of these are non-......................., solitary sports, which involve certain risks or are clearly dangerous. I'm sure a psychologist could draw far-reaching conclusions from this, but, as I see it, these are just .... I have never tried my hand at. For example, it has always been one of my dreams to be able to experience one of the sports that involve .... In fact, once I was a "passenger" on a ...., and it was an absolutely fantastic experience – flying without an engine in that deadly silence up there, the fast movement, the void on both sides as you look out of the windows, well, that was a truly exhilarating sensation. I can imagine how fantastic it might be to do hang-....................... where there isn't even a capsule to separate you from the void around you, or .... where you haven't even got a metal bar to hang on to. I wonder, however, whether I could ever jump out of a plane.

Rock-....................... is another sport I would always have liked to try, in spite of the fact – or just because of it? – that once I had quite a frightening experience of it; not knowing the climb up is always easier than the descent, me and my friends almost got stuck on a cliff at Békás-szoros.

There are some sports, however that I'm not interested in at all, and I will switch off the telly when they come on. This is the situation with all .... sports, – particularly .... One car-....................... . I find them so boring that I'm sure most people just watch them because they look forward to the inevitable accidents. I don't particularly like sports that are almost exclusively based on physical strength and endurance, for example long .... running or cross-...................... skiing, and some other sports that I find very artificial or ridiculous, like .... skating, aerobics, and body building.

GRAMMAR FOCUS
p r e v i e w

Auxiliaries 3

The auxiliaries in this group are used in particular situations with a special meaning. Some of them have both present and past forms, but most of them are only used in the present in certain speech acts or functions. We can use

will

to ask someone to do something *(legyen szíves)*

➢ *Will you sign this sheet here, please? Sign this sheet here, will you? If you will sign this sheet here, please.*

to talk about habits *(mindig így szokta)*

➢ *On Sundays he will get up at about 10.*

to talk about characteristic behaviour *(képes ezt tenni!)*

➢ *He is really mad about cartoons; he will watch Cartoon Network for ten hours at the weekend.*

to invite somebody to do something *(parancsol ...?)*

➢ *Will you have a cup of coffee? Won't you take a seat?*

to offer to do something *(majd én ...)*

➢ *I will pay for the tickets.*

won't

to talk about people or things that refuse to do something *(nem hajlandó, nem akar)*

➢ *This bloody door won't open. She won't help anyone. I won't say a word.*

shall *(should* has all these meanings, too)

to suggest something *(csináljuk ezt és ezt!)*

➢ *Shall we go to the cinema? Let's go to the cinema, shall we?*

to offer to do something *(kinyissam ...?)*

➢ *Shall I open the window?*

to ask for advice *(tegyem ezt/mit tegyek?)*

➢ *What shall I do now?*

would

to politely ask someone to do something *(ha lenne olyan kedves, és ...)*

➢ *Would you turn down the volume a bit, please? If you would take a seat.*

to talk about habits in the past *(és akkor mindig ...)*

➢ *When I was a kid, we would get up early on Sundays and go to the Zoo. We would be back home by noon, and we would have lunch. Then we would ...*

to criticise something that somebody did *(jellemző rád, hogy ...)*

➢ *You would call me at a time like this. Do you know what the time is?*

wouldn't

to talk about someone or something that refused to do something in the past (*nem akart/nem volt hajlandó*)

➢ *She wouldn't answer my question. The door wouldn't open.*

could

to politely ask someone to do something (*legyen/légy szíves .../tudna/nál ...?*)

➢ *Could you lend me you pen, please?*

should

to ask for advice, to make offers\suggestions (*tegyem/tegyük ezt?*) (almost the same as *shall*)

➢ *What should I do now? Should I help you with ...?*

to make something sound less probable (if, by any chance ...) (*ha netán/ha véletlenül*)

➢ *If you should have some news, let me know immediately. Should you have some news, let me know immediately. I'll take an umbrella, in case it should rain.(or: ... it rains) I took an umbrella, in case it should rain. (or: ... it rained)*

to say that something will probably happen/be the case (*ought to* is also possible in this meaning) (*valószínűleg*)

➢ *It's not very expensive; it shouldn't be more than £10. He should/ought to be home in a few minutes.*

after certain verbs that take the infinitive, particularly when the subject of the second verb is different: *advise, agree, ask, demand, insist, order, propose, recommend, etc.*; and also after *suggest* (which normally takes the *gerund*)

➢ *They insisted (that) I should be the leader of the team. The demonstrators demanded (that) the government should do something about unemployment. My doctor suggested (that) I should see a dentist as soon as possible.*

Other structures are also possible here: we can use the simple present/simple past or we can simply leave out *should*.

➢ *What do you suggest I do now? Vivien suggested I wrote a book. I recommend that she gives up smoking.*

after certain adjectives (which express that something is important and must be done): *important, essential, necessary, vital, crucial*

➢ *It is crucial that I (should) be informed in time. It is important that both of you should be there.*

after certain adjectives (which express personal reactions to things): *strange, odd, funny, interesting, amazing, natural, typical, normal, surprising, it's a shame, surprised, shocked, sorry* (*..., hogy ilyesmi történjen*)

➢ *It is strange that he (should) say such a thing. I'm sorry you (should) believe these stories. I don't think it is normal that she (should) be so rude to her parents.*

with *so that* and *in order that* in past sentences (*azért, hogy [nehogy] ...*)

➢ *I tiptoed down the stairs so that I shouldn't wake up the kids.*

may

to express a (formal) good wish (*szívből kívánom, hogy ...*)

➢ *May you stay forever young.*

used to

to talk about past habits and states/situations that are not true any longer (*régebben ..., de már nem*) N.B.: *Would* is only used for past habits! Do not use *used to* or *would* to say how often or how long something happened in the past.

➢ *I used to have (long) hair. Did you use to be slim when you were young? He didn't use to be so rude before the wedding.*

dare

to say that someone is cheeky enough or has enough courage to do something in the present (*mer, merészel, van képe, hogy*)

➢ *I daren't tell her that I love her. How dare you read my letters you cheeky so-and-so?*

dare can be used like an ordinary verb, too, but in this case it usually (but not always) takes an *infinitive with* 'to' – there's some inconsistency in the usage here.

➢ *I don't/didn't dare to tell him the truth. Don't you dare say that again!*

I dare say/daresay means 'I think/guess/suppose' or 'probably'.

➢ *I daresay it'll be pretty expensive.*

LESSON 2

VOCABULARY survival kit checkpoint

a **Check the fill-in-the-blank homework task with the rest of the class.**

b **What are the "opposites" of the following words and phrases?**

- to do a lot of sport
- to take up a sport
- indoor games
- professional sports
- spectator sports
- leisure sports
- team sports
- heat
- Hungary defeated England
- to come in first

c **Identify the sports and games by the "tools of the trade".**

- club, green, fairway
- corner, ropes, gloves
- goalpost, penalty area, kick-off spot
- table, bat
- net, racket
- oar
- board, piece, clock
- hook, line, rod
- hurdle, lane, starting block
- sabre, piste
- bow, arrow
- table, cue
- sail, mast
- net, shuttlecock
- goal, stick, puck
- reins, stirrup, saddle

d **What sports and games do you think the following geographical names can be associated with?**

- St Andrews *(Scotland)*
- Epsom *(south of London)*
- Las Vegas *(Nevada, US)*
- Wimbledon *(South London)*
- Silverstone *(Northamptonshire, England)*
- Wembley *(London)*
- Ascot *(near Windsor)*
- Indianapolis *(Indiana, US)*

e Complete the definitions.

- When a game or match ends without either side winning, it is a ....
- When you do a programme of exercises on a regular basis to make your body fit and strong you ....
- A .... is someone who regularly goes to watch a particular sports team play.
- Someone who plays for one of their country's sports teams is an ....
- .... is the activity of making and repairing things yourself instead of buying them or paying someone else to do it.
- A .... is a system in which people buy tickets with different numbers on them; several numbers are then chosen at random and the people whose tickets have these (or some of these) numbers on them win money.

GRAMMAR FOCUS

translation into English

Auxiliaries 3

Translate the following sentences into English, discussing each section with the rest of the class as you progress.

❶ – Együnk egy hamburgert, jó?
– Jó. Igyunk kólát is?
– Hát persze. Rendeljek?

....

....

❷ Legyen szíves nyissa ki a bőröndjét. Nyissa ki a bőröndjét, legyen szíves. Ha lenne olyan szíves itt helyet foglalni. Valami baj van; nem akar indulni a motor. *(engine)* Minden reggel kocogok; mindig lefutok a folyópartra, ott mindig gimnasztikázok egy kicsit, majd hazafutok. Kérsz egy sört? Majd én hazaviszlek. Olyan szorgalmas – mindig hajnalig tanul/ képes hajnalig tanulni dolgozatok előtt.

....

....

....

....

....

❸ Ha netán látnád őt, mondd meg neki, hogy még mindig szeretem. Fontos, hogy tudja, hogy még mindig szeretem. Ragaszkodom hozzá, hogy maradj itt vacsorára. Azt javasolom, hogy ne mondjon egy szót sem a tárgyaláson. Mercedest vegyek, vagy BMW-t? Valószínűleg kész leszek tízre.

....

....

❹ Lenne olyan kedves segíteni nekem? Nagyon hálás lennék, ha lennének szívesek küldeni nekem egy prospektust. *(brochure)* Nem akart indulni a motor. Minden reggel kocogtam; mindig lefutottam a folyópartra, ott gimnasztikáztam egy kicsit, majd hazafutottam. Ez jellemző rád: kidobsz tízezer forintot egy ilyen marhaságra. *(to splash out on, silly)*

❺ Kívánom, hogy minden kívánságod váljon valóra! *(to come true)*

❻ Ez a műsor régebben egész jó volt. Régebben nem panaszkodtál ennyit. Gyerekkoromban minden vasárnap templomba jártam.

❼ Hogy mersz ilyen dolgokat mondani? Ne merészelj még egyszer patkánynak nevezni! *(rat)* Nem mertem neki megmondani az igazat.

L I S T E N I N G

Events, heroes, results

BBC sports news

a Read the questions and try to answer them after you have listened to the recording once. Discuss your answers with your partner.

- What sports and games are mentioned in the news? (There are 6 different sports and games mentioned.)
- What international sporting events are mentioned in the news? (There are 4 such events mentioned.)
- Are you familiar with any of the names that are mentioned in the news?

b Answer the following questions as you listen to the tape for the second time. Discuss your answers with the rest of the class.

- What three medals did British athletics win in Gothenburg (Göteborg, Sweden) on that particular day? In what sports?
- Why is Hungary mentioned in the news?
- Who was the winner there, and what does he say about his victory?
- Who was the big loser there and why?
- How do British authorities plan to deal with foreign troublemakers at next year's European Championship?
- What is the purpose of the police Football Intelligence Unit's telephone Hotline?
- What makes Jonathan Edwards's victory a historic event?
- Whose world record did he break, and what was the old world record (not mentioned in the report directly!)?

HOMEWORK

TRANSLATION
English into Hungarian

Use a dictionary to read the following article, and translate the *highlighted* part of the text into Hungarian in writing. Pay particular attention to the underlined words and phrases.

The Big Game

There are big games, and then there is The Big Game – the Superbowl. The superbowl is the most important event in the world, probably in the universe. A lot of sports fans argue that this annual American football game is the most important event of any kind ever held anywhere, certainly more important than the invasion of Normandy or the inauguration of a new President.

This end-of-January extravaganza purports to be the World Championship of a game that is only played professionally in North America. (There is a World League of American Football, but the chances of one of its teams playing in the Superbowl any time soon are thinner than a cheerleader's panties.)

The game's promoters select a stadium that's as large as possible in a city that's warm enough so that wealthy fans won't freeze to death, usually somewhere in Florida, or Texas. For maximum dollar impact, the game is scheduled to allow easy viewing in all the main American time zones, and advertisers trot out their most innovative commercials for the Superbowl, paying upwards of $1,800,000 a minute for the privilege of showing them. This may well be worth it, since on Superbowl Sunday more than half of all American televisions are tuned to The Game.

On Superbowl Sunday, Americans hold parties to watch television and consume beer, and pizza. In a city that has a team playing in the Superbowl, all public activity stops and traffic disappears. When the game is over, riotous celebrations, or sometimes just riots, break out in the neighbourhood with the most bars.

The Xenophobe's Guide to The Americans, by Stephanie Faul, Ravette Books, London 1994

LESSON 3

TRANSLATION
English into Hungarian
checkpoint

The Big Game

a **What kind of translations have the different people in the class come up with for the following words and phrases in the context of the passage?**

- the game's promoters
- this may well be worth it
- for maximum dollar impact
- all public activity stops
- the game is scheduled to allow easy viewing
- riotous celebrations
- innovative
- just riots

b **Compare and discuss the possible translations for each and every sentence with the whole class.**

c **Choose three new words or phrases from the text that you think are worth remembering.**

READING & VOCABULARY
a r t i c l e s

a **Read through the articles and try to answer the following questions without using a dictionary. When you have finished, discuss your answers in pairs.**

- Where did the judge leave his car?
- Where did he leave his canoe?
- How long did it take for him to get home?
- What kind of collector's items is New York planning to sell, for how much, and why?

Judge paddles his own canoe to court

A judge yesterday followed the Government's advice to leave cars at home – and paddled his canoe to court.

His Honour Judge John Bull astonished officials when he turned up at Guildford Crown Court after navigating six miles down the River Wey from his home.

Dressed in jeans, T-shirt and trainers, Judge Bull, 61, dragged the canoe 40 yards up the river bank to his reserved spot in the car park and left it alongside the BMWs and Rovers of other judges and court officials. No one doubted to whom it belonged, for on its bow is a small brass plaque depicting Big Chief Sitting Bull.

The canoe safely berthed, Judge Bull then slipped into his suit and robes before presiding over a trial and two appeals. Last night, before paddling off into the sunset, he said: "I had always wanted to do this, so this morning I thought 'why not?' ".

Judge Bull's return journey took three and a quarter hours; by car it takes 20 minutes.

The Times

New York strapped for cash

New York City, USA — Two of the world's most morbid collector's items may be sold at auction to reduce New York's huge budget deficit.

The governor of NY says he may sell two electric chairs, known as "The Old Sparkies", which were used in the city's prison between 1890 and 1963. The bulky chairs come complete with stainless steel hand cuffs and heavy leather straps, but no recline-function. If sold as a pair, the chairs are expected to raise $0.5 million.

"Over 700 people have sat in those chairs" said an auctioneer, "and not one of them ever complained. These could be the most collectable instruments of capital punishment this century. It's very exciting."

The Daily Telegraph

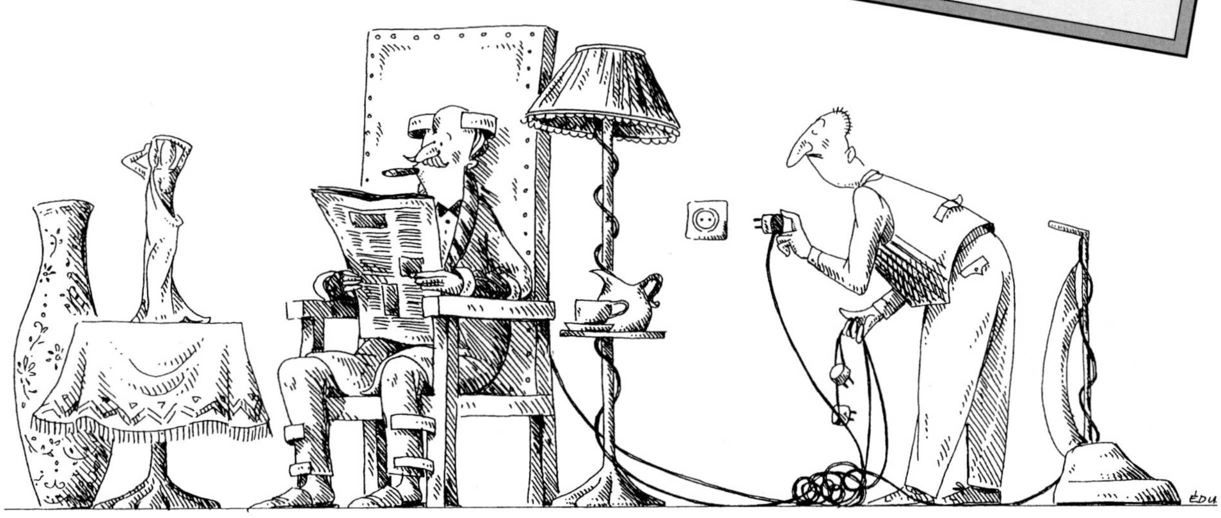

b Now try and find the English for the following words and phrases in the text, and make guesses about the possible derivatives. When you have finished, discuss them with the rest of the class.

bíró úr

....

edzőcipő

....

vonszolni ⇒ dögunalom

....

folyópart

....

fenntartott hely ⇒ azonnal/helyben

....

ábrázolni

....

sárgaréz

....

főnök ⇒ főbb/legfőbb ⇒ főleg/elsősorban

....

belebújni ⇒ csúszás ⇒ nyelvbotlás ⇒ csúszós

....

elnökölni ⇒ elnök ⇒ elnöki ⇒ elnökség(e valakinek)

....

valakié/valakihez tartozni ⇒ holmi

....

tárgyalás

....

fellebbezés ⇒ fellebbezni

....

naplemente

....

talár

....

hajóorr

....

kikötni/lehorgonyozni

....

(fém)tábla

....

bilincs ⇒ mandzsetta

....

hozni/előteremteni (pénzt)

....

terjedelmes ⇒ a zöme valaminek

....

szikra (!) ⇒ szikrázni ⇒ szikrázó

....

....

csökkenteni ⇒ árleszállítás

....

kormányzó ⇒ kormány

....

elektromos ⇒ ~ energia ⇒ ~ áram ⇒ elektromérnök ⇒ villanyszerelő

....

....

halálbüntetés

....

árverés ⇒ elárverezni ⇒ ~vezető

....

...-val együtt kapható/árulják/gyártják

....

rozsdamentes acél

....

különleges/gyűjteménybe való darab

....

szíj

....

gyűjtésre érdemes ⇒ gyűjthető tárgy

....

„megszorulni" (pénzügyileg)

....

állítható támlájú

....

c Now read the following questions and answer them in writing after reading the articles again. When you have finished, discuss the answers with the rest of the class.

Why were court officials astonished when Judge Bull arrived at work yesterday?

....

....

How was he dressed before and after arrival?

....

....

What kind of distinguishing feature has his canoe got?

....

....

Why does he say he did that and what does the article suggest about this?

....

....

How does the length of this journey compare to the length of the journey by car?

....

....

What does the article say about the history of the electric chairs?

....

....

What do the chairs look like, and how much are they expected to raise?

....

....

PRONUNCIATION 2

stress, rhythm & intonation

Stress & rhythm

- The strong form of the preposition is used before pronouns and at the end of the sentence.
- Adverbs do not have a weak form.
- The strong form of *that* is used when it is a demonstrative pronoun.
- The strong form of the *to* of the infinitive is used at the end of the sentence.
- The strong form of *some* is used when it means ‘certain, not all’.

Listen and repeat.

Where do you come from?	Do you know that man?
What are you looking at?	I didn't know that.
What's this for?	Did she really want to?
What's it made of?	Some people like soap operas.
Where are you going to?	I like some jazz.
When did you get up this morning?	I've seen some of them.

Intonation

☞ Orders and exclamations normally have a falling tune. However, a command can be turned into a request by giving it a rising tune.

Listen and repeat.

Shut ↘up!	Wait a ↗moment!
↘Stop it, please!	Don't be a↗fraid!
It ↘hurts!	Don't ↗cry!
What a ↘show!	Let's have a ↗beer!
How ↘lovely!	Hurry ↗up!
What a beautiful ↘girl!	Take a↗nother one!

LINK WORDS

Make sure you know what the following link words mean, and working in pairs, use as many as you can to make the text below sound more natural and dynamic. When you have found a suitable place for all of them, take turns to read out the new text.

(1) secondly (2) and lastly (3) admittedly (4) for example (5) to the best of my knowledge (6) anyway (7) for some reason (8) like/such as (9) in my opinion/if you want my opinion/as far as I can judge (10) and things like that (11) I'm convinced/I have no doubt in my mind (12) furthermore/in addition to this (13) in fact/as a matter of fact

Collectibles:

Some friends of mine think I am a collector. ...., I am actually not one – against all appearances.

........................, a real collector is a person who feels an irresistible urge to obtain the missing items of her/his collection, and is ready (and can afford) to make sacrifices to that end. I don't really feel this urge, and I can't afford to spend large sums of money on such things ...., I have never collected stamps, works of art, or anything at all purely and simply for their material value. As for the things I have, well, I think I can give you a reasonable account of how they have come into my possession.

➢ In the first place, I've inherited the complete furnishings and decorations of a smaller flat, and I am trying to find "new" pieces that go with the old ones.

........................, I like old things. In this category I will hunt for different pieces of furniture, ... tables, chairs, missing pieces of a lovely old dinner service, lamps, etc.

➢ ...., I received the first items of other "collections" as a present. I got a nice brass bell from my students some 15 years ago. I liked it a lot, so I got another one on another occasion. When other students came to see me, they saw the bells, and .... they thought I collected them, so I got another one as a present. In this way I've been presented with at least ten bells over the years. ...., I've already bought some myself, as well. In this group I have collectibles like large brass keys, dice, rocks, fossils, ...

➢ ...., there are other things that have simply piled up over the years, books, records, cassettes, family/school memorabilia like photographs, school badges, etc.

.... that all this has a lot more to do with feelings and emotions than with a desire to possess things.

HOMEWORK

VOCABULARY
articles
study tasks

Judge paddles his own canoe to court/New York strapped for cash

a Read the articles again and memorise any vocabulary items that are new to you. When you have finished, use the words in the box to fill in the gaps in the passage below. Change the form of the words if necessary.

A few weeks ago we were a bit .... for cash, so we decided to sell the .... piano that took up far too much space in our tiny sitting room. It was a classic example of a white elephant; it wasn't only ugly, but also completely useless as none of us can play the piano. Well, to cut a long story short, I eventually called a dealer to appraise the thing. As it turned out, it was a real collector's .... , more than a hundred years old, and we sold it at .... managing to .... an incredible 1.5 million forints. Needless to say, the transaction has considerably .... the family's huge budget ...., what is more, I might also be able to buy a small car. This would be a fantastic change, because now I .... my own canoe to work every day. I am a judge by profession, and quite honestly, I've had enough of having to wear jeans, T-shirt and .... during the journey, and having to .... into my suit and .... before .... over my trials and .... If I can buy a car at long last, I won't have to .... my canoe 200 meters up the river .... to my reserved .... in the car park of the court, and "park" it alongside fancy BMWs and Rovers, which is quite ridiculous. The .... advantage, of course, is that the journey will only take twenty minutes instead of the ususal three hours. This paddling has become quite a ...., as now I hardly ever get home before ....

to raise
spot
robes
sunset
trainers
to reduce
to slip
auction
bulky
item
to drag
to paddle
appeal
chief
to be strapped
drag
deficit
to preside
bank

b **Use the following guidelines to prepare for a short oral summary of the articles about the judge and the chairs in a few sentences.**

The canoeing judge: → the person → the journey → "parking" → clothes → comparison
The electric chairs: → description → the reason → the price → their history + joke

WRITING
composition

Few, if any events attract quite as many spectators as sporting events, particularly international contests. What could be the secret? It would be interesting to know what the class thinks about the possible reasons. In order to find out about this, write your teacher a short essay containing your ideas about this phenomenon, so that s/he can add your views to what the rest of the class has to say.

Step One	Step two	Step three
General outline:	Brainstorming:	Details:
Introduction	introducing topic, some kind of a general judgement about the phenomenon	*e.g.: "Panem et circenses" – "bread and circuses" wrote the Roman poet Juvenal almost two thousand years ago, ... e.g.: A third-rate football match will attract more people than a first class classical music concert, ...*
Possible reasons	e.g.: a chance for people to "let off steam" a bit/to belong to group/to be part of a victory or defeat/to meet other people/to enjoy the excitement/to go out/to see celebrities live/etc. it is easy to understand/ spectacular/relatively cheap/ etc.	*As I see it // Personally I feel // The way I see it ... // There're a number of different reasons why ...* *No wonder ...* *First and foremost, // Most important of all, ...* *This is the feature that ...* *Similarly, ...* *In addition to ...*
Conclusion	summary	*In conclusion ...*

☞ When you have finished, don't forget to check your work for grammatical mistakes.

LESSON 4

VOCABULARY
articles
checkpoint

Judge paddles his own canoe to court/New York strapped for cash

a **Compare your solutions to the fill-in-gap homework task with the rest of the class.**

b **Discuss with the rest of the class what you think the English would be for the following Hungarian sentences.**

Bocs, ez csak nyelvbotlás volt; valójában azt akartam mondani, hogy szeretem a kekszet.

....

....

Ez a buli egy dögunalom, akár haza is mehetünk.

....

....

Ez az ajtó rozsdamentes acél és sárgaréz kilinccsel is kapható.

....

....

Nem lesz könnyű elég pénzt előteremteni erre a programra. (*project*)

....

....

Egy bulin találkozott vele először, és ott helyben meg is kérte a kezét.

....

....

Egy csomó különleges/gyűjteménybe való tárgyat árvereztek el, főleg festményeket.

....

....

Sokan úgy gondolják, hogy a halálbüntetés segítene visszaszorítani (csökkenteni) a bűnözést.

....

....

c **Working in pairs, give a brief summary of the articles we read last lesson.**

GRAMMAR FOCUS
m i n i t e s t

Auxiliaries 3

Do the following test and check it with the rest of the class.

1. It is typical of him that he ... be late for his own wedding.
- **A** would
- **B** should
- **C** shall
- **D** can

2. ... have enough time, please come and see us.
- **A** If you would
- **B** If you will
- **C** Should you
- **D** Would you

3. Oh dear, this goddamn car ... start! It ... do that, just as I am trying to catch my plane.
- **A** won't // would
- **B** doesn't // should
- **C** wouldn't // shouldn't
- **D** won't // should

4. "... I give you a hand with those bags?" "No, it's OK, I can manage."
- **A** Will
- **B** Would
- **C** Shall
- **D** Won't

5. I ... be very grateful if you ... send me further information about the conditions.
- **A** will // could
- **B** would // would
- **C** shall // shall
- **D** should // —

6. They agreed ... up later and talk things over once again.
- **A** that we must meet
- **B** we met
- **C** that we shall meet
- **D** we will meet

7. It is rather strange ... my car without saying a word.
- **A** he would take
- **B** that he takes
- **C** he take
- **D** that he should take

8. "I wonder why she takes ages to get out of the bathroom."
"Don't worry, she ... be ready in a few minutes."
- **A** should
- **B** shall
- **C** would
- **D** must

9. Although he is quite old now, he ... a fantastic sportsman; he ... the Hungarian heavy weight champion for more than ten years. He ... out most of his opponents in the first round.
- **A** was // would be // used to knock
- **B** used to be // was // would knock
- **C** would be // used to be // knocked
- **D** was // used to be // would knock

10. When I was in my mid teens I ... very shy; for example, I ... out with Márti, my first love for more than a year, and I ... kiss her.
- **A** would be // used to go // didn't even dare
- **B** was // would go // daren't even
- **C** used to be//went//didn't even dare to
- **D** was // used to go // even daren't to

SPEAKING
discussion

a **Discuss in pairs whether you would ever give the following sports a try (i.e. if you haven't so far). Give reasons.**

- water skiing
- roller skating
- car-racing
- archery
- bungee jumping
- scuba-diving
- horse-riding
- parachuting
- competitive dancing
- golf

b **If you had a daughter and a son, would you like them to do the following sports and games on a competitive basis? Discuss your answers in pairs (give reasons!), and then compare them with the other pairs in the class.**

BOYS

car racing
body building
football
aerobics
hang-gliding
boxing

GIRLS

handball
parachuting
chess
gymnastics
swimming
boxing

c **A lot of spectator sports and games are criticised for not being interesting or spectacular enough, particularly on TV. Read the following remarks, and in small groups, try and think of possible ways of "improving" the entertaining potential or quality of the corresponding sports.**

Football: there are far too few goals.

Handball/Water-polo: there are far too many stops in the game because of faults.

Basketball: height is far too important.

Ice-hockey: it is very difficult to see the puck.

Formula One car-racing: the technical quality of the cars is more important the skill of the driver; very little happens during the race, except for accidents.

Gymnastics/Figure skating/etc.: the scoring is far too subjective.

d **What's your opinion about the following statements? Think of some reasons to support your view and then compare your ideas with your partner's.**

1. Sporting stars are the heroes of our times.
2. Sport is healthy.
3. The number of medals (or points) particular countries win at the Olympic Games is a good measure of how talented the peoples of these countries are.
4. Sport has fantastic character-building qualities.

e **Using your ideas from your homework essay, discuss with the rest of the class why you think sporting events are so enormously popular.**

HOMEWORK

VOCABULARY survival kit preview

Read through the new vocabulary list on page 195-196, and consult a dictionary if you come across something that is unfamiliar or unclear to you.

EXAM TIPS

The guided interview (The conversation)

☞ This is the first task of the oral exam. You are supposed to carry on a short (maximum 5–8-minute-long) conversation with the examiner, with her/him asking the questions. These questions are meant to keep the conversation going, and they should cover at least two of the main topic areas, formulated in a way that they sound quite personal and/or topical, e.g.: *How did you get here from home? Do you suffer from environmental problems in any way? What's the weather like today?* You will be evaluated on the basis of your fluency, vocabulary and accuracy.

As this task also has a warm-up/introductory function, some topic areas will crop up more frequently than others. Students, for example, are quite likely to be asked questions about their *studies*, *future plans*, etc., other people can expect a question or two about their *jobs*. The least one can do to cope with this part of the exam is to prepare for all possible questions about *personal particulars* in general. Quite obviously, anything unusual about these (a strange name, a funny photo in your ID card, etc.) might result in some questions, too.

As for examination strategies, there is a very simple rule here: although you shouldn't normally ask questions, you are supposed to *take a fairly active part in the conversation*, which means avoiding simple yes or no answers and being as willing as possible to answer the examiner's questions. You shouldn't be "offended" by the questions (even if you think they are uninteresting or difficult) and you shouldn't try to be very funny, either.

UNIT 8 Weather and clothes

LESSON 1

VOCABULARY survival kit

Weather
Nice, fine, good, fair, sunny, mild, warm, clear day\sky, lovely day
Bad, nasty, foul, rotten, cool, (freezing/bitterly) cold, chilly, changeable, unpredictable
Hot, boiling/scorching/baking/roasting hot, (unbearable) heat, heatwave, sweltering, sultry/ close, muggy, sticky
Cloudy, foggy, dull, overcast, sunny spells, wet, moist, damp, humid, humidity
to cloud over, to clear up, fog, to fog up, smog, mist, haze, dew, vapour, to evaporate
Rainy, (heavy) rain, outbreaks of rain, to pour, raindrop, (to) sleet, (to) drizzle, (to) hail, hailstone, (to) shower, snow(flake), ice, (to) frost, to freeze over, to thaw, to melt, slush, mud, flood(ing), drought
Windy, strong\slight\north wind, (light) breeze, gale, (thunder)storm, thunder(bolt/clap), lightning
Effects: to be/feel/get hot\cold, to get wet/ drenched/soaking wet, to be wet through/ drenched to the skin, to slip, slippery
Weather report: temperature, ... degrees Celsius/ Centigrade\Fahrenheit (below\above zero), thermometer, weather forecast, cold front, (temperate) climate

Clothing
Something to wear: (formal\informal) clothes, outfit, gear, garment, dress, uniform, made-to-measure, ready-made, taylor, dressmaker, seamstress, designer
Fashion: to be in/out of fashion, to be in\out, (un)fashionable, to come into ~, to go out of ~, trendy, chic, stylish, latest fashion, brand, fashion-show, model, catwalk
well/smartly\fashionably dressed, to be elegant, to be smart, to be immaculate, to be dressed to kill, to be badly/shabbily dressed, smart/elegant clothes, sporty clothes
Wearing clothes: to wear (clothes, accessories, colours), to have sg on, to be sporting sg, to dress (for work\dinner), to get (un)dressed, to put sg on, to take sg off, to get changed, to change into sg, to fit, to suit, to match, to go with
Materials: materials/fabrics, woollen, cotton, corduroy, silk, velvet, satin, lace, tartan, linen, denim, tweed, knitted, nylon, leather, fur, man-made/synthetic fabrics

Patterns, styles & sizes: colour, plain, check *[BrE]*/plaid *[AmE]*, striped, dotted, patterned, embroidered, style, size, loose\tight-fitting, to try on, too loose\tight, to take in, to let out
Fasteners: belt, buckle, zip\Velcro-fastener, to do/zip\button up, to undo/unzip\unbutton, fly
Garments/Clothes/Items of clothing:
Trousers/slacks *[AmE]*/pants *[AmE]*, jeans, shorts, straight\flared trousers, turn-ups
Coats: overcoat, raincoat, jacket, fur coat, anorak, pocket
Suits & dresses:(two-piece) dress, full evening dress, suit, collar-and-tie, jacket, dinner jacket, tuxedo, blazer, waistcoat
Shirts: blouse, top, T-shirt, sweat-shirt, short\long-sleeved\sleeveless\open-necked\collarless shirt, button-down collar, cuffs
Skirts: straight\pleated\mini\long skirts
Pullovers, sweater, jumper, jersey, cardigan, V\polo *[BrE]*/turtle *[AmE]*\crew\scooped-necked
Underclothes/underwear/undies, pants *[BrE]*, vest, panties/knickers, camisole, body, tights/ pantihose *[AmE]*, leggings, socks, stockings, bra, slip, night-dress/nightie, pyjamas, gown
Swimsuit/bathing suit, swimming costume, swimming trunks, bikini, bathrobe
Shoes: boots, shoelaces, wellingtons/wellies, clogs, sandals, slippers, sports/tennis/gym shoes, plimsolls, trainers *[BrE]*/sneakers *[AmE]*, flat\high-heeled\rubber\thick soled/platform shoes
Other: gloves, mittens, scarf, cap, hat, hood, (bow) tie, jogging suit, tracksuit *[BrE]*/warm-up suit *[AmE]*, dungarees

SPEAKING
conversation

Taking turns with your partner, use the following guidelines to describe a) the clothes you are wearing at the moment, and b) what the weather is like today.

the weather: general quality ➜ the air (temperature, humidity, wind) ➜ the sky (clouds, rain)
clothes: items of clothing: ➜ colour ➜ pattern ➜ material ➜ special features

SPEAKING
pictures

A

B

a **Discuss with the class what vocabulary you need to describe the pictures.**

Verbs:	Nouns:	Adjectives:

b **Agree with your partner which one of you has picture A and B, take turns to describe what you can see in them, and make guesses about the situation.**

c **Looking at both pictures now, discuss what you think is relevant of the following questions in pairs (It is your personal experience/judgement/opinion/etc. that is important here!):**

- Have you ever been in a situation like this?
- What do you think it is/could be like to be in a situation like this?
- What do/would you do if you are/were in a situation like this?
- What do you think of what you can see and/or what is happening in the picture?

You may find the following phrases useful here: I (can still) remember ...-ing ... ➺ I've already been in a situation like this. ➺ That reminds me of ... ➺ If I were in a situation like this ... // If such a thing happened to me ..., I would ... ➺ I think/guess ... ➺ In my opinion/view ... ➺ As far as I'm concerned ... ➺ The way I see it ... ➺ From my point of view ... ➺ It seems to me that ... ➺ I'd say ... ➺ If you ask me ... ➺ To my mind ...

FUNCTIONS
role-play

a **Read both role-cards and agree with your partner who's A and who's B.**

A You are going out on a date, and you are rather cold in your shorts, T-shirt and sandals. The weather has fooled you; it looked so sunny and warm from inside your room, but in fact it is only 20 degrees Celsius. When your boyfriend turns up, you notice that he has been fooled, too; he is wearing a thick jumper and a warm jacket, and looks rather hot.

- Greet your boyfriend.
- Tell him about the mistake you made, and tell him how cold you are.
- Accept the offer, tell him that you feel a lot better, and thank him for the jumper.
- Ask your friend whether he thinks you look rather ridiculous in his large jumper.
- Thank him for his compliments.

B You are going out on a date, and you are rather hot in your thick jumper and warm jacket. The weather has fooled you; it looked sunny but rather cool from inside your room, but in fact it is about 20 degrees Celsius. When your girlfriend turns up, you notice that she has been fooled, too; she is wearing shorts, a T-shirt and sandals, and looks rather cold.

- Greet your girlfriend.
- Tell her about the mistake you made, and tell her how hot you are.
- Peel off your jumper and offer it to her.
- Tell her that you feel a lot better, and ask her whether she feels any better in your jumper.
- Reassure her that she looks lovely in your jumper.

b Try and agree with the rest of your class how you could use the following phrases in this situation; complete the phrases and answer the questions.

X: Hi/Hello (there, Judy/Peter)!

X: Oh dear/damn/blast/(bloody)hell! // I'm/You look freezing/so cold/chilled to the bone. // You look/I am awfully/rather hot.

X: Oh I am very cold/hot.

X: I was such a fool/idiot ... // How stupid/silly of me to have ... // ...,which was a pretty silly thing to do.

B: *Why don't you have ...? // Please take ... // Would you like ...?*

A: ***Thank you I will. // That would be very nice/great. // Thank you I would. // Lovely. // Great!***

B: *Here you are. // Here. // Is it any better?*

A: ***Thanks. // Great. // Cheers. // Hey, that's great. // It's a lot better now.***

A: ***I'm sure I look ... // I must look ... // Don't I look ...?***

B: *There's nothing to worry about ... // It suits you very well. // You're looking/You look really/extremely/very smart/great/terrific/fantastic!*

A: ***Thanks.***

c Rehearse the situation in pairs. Read the cards again before starting but try and rely only on the notes below while practising.

greeting ➜ feeling cold/warm ➜ offering/accepting pullover ➜ ridiculous/compliment

PRONUNCIATION 1

sounds & word stress

Sounds

☞ In British English, the [r] sound is not pronounced at the end of a word, unless the next word in the sentence begins with a vowel sound. This [r] is called *linking r*.

Listen and repeat.

- father and mother
- the farmer and his son
- there is enough time
- a pair of socks
- poor old guy
- some more of this
- never again
- more or less
- here it is
- for instance

☞ Interestingly, something similar might happen if there is no *r* at the end of a word, but the word ends with a vowel, and the next word begins with a vowel sound. This is called *intrusive r*.

Listen and repeat.

- Asia*[r]* and Africa
- Anna*[r]* and Peter
- the idea*[r]* of a winter holiday
- I saw*[r]* it in London.

☞ When there is an [r] after [t] or [d] in a word, the result is a rather "wet" sound.

Listen and repeat.

- train
- tree
- try
- trick
- true
- truck
- dry
- drag
- dress
- drug
- drink
- dream

Word stress

Listen and repeat.

[ɪk's...]	[ɪg'z...]	['/,eks...]	[ɪ]	[e]	[iː]
ex'treme	ex'am	'exercise	re'peat	'recognize	,re'build
ex'citing	ex'actly	'excellent	re'act	'relative	,re'open
ex'pect	ex'amine	'expert	re'main	'president	,re'write
ex'ternal	ex'aggerate	,expe'dition	pre'fer	'demonstrate	,de'moralize
ex'traordinary	ex'ample	,exhi'bition	de'cide	'rescue	,pre'heat

HOMEWORK

VOCABULARY
survival kit
study task

Study the word list on page 195-196, and memorise the words and phrases that you think are important and relevant to your circumstances. When you have finished, put the following words in their correct places in the passage below to check your knowledge. (You might try and do the task without using the box.)

garments, dressmakers, elegant, breeze, brand, dress, looks, immaculate, silk, pouring, collar, heatwave, sporting, leather, evening, gale, piece, outfit, casual, designer

If you want to be a successful businessman, you should also *look the part*, that is to say, you should behave and .... like one; only the real superstars can afford to look .... This is because success attracts success, in other words someone who has money will have more confidence in someone who is successful himself.

The *yuppie*, the young (urban) professional careerist is the embodiment of this stereotypical image of the successful businessman; he is the ....-looking guy in shampoo commercials, who is playing with his lovely kids (and dog) .... a smart ....-and-tie .... in the light .... His female counterpart is the businesswoman sporting an elegant two-........................ outfit, whose hair looks equally perfect in the .... rain in London, in the .... in Berlin and in the .... in Rome. Needless to say, there is a price to pay for this, and a very high price at that: most ordinary people would probably not believe their eyes if they saw the price-tags to .... suitable for this class of people. Incredible as it may sound, a .... tie might cost you as much as HUF20,000, and a pair of .... socks could very well be around 4 or 5,000. Shops like Hugo Boss in Párisi utca, Budapest will charge you more than 50,000 for an acceptable pair of .... shoes, over 15,000 for a shirt, and an .... suit begins at 100,000. The same refers to women's wear, an .... dress that you wear only on one or two occasions could cost you more than 200,000 at top-class .... like Lucia's.

It is very important to know that you can't fool those within the circle. The fact that something .... good, or even that it is of very high quality does not really matter: it must be the right ...., it must be expensive.

GRAMMAR FOCUS

p r e v i e w

Reported Speech

In **reported speech**, we quote/report original statements, questions, orders, etc. (i.e. *direct speech*) by connecting them to our own (new) sentence. This new construction may be different from the original sentence in terms of *person, place, word-order and time (tense), and certain words may disappear or be expressed in other ways.*

- When we report orders, requests, negative requests, warnings, advice, invitations, offers, promises, and threats, we use a reporting verb (*tell, ask, warn, advise, invite, offer, promise, threaten, agree, refuse, remind*) plus an *infinitive*. After certain verbs (*e.g. tell, warn, offer, promise, threaten, agree, suggest*) a *that (should)* clause is also possible.
  ➢ *I told him to shut up and listen to me. She reminded me to switch off the light before leaving. You promised to be true to me. I offered to help her with the translation. He advised me to stay away from his girlfriend. I warned them to leave me alone.*

- After *admit, insist on, apologize for* and *suggest* (when the person who suggests is also involved) we can use the *Gerund*.
  ➢ *I suggested going to the cinema. He apologized for being late. He insisted on carrying my bag.*

- In reported questions, we get rid of the question form (word-order, *do*, etc.) after the reporting verb (*ask, want to know, wonder*) or the introductory phrase (*Can you tell me ...?, Do you happen to know ...? Have you got any idea ...? Do you think ...?*), and use the *question word* or, in yes/no questions, *if* or *whether* to connect the sentence.
  ➢ *He wants to know where the pub is. I wonder how old she is. She wants to know if you are interested in the offer. Could you tell me how much these apples are?*

- Note the special structure in *When/Why/How old/What colour/etc. do you think/did you say ...?* type sentences.
  ➢ *How much do you think the whole thing will cost? How old did you say you were at the time?*

- When the reporting verb is in the *present*, the tense does not change in statements and questions.
- When the reporting verb is in the *past*, simultaneous things are in the past, too. If the statement is still up to date when we report it, we can choose between the *present* or the *past*.
  ➢ *My wife said (that) she wasn't interested in my excuses. I told her I was telling the truth. The Prime Minister said the economy was/is in a perfect state. I told him our flat was/is too small for a party like this.*
- When the reporting verb is in the *past*, things that had happened earlier than that will be in the *past perfect*. If the "original" statement was already in the *past*, the *past* is also possible.
  ➢ *I told her I had never seen such a beautiful girl before. She asked me if I had liked/liked the film. He told them he was born in 1982.*
- When the reporting verb is in the *past*, future things will change according to their structure, but *will* becomes *would*.
  ➢ *She said she was having a party on Saturday. He told me he was going to sell his car. My boss told me I would be appointed head of the department.*
- When the reporting verb is in the *past*, *Type 1 auxiliaries* change in a regular way, except for *may*, which becomes *might*, and *must*, which either changes to *had to* or remains *must*. *Type 2 and 3 auxiliaries* (including the *conditional auxiliaries* and *'if' clauses)* do not change, except for *may*, which becomes *might*, and *shall*, which changes to *should*.
  ➢ *I told the teacher (that) I had been able to do my homework. He said he couldn't wait any longer. I asked him if I might ask a favour of him. He told his boss he had to/must leave a bit earlier. I asked him whether he would buy that car if he had enough money. The teacher said she might fail me. He asked me if he should help me with my luggage.*
- When the reporting verb is in the *past*, *'here-and-now' words* may change, depending on the situation. You can simply use your common sense in these cases.
  ➢ *He said he was there on business. She said she had tried to call me the day before, too. Our maths teacher said he didn't/doesn't like teaching in this class because we are very lazy. Our boss told us we would have a very busy day today, and he was right.*

  If it is necessary, we have to change *here* to *there*, *this* to *that*, *now* to *then*, *today* to *that day*, *tonight* to *that night*, *this morning* to *that morning*, *yesterday* to *the day before/the previous day*, *last week* to *the week before/the previous week*, *ago* to *before*, *tomorrow* to *the next day/the following day*, and *next week* to *the following week*.

LESSON 2

VOCABULARY survival kit checkpoint

a **Check the fill-in-the-blank homework task with the rest of the class.**

• sunny (weather)	• flooding	• ready-made	• to take a blouse in
• lovely (weather/day)	• above zero	• to come into fashion	• loose-fitting
• boiling hot	• dry	• to be elegant	• flat-heeled shoes
• to freeze	• strong wind	• to put clothes on	• mini skirt
• to cloud over	• to be cold	• patterned	• to do up a coat

b **What are opposites of the following words and phrases?**

c **What is the corresponding word or phrase with a similar meaning?**

scorching hot	→	**b...... hot**	outfit	→	**g...**
sultry	→	**c....**	fashionable	→	**t....**
mist	→	**h...**	pullover	→	**j....**
(light) wind	→	**b.....**	underclothes	→	**underw...**
to get drenched	→	**to get s...... wet**	polo-necked *[BrE]*	→	**t.....-necked** *[AmE]*
weather report	→	**weather f......**	trainers *[BrE]*	→	**s.......** *[AmE]*

d **Complete the definitions.**

- Weather that is .... changes a lot so it is impossible to know what it will be like.
- A .... is a short period of (rather heavy) rain (or snow).
- A .... is a part of a coat or sweat-shirt that you can pull up to cover your head.
- .... is a thick, fairly strong cotton cloth with thin raised lines on it.
- .... is a special fastener, which sticks together when you press a piece with rough surface against a piece with a soft surface.

GRAMMAR FOCUS

translation into English

Reported Speech

Translate the following sentences into English, discussing each section with the rest of the class as you progress.

❶ Mondd meg, hogy miért nem szeretsz. Azt szeretném tudni, hogy mi a probléma. Meg tudná mondani, hogy mennyi az idő?

....

....

❷ Legyen szíves megmondani, hogy van-e egyáltalán esélyem. Kérem, értesítsenek, hogy szükségük van-e rám. *(to let sy know)* Kíváncsi vagyok, mennyibe fog kerülni. *(I wonder)*

....

....

....

❸ Az ügyvéd azt tanácsolta, hogy ne válaszoljak egyetlen kérdésre sem. Megkértem a főnökömet, hogy engedjen el egy órával előbb. *(to let sy leave)* Azt mondta, hogy fogjam be a számat. Felajánlotta, hogy segít nekem. Azt ígérte, hogy feleségül vesz.

....

....

....

....

❹ Azt mondta, hogy nem szeret. Azt kérdezte, hogy van-e most időm. Azt írta az újság, hogy Magyarország lakosságának 30%-a a létminimum alatt él. *(below the poverty-line)* Megmondtam a rendőrnek, hogy már elmúltam 18 éves. *(over)*

....

....

....

....

❺ Amikor beszéltem vele, azt mondta, hogy már egy órája szerencsétlenkedik a fordítással, de még nem fejezte be. *(to tinker with)* Azt mondta, hogy előző nap evett utoljára. Megkérdeztem tőle, hogy hallott-e már valaha az elsőbbségadásról. *(right of way)* Azt mondta, hogy még soha nem hallotta a nevemet. Azt írta, hogy egy hónapja súlyos balesete volt, de már felgyógyult. *(to recover)*

6 Azt írta, hogy másnap meglátogat. Azt mondta, hogy szombaton moziba megy. Azt mondta, hogy vesz egy új autót. Megkérdeztem tőle, hogy mikor lesz rám egy kis ideje.

7 Azt mondta, hogy tud gitározni, de nem volt hajlandó. Azt mondta, hogy már mennie kell. Azt kérdezte, hogy feltehet-e egy személyes jellegű kérdést. *(personal)* Azt mondta, hogy lehet, hogy egy kicsit késni fog.

8 Azt kérdezte, hogy én mit tennék, ha ilyen helyzetben lennék. Az orvos azt mondta neki, hogy nem lenne szabad ennyit ennie. Azt mondta, hogy tudna nekem segíteni.

9 Mit mondott, mikor fog kezdődni a film? Mit mondtál, hány éves vagy? Mit mondtál, mióta vagy házas?

10 Azt javasolta, hogy beszéljük meg a problémát még egyszer. Ragaszkodtak hozzá, hogy én elnököljek a konferencián.

LISTENING

1. Rain or shine

Weather forecast for Britain

Listen to the recording twice, and fill in the grid with the information from the forecast. When you have finished, compare your grid with the rest of the class. (Note that you won't be able to fill in some of the boxes.)

	England & Wales		Northern Ireland		Scotland	
	south & east	north & west	Down/Armagh	north	south & east	north & west
temperature						
sunshine/cloud						
rain						
wind						

2. Bizarre outfits

Interview with a fashion designer

a **Read the question and try to answer it when you have listened to the recording once. Discuss your answer with your partner.**

- What is the word the designer would be careful to use in connection with fashion, and why?

b **Answer the following questions as you listen to the tape for the second time. Discuss your answers with the rest of the class.**

What kind of outfits did the interviewer find bizarre at last night's fashion show?

What examples does the designer give to support his point?

Why does he say people laugh at fashion twice?

HOMEWORK

TRANSLATION

English into Hungarian

Use a dictionary to translate the following article into Hungarian. Pay special attention to the underlined words and phrases.

English Weather

Without the topic of the weather, the English would be without one of the most useful weapons in their conversational armoury.

Rather like the inhabitants, the weather in the British Isles is particularly unpredictable. The geographic location of the country makes it prey to momentary atmospheric changes, and forward planning of any outdoor event is fraught with dangers.

The English have, of course, lived with this situation for hundreds of years. Nevertheless, it appears that the changeability of the weather always takes them by surprise. If it snows, the country's transport systems grind immediately to a halt while negotiations are made to import snow-ploughs from abroad. In the spring, flash flooding annually drives householders up on to their roofs, and the innocent falling leaves of autumn cause the railways to seize up completely. But while late frosts kill cherished plants and cloudbursts wash away the tea tents at village fêtes in high summer, they have, in English eyes, a higher purpose – to furnish conversation. The weather is not just their preferred conversational topic, it is their favourite gripe. If it is hot, it is always 'too hot'. If cold, it is 'freezing'.

The Xenophobe's Guide to The English, by Antony Miall, Ravette Books, London 1993

LESSON 3

TRANSLATION
English into Hungarian
checkpoint

English Weather

a What kind of translations have the different people in the class come up with for the following words and phrases in the context of the passage?

- conversational armoury
- rather like the inhabitants
- unpredictable
- the country's transport systems
- cause the railways to seize up completely
- at village fetês
- a higher purpose
- to furnish conversation
- their preferred conversational topic
- their favourite gripe

b Compare and discuss the possible translations for each and every sentence with the whole class.

c Choose three new words or phrases from the text that you think are worth remembering.

READING & VOCABULARY
articles

a Read through the articles and try to answer the following questions without using a dictionary. When you have finished, discuss your answers in pairs.

- Why was the man sent to jail?
- How does he explain the incident?
- What did Mary Benton and her family do that pool attendants and council officials were so upset about?
- What are her reasons for doing that?

Swimsuit man must face trial

A Briton who spent nearly two weeks in a Spanish jail for wearing transparent swimming trunks was yesterday advised to return to Spain next week so that he can be sentenced formally to a three-month term of imprisonment, plus a fine of 30,000 pesetas (£140).

Mr Ralph Appleby, aged 34, of Chellaston Road, Derby, said: "I bought the white swim trunks in a chain store in Derby and I had no idea they would become transparent in the water."

According to the lawyer, even if Mr Appleby were found guilty, he would not actually have to serve a term of imprisonment. If Mr Appleby did not appear for the trial, he would lose his bail money and would probably be in contempt of court, with a consequent risk of imprisonment should he return to Spain in the next five years.

The Times

Modest Mary

Housewife Mary Benton's swimming outfit upset the attendants at the local pool. Not that it was too revealing. On the contrary – they thought she was wearing too much. Mary, 33, the mother of four children, was wearing a black one-piece swimsuit with a black nylon V-necked cardigan buttoned at the front. Her husband, Eddie, a heating engineer, of Abbotsweald, Harlow, Essex, was also accused of being overdressed. He wore bathing trunks and a T-shirt.

A Harlow council spokesman said: "Some people have wanted to wear all kinds of clothing in the pool, such as cut-down denim trousers. These were often dirty, and clearly presented a health hazard. We accept this was not the case with Mr and Mrs Benton's costumes, but if we make one exception we will have trouble with others."

Now Mr and Mrs Benton and their children – boys aged 12, 11, 7 and a daughter aged three – have been told they will be barred unless they wear acceptable bathing suits.

Said Mrs Benton: "We are modest people and want to wear more than skimpy modern swimsuits. I think that girls in bikinis just show their bodies to flirt."

Sunday Mirror

b Now try and find the English for the following words and phrases in the text, and make guesses about the possible derivatives. When you have finished, discuss them with the rest of the class.

- óvadék

....

- pénzbüntetés ⇒ pénzbüntetésre ítélni

....

- kockázat ⇒ kockáztatni ⇒ kockázatos ⇒ kockázatvállalás

....

- átlátszó

....

- bűnösnek találni

....

- valamiből következő/eredő

....

- szabadságvesztés ideje ⇒ letölteni a börtönbüntetést

....

....

- áruházlánc

....

- azért/abból a célból, hogy ...

....

- számolhat valamivel/valami vár rá/ valaminek elébe néz

....

....

- „papíron" ⇒ hivatalos ⇒ külsőségek

....

- börtön ⇒ bebörtönözni

....

- „bíróság megsértése"

....

- kivétel ⇒ kivételt tenni ⇒ kivéve ⇒ kivételes

....

- tanács/önkormányzat

....

- kockázatot/veszélyt jelenteni/okozni

....

- személyzet ⇒ parkolóőr; ruhatáros; benzinkutas

....

- „merész"/leleplező/árulkodó ⇒ feltárni/ leleplezni

....

- szóvivő

....

- szemérm(et)es/szolid/szerény ⇒ szemérmetlen/szerénytelen ⇒ szemérmesség/ szerénység

....

....

- flörtölni ⇒ flörtölés ⇒ kihívó ⇒ játszani a gondolattal ⇒ rövid ideig érdeklődni valami iránt

....

....

- megvádolni ⇒ vád/vádaskodás ⇒ vádlott

....

- felzaklatni/kihozni a sodrából ⇒ felfordulás

....

- „tenyérnyi" ⇒ spórolni valamin

....

- kitiltani/eltiltani

....

c Now read the following questions and answer them in writing after reading the articles again. When you have finished, discuss the answers with the rest of the class.

What does the lawyer suggest Mr Appleby should do?

....

....

What sort of a sentence is Mr Appleby likely to get?

....

....

What would happen if Mr Appleby did not appear for the trial?

....

....

What background information have we got about the Bentons?

....

....

What were they wearing in the swimming pool?

....

....

What decision did the Harlow council make about the case?

....

....

Why did the council spokesman say they were so strict?

....

....

PRONUNCIATION 2

stress, rhythm & intonation

Stress, rhythm & intonation

☞ There's one rule that can overrule all other rules of sentence stress and intonation: the rule of emphasis. If we want to emphasise something in a sentence, we will put a strong stress there, regardless of anything else.

Listen and repeat.

This is **the** [ði:] music for me. *(the kind I really like)*
Is this **your** car??? *(you don't look so rich)*
I put this letter on the table. *(and not somebody else)*
I **put** this letter on the table. *(and didn't throw it)*
I put **this** letter on the table. *(and not the other letter)*
I put this **letter** on the table. *(and not a dictionary)*
I put this letter **on** the table. *(and not under it)*
I put this letter on **the** table. *(the most important table)*
I put this letter on the **table**. *(and not on the chair)*
I kissed her yesterday. *(and not another boy)*
I **kissed** her yesterday. *(and did not bite her)*
I kissed **her** yesterday. *(and not another girl)*
I kissed her **yesterday**. *(and not today)*

LINK WORDS

Make sure you know what the following link words mean, and working in pairs, use as many as you can to make the text below sound more natural and dynamic. When you have found a suitable place for all of them, take turns to read out the new text.

(1) that is not to say (2) on top of everything else (3) I wonder (4) let alone (5) to make things worse (6) after all (7) having said that (8) mind you (9) for that matter (10) hardly (11) at any rate (12) honestly/frankly (13) for example/instance

Ode To Our Climate:

.... if you have ever imagined what it might be like to live in parts of the world where the climate is completely different from ours. Let's take Brasil, ..., they never have snow, and the temperature very rarely drops below 20 degrees Celsius in most places. ...., these people haven't even got coats or pullovers, ... gloves and caps! And, ..., they have Christmas in tropical heat! Or, ..., let's imagine what it can be like in winter in the north of Europe,for example; they .... have any sunlight for six months, and, ..., it is bitterly cold, as well. .... that I am always happy with our climate: sometimes I am quite fed up with our dull, snowless but damp and slushy winters, windy springs, or boiling hot summers, but – .... – quite ...., I don't think I could live in a place where you never have these horrible things, if you see what I mean. ...., we have variety. And, ..., isn't waiting for summer almost as much fun as summer itself?

HOMEWORK

VOCABULARY
articles
study tasks

Swimsuit man must face trial/Modest Mary

a **Read the articles again and memorise any vocabulary items that are new to you. When you have finished, use the words in the box to fill in the gaps in the passage below. Change the form of the words if necessary.**

I can't say I am particularly lucky with swimming these days, I've had two rather embarrassing incidents in connection with my swimming .... recently. Earlier this summer I was in Spain on holiday. On the very first day of my stay there I was coming out of the water after a nice swim in the sea, when two policemen walked up to me and said I was arrested. I had no idea what had happened, when they pointed at my swimming .... I looked at them myself, and I must admit they were pretty ....: to my astonishment they'd become .... in the water! Of course, I protested that I wasn't ...., and I explained to them that I'd bought my trunks in a .... store back home, but they wouldn't believe me; they .... me of deliberate .... behaviour and sent me to .... Thanks to my lawyer, I eventually got off with a formal term of .... and a .... of £140, but this incident taught me to be more careful with my swimming outfit. So, when I got back from Spain and went to the local pool, I didn't want to take a .... and I put on a pair of cut-down denim trousers istead. To my surprise, the pool .... got rather .... this time, too, and, saying that my trousers were dirty and presented a health ...., they .... me from the pool unless I wore real swimming trunks. Now I really don't know what I should do, in fact I am .... with the thought of becoming a nudist, at least they don't need to worry about their outfits.

upset
to flirt
attandent
fine
hazard
immodest
chain
to bar
risk
transparent
jail
guilty
revealing
imprisonment
trunks
to accuse
outfit

b **Use the following guidelines to prepare for a short oral summary of the articles about the swimsuit man and modest Mary in a few sentences.**

The swimsuit man: → the offence → the guy's explanation → the probable sentence → the lawyer's advice → his reasons
Modest Mary: → the offence → Mary's reasons → the council's decision → their reasons

WRITING
letter

A British friend of yours is coming to see you in a few weeks. He has never been to our part of the world before, so s/he has written a letter to you to inquire about the weather conditions in Hungary at this time of the year, so that s/he knows what sort of clothes s/he should pack for the journey. Using the guidelines below, write her/him a letter in which you inform and advise her/him about these things.

Step One	Step two	Step three
General outline:	Brainstorming:	Details:
Introduction	reference to letter/visit	*I have just this moment received your letter and I am writing at once because …*
About the weather/ advice on clothing	temperature, rain, etc. any special clothes? (formal, sports, etc.)	*In your letter you asked me to write about …* *Now I'll try to summarise the most important things in a few sentences.*
Conclusion	summary, reference to visit	*Well, I hope I have remembered everything, but if I haven't, please do not worry, I can …* *Looking forward to seeing you soon.* *All the best // Best wishes // My best wishes to you and your … // Love\Yours*

☞ When you have finished, don't forget to check your work for grammatical mistakes.

LESSON 4

VOCABULARY
articles
checkpoint

Swimsuit man must face trial/Modest Mary

a Compare your solutions to the fill-in-gap homework task with the rest of the class.

b Discuss with the rest of the class what you think the English would be for the following Hungarian sentences.

Nem gondolod, hogy nagyon kockázatos dolog puskázni egy ilyen fontos vizsgán?

....

....

A szóvivőt azzal vádolták, hogy hazudott a sajtónak.

....

....

Fogalmam sincs, mi hozta őt ki ennyire a sodrából.

....

Az újságcikk leleplezte, hogy az önkormányzat súlyos hibát követett el az üggyel kapcsolatban.

....

....

A bíróság bűnösnek találta lopás vétségében, és két évre ítélték.

....

Szembe kell néznünk azzal a ténnyel, hogy a magyar labdarúgás reménytelen helyzetben van.

....

....

c Working in pairs, give a brief summary of the articles we read last lesson.

GRAMMAR FOCUS

m i n i t e s t

Reported Speech

Do the following test and check it with the rest of the class.

1. It was at that moment that I realised I ... lose everything if I told the truth.

A can | **C** may
B might | **D** ought

2. I was extremely tired because I ... hard all morning.

A have worked | **C** had been working
B had to work | **D** have been working

3. I was wondering what ... to do about the problems.

A the management wanted | **C** wanted the management
B did the management want | **D** does the management want

4. My wife suggested ... to the cinema.

A to go | **C** go
B going | **D** we should have gone

5. I wasn't quite sure how much money ...

A in my pocket was. | **C** was there in my pocket.
B there was in my pocket. | **D** in my pocket there was.

6. Last week the mechanic said ...

A he'll repair the car that afternoon. | **C** he already repaired the car.
B he'll repair the car by the end of next week. | **D** he repairs the car immediately.

7. The stewardess said we ... sit wherever we ... to.

A would // want | **C** could // wanted
B can // wanted | **D** might // want

8. What do you think ...

A what can be the reason for her not coming? | **C** why hasn't she come?
B could be the reason for her not coming? | **D** why she hasn't come?

9. I wondered what ... if he discovered that his wife ... him any longer.

A he would do // didn't love | **C** would he do // not loved
B would he have done // had loved | **D** he would have done // hadn't loved

10. The doctor asked the patient how long ... sleep.

A couldn't she | **C** she hadn't been able to
B hasn't she been able to | **D** she couldn't

SPEAKING
discussion

a **Discuss in pairs what kind of outfit you would wear on the following occasions at this time of the year. Think of real items of clothing you have at home, and say if you'd have to buy/borrow particular things. If necessary, give reasons, as well. (Try and be serious!)**

- your sister's/brother's wedding
- a night at the opera
- a job interview
- your friend's birthday party
- the oral English exam
- a hike in the woods

b **In groups of three, discuss what you think of the following articles/ phenomena of fashion. (Do you like them? Would you wear them? Would you like your girl/boyfriend/ wife/husband to wear them?) Try and find out what the most and the least acceptable things are with the three of you. When you have finished, compare your views with the rest of the class.**

- ear-rings for men
- very short mini skirts
- platform shoes
- bermudas
- leggings
- lady's tops that reveal the wearer's belly
- high heeled shoes
- bow ties

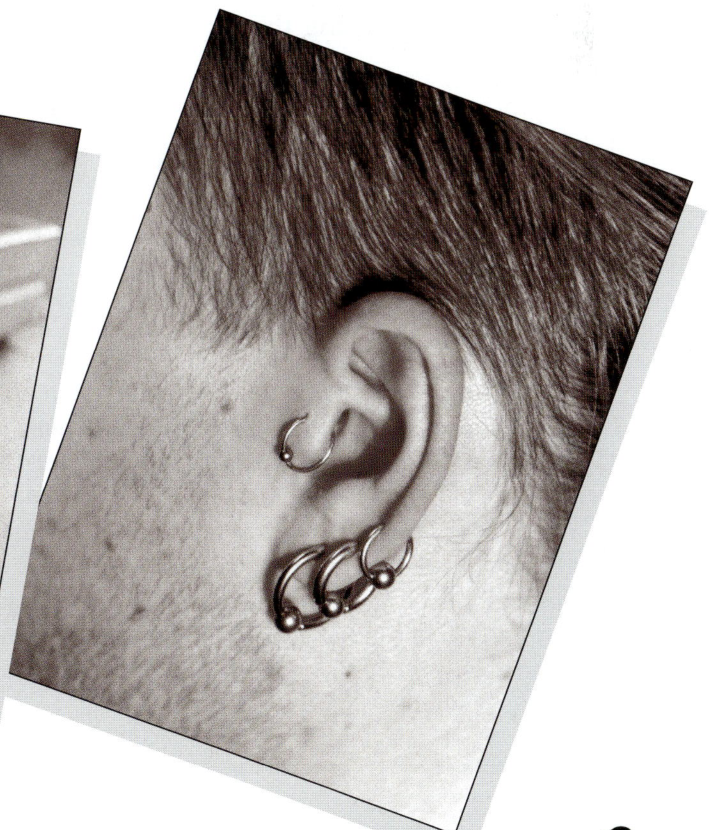

c **Discuss with the rest of the class whether you think you can judge people by the clothes they wear. If yes, do you think there are any limitations or dangers here? If no, does it mean you would wear anything or that you are equally tolerant of other people's choice of clothes? In any case, give reasons, as well.**

d **Discuss in pairs what you think are the advantages and disadvantages of the following things compared to each other.**

- jeans vs. skirts
- spring vs. autumn
- gloves vs. mittens
- bikinis vs. one-piece swimsuits
- zips vs. buttons
- ready-made vs. made-to-measure clothes
- coats vs. jackets
- trainers vs. sandals
- shorts vs. trousers
- snow vs. rain
- wool vs. cotton
- caps vs. hats

HOMEWORK

VOCABULARY survival kit preview

Read through the new vocabulary list on page 225-226, and consult a dictionary if you come across something that is unfamiliar or unclear to you.

EXAM TIPS

The multiple choice test

☞This is the first task of the written exam, and the only component where the use of dictionaries is *not* allowed. There are 30 minutes to complete the task, so you only have a little more than 30 seconds for each item, which means you have to be pretty fast if you are to get to the end before your time is up.

One of the standard ways of doing multiple choice tests is to arrive at a solution by a *process of elimination*, i.e. by carefully examining and rejecting each possibility until only one is left. Obviously, you can't afford *not* to pick any of the four possibilities (after all, if you just marked the answer sheet at random, you could have as many as 12.5 good answers!), which means that if you do not really *know* the correct answer, you should at least have an intelligent *guess* based on a process of elimination.

REVISION Test 2

A

Do the following multiple choice test, and when you have finished, discuss it with the class.

1. I am not sure I ... pay back my debts in the near future. I ... spend far too much on my car recently.

A won't be able to // had to
B will able to // must
C can // have had to
D will be able // have to

2. No news ... good news.

A is
B are a
C is a
D are

3. She ... leave her sick-bed since she had that car accident. Needless to say, she ... take an awful lot of medicine as well.

A couldn't // must
B hasn't been allowed // has had to
C mustn't // had to
D isn't allowed // has to

4. There's no need to hurry, we've got ... time left.

A lots of
B plenty
C a great deal
D a few

5. Although they were both very tired, and ... walk, they somehow ... reach the peak.

A hardly could // succeeded to
B were hardly able to // could
C hardly able to // weren't able to
D could hardly // managed to

6. Both of my parents speak good German but ... of them speak any English at all.

A either
B none
C not any
D neither

7. "... I have a word with you, Peter?" "Yes, of course you ... ."

A must // might
B might // can
C could // could
D can // could

8. He kept buying those expensive gifts, ... it was obvious that he couldn't afford them.

A despite
B although
C in spite of
D no matter

9. You ... have sent him a letter. Judy has already given him a ring. She ... him all the necessary information.
A wouldn't // could give
B needn't // must have given
C mustn't // should have given
D oughtn't // must give

10. I don't know much about business, but the idea of opening a public toilet ... to me.
A is not sounding very good
B is not sounding very well
C doesn't sound very well
D doesn't sound very good

11. I ... speak to him as soon as possible, he ... have heard anything about the case at all.
A would // may
B could // might
C ought to // may not
D need // couldn't

12. It was silly to stay indoors in ... wonderful weather.
A so
B such a
C such
D so a

13. I know her very well, believe me, she ... have done so well at the test. She ... have been cheating!
A can't // must
B mightn't // can
C mustn't // should
D oughtn't to // needn't

14. The guide book contains ... you need to know about the area.
A every information
B the whole information
C each information
D all the information

15. I ... understand people who are ready to do this job for so little money. They ... be crazy!
A could // mustn't
B can't // must
C ought to // have to
D should // can

16. A Cadillac takes up at least four times ... a small Polski Fiat.
A as big place than
B as much space as
C so much place as
D as many spaces as

17. If they ... the preparations in good time, they ... in such a hurry now.
A would have started // weren't
B have started // wouldn't have been
C had started // wouldn't be
D would start // may not be

18. Not only ... the car, but he also lost his driving licence for two years.
A he did wreck
B had he wrecked
C did he wreck
D he wrecked

19. He is a real chain smoker; if he ... smoke a cigarette for more than half an hour, he ... restless and quite unable to concentrate.
A didn't // will get
B wouldn't // got
C mustn't // would get
D can't // gets

20. Peter found work on one of the farms ...
A nearly.
B closely.
C near.
D nearby.

21. I wish you ... a bit more attention to these seemingly unimportant things; you ... get into serious trouble one day.

A pay // can
B would pay // might
C have paid // must
D will pay // would

22. ... had she had the font of the car fixed ... she damaged the rear.

A No sooner // when
B Hardly // then
C Hardly // when
D No sooner // that

23. "... need any more information, just let me know." "Great. ... I write a letter, or just give you a ring?"

A If you would // Can
B If you will // May
C Should you // Shall
D Would you // Will

24. Although it was August, my mother put three pullovers into my bag, ... it was cold.

A if
B in case
C in the case
D if perhaps

25. Oh blast, this bloody zip ... open! It ... do that, when I am in such a hurry.

A wouldn't // shouldn't
B won't // should
C won't // would
D doesn't // should

26. Why is this girl looking at me ... she knew me? I've never seen her before in my life.

A although
B as
C as though
D if only

27. We ... really be very grateful if you ... briefly explain the situation to us.

A should // —
B would // could
C shall // shall
D will // would

28. It's ... expensive to own a car these days.

A such
B terrible
C rather
D enough

29. It is true that she is not a spring chicken any more, but she ... an extremely pretty woman; men ... turn and stare wherever she went.

A would be // used to
B used to be // should
C would be // would
D used to be // would

30. ... it was early September, it was quite cold for the time of the year.

A Despite
B However
C In spite of
D Although

31. It was quite understandable that they ... so angry; after all they ... for their turn for more than three hours.

A are // have been waiting
B had been // were waiting
C were // had been waiting
D are // were waiting

32. The dentist examined all my teeth, but, thank God, ... was all right.

A every one
B every
C the whole
D all

33. I don't really understand why ... me. On Friday she promised that … me a ring sometime during the weekend.
A she didn't call // she would give
B didn't she call // she will give
C she called // she would have given
D did she call // will give

34. At 50 ... has the face he deserves.
A each
B everyone
C all
D most

35. The advertisement said that customers ... eat as much as they ... for HUF600.
A might // wish
B could // wished
C can // wished
D would // wish

36. You're only young once. After that you'll have to find ... excuse.
A other
B different
C else
D another

37. What would you say ... if he ... in such a situation?
A what would he do // were
B he would have done // had been
C would he do // weren't
D would he have done // hadn't been

38. Each generation imagines itself to be ... the one that went before it, and ... the one that comes after it.
A intelligenter than // more wise than
B more intelligent than // wiser than
C more intelligent as // wiser as
D intelligenter as // more wise as

39. It's no good waiting for the tram. We ... walk.
A might
B might as well
C might well
D may

40. I don't deserve this award, but I have arthritis and I don't deserve that ...
A nor.
B too.
C neither.
D either.

B

Read the definitions and supply the appropriate words or phrases.

1. If we describe a husband as .... we mean that he is completely dominated by his wife, who orders him about and tells him what to do.

2. The .... of a novel, a film, etc. is the story it is based on.

3. If you .... money for a particular purpose, you manage to get the necessary amount by cashing your savings, selling something, collecting from other people or by borrowing.

4. .... is lack or serious shortage of rainwater.

5. If you .... a business, a company, etc., you make the necessary arrangements and preparations to start it.

6. A .... is an advertisement that is broadcast on television or radio.

7. Someone who has won the first prize in a competition, or who has beaten everyone else in a contest or fight is a ....

8. .... are small-sized newspapers in which the news stories and articles are short and sensational, usually with a lot of photographs.

9. An .... is a formal request to a court of law for an earlier decision to be changed.

10. .... If you do something on ...., you do it immediately, without any delay.

11. Weather that is .... makes you feel uncomfortable because the air feels very hot and wet.

12. .... is something that you do to hurt or punish someone who has done something bad to you.

13. A .... is an elected organisation that is responsible for local government in a particular area.

14. .... are a kind of clothing worn by women that fit closely round the hips, legs and feet, and are made of thin, stretchy material.

15. A .... is a book that gives information for tourists about a particular area.

16. A .... is a narrow platform that models walk along to display clothes in a fashion show.

17. The place in a theatre, cinema, or concert where the tickets are sold is called the ....

18. A .... is a period of physical exercise which you do as training for a sport.

19. If something is ...., it is smooth, wet, or greasy so it is difficult for you to hold or walk on.

20. .... is a special material used for fastening clothes, which sticks together when you press a piece with a rough surface against a piece with a soft surface.

C

Translate the following text into English.
(Use a dictionary if necessary.)

✓ Te jó ég, mi történt az autóddal?

....

✓ Na, átmentél végre a vizsgán?

....

✓ Bárcsak átmentem volna, de sajnos nem sikerült! A vicc az, hogy a vizsgán úgy tűnt, hogy jól mennek a dolgok. Azt hittem, most végre sikerülni fog.

....

....

✓ Á, az előző hét vizsgán is így volt, és azokon sem sikerült átmenni.

....

✓ Igazad van. Biztosan jó nagy hibákat csináltam. Elég rossz lehettem, ha csak 10 pontot kaptam. Mit gondolsz, mit csináljak most? Megpróbáljam még egyszer?

....

....

....

✓ Hát, én a helyedben beiratkoznék még egy tanfolyamra. Szerintem nem kellett volna a hetedik vizsga után ilyen hamar újra megpróbálnod. El kellett volna végezned még egy vagy két szemesztert a nyelviskolában, és akkor talán több esélyed lett volna.

....

....

....

....

✓ Hát, lehet, hogy igazad van. Mit gondolsz, tudnál nekem segíteni? Azt hiszem, át kellene ismételnem az egész nyelvtant. Ha jobban tudnám a nyelvtant, sokkal magabiztosabb lennék, és akkor már csak a szókincsemet kellene egy kicsit fejleszteni.

....

....

....

....

UNIT 9 Shops and goods

LESSON 1

VOCABULARY survival kit

Shopping for food

Shops: hypermarket, supermarket, grocer's, greengrocer's, butcher's, baker's, dairy, sweet shop, confectioner's, market, shopping complex, shopping centre/shopping mall *[AmE]*
Selling and buying: shop assistant, shopper, customer, to sell (sold), to buy, to purchase, cash desk, cashier, receipt, shopping bag
Goods: item, foodstuff, ready made\tinned\frozen\microwavable food, a carton\jar\packet\box\tube\loaf\bottle\roll of ...

Meat
pork
veal
beef
mutton, lamb
mince
poultry:
chicken, duck, goose, turkey
freshwater fish:
pike, carp, trout
seafish:
cod, salmon, lobster
game
sausage
bacon, ham
salami
cold meat/cuts *[AmE]*

Vegetables
cabbage
brussels-sprouts
carrot, parsnip
cauliflower, broccoli
beans, peas
rice, tomatoes
potatoes, corn cobs
spinach, sorrel
marrow, mushrooms
lettuce
(spring) onion
garlic
beetroot
green peppers
radishes
cucumbers
celery, parsley

Fruit
strawberries
raspberries
cherries
pears
peaches
apricots
lemons
pineapple
grapes
plums
currants
walnuts, peanuts
dates, bananas
almonds
watermelon
cantaloup
oranges, figs

Groceries
dairy products: yoghurt, margarine
butter, sweet\sour\whipped cream
cottage cheese, chocolate milk
white coffee, bread, roll, cereals
cornflakes, flour, breadcrumbs
biscuits, crackers, instant coffee
oil, granulated\castor\lump sugar
sweetener, vinegar, pickled onions
spices: salt, pepper, paprika
nutmeg, clove, cinnamon, caraway
mustard, mayonnaise
jam, marmalade, preserved fruit
soft drinks:
still\sparkling, soda *[AmE]* juice
hard (alcoholic) drinks:
brandy, sherry, dry\sweet wine,
beer, champagne

A healthy diet

to have high\low cholesterol\fat\sugar\starch\vitamin\fibre content, to contain, to be high\low in cholesterol\fat\etc., (artificial\natural) ingredients, chemicals, to avoid, to cut down on ..., health food, organic food, a balanced/healthy/correct\special diet, a salt\etc. -free diet, to be on a diet/to diet/to slim, vegetarian/veggie/vegan, semi-veg, to fry (in breadcrumbs) in oil, to roast meat in the oven, to grill meat, to bake a cake, to boil vegetables, to cook dinner/a meal, roux

Dishes: Hungarian cuisine, starter, main course, dessert, Goulash\chicken\etc. soup, breaded fried chicken\pork chops\mushrooms\cheese, chicken paprika with dumplings, beefsteak, turkey breast Kiev style, pork stew, stuffed cabbage, noodles with cabbage\cottage cheese, pancakes with meat filling, pickled salad, lettuce with dressing, sponge cake Somló style

Shopping for other articles

store *[AmE]*, chain store, shop window, window-shopping, price-tag, cash, credit card, wide choice/variety of goods, bargain, consumer goods\durables, sale, to reduce prices, at a reduced price, to include VAT, to buy sg on hire purchase (H.P.)/on the installment plan *[AmE]*, leasing, part-exchange/trade-in *[AmE]*, deposit, monthly instalments, mail order, catalogue

department store
chemist's
florist's
tobacconist's
haberdasher's

sportswear shop
book shop
furniture shop
china shop
hardware shop

stationer's
souvenir shop
shoe shop
optician's
toy shop

news stand
kitchenware shop
electrical appliances shop
ladies'\men's wear shop
drugstore

SPEAKING
conversation

Use the vocabulary list and the guidelines to talk to your partner about the following issues.

1. **How is the shopping for basic foodstuffs taken care of in your family?** Who? ➜ When? ➜ Where?
2. **Suppose you won the first prize in an advertising campaign and you were given a gift voucher that you can use to buy any single item of goods at all the different departments of a department store. Taking your real needs (rather than mere value) into account, go ahead and take your pick!** What department? ➜ What particular good? ➜ Why?
3. **Can you cook?** What kind of typical Hungarian dishes could you prepare? ➜ What are the favourite dishes in your family? ➜ What are your personal favourites? ➜ What are the things you don't like?
4. **Study the columns of different foodstuffs in the vocabulary list, and tell your partner about any items that you a) particularly like, and b) dislike.** Meat? ➜ Vegetables? ➜ Fruit? ➜ Groceries/Drinks?
5. **Name some goods that you can buy in the different types of shops listed at the bottom of the previous page.**

a **Discuss with the class what vocabulary you need to describe the pictures.**

Verbs:	Nouns:	Adjectives:

b **Agree with your partner which one of you has picture A and B, take turns to describe what you can see in them, make guesses about the situation, and tell each other about the thoughts, feelings, memories, etc. they evoke in you.**

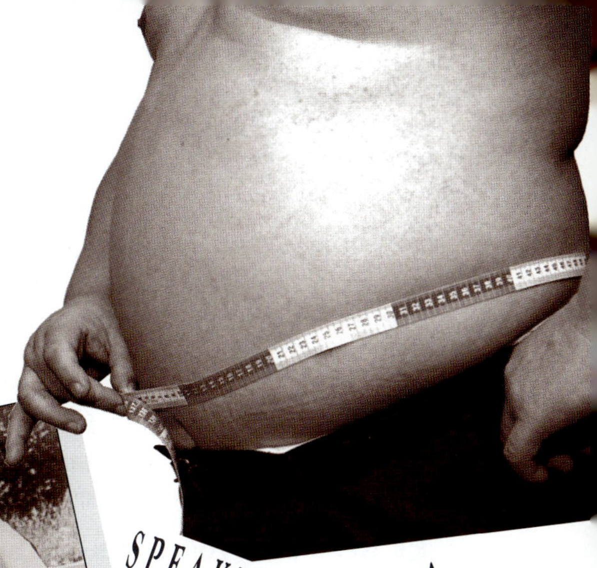

SPEAKING pictures

A

B

c **Looking at both pictures now, say a few words about the subject in general, viewing the contents of the pictures from a wider – national or even global – perspective. The following questions might help you to come up with some ideas:**

- How widespread and important is the phenomenon depicted in the picture? Is it characteristic of a particular area/social group/age group/etc.?
- What do you think the individual should/could do about the problem?
- Is there anything that could/should be/have been done about the issue on a national/global level? (Apart from everybody's personal responsibility.)

You may find the following phrases useful here: This is one of the ... issues of our times, and ... ➾ The issue of ... has now become the focus of national/worldwide media attention, and ... ➾ ... has focussed public attention on ... ➾ I think people/the government/etc. should ... ➾ Generally speaking, ...

FUNCTIONS
role-play

a Read both role cards and agree with your partner who's A and who's B.

A You're travelling to Britain next week and your daughter asks you to bring back a number of things for her. You aren't particularly good at shopping, so you need detailed information about a few important things. With each item, ...

- ask your daughter why she doesn't buy it in Hungary.
- ask your daughter where you could buy it.
- ask her how much she thinks it might be.
- ask her some for some details about it (title/size/brand/colour/etc.).

B Your father is going to Britain next week and you think you could ask him to bring back a few things for you.

- Tell your father that you'd like him to buy a CD: Christy Moore's Ordinary Man (Irish songwriter/singer/guitarist, not much known in Hungary). The best place to buy it is HMV's or Our Price, the largest record shops (approx. £15).
- Ask him to buy an electric kettle (Philips, the cordless type; scarcely ever available in Hungary, and even if it is, it's rather dear; electrical appliances shops, or Argos stores, £22.50).
- Tell him that you would like a nice pullover (thick, knitted, natural colour, pure wool, size S; any boutique [bu:'ti:k] or the ladies'wear department of any department store, about £20–40).
- Ask him to bring back some tea (Lipton, available here, but ridiculously expensive; any grocer's or supermarket, £2–5).

b Try and agree with the rest of your class what phrases you could use in this situation.

c Rehearse the situation in pairs. Read the cards again before starting but try and rely only on the notes below while practising.

A	B
why? ➜ exactly? ➜ where? ➜ how much?	introduction ➜ CD ➜ kettle ➜ pullover ➜ tea

HOMEWORK

VOCABULARY survival kit study task

Study the word list on page 225-226, and memorise the words and phrases. When you have finished, put the following words in their correct places in the passage below to check your knowledge. (You might try and do the task without using the box.)

> *shopper, malls, goods, catalogues, butcher's, item, centres, credit card, foodstuffs, mail order, baker's, supermarkets, shopping, customers, greengrocer's, department, sell, dairy, variety, window*

Until a few years ago the English used to buy their basic .... at the local shop; they bought bread at their local ...., beef at their local ...., vegetables at their local .... and so on. Now these small shops have all but disappeared as their .... get into their cars and get everything they need at huge out-of-town-centre shopping .... filled with almost everything a .... could ever want to buy.

The only shops that have survived the spread of .... are 'the corner shops', which are usually run by Asian immigrant families. These corner shops are often supermarkets in miniature and .... anything from bananas to postcards, or from .... products to newspapers. Many of them are also open all day and half the night.

American shopping .... are vast labirynths of shops and .... stores. They are surrounded by huge car parks, they are clean and safe, and, of course, they are filled with an incredible .... of expensive .... from all over the world. No wonder .... isn't a chore for the Americans, in fact it's a pleasure, an amusement, a way to spend time. Friends will make a date to go ....-shopping together and happily return home empty-handed.

The most comfortable way of shopping is, of course, ... Every home receives hundreds of coloured .... offering every imaginable .... (and sometimes unimaginable ones) through the mail. Armed with a catalogue, a telephone, and a ...., an American can outfit a complete household.

GRAMMAR FOCUS
p r e v i e w

Relative Clauses

1. Adding (non-identifying) [bővítő] relative clauses add extra information to something already identified or something unique. The sentence is actually meaningful on its own without the relative clause. The clause is separated from the noun by a comma, and, if the sentence continues after the clause, there is another comma. These sentences sound rather formal, and are a lot more common in writing (particularly in news reports) than in conversation.

To add such a clause, you can use

who, which (*aki, amely*) for the subject.

➢ *My grandma, who is 94 years old, doesn't really like heavy metal. Nyírbátor, which is famous for its beautiful Calvinist church, is about 400 kilometers from Budapest.*

whom/who, which (*akit, amelyet*) for the subject.

➢ *Peter, whom we saw at the concert yesterday, is a colleague of mine.*

whose, ... of which (*akinek a ..., amelynek a ...*)

➢ *The English National Anthem, the authorship of which is disputed, is at least 250 years old.*

for/about/etc. whom, for/about/etc. which or **who ... for/about/etc., which ... for/about/etc.** (*akinek/akiről, amelynek/amelyről*).

➢ *Mr Savage, for whom my son works, is a very nasty man./Mr Savage, who my son works for, is a very nasty man.*

2. Identifying [szűkítő] relative clauses identify which particular one we mean (out of a choice). Without the clause the sentence would be incomplete. As it is an essential part of the sentence, the clause does not have commas round it. This is the most common type of relative clause, especially in spoken English.

To start such a clause, you can use

who (that), that (which) *(aki, amely)* with nouns and **that** *(amely, ami)* after superlatives and pronouns like *every(thing), all, some(thing), any(thing), no(thing), none, little, few, much, only,* if the pronoun is the **subject** of the clause.
➢ *The woman who (that) lives upstairs from me is quite crazy. The film that (which) won the most Oscars this year is a slightly slushy war movie. I'm afraid this is all that is left.*

who, which (except for superlatives and pronouns), **that** or, even better, **leave out the relative pronoun** *(akit, amelyet)* if the pronoun is the **object** of the clause.
➢ *She is the most exciting girl (that) I have ever gone out with. The football team (which, that) I supported came in last this year.*

whose *(akinek a …, amelynek a …)* with both people and objects.
➢ *I don't like people whose cars are bigger than mine. In front of us was a car whose driver was clearly as drunk as a lord.*

for/about/etc. whom, for/about/etc. which or, better, **which, who, that … for/about/etc.** or, even better, **leave out the relative pronoun** and put the preposition at the end of the clause.
➢ *That was the argument on which Ms Dotras's claim was based./That was the argument that/which Ms Dotras's claim was based on./That was the argument Ms Dotras's claim was based on.*

where, why *(ahol, amiért)* instead of *in which* and *the reason for which.*
➢ *The town where we live …, That's why I went on to university.*

3. What as a relative pronoun means *the thing(s) that (hogy mi[t], az[t], hogy mi[t], ami[t], az[t] ami[t]),* so it cannot ever refer to a noun. Note that there's no comma here.
➢ *I didn't know what to do. His voice was so weak that I couldn't hear what he was saying. What I found was rather disappointing. What I really want is a nice cup of tea. What I'd like to do is have a shower.*

4. Which is a sentence relative, and it refers to a whole sentence, not just a noun *(ami, amit).* The *which*-clause is a kind of a judgement about the first sentence, and it is separated by a comma.
➢ *He is always blowing smoke into my face, which is rather annoying. He is already married, which is a pity.*

To sum up:

- Never use *what* for a noun.
- Use *, which* … to make a judgement about a whole sentence.
- Use the "traditional" pronouns, and commas to add extra information to an identified noun. (You can't leave out the pronouns, and you can't use *that.*)
- *That* is always an acceptable solution when you want to identify a noun.
- You can only *leave out* a pronoun if you use the clause to identify a noun and it is the object of the clause or the preposition.

LESSON 2

VOCABULARY survival kit checkpoint

a **Check the fill-in-the-blank homework task with the rest of the class.**

b **What shops would you go to to buy the following goods? (Forget supermarkets and departments stores for a minute.)**

- a microwave oven
- a bottle of Bailey's Irish Cream
- a bunch of roses
- a slice of cake
- a bar of soap
- a carton of milk
- a pair of men's gloves
- some nails
- a can of Coke
- a box of chocolates
- a packet of cigarettes
- a loaf of bread
- a reel of white thread
- a jar of honey
- a tube of toothpaste
- a pair of trainers
- some sheets of wrapping paper
- crockery and cutlery
- a pound of pork
- two pounds of apples

c **What do you think the following could be?**

- A dairy product, thought to be very healthy, perhaps even lengthening people's lives.
- Meat orthodox Muslims and Jews are not allowed to eat.
- The "Hungarian" spice.
- The non-alcoholic drink the British consume most of. (!)
- A meat product the Hungarian version of which a British or American person would never even taste.
- A dairy product that the British never have for breakfast, but often have after lunch.
- The bitter "jam", which the British only eat for breakfast.
- Strong Spanish or Portugese wine, the most formal drink besides champagne (at least in Britain).
- The most "elegant" of fish foods.
- The spice of Zanzibar.
- The "American" vegetable.
- The fish of fast-flowing mountain streams.
- The Russian/German national vegetable.
- The traditional Christmas and Thanksgiving meat.

d Complete the definition.

- .... are regular payments we have to make until we have paid all the money we owe.
- A .... is a vegetarian who occasionally eats eggs, fish or even chicken.
- If you say that something was a real ...., you mean that it was bought cheaply or for less than its usual price.
- If you buy something on ...., you pay a deposit and then small amounts over a longer period of time.
- The .... of a particular dish are the types of food that are used to make it.

GRAMMAR FOCUS

translation into English

Relative Clauses

Translate the following sentences into English, discussing each section with the rest of the class as you progress.

❶ Rendszeresen rólam másolja a házi feladatát, ami nagyon veszélyes dolog ennél a tanárnál. *(to copy off/from sy; a … thing to do; with)* Tegnap megint késett vagy negyven percet, ami rettenetesen feldühített. *(to make sy angry/cross/furious)* Foglalkozására nézve tanár, ami azt jelenti, hogy nincsenek anyagi gondjai. *(financial/material)* A miniszoknyáját vette fel, ami nagyon bölcs döntésnek bizonyult. *(clever/wise)*

....

....

....

....

....

❷ Fogalmam sincs, hogy mit vegyek fel. Nem egészen értettem, hogy mit mond. Nem volt világos, hogy mi a probléma. Miért nem mondod meg őszintén, hogy mit akarsz? Amire igazán szükségem lenne, az egy csomó pénz. Amit igazán szeretek benned, az az, hogy olyan szép nagy fejed van. *(about you)*

....

....

....

....

....

❸ Ez itt a Duna, amely Közép-Európa legpiszkosabb folyója. A mamám, aki hatvanas évei vége felé jár, fiatalabbnak néz ki, mint sok negyvenes. *(in her late sixties)* A XX. század egyik legnagyobb angol regényírója Joseph Conrad, aki Lengyelországban született, és felnőtt fejjel tanult meg angolul. *(as an adult)* Négy feladat volt, amelyek közül kettő nagyon nehéz volt. Odaadtam neki a kabátom, amit azonnal fel is vett. Ez itt a gyűjtemény legértékesebb darabja, amelynek ára több mint egy millió font. *(valuable)* Madonna, akiről a sajtónak előzőleg nem volt valami nagyon jó véleménye, egész jó színésznőnek bizonyult. *(to have a high opinion of)*

....

....

....

....

....

....

....

....

4 Különösen tetszett az a novella, amely Rómában játszódik. Szívesebben vennék olyan lakást, amely a zöldövezetben van. Hol van az a lány, aki ezeket a képeket festette? Olyan fiúhoz akarok feleségül menni, aki tud főzni, és szeret takarítani. Az egyetlen dolog, ami igazán számít, az az, hogy szeretjük egymást. Ő a leghíresebb diák, aki valaha is ebbe a gimnáziumba járt. Semmi, ami ebben a könyvben áll, nem igaz.

....

....

....

....

....

....

....

5 Ez a legnagyobb hazugság, amelyet valaha is hallottam. Minden, amit mondtam, igaz. Ez az a lány, akit tegnap láttam a vizsgán.

....

....

....

....

6 Az emberek, akikkel együtt dolgozom, mind kedvesek és segítőkészek. Ez az a könyv, amelyről meséltem neked. *(to tell sy)* Ki az a személy, akitől ezt az információt kaptad? Az egyenlőség egy olyan eszme, amelyben én hiszek. *(idea)*

....

....

....

....

7 A pasas, akinek a kutyája megharapott, azt állítja, hogy én voltam az, aki először megharapta az ő kutyáját. *(to bite, bit, bitten)* Melyik az a magyar város, amelynek a fele külföldön van? Ez az a ház, amelyben *(ahol)* lakom. Ez a fő oka annak, hogy szeretlek. A nagymamám volt az, aki ezt a pulcsit kötötte. Szombaton történt, hogy felhívott, és találkoztunk.

....

....

....

....

....

....

LISTENING

Russian bistro

A report about the first genuine Russian fast food outlet

a Read the question and try to answer it after you have listened to the recording once. Discuss your answer with your partner.

- What different features of the new Russian fast food outlet and McDonald's does the interview compare?

b Answer the following questions as you listen to the tape for the second time. Discuss your answers with the rest of the class.

- What examples of traditional Russian food does Ms Ingram mention?
- What does Ms Ingram call "an ace up their sleeve"?
- What kind of duality characterises the atmosphere inside Russko-bistro?
- How fast is the service compared to McDonald's?
- Who are the most important customers of McDonald's now?
- How do the prices compare between Russko-bistro and McDonald's?
- What political trend does Ms Ingram mention in connection with the opening of Russko-bistro?
- What is the "story" of the word *bistro?*

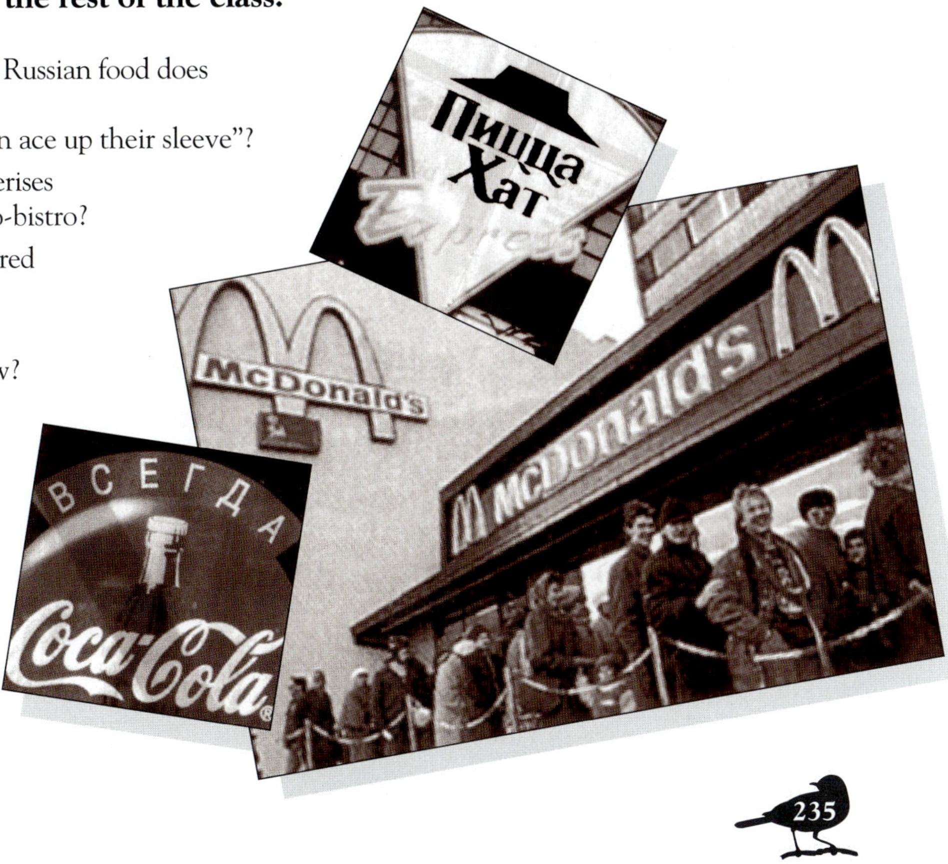

HOMEWORK

TRANSLATION

English into Hungarian

Use a dictionary to translate the following article into Hungarian.

All I Want for Christmas Is an Underwater Joy Ride

Want to give someone a nice surprise for Christmas? Then consider buying his-and-hers underwater scooters for a mere $7,500 each.

That's this year's highlighted gift in the Neiman Marcus Christmas catalog, which features pricey, whimsical and outrageous items among dresses and pajamas. The scooter, the Breathing Observation Bubble, better known as BOB, resembles a standing dryer at a hairdresser. You sit on a seat, place your head into a Plexiglas air-filled dome and plunge, James Bond-like, 40 feet underwater.

More than 3 million copies of the 140-page Christmas Book started reaching customers last week. Carolyn Cobb, a spokeswoman for the catalog, said Neiman Marcus has already taken an order for a yellow BOB ("no one wants that pink one") and has sent videos to 25 other interested divers. The beauty of BOB – designed by British inventor Andrew Sneath and made by Bellaqua in Palm Beach, Florida – is that you don't have to carry diving equipment. For another $1,500, BOB comes with a fancy walkie-talkie.

Neiman Marcus also offers a 10-foot-tall, elephant shaped aquarium for $120,000. Fish are not included. One customer bought it, and another wants one custom-made in the shape of an eagle, Cobb said.

Neiman Marcus has not yet sold its $200,000, 18-carat, yellow-gold teddy bear encrusted with 200 diamonds, 36 rubies and other jewels, but don't despair. There are still 85 shopping days and the store has received several inquires. The $14,000 cigar-box custom-made by Viscount David Linley, a member of the British royal family, went immediately, and cowboy boots studded with gold have flown off the shelves.

New York Newsday

LESSON 3

TRANSLATION
English into Hungarian
checkpoint

All I Want for Christmas Is an Underwater Joy Ride

a **What kind of translations have the different people in the class come up with for the following words and phrases in the context of the passage?**

- joy ride
- this year's highlighted gift
- the catalog features pricey items
- Breathing Observation Bubble
- James Bond-like
- custom-made
- but don't dispair
- have flown off the shelves

b **Compare and discuss the possible translations for each and every sentence with the whole class.**

c **Choose three new words or phrases from the text that you think are worth remembering.**

READING & VOCABULARY
article

a **You are going to read an article about different foodstuffs. Before reading the text, decide if the following statements are true or false, and after comparing your answers with your partner, read the article to check whether your guesses were good.**

	TRUE	FALSE
1. Honey is healthier than sugar.	❑	❑
2. Natural vitamins are better than synthetic ones.	❑	❑
3. Raw sugar is healthier than white sugar.	❑	❑
4. Brown bread is healthier than white bread.	❑	❑
5. Red meat is fatty and leads to heart disease.	❑	❑
6. Vitamins help you cope with stress.	❑	❑
7. Alcohol is bad for your heart.	❑	❑
8. Vitamin pills give you energy.	❑	❑
9. Vegetarians are healthier than meat eaters.	❑	❑
10. Too much oil is bad for you.	❑	❑
11. Starches are bad for you.	❑	❑

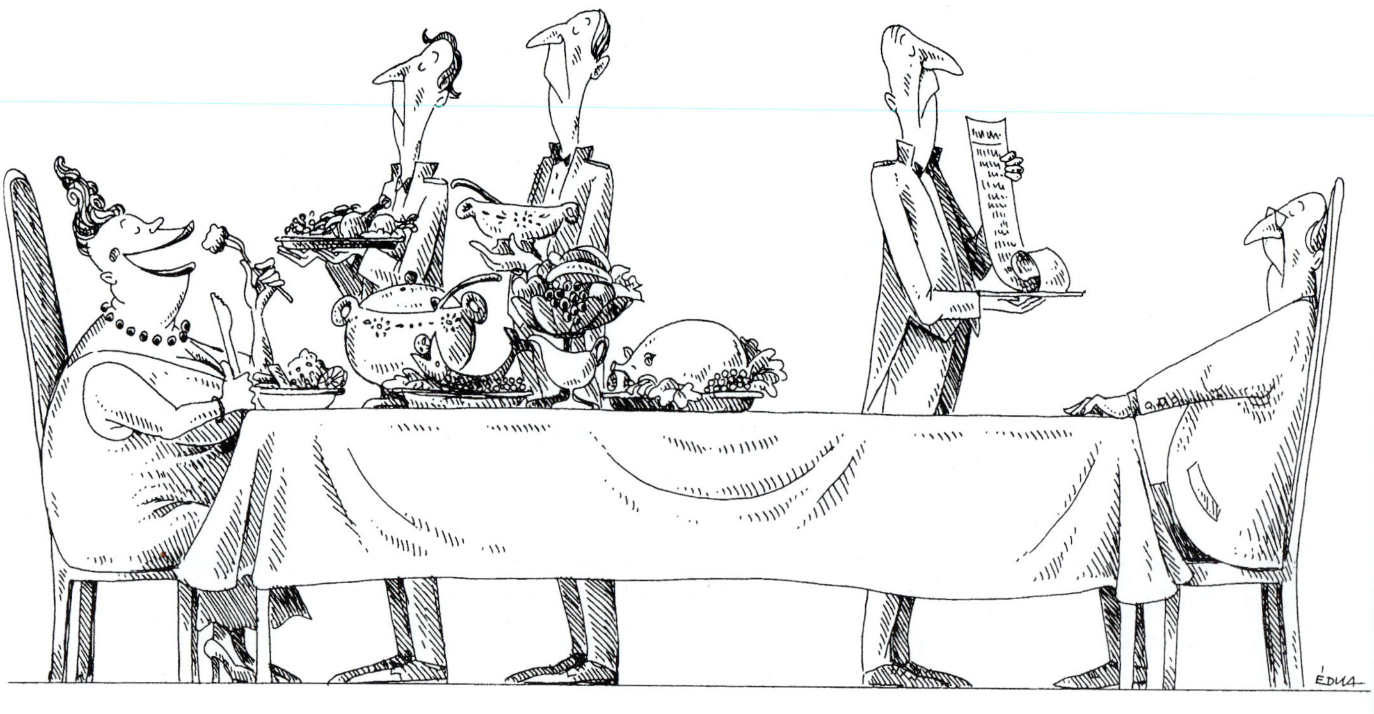

Great Food Myths

Great Food Myths

We're given so much advice about healthy eating these days, it's sometimes difficult to know what to believe. Greg Breadbury takes a look at some of the popular myths and the latest thinking.

(Woman)

1 Honey is better than sugar. The Bible described Israel as the land of milk and honey and this sweet, sticky substance has been considered extremely healthy ever since. It's often used in cold cures, and has also been credited with curing asthma and insomnia and providing vitamins. Yet Professor Arnold Bender, professor of nutrition at London University, points out that honey contains only traces of nutrients and is nothing more than pleasant-flavoured sugar

2 Natural vitamins are better than synthetic ones. The body doesn't care whether vitamins come from a laboratory or the garden. Catherine Collins a dietician at St George's Hospital, London, says: 'A vitamin is simply a chemical required by the body for certain activities.'

3 Raw sugar is better than white. Raw sugar is just sugar with dirt – it has no added nutritional benefits.

4 Brown bread is better than white. Most white bread now contains added calcium and B group vitamins – some experts believe it's better for us than supposedly 'healthier' brown bread.

5 Red meat is fatty and leads to heart disease Red meat has been branded by health gurus as the root of all dietary evil. Yet lean red meat, with the fat removed, contains only five per cent fat. Also, as Dr Ian Baird, medical spokesman for the British Heart Foundation, points out, we probably consume more fat from biscuits than from meat. He says: 'In moderation, red meat is a good idea – it's very nutritious. There's no need to go completely vegetarian.'

6 Vitamins help you cope with stress. This is a ludicrous idea! Emotional stress is only likely to deprive the body of vitamins if it actually stops you eating.

7 Alcohol is bad for your heart Medical expert Sir Richard Doll found last year that people who drank up to four pints of beer a week were less likely to die from heart disease. His findings reinforce the evidence that heart disease levels are lower among the French, thanks to their love of red wine.

8 Vitamin pills give you energy. Vitamins aren't pick-me-ups – energy, of course, comes from calories.

9 Vegetarians are healthier than meat eaters The British Nutrition Foundation warns that people who abandon all meat in favour of a vegetarian diet, without seeking nutritional advice, may risk malnutrition through deficiencies in zinc and vitamin B_{12}. Vegans are even more susceptible.

10 Too much oil is bad for you The taboo on fried foods has convinced people that oil is unhealthy. In fact, the opposite is true. Three years ago, a study showed that men who ate herring had lower death rate from all causes than those who reduced their fat consumption – this is because the fish oils helped lower their cholesterol levels. The traditional Mediterranean diet is good news precisely because it uses a lot of olive oil, which is high in vegatable fat and therefore good for you.

11 Starches are bad for you The image of an Italian mamma made fat from a life-long diet of spaghetti haunts the popular imagination. Yet the Government, backed by nutritionists, advises that pasta, potatoes, bread and rice are filling and fibrous rather than fattening or heavy.

b Now try and find the words and phrases for the following definitions in the text, and make guesses about the possible derivatives. When you have finished, discuss them with the rest of the class.

solid, powdered or liquid material

....

a chemical or food that provides what is needed to live or grow ⇒ the process of giving or getting the right kind of food for good health and growth ⇒ a specialist in ~ ⇒ related to the food we eat ⇒ not proper or satisfactory ~ ⇒ food that is full the natural substances that the body needs to stay healthy and grow properly

....

....

having a particular taste

....

to eat or drink sg or use sg up ⇒ the act of eating or drinking sg or using sg up ⇒ the amount of what is eaten, drunk or used up

....

to support

....

something that has a harmful or unpleasant influence or effect

....

in a controlled way; not too much

....

a very small amount that is difficult to see or notice

....

to succeed in dealing with problem or situation

....

in a natural state; not processed; not cooked

....

to give or supply

....

the good result of something that makes life better for you

....

Italian food made from flour, eggs, and water

....

an idea or explanation that many people believe, but which is not true

....

to tell someone that something bad or dangerous might happen

....

to look for or try to get something

....

instead of

....

facts or objects that make you believe that something is true or has really happened

....

information we get as a result of an investigation or some research

....

making you feel full when you have eaten it

....

containing fibres

....

a person who knows a lot about a particular subject, and to whom people go for advice

....

likely to suffer from illness or be affected by a problem

....

to stop doing sg; to give sg up

....

to (unfairly) describe sg as a very bad type of thing ⇒ a name given to a product by the company that makes it

....

to be said or believed to have a particular good quality

....

a drink or medicine that makes you feel more cheerful and gives you more energy

....

someone whose job is to advise people about food and eating

....

ridiculous; completely unreasonable or stupid

....

lack of something that is necessary

....

to make someone worry or sad

....

to take from someone something that they need

....

to make it stronger; to make it more likely to be true

....

c Now read the following questions and answer them in writing after reading the article again. When you have finished, discuss the answers with the rest of the class.

What does Professor Arnold Bender say about honey?

....

....

What does Dr Ian Baird say about lean red meat?

....

....

What evidence do Sir Richard Doll's findings reinforce?

....

....

What are the dangers of being a vegan?

....

....

Why is oil thought to be healthy?

....

....

What do nutritionists say about foodstuffs that have a high starch content?

....

....

HOMEWORK

VOCABULARY
article
study tasks

Great Food Myths

a Read the article again and memorise any vocabulary items that are new to you. When you have finished, use the words in the box to fill in the gaps in the passage below. Change the form of the words if necessary.

nutritionist
ludicrous
evidence
fattening
consumption
to cope with
moderation
to provide

Have you ever eaten kangaroo meat? Well, ... as it may sound, a surprisingly large number of Hungarians have!

Mavadker, the importer says that sales of kangaroo meat are literally jumping. "Hungarians are not going to eat the most kangaroos in the world, but .... is definitely increasing," said the manager of the company.

But what does kangaroo taste like? "It's a little bit gamey, but, in ...., it's not too bad," says an expatriate from Down Under. "It's usually pet food in Australia. Dogs love it."

Mavadker is, quite understandably, emphasising the health .... of kangaroo. .... by ...., they say the meat contains less than 2 per cent fat and there's .... that it is low in cholesterol.

The .... meat comes in packs of thighs, backs and tail steaks. Mavadker also offers mixed packs, which include parts of shoulders and necks. For those who can't .... the task of preparing kangaroo dishes or for those in a hurry, the company .... prepackaged microwavable portions. The recipe was developed by the kitchen at the Kempinski Hotel. The kangaroo is prepared in a pleasant-........................ white wine sauce and is accompanied by rice and corn.

Unfortunately, contrary to popular ...., healthy living doesn't come cheap. Supermarkets in Budapest sell kangaroo meat for about 2,000 forints a kilo. Still, the importer thinks Hungarians are hungry for exotic meat that is not .... Later this month, the company will start importing ostriches.

benefit
flavour
raw
myth
to back

b Use the following guidelines to prepare for a short oral summary of the article about food myths.

honey ➜ bread ➜ sugar ➜ red meat ➜ alcohol ➜ oil ➜ starchy food ➜ vegans ➜ vitamins

WRITING
composition

Hungary's conversion to market economy has radically changed the face of the retail trade in this country. There are a lot of revolutionary processes going on, which are very often contradictory in nature, and, needless to say, divide the public:

1. Small shops and butiques have mushroomed in the past few years: ➜ some are open around the clock, some have a special choice of goods, some have a friendly atmosphere, they give work to a lot of people ➜ some are surprisingly expensive, some are very crowded

2. The number of huge super/hypermarkets and shopping centres has multiplied: ➜ you can buy everything under one roof, they have a wide choice of goods, they are modern and well equipped, they can be pretty cheap ➜ they may be a long way away from the city centre, they kill small shops, i.e. a lot of shopkeepers go bankrupt

3. Marketing has become more intensive: advertisements (brochures through the post, leaflets, posters), TV and radio commercials, complex advertising campaigns, sponsoring: ➜ you get a lot of information about goods and shops, some of them are funny ➜ they are far too aggressive (giant posters, TV commercials during films, tele-marketing), they are very expensive and we pay the price, nothing is sacred: everything becomes commercial

4. Mail order shopping is getting more and more important: teleshopping, catalogue shopping, shopping through the Internet: ➜ it's extremely comfortable ➜ it's far too slow, it may be risky

5. There are new loan schemes: leasing, hire purchase, part-exchange: ➜ you can buy something and pay for it later, more people can afford to buy things ➜ it's often more expensive, it may be a burden on the family for years

Use (whatever you want from) the information above and the guidelines below to give your opinion about shops and shopping in Hungary.

- How has the general state of the retail trade changed in Hungary under the new regime?
- How has the structure of shops changed, and what do you think about these changes?
- What are the most important changes in marketing techniques, and what's your opinion about them?
- What new forms of shopping and what financial techniques have appeared, and how important do you think they are or might be in the future?

☞ When you have finished, don't forget to check your work for grammatical mistakes.

LESSON 4

VOCABULARY
article
checkpoint

a Compare your solutions to the fill-in-the-gap homework task with the rest of the class.

b Discuss with the rest of the class what you think the English would be for the following Hungarian sentences.

Még soha nem vezettem buszt, de azt hiszem azért menne.

....

Sokan a munkát szükséges rossznak tartják.

....

A vitaminhiánynak súlyos következményei lehetnek.

....

A kormány megígérte, hogy támogatni fogja javaslatot.

....

Bizonyíték van arra, hogy az aerosolos spray-k is felelősek az ózonlyukért. *(the hole in the ozone layer)*

....

Valami olasz tésztát ennék; mit szólnál egy jó kis spagettihoz? *(a nice dish of ...)*

....

Sajnos, az csak egy tévhit, hogy a magyarok tehetségesebbek más népeknél.

....

A felmérés eredménye nagyon érdekes volt; kiderült, hogy az emberek több mint kilencven százaléka lopott már valamit életében.

....

....

Imádom az eperízű joghurtot.

....

Talán ez az egyetlen dolog az életben, amit nem kell mértékkel/módjával csinálni, és mégis jó.

....

c Working in pairs, give a brief summary of the article we read last lesson.

GRAMMAR FOCUS
m i n i t e s t
Relative Clauses

Do the following test and check it with the rest of the class.

1. I got a bonus of ten thousand forints last week, ... I spent on books immediately.
A that **C** which
B what **D** —

2. We need a secretary ... is younger than 25 and has at least 20 years of office experience.
A — **C**, who
B, that **D** who

3. It was only in the 89th minute ... the Hungarian team managed to score a goal.
A that **C** which
B when **D**, when

4. The place ... we stayed at wasn't exactly ... I'd call a first class hotel.
A what // which **C** which // that
B — // what **D** where // —

5. The deadline is 10 December ... means that I have another three months to work on this book.
A, which **C** which
B, what **D** that

6. Patrick Brontë had three daughters, all three of ... became famous writers.
A which **C** whom
B who **D** whose

7. He will sharply criticise anything ... is better than his own work.
A what **C** —
B, which **D** that

8. If only I could still put on the suit ... I took my school-leaving exams.
A in which **C** in that
B in what **D** which

9. Why is it that politicians forget everything ... they promised in opposition the moment they've been elected to power?
A — **C**,which
B what **D**, that

10. A Rolls Royce seems to be the only car ... is good enough for my girlfriend.
A which **C** that
B what **D** —

SPEAKING
discussion

a What's your opinion about and/or your usual reaction to the following things? Think of some reasons to support your view and then discuss the issue with your partner.

- television commercials on Hungarian TV *(quality, quantity, timing)*
- free food tastings in shops *(coffee, ice cream, beer)*
- cash machines/dispensers/points *(cash cards as opposed to carrying cash)*
- window-shopping *(just looking and not buying anything, as a pastime)*
- mail order *(e.g. household appliances, books chosen from a catalogue and then delivered)*
- door-to-door marketing *(salesmen coming to your home trying to sell things)*
- hire purchase *(paying a deposit, and then paying the rest of the money for e.g. comsumer durables by instalments over a period of time)*
- shopping complexes/malls *(Duna Plaza and the like)*

b In groups of four, try to agree what raw materials (ingredients) you would have to obtain to prepare the following dishes.

- a nice bowl of mixed/ tossed salad
- scrambled eggs
- bean soup Jókai style
- a nice bowl of fruit salad
- Tartare beafsteak
- pancakes

c Suppose this group of yours wanted to have a party. You and your partner have been appointed to make arrangements for the necessary food and drink supplies. Plan what you think will need to be bought to ensure that no one dies of starvation and thirst at the gathering. Suppose you collect 200 forints from each participant to cover costs.

HOMEWORK

VOCABULARY
survival kit
preview

Read through the new vocabulary list on page 249-250, and consult a dictionary if you come across something that is unfamiliar or unclear to you.

EXAM TIPS

The Hungarian into English translation task

☞ This component contains about ten Hungarian sentences in some sort of a context (either a dialogue or a narrative passage). The main aim of the task is to assess the candidates' ability to *use grammar*, so it is not a translation task in the strict sense of the word. The use of dictionaries is allowed, but as the focus is on structures rather than vocabulary here, there is normally no need to use the dictionary at all.

Though the text is a continuous passage, the individual sentences are *typical "grammar sentences"*, which means that in most cases you are supposed to recognise the "grammatical content/focus" of the sentence immediately. This is the crucial point here; once you have determined this "focus", you can just go ahead and translate it, or, if there is no obvious equivalent for the original sentence, you should try to *reformulate* the original Hungarian sentence (while keeping the original meaning, of course), so that it becomes "translatable", i.e. so that you can use an English structure that you are familiar with. Remember that in most cases a word by word (or rather, structure by structure) translation will not be suitable; you should come up with the English equivalent of the Hungarian sentence and not a word for word translation. [e.g.: ***Tudod, éppen építkeztünk, és nagy szükségünk volt a pénzre.*** → *éppen:* Past Continuous → *építkezni:* házat építtetni: to have sg done → *szüksége van:* kell: Black List verb → *nagy:* nagyon (kellett): *borzasztóan:* badly/desperately → *a pénz:* uncountable: money → ***You know/see, we were having a house built, and we (badly/desperately) needed money (badly/desperately)./... and we were in dire need of money.]***

The fact that the text is a continuous passage might be quite important, both in terms of the meaning and in terms of the necessary grammatical structures. [e.g. ~ ***Miért, mi lett azzal a pénzzel, amit a lottón nyertetek?*** → ***Why, what <u>had</u> happened to the money you <u>had</u> won in the lottery?]***

In the marking, the examiners draw a distinction between "big" and "small" mistakes: while you can get off with a loss of one or two points [e.g. **<u>with</u> the money]* or even with no loss of points at all [e.g. failing to use a comma, or **<u>on</u> the lottery]* in the case of minor errors, you will lose all the points if you miss the "key grammar point" in the sentence.

UNIT 10
A picture of health

LESSON 1

VOCABULARY
survival kit

General condition

In good shape: to be healthy/(fighting) fit/fit (as a fiddle)/in (great) shape/a picture of health/well/fine/OK

In poor shape: to be unhealthy/unwell/unfit/ill/out of shape, to be in terrible shape/condition, to be in serious but stable condition, to be in life-threatening condition

Handicaps: to be mentally ill/(physically\mentally) handicapped ⇒ lame, deaf, hard of hearing, dumb, to stammer, blind, short\longsighted

Problems

Illnesses: trouble, problem, disease, infectious/contagious disease, epidemic, to infect, infection, immune system, immune to ..., to immunise sy against ..., disability, mental illness, handicap, incurable, fatal

Becoming ill: to become/fall ill *[BrE]*/to get sick *[AmE]*/to be taken ill, to develop a disease, there's something wrong with ..., to suffer from ...

Injuries: to be\get injured/hurt, to hurt/injure sy\your arm\etc.\yourself ⇒ (minor\major) injury, wound, to break/fracture, to sprain, to bruise, to strain, ⇒ fracture, bruise, sprain, strain

The body — weak points

Flesh & blood: skin, joints, muscle, tissue, nerve, the nervous system, blood-vessels, artery, vein

Bones: skull, jawbone, spine/backbone, rib, shin bone, collarbone, thigh bone

Head: chin, cheek, forehead, temple, nape, neck, nose, nostril, eyebrow, eyelashes, eyeball, ear, mouth, lip, tongue, tooth (teeth), gum

Trunk: chest, breast, back, shoulder, buttocks/bottom, waist, hip, abdomen/belly

Limbs: thigh, knee, ankle, heel, sole, toe, upper\forearm, elbow, wrist, palm, thumb, fore\middle\ring\little finger, nail

Organs: brain, heart, stomach/tummy, bowels, lungs, kidneys, bladder, liver, genitals, womb

Symptoms

Feeling bad: to feel poorly/terrible\funny\dizzy\shivery\run-down\a bit under the weather, an upset stomach/tummy, to feel\be sick, to vomit/bring up/throw up/to puke (up)

Fainting: to lose consciousness, to be unconscious, to come to

Sounds: (to) cough, to have a (bad) cough, (to) sneeze, (to) hiccup, (to) sigh, (to) wheeze

Telltale signs: to have a temperature of ..., fever, to have high\low blood pressure, to have a runny nose, to have a cavity, to swell (swelled, swollen), to be inflamed, ⇒ swelling, inflammation

Aches & pains: to hurt, to ache, to have a pain in ..., to have/get a sore throat\a headache\backache\stomach ache\toothache\earache\chest pains, ⇒ painful/sore, a sharp\dull pain; suffering

Skin: to have a rash/spots on ..., to come out in a rash, to have a sty, pimple, wart, corn, scar, birthmark, blister(-ed), burn

Stomach: to have diarrhoea\constipation\heartburn

Depression: to be depressed\exhausted\strained/nervous/nervy/jumpy, to lose your appetite\voice, insomnia

Diagnosis

to have\catch a cold, (the) flu, pneumonia, measles, chickenpox, whooping cough, scarlet fever, mumps, an ulcer, cancer, a heart attack/failure, a virus, an allergy, rheumatism, indigestion, a poisoning, a nervous breakdown, A(cquired) I(mmune) D(eficiency) S(yndrome), tooth decay, to be allergic to ..., to be pregnant, to be a hypochondriac, travel sickness, to be addicted to ...

Treatment

Therapy: to see\call a doctor, to examine, to treat, to cure, to operate on sy, to have an operation, to undergo surgery, to have your tonsils\appendix\a tooth out, to fill a tooth, filling, crown, to drill, to take sy's temperature\pulse, to be X-rayed, to put on a bandage, to heal, to recover, to get well/better, to die of ... ⇒ examination, cure, treatment, (plastic) surgery, first aid, care, recovery, therapy, checkup, euthanasia

Doctors & patients: doctor/physician, specialist, general practitioner/GP, family doctor, surgeon, psychiatrist, psychologist, dentist, naturopath, naturopathy, nurse, patient, casualty, victim

Medication: to stay in bed, to take medicine/medication, ⇒ drug, pill, tablet, (to apply an) ointment, antiseptic, antibiotic, pain-killer, sedative/tranquilliser, sleeping pill, (to be on) the Pill/contraceptive, placebo; injection/jab *[BrE]*/shot *[AmE]*, syringe, needle, cotton-wool, bandage, plaster/Elastoplast *[BrE]*/Band-Aid *[AmE]*, in plaster

Hospitals and surgeries: to be in\taken to hospital, ambulance, stretcher, clinic, ward, (dental) surgery, consulting room *[BrE]*/doctor's office *[AmE]*, operating theatre, casualty department, waiting room, to have an appointment, consulting hours, to prescribe medicine, prescription, (doctor's) fee

Health insurance: medical certificate, to be off sick, to call in sick, sick note, to put sy on the sick list, sickness benefit, health insurance, (under) the public/national health service, prevention

SPEAKING
conversation

Use the vocabulary list and the guidelines to discuss the following health-related issues with your partner.

1. **Have you ever had a broken bone?** If yes: When? ➜ How did it happen? ➜ Was it painful? ➜ What did you (or other people) do?
2. **What kind of diseases have you had in the past 12 months?** How bad were they? ➜ Did you see a doctor? ➜ What was the treatment?

3. **What would you say are the differences between the symptoms of the flu and a cold?** Temperature? Runny nose? Pain in the limbs? Feeling unwell? Headache? Sore throat? Feeling sick? Anything else?
4. **What would you do if you woke up in the morning and you had a) a nasty headache, b) a high temperature, c) a sharp pain in your tummy?** Medication? ➜ Doctor? ➜ Off sick?
5. **What would you say are a) the most common, and b) the most dangerous diseases of our times? Make two lists.**

A

SPEAKING pictures

a Discuss with the class what vocabulary you need to describe the pictures.

Verbs:

Nouns

Adjectives:

B

b **Agree with your partner which one of you has picture A and B, take turns to describe what you can see in them, make guesses about the situation, and tell each other about the thoughts, feelings, memories, etc. they evoke in you.**

c **Looking at both pictures now, say a few words about the subject in general, viewing the contents of the pictures from a wider – national or even global – perspective. The following questions might help you to come up with some ideas:**

- How widespread is the problem depicted in the picture? Is it characteristic of a particular age/social group/etc.?
- What do you think the individual should/could do about the problem?
- Is there anything that could/should be/have been done about the issue on a national/global level? (Apart from everybody's personal responsibility.)

You may find the following phrases useful here:

Thank God ... ➻ Unfortunatelly, ... ➻ It is in everyone's best interest to ... ➻ You may have to pay very dearly for ... ➻ You/The government should ... ➻ It is crucial/extremely important that ... should ... ➻ There has been a lot of progress made in ... ➻ Generally speaking, ...

FUNCTIONS
role-play

a **Read both role-cards and agree with your partner who's A and who's B.**

A You've noticed that whenever you come out of the bath, your skin behaves in a very strange way: it is raised up in small points, the hairs on it stand up so that it is covered with tiny bumps. You've also noticed that the same thing happens whenever you are cold, frightened, or when you see certain people. You are worried that you have developed an allergy of some kind, and you turn to a doctor for medical advice.

- ♣ Tell the doctor about your problem.
- ♣ Ask her/him what s/he thinks the problem is.
- ♣ Ask the doctor whether s/he thinks this condition is serious.
- ♣ Ask her/him whether hospital treatment would be necessary.
- ♣ Ask her/him if you should take any medication.
- ♣ Ask her/him what you should do.
- ♣ Ask the doctor what her/his fee is.

B You are a doctor, and a patient turns to you with something s/he thinks is a medical problem. S/he asks for your expert advice on the possible treatment.

- ♠ Ask the patient to briefly describe her/his symptoms.
- ♠ Having listened to the description, ask her/him to turn up her/his sleeve so that you could examine the skin.

- ♠ Tell your patient that you haven't seen anything, but you think the name of this condition is goooseflash.
- ♠ Tell her/him that this condition is not serious at all.
- ♠ Tell her/him that no hospital treatment is necessary.
- ♠ Tell him/her that no medication is necessary.
- ♠ Tell your patient that this condition is absolutely natural, and that there isn't much s/he can do about it; perhaps she could dry her/himself as soon as possible after coming out of the bath, s/he should put on a pullover when s/he is cold, and s/he should avoid frightening situations and people s/he doesn't like.
- ♠ Tell the patient that a consultation is HUF5,000.

b Try and agree with the rest of your class what phrases you could use in this situation.

c Rehearse the situation in pairs. Read the cards again before starting, but try and rely only on the notes below while practising.

A	B
greeting → symptoms → seriousness? → hospital? → medication? → advice → fee?	what's the matter? → examination → comforting words → advice → fee

HOMEWORK

VOCABULARY
survival kit
study task

Study the word list on page 249-250, and memorise the words and phrases. When you have finished, put the following words in their correct places in the passage below to check your knowledge. (You might try and do the task without using the box.)

medical, blistered, symptoms, virus, tissues, care, surgical, injury, prevent, treatment, healing, ointment, cold, medicine, feel fine, blood, fever, drugs, checkups, antibiotics, thermometer, chemist, skin, infection

I don't know where or when the following bits of medical advice originated. I suspect that they have just been passed down over the years like other bits of family folklore. Besides being widely accepted, however, all are myths, so there's an important message: the wrong advice can get you into real trouble by prolonging unpleasant ...., delaying proper .... or leading to unexpected complications. Here are the most common myths along with the right .... advice:

Put yoghurt or cream on a burn: Oily things like these tend to deepen the area of ....; yoghurt and cream are also nonsterile and can delay .... and lead to .... *Better advice:* Wash a minor burn with soap and cool water. Apply an antibiotic .... to prevent infection. See your doctor for large, deep or .... burns.

You'll catch cold if you get chilled: Colds are .... infections. You stand a better chance of catching a .... in a warm room with other people than you do by going outdoors with wet hair or light clothing. *Better advice:* To .... a cold, wash you hands frequently, and avoid finger-to-nose contact. Eat well, get enough sleep and rest and drink plenty of fluids.

You can stop a medication once you feel better: That's true for .... that control symptoms, such as cough and cold medicines. Other drugs, however, like .... should be taken for their full course. *Better advice:* Ask your doctor or .... to explain the right way to take a .... and for how long.

Get a complete medical examination every year: Complete annual .... for everyone are a waste of time and money. *Better advice:* If you ...., it's enough to get a complete exam every five years after 40, every two years after 60 and annually after 75.

Feel the forehead to check for ....: That is highly inaccurate, particularly if you or the other person have just come in from outdoors. *Better advice:* Use a ...., leaving it in place at least 10 minutes for a proper reading.

Squeeze a pimple to help it drain: Such .... for these localized infections actually may force the material deeper into the .... and worsen the problem. *Better advice:* Apply warm soaks several times a day to soften the ...., increase .... flow and hasten drainage. If the infection won't drain, see your doctor for antibiotics or .... treatment.

You need eight hours of sleep each night: There's no one right amount for everyone. Some people do just fine on 5 hours; others require 9 to 10. *Better advice:* Get enough sleep so that you wake up feeling rested and refreshed.

By James Wasco, M.D., Woman's Day

GRAMMAR FOCUS

preview

The Gerund

The *Gerund* has features that are characteristic of a verb and a noun at the same time. It can, for example, be followed by an object and it can be passive like a verb, and it can stand with a preposition and can be the subject or object of a sentence like a noun.

The *Gerund* has a *Present* and a *Perfect* (for finished actions) form, but we can also use the *Present* for finished actions, so the *Perfect* is not compulsory.

	active	*passive*
Present	delaying	being delayed
(Perfect)	(having delayed)	(having been delayed)

1. The Gerund can be the subject of the sentence:

➢ Watching too much television makes you shortsighted. Smoking is a nasty habit.

2. The Gerund can be the object of the sentence (i.e. certain words are followed by a Gerund). Some verbs always take the *Gerund* (and <u>not</u> the *Infinitive*):

to admit* (to)	**enjoy**	**mention***	**tolerate**
appreciate*	**escape**	**mind****	**miss**
avoid	**enjoy**	**postpone**	**go shopping/swimming/walking/etc.**
can't help	**excuse**	**practise**	**spend\waste time/money doing sg**
can't stand	**fancy**	**quit**	**keep sy waiting**
consider	**finish**	**recollect**	**keep (on) doing sg**
delay	**imagine***	**resist**	**prevent\stop sy (from) doing sg**
deny*	**involve**	**risk***	**burst out crying/laughing**
dislike	**justify**	**suggest***	**need, require, want**

➢ *Don't delay seeing a dentist. I could't help laughing. Your hair needs cutting. You mentioned seeing him at that party. Excuse my asking ..., I must quit smoking. Imagine being in Italy now. You shouldn't risk losing your money. This job involves getting up early in the morning. Have you considered marrying her?*

*With these verbs we can also use a **that-clause**:

➢ *You mentioned that you had seen him at the party. I appreciated that she was so helpful.*

With *mind* we can also use an **if-clause:

➢ *Would you mind if I asked you a personal question? Do you mind if I ask you a question?*

3. The Gerund is used after all prepositions (including *to*, when it is one!).

verb + preposition: ***to insist on, to put off, etc.; to look forward to, to object to, etc.***
➢ *I am dreaming of buying a house in the country. I look forward to hearing from you.*

adjective + preposition: ***to be fond of, to be good at, etc.; to be used to, to be accustomed to, to be allergic to, to be essential to, to be similar to, etc.***
➢ *I am quite used to getting up early in the morning.*

noun + preposition: ***point in, thought of, possibility of, etc.; objection to, in addition to, etc.***
➢ *There's no point in waiting any longer. Is there any point in …? There's a possibility of us spending the summer in Spain this year.*

4. Special cases with the Gerund

to be worth, it's no use/good, to feel like, busy, difficulty (in), like, than, as, after, before, without, instead of, by, how/what about
➢ *I feel like going to bed. He was busy copying my homework when the teacher came in. This book is really worth reading./It's worth reading this book. It's no use trying it again. Is it any use trying it again? Did you have any difficulty (in) finding the address? There's nothing I hate more than being woken up by an early morning phone call. She is watching TV instead of helping her mother. How about drinking some wine?*

LESSON 2

VOCABULARY
survival kit
checkpoint

a **Check the fill-in-the-blank homework task with the rest of the class.**

b **What are the corresponding words and phrases with a similar meaning?**

to be in poor shape	→	**to be in poor c……..**
infectious	→	**c……..**
to become ill	→	**to f… ill**
abdomen	→	**b…**
stomach	→	**t….**
to lose consciousness	→	**to f….**

disability	→	**h......**
to break a bone	→	**to f....... a bone**
to be nervy	→	**to be j....**
operation	→	**s......**
backbone	→	**s....**
doctor	→	**p........**
medicine	→	**m.........**
tranquilliser	→	**s......**
injection	→	**s...** *[AmE]*
plaster	→	**E...........** *[BrE]* / **B...-...***[AmE]*

c Name a medical condition that is typical of the following organs.

- the lungs
- the skin of the face
- the stomach
- the ears
- the back
- the bones
- the heart
- the nose
- the nervous system
- the teeth

d What would you say are the most obvious symptoms of the following medical conditions?

- food poisoning
- nervous breakdown
- travel sickness
- allergy
- mumps
- chickenpox

e Complete the definitions.

- .... is simple medical treatment that is given as soon as possible to someone who is injured or who suddenly becomes ill.
- If you speak or say something with a lot of pauses and repeated sounds (either because you have speech problem, or because you are nervous or excited), you ....
- Your .... are your arms and legs.
- If your nose is ...., liquid is flowing from it, usually because you have a cold or you are allergic to something.
- A .... is a painful swelling on your skin, which contains clear liquid and can be caused by burning or by rubbing constantly against the skin.
- The .... is the system in certain countries which provides free or cheap medical care to everybody.

GRAMMAR FOCUS
translation into English

The Gerund

Translate the following sentences into English, discussing each section with the rest of the class as you progress.

1. Tagadta, hogy látott vagy hallott volna bármit is. A diákok 85%-a beismerte, hogy időnként puskázik dolgozatírásnál. Nem szeretem, ha valaki napszemüveget hord, amikor nem is süt a nap. *(people)*

2. Egy időre elhalasztottam, hogy BMW-t vegyek. *(for a while)* Egyszerűen nem tudtam ellenállni (a kísértésnek), hogy belessek a kulcslyukon. *(to peep through)* Semmi sem indokolhatja egy másik ember megalázását. *(to humiliate)*

3. Beosztottakat megvárakoztatni bunkóság, feletteseket megvárakoztatni öngyilkosság. *(subordinates, uncouth/ness [ʌn'ku:θnəs] superiors, suicide/suicidal)* Ezekre a falakra igencsak ráférne a festés. Semmi nem akadályozhat meg abban, hogy megegyem ezt süteményt. Amikor beléptem a terembe, mindenki nevetésben tört ki.

4. Azt tervezem, hogy egy másik városba költözöm. *(to think of)* Már feladtam, hogy abban reménykedjem, hogy egyszer meggazdagszom. *(to give up, one day)* Az összes lakó tiltakozott az ellen, hogy több lakbért kelljen fizetni.

5. Nem vagyok hozzászokva ahhoz, hogy megvárakoztassanak. Azon kívül, hogy rendkívül okos, nagyon szép is. Mi értelme van ilyen sokat költeni egy ilyen marhaságra? *(useless thing)*

❻ Gondolod, hogy érdemes megnézni ezt a filmet? Amilyen csinos, nem hiszem, hogy bármilyen gondja lesz egy jó állást találni. *(Pretty as she is)*. Nem érdemes vele vitázni, (úgysem) hajlandó senkire hallgatni. *(won't)*

❼ Soha ne kezdj el fordítani egy szöveget anélkül, hogy elejétől a végéig elolvasnád. *(from beginning to end)* Mi lenne/mit szólnál ahhoz, ha zöldre festenénk a hajunkat? *(to dye)* Valahogy ma nincs kedvem iskolába menni. *(somehow)*

LISTENING

Bless you!

Interview with a GP about the flu

a Read the question and try to answer it after you have listened to the recording once. Discuss your answer with your partner.

How serious an illness is the flu today, and how good is the medical science at protecting us from it?

b Answer the following questions as you listen to the tape for the second time. Discuss your answers with the rest of the class.

- What are the typical symptoms of a cold according to the doctor?
- What additional symptoms do you have when you've got the flu?
- What does the interviewer say about the origin of the word *influenza?*
- What can we do to protect ourselves from the flu?
- What groups of people are particularly in danger?
- What does Dr Summers say about this century's worst epidemic?
- When was the influenza virus discovered?
- Why is it so difficult to ward off the flu?

HOMEWORK

TRANSLATION
English into Hungarian

Use a dictionary to translate the following article into Hungarian.

I Bought Myself a New Body

Cosmetic surgery is now a booming business and most operations are performed to reverse the signs of ageing. This year, more than 60,000 women will go under the knife in an attempt to improve their looks. It can cost anything from £200 for a collagen implant in the lips to £2,000 to remove eyebags. And there are risks – silicone implants can leak and, in the US, have been blamed for cancer. But more and more women are saving money to pay for private surgery. And nothing will put off those in pursuit of a perfect body.

Sue Fogden, 46, from Buckingham, had always hated her big thighs and bottom. "Big hips and thighs seem to run in my family and, from my teens onwards, I was always pear-shaped. I tried every diet and exercise plan under the sun but nothing worked. It was a total misery. I even had to make my own clothes because I could never buy anything off the peg.

Then, three years ago, I saw an advert for plastic surgery in a magazine and I began to think seriously about it. Eventually I went along to see the surgeon at the clinic, and he seemed so down to earth that any nerves I had simply disappeared. I opened a bank account to save up for the operation, and put money in for a year until I'd got enough. Just before Easter 1991, I went in for the op.

After the surgery, my legs were black down to my toes and they looked horrendous. I felt as if I'd fallen down stairs – I was sore and it was difficult to sit down. But at the end of the month when the swelling had gone down, I'd lost two inches off my hips, and that made the pain worthwhile. Now I am a totally different shape and I just buy size 10 or 12 clothes and I feel comfortable in shorts. It's changed the way I feel about myself."

Best

LESSON 3

TRANSLATION
English into Hungarian
checkpoint

I Bought Myself a New Body

a What kind of translations have the different people in the class come up with for the following words and phrases in the context of the passage?

- a new body
- to reverse the signs of ageing
- to go under the knife
- in attempt to improve their looks
- those in persuit of a perfect body
- seem to run in my family
- every diet under the sun
- to buy clothes off the peg
- that made the pain worthwhile
- the way I feel about myself

b Compare and discuss the possible translations for each and every sentence with the whole class.

c Choose three new words or phrases from the text that you think are worth remembering.

READING & VOCABULARY
article

a Read through the article and try to answer the following questions without using a dictionary. When you have finished, discuss your answers in pairs.

- What *is* and what *isn't* the value of a dead parrot?
- What was the bird like?
- Why did the case get before court?

This dead parrot is *difunto*

By John Hooper in Madrid

A QUESTION left hanging in the air by John Cleese – what is the value of a dead parrot? – has finally been resolved by a Barcelona judge. His honour Antonio Nuñio de la Rosa has ruled that a dead parrot is worth 150,000 pesetas ($815).

He was awarding damages to Maria del Carmen Dotras, whose parrot (male, green) died, passed away, ceased to exist and, in short, became defunct two years ago in the city's Vall d'Hebron hospital. Ms Dotras, who lives with her mother, had owned the bird for 23 years, since she was 12.

Her family doctor suspected the parrot might be the cause of an allergy her mother had developed. He wanted it to have a blood test, and told her it would be better done by a doctor than a vet. This didn't prove to be a very good idea.

According to Ms Dotras, the doctors virtually suffocated the bird by putting a towel over its head, and took six times as much blood as they were told to.

Eventually, a consultant ordered it to be put out of its misery.

Ms Dotras put the dead bird in the freezer, to facilitate an autopsy. In fact, the deep freezing made it impossible to determine the cause of death.

But, as judge Nuñio de la Rosa said in his judgement – passages of which might have come from a Monty Python show: "The parrot has deceased, and cannot be revived." He decided the hospital authorities and the doctor responsible should pay a sum equivalent to the price of a new bird. He dismissed Ms Dotras's claim for damages of one million pesetas ($5,435). This had been based, in part, on the argument that her parrot could talk.

Drawing a fine distinction, the judge ruled that the bird merely "articulated sounds similar to those of people". If the parrot had been able to talk, he said, "It would have complained".

Guardian Weekly

b Now try and find the words and phrases for the following definitions in the text, and make guesses about the possible derivatives. When you have finished, discuss them with the rest of the class.

to make a decision about a legal problem ⇒ such a decision ⇒ a King or Queen

....

....

a short part of a book, poem, play, etc.

....

....

money someone has to pay to someone else in compensation for harming them or their property

....

....

someone who is trained to give medical care and treatment to sick animals

....

....

to die

....

....

almost

....

....

to officially decide that someone should receive a payment, a judgement, a prize, etc.

....

....

only

....

to say that two things are slightly different ⇒ to be able to recognise and understand the difference between two different things, and also to be the thing that makes someone or something different from other people or things

....

....

....

to find or provide a solution to a (difficult) problem

....

....

terrible suffering ⇒ to kill an animal in order to end its suffering

....

to find out the exact details or facts about something

....

to bring back into life ⇒ the process and the fact of something becoming active, strong, popular, etc. again

....

....

having the same value as something else ⇒ to be exactly the same in size, number, amount, etc. as something else ⇒ a position or situation in which people have the same rights ⇒ to the same degree ⇒ to make two or more things the same in size, value, amount, etc.

....

....

....

a set of reasons that show that something is true or untrue, right or wrong, etc.

....

....

to make it easier to happen ⇒ rooms, equipment, or services that are provided for a particular purpose

....

....

to refuse to accept

....

....

to fail to make a definite decision about a question

....

....

to make someone die by preventing them from breathing

....

....

an examination of a dead body to discover the cause of death

....

....

c Now read the following questions and answer them in writing after reading the article again. When you have finished, discuss the answers with the rest of the class.

Why was a blood test taken?

....

....

How did the bird actually die?

....

....

Why was it impossible to determine the cause of death?

....

....

How did the judge rule?

....

....

Why did he dismiss Ms Dotras's claim?

....

....

HOMEWORK

VOCABULARY
article
study tasks

This dead parrot is difunto

a Read the article again and memorise any vocabulary items that are new to you. When you have finished, use the words in the box to fill in the gaps in the passage below.

It all began two years ago when mum developed that allergy. We went to see Dr Iglesias, but he couldn't .... what mum was allergic to. Suspecting our 23-year-old talking parrot Fridi might be the cause, Dr Iglesias wanted him to have a blood test, and said it could be done in the Vall d'Hebron hospital. Naturally, I protested and said it would be better done by a ...., but he reassured me that it was just a routine job, and real doctors knew better, anyway.

Needless to say, those clever guys made a real mess of the whole intervention: they virtually .... the poor thing with a towel, and took so much blood that it would've been enough even for an elephant. In the end they were left with no choice but to put Fridi out of his .... by giving the poor bird an injection.

Of course, I knew that Fridi had .... and he couldn't be ...., but I was so outraged that I decided to go to court to get ....; after all, Fridi had been a truly special bird with his amazing vocabulary.

Well, to cut a long story short, the trial was a complete joke. The judge just wouldn't draw a .... between an ordinary green parrot and fantastic bird that could actually talk, and .... my claim. Eventually he ruled that the hospital should pay a sum .... to the price of a new bird, saying that Fridi had not really been able to talk.

I wonder what my dear bird would've said if he had heard this ridiculous ....

misery
damages
equivalent
to determine
argument
to decease
to suffocate
to dismiss
vet
to revive
distinction

b Use the following guidelines as you prepare to summarise the article about the poor parrot.

allergy → blood test → mercy killing → freezer → judge's ruling → reasons

WRITING
composition

Hungary has notoriously poor medical statistics: Hungarians spend a record time off sick, and our life expectancy is one of the lowest in the developed world. Most scientists agree that it is chiefly the following factors that are responsible for the present situation:

1. Individual responsibility:
traditional lifestyle

a) **Unhealthy cuisine and eating habits:** *unhealthy raw materials:* too much animal fat: bacon, pork, not enough fruit and vegetables,etc.; *unhealthy technologies:* frying, roux, too much salt, etc.

b) **Extremely high consumption of potentially dangerous things** like alcohol, tobacco, coffee, sweets, and medicine (sleeping pills, sedatives), etc.

c) **The "rat-race":** overwork, lack of relaxation, the stresses and strains of everyday (working) life.

d) **Lack of regular physical exercise.**

e) **Attitude problem:** not enough attention paid to health-related issues, particularly prevention.

2. Governmental responsibility:
a prolonged decline in the country's living standards

a) **Widespread poverty:** unhealthy housing conditions, lack of personal hygiene, etc.

b) **Unsatisfactory medical services:** *lack of financial resources:* lack of modern equipment and medication, etc.

c) **Environmental issues:** unhealthy drinking water, pollution, etc.

d) **Lack of popular medical education.**

Use (whatever you want from) the information above and the guidelines below to write an account of what you think the Hungarian goverment and the Hungarian citizen should do to improve the present situation.

- What is the present situation like?
- Who are responsible for the present situation?
- What are the most important factors that contribute to the present situation, and what should be done about them?
- What do you think are the chances of the situation getting better in the near future?

☞ When you have finished, don't forget to check your work for grammatical mistakes.

LESSON 4

VOCABULARY
article
checkpoint

This dead parrot is difunto

a Compare your solutions to the fill-in-the-gap homework task with the rest of the class.

b Discuss with the rest of the class what you think the English would be for the following Hungarian sentences.

Néhány millió forint megoldaná minden problémámat.

....

A rendőrségnek nem sikerült kiderítenie a baleset pontos okát.

....

Mi lehet a spanyol *difunto* szó angol megfelelője?

....

Ne haragudj, de ezt az érvelést nem tudom elfogadni.

....

A kormány szerint Magyarországnak külföldi tőkére van szüksége a // gazdasági növekedés beindításához. // a gazdaság fellendítéséhez. (*to facilitate; growth*)

....

....

Az igaz, hogy magas tandíjat kell fizetni, de fantasztikus tanulmányi és sportolási lehetőségek vannak.

....

....

Miért van az, hogy ugyanazokat, akik sírva fakadnak egy kóbor kutya láttán, gyakran egyáltalán nem érdekli az emberi szenvedés? (*to burst into tears, stray dog*)

....

....

Hány Oscar-díjat ítéltek oda *Az angol beteg* című amerikai filmnek?

....

Ezek az új autók annyira hasonlóak, alig lehet különbséget tenni egy Opel és egy VW között.

....

c Working in pairs, give a brief summary of the article we read last lesson.

GRAMMAR FOCUS
m i n i t e s t

The Gerund

Do the following test and check it with the rest of the class.

1. ... thinking that I made a big mistake when I bought this car.
- **A** I can't afford
- **B** I can't help
- **C** There's no use
- **D** It's no point

2. If I were you, I would ... applying for admission to an American university.
- **A** attempt
- **B** not hesitate
- **C** consider
- **D** need

3. If you drive when you are drunk, you don't just ... from driving for long years but you also endanger yourself and others.
- **A** risk banning
- **B** risk having banned
- **C** risk being banned
- **D** risk having been banned

4. It's silly of him to ... having this car repaired; it could break down at any moment.
- **A** delay
- **B** urge
- **C** neglect
- **D** miss

5. Quite honestly, I'm fed up with my boss; simply I ... like this.
- **A** am not used to treating
- **B** didn't use to treat
- **C** am not used to be treated
- **D** am not used to being treated

6. Couldn't we just put off this test? Somehow we ... writing it today.
- **A** aren't ready
- **B** don't want
- **C** don't feel like
- **D** couldn't manage

7. Eventually he admitted ... the alarm clock.
- **A** that he had forgotten to set
- **B** having forgotten setting
- **C** forgetting setting
- **D** failing setting

8. Most reviews agreed that this film simply ... seeing.
- **A** wasn't good enough
- **B** wasn't worth
- **C** was no good
- **D** was no point in

9. The test was so easy that no one had any difficulty ... at least sixty points.
- **A** scoring
- **B** having scored
- **C** in having been scored
- **D** to score

10. Do you mind ... a red pen to correct your mistakes?
- **A** if my using
- **B** if I used
- **C** I using
- **D** if I use

SPEAKING
discussion

a What's your opinion about the following statements? Think of some reasons to support your view and then compare your ideas with your partner's.

1. "If I had to choose between 50 million forints and a guarantee that I will not be taken seriously ill for 50 more years, I would go for the money. After all, statistically speaking, I have a better chance of remaining healthy than of ever getting so much dough. Nothing ventured, nothing gained!"
2. "With these campaigns for healthier lifestyles, doctors and politicians try to put the blame on us for our state of health, because they can't cure us or they are not willing to pay for our treatment. Let's face it: no matter how healthy your lifestyle is, there's no guarantee of anything; you may fall ill like anybody else."

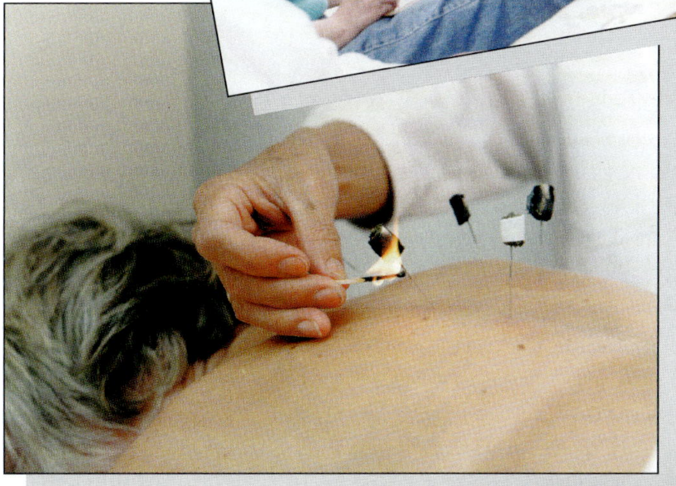

b Answer the following questions in pairs.

Would you ever undergo cosmetic plastic surgery? (to have a wart/a roll of fat removed, to have a facelift, etc.)
Would you tip the doctor and the nurses if you or a close relative were in hospital? Why (not)?
Do you believe in naturopathy? Have you experienced such a treatment at first hand?

c If you go to Britain or the USA, you'll be surprised to see far more physically handicapped people in the street than in Hungary. Of course, it's not that there are more disabled people in these countries, it's only that those societies pay more attention to them and provide them with better facilities so that they can have a lot more freedom in movement. Thinking of your school/place of work, public transportation, etc., make a list of the steps that should be taken to make life easier for handicapped people in this country. Work in pairs.

HOMEWORK

VOCABULARY

survival kit

preview

Read through the new vocabulary list on page 271-272, and consult a dictionary if you come across something that is unfamiliar or unclear to you.

EXAM TIPS

The picture-based task

☞ Believe it or not, *there is no such thing as a terrible picture at the exam.* At the same time, however, there *is* such thing as an applicant who does not know what to do with a picture. To make sure you do not run out of ideas, try and follow the steps described below as closely as possible:

- Determine what type of picture/s you have; it/they could be *snapshots* (informal photographs taken of everyday things), *press photos* (pictures reporting on events), *advertisements*, *portraits*, *landscape photos*, *cartoons*, *stills from a film*, etc.
- *Give a short description* of the picture(s), focusing on the most important features. Start with a general description of the picture as a whole, don't start with details: add these later if you think they are necessary.
- If you have a single picture, and it is not clear what the "message" is, make *intelligent guesses* about the situation.
- Establish some sort of a logical relationship between your picture(s) and one of the main *topic areas*, and talk about the issue in general terms, looking at the problem from a *global/national perspective*. (Healthy lifestyles, social problems, sports and entertainment, travelling, and environmental problems seem to be particularly popular with the ÁNyB*.)
- Finish off by adding a *personal touch* to the whole issue; give your own opinion, tell them what you would do in a situation like this or whether you have ever been effected by the problem in any way, etc.

If you go through all these stages or steps, you will not be at a loss whatever you see in your picture(s). Furthermore, you have a choice of *two* (sets of) pictures (in other words, a choice of two topics). Make your decision on the basis of the above.

Remember that you are not expected to recognise anybody or anything in your picture(s), and that it is basically your choice what you say about any picture. In fact, examiners do not even ask any questions during the task. You are supposed to keep talking for about three or four minutes.

* Állami Nyelvvizsga Bizottság (State Foreign Languages Examination Board)

UNIT 11 Transport and travelling

LESSON 1

VOCABULARY survival kit

Cars

Vehicles: vehicle, lorry *[BrE]*/truck *[AmE]*, van, motor bike, What make is this car?

Parts of the car: numberplate, bumper, headlight, indicator, bonnet, windscreen *[BrE]*/windshield *[AmE]*, tyre, boot *[BrE]*/trunk *[AmE]*, rear light, rear window, rearview mirror, driver's\passenger\back seat, to fasten your seat belt, steering wheel, ignition, gear stick, handbrake, accelerator, clutch, horn, petrol *[BrE]*/gas *[AmE]*

Driving: by car\road, to drive, to travel/go/ride *[AmE]* in sy's car, to turn the ignition key, to start the engine, to put on\release the handbrake, to indicate/signal right/left, to change up into second gear, to press the accelerator, to pull away, to accelerate, to slow down, to change lanes, to pull out and overtake, to pull out into traffic (from a side-street), to pull up (at the red\amber\green light), to pull over (by the pavement), to park the car

The Highway Code: motoring, motorist, driving licence, driving test, to have\give the right of way (over), dead-end (street), one-way street, pedestrian crossing, (a set of) traffic lights, speeding, at 60 miles per hour, breathalyser, to park illegally, wheel clamp *[BrE]*/Denver boot *[AmE]*, to tow away, to have an accident, to crash into, to run sy over, to knock sy down, to wreck the car, a write-off, motorway *[BrE]*/freeway *[AmE]*, toll road/turnpike *[AmE]*

Maintenance: filling/petrol/gas *[AmE]* station, garage, to break down, to have the car serviced

Public transport in the city

A means of transport: by bus, (the N°6) tram, trolley bus, (the blue line of) the underground/the metro/the subway *[AmE]*, on the yellow line, local/suburban train, cogwheel railway, taxi/cab, bus/tram stop, underground station, terminus

Getting about: journey/ride, to travel/go/ride *[AmE]* on the N°7 bus, to take/get/ride *[AmE]* a bus to get on\off, to change (to), to go as far as ..., to go 3 stops

Fares: (bus)fare, to dodge the fare, to punch your ticket, monthly pass

Rush hours: to be/get stuck in a traffic jam, overcrowded

Trains & coaches

ticket office, platform, train services, single\return ticket, carriage, compartment, to take /catch/get a train\bus\etc. to ..., to board/get on, to get off, to miss, conductor, ticket inspector

Air travel

(aero *[BrE]*/air)plane, airport, terminal, departure lounge, air ticket, flight, to check in\out, check-in counter, boarding pass, to check in luggage *[BrE]*/baggage *[AmE]*, excess luggage, to take off, to land

Holidays

summer\winter holiday/vacation *[AmE]*, trip, excursion, package holiday, holiday resort, a holiday by the sea, a skiing\camping holiday, a tour of ..., a sea-cruise, hitch-hiking, travel agency/bureau, tourist

Going abroad

to apply for a passport\visa, to expire, to have sg renewed, immigration control, to check documents, to clear customs, to declare, to pay duty on ..., security check, to cross the border, to enter a country

Accommodation

to reserve accommodation, to make a reservation in advance, to book a room, hotel, motel, full\half board, guesthouse/bread and breakfast/B & B, youth hostel, camp(ing) site, to put up/pitch a tent, a paying guest, to stay at a hotel, to stay with friend\relatives, to put sy up, to put up somewhere, a single\double room, to check in\out, to pay/settle the bill, reception desk

SPEAKING
conversation

Use the vocabulary list and the guidelines to talk to your partner about the following issues.

1. **Have you or your family got a car?** What make is it? ➜ Who drive(s) it? ➜ Can/Do you drive?
2. **What are the steps of starting a car and pulling away?**
3. **What public transportation (if any) do you use on an everyday basis?** How satisfied are you with the services? ➜ Do you have any preferences for any particular means of public transport?

4. **What would you say are the pros and cons of travelling long distances by a) coach, b) train and c) plane?**

5. **Where did you go for your holidays last summer? How was it?** For how long? ➜ Where did you stay? **Are you going/planning to go anywhere this summer?**
6. **What arrangements would you make if you wanted to spend a weekend in London, but you didn't have any of the necessary documents, tickets and reservations? Make a list of the things that would have to be taken care of.**

SPEAKING pictures

A

B

a Discuss with the class what vocabulary you need to describe the pictures.

Verbs:	Nouns:	Adjectives:

b Agree with your partner which one of you has picture A and B, take turns to describe what you can see in them, make guesses about the situation, and tell each other about the thoughts, feelings, memories, etc. they evoke in you.

c Looking at both pictures now, say a few words about the subject in general, viewing the contents of the pictures from a wider – national or even global – perspective. The following questions might help you to come up with some ideas:

- How widespread and important is the phenomenon depicted in the picture? Is it characteristic of a particular age group/social group/type of vehicle/type of road/etc. (picture A) and area/time of the day/etc. (picture B)?
- What do you think the individual should/could do about the problem?
- Is there anything that could/should be/have been done about the issue on a national/global level? (Apart from everybody's personal responsibility.)

You may find the following phrases useful here: This is one of the ... issues of our times, and ... ➻ This issue has been hotly debated for some time, and ... ➻ There has been a lot of (heated/fierce/intense) public debate on this issue, and ... ➻ The issue of ... has now become the focus of national/worldwide media attention, and ... ➻ ... has focussed public attention on ... ➻ Unless we/the government/etc. do something about this problem, ... will ... ➻ There are a number of things we could do about this problem ... ➻ The only thing we can do is to ... ➻ The only way out of this situation seems to be ...-ing ... ➻ The only solution to this problem seems to be ...-ing ... ➻ We are left with no choice, but to ... ➻ ... before it's too late.

FUNCTIONS
role-play

a Read both role-cards and agree with your partner who's A and who's B.

A Summer is coming and you raise the question of holidays to your husband. You would like to go to Lake Balaton for a fortnight as usual.

- Tell your hubby that you would like to go to Lake Balaton again.
- When he says that he would prefer a skiing holiday somewhere abroad, tell him that you are not particularly keen on the idea, because ...
  - you can't ski..
  - you'd have to go abroad and that's quite expensive.
  - skiing resorts aren't very cheap either.
  - you'd have to buy skiing equipment.
  - it might be very cold.
  - you're interested in sunbathing.
  - there's not much you can do if there's no snow.

- Listen to your husband's arguments for a skiing holiday, and then try to convince him that a holiday by the lake would be great, because ...
  - it's so nice to go back to a place you know so well.
  - after all it's not more expensive than going abroad.
  - it's great to be near water when it's so hot.
  - there are lots of interesting places to visit if it's not sunny.
- Suggest that you should spend a week at Lake Balaton, and another week skiing in Austria.

B Your wife raises the issue of this year's holidays. You would like to have a winter holiday instead of your usual summer fortnight by Lake Balaton.

- When your wife says she would like to go to Lake Balaton, tell her that you're fed up with the idea of a summer holiday, because ...
  - Siófok is a bit boring after all these years.
  - prices are ridiculously high.
  - the weather is too hot.
  - there's not much you can do if it's not warm and sunny.

  Tell her that you think a skiing holiday somewhere abroad would be better.
- Listen to her arguments against the idea, and then tell her that you still think a skiing holiday would be a good idea, because ...
  - you could learn how to ski.
  - things aren't any cheaper in Hungary either.
  - you can hire skiing equipment.
  - there's nothing more beautiful than the snowy hills.
  - you can get a nice suntan while skiing, too.
  - you can go hiking if there's no snow.
- Agree to your wife's suggestion.

b **Try and agree with the rest of your class what phrases you could use in this situation.**

c **Rehearse the situation in pairs. Read the cards again before starting but try and rely only on the notes below while practising.**

A

raising the question ➜ SKIING: can't ski; cost of going abroad; expensive resorts; buying equipment; cold; sunbathing; no snow ➜ LAKE BALATON: familiar place; costs; water; if it's not sunny ➜ COMPROMISE

B

saying you're not keen ➜ LAKE BALATON: boring; costs; heat; bad weather ➜ SKIING: learning how to ski; not dearer; hiring equipment; snowy hills; tan; hiking ➜ COMPROMISE

HOMEWORK

VOCABULARY

survival kit

study task

Study the word list on page 271-272, and memorise the words and phrases. When you have finished, put the following words in their correct places in the passage below to check your knowledge. (You might try and do the task without using the the box.)

luggage, lounge, vehicles, accommodation, terminus, immigration, coach, checking, change, transport, applying, customs, catch, Terminal, bus, board, journey, flight, visa, travelling

"I'm travelling to Oxford next week." It should be so simple, after all, we are at the turn of the millennium, and the approximately 1750 kilometer distance between Pécs and Oxford is no distance in global terms at all.

But the reality is that the .... is time consuming, tiring, expensive and it requires an awful lot of careful arrangements like .... for a passport (thank God we don't need a .... any more!), buying your airline ticket, changing money, reserving ...., and doing the packing, to mention but a few.

If you have taken care of all this, and you are still alive, you're ready for the actual journey. When the day comes, you should get up at about 4 so that you can get an early bus to the railway station and .... the 6.00 Intercity train to Budapest. From Déli Station you should take the Red line of the underground, ... for the Blue line at Deák tér, and then go as far as the Kõbánya-Kispest .... There you should change for the red 154 bus which takes you to .... 1 at Ferihegy airport. Note that you have used 3 different means of ...., you have taken 5 different ...., and you have spent three and a half hours ...., and you haven't even started your journey yet.

After .... in, clearing .... and passport control, you will have to wait another hour or so in the departure .... before finally you can .... the plane. The .... itself is shorter than the train journey from Pécs, but the .... control procedures and reclaiming your .... at Heathrow will take at least 45 minutes. At least you're in Britain now!

If you get lucky, you will have a National Express .... to Oxford from Heathrow Coach Station within an hour, and the 56 mile ride shouldn't take longer than one and a half hours. Once you're in Oxford, all you have to do is take a .... or a taxi to your hotel from the coach station and your 10-12 hour trials and tribulations are over. Welcome to Oxford!

If only I could undergo this terrible ordeal a few more times in the near future!

GRAMMAR FOCUS
preview

The Infinitive

The *Infinitive* also has features that are characteristic of a verb and a noun at the same time. It can be followed by an object and it can be passive like a verb, and it can be the subject or object of a sentence like a noun.

The *Infinitive* has a *Present* and a *Perfect* form, and it can be *Simple* or *Continuous*. In this case, the *Perfect* is compulsory for finished actions.

	active	***passive***
Present	to do	to be done
Present Continuous	to be doing	—
Perfect	to have done	to have been done
Perfect Continuous	to have been done	—

1. The Infinitive (with *to*) after verbs:

to advise sy**	**dare**	**intend**	**persuade sy**	**tell sy* how**
afford	**decide****	**invite sy**	**plan**	**tempt sy**
agree**	**demand****	**get sy**	**pretend***	**tend**
appear*	**enable sy**	**learn (how)**	**promise***	**threaten**
attempt	**entitle sy**	**leave**	**prove***	**not trouble**
ask sy	**expect (sy)***	**manage**	**refuse**	**turn out***
beg sy	**fail**	**neglect**	**remind sy***	**undertake**
not bother	**force sy**	**need (sy) (!)**	**request sy**	**urge sy**
cause sy/sg	**happen***	**oblige**	**seem***	**volunteer**
choose	**hesitate**	**occur to sy**	**swear**	**want (sy)**
claim**	**help (to)**	**offer**	**show sy* how**	**warn sy**
command sy	**hope**	**order sy**	**teach sy* how**	**wish (sy)**

➢ *I can't afford to buy such expensive things. American doctors claim to have discovered a cure for AIDS. Should you have any problems, don't hesitate to get in touch with me. Everything seems to be OK. I promised not to tell anyone. Has it ever occurred to you to apply for this post? I happened to meet her on my way home. They failed to notice an obvious symptom. He didn't even bother to check the address. He is not entitled to use the company car. I didn't expect to be admitted to university. The money he'd won in the lottery enabled him to travel to America. Your hair needs to be cut.*

* These verbs may also be followed by a *that-clause*.
** These verbs may also be followed by a *that sy should* structure.

2. The Infinitive after adjectives:

it's possible, impossible, important, dangerous, awful, strange, funny, terrible, exciting, easy for you, good for you, good/nice of you, etc.

➢ *It was impossible to leave any earlier. It's easy for you to talk, you don't have to make a decision. It was really nice of them to help us. It's so nice to be sitting here with you.*

to be happy, stupid, fortunate, lucky, ashamed, certain, (un)able, sure, likely, unlikely, ready, anxious, due, fit, inclined, willing, bound, determined, expected, pleased, shocked, delighted, prepared, etc.

➢ *I was so happy to see them there. They are lucky to have such a good job. He's inclined to judge people by their appearence. I'm anxious to see her again. The film is due to start at six. He's not willing to pay. This book is quite easy to read. They're bound to win the elections. They are quite unlikely to have arrived yet. He's likely to have forgotten about it.*

3. The Infinitive after certain nouns:

agreement, ability, ambition, decision, demand, desire, eagerness, effort, failure, offer, plan, promise, refusal, request, scheme, way, willingness, wish, etc.

➢ *His ability to understand other people's problems is really fantastic. He made an effort to get on his feet, but he proved to be far too weak. Their plan to change the entrance exam was rejected by the authorities.*

4. Some special uses of the Infinitive:

it's (about *or* high) time (for sy) to do ... <u>BUT</u>: it's time <u>sy</u> + *Past Tense*

➢ *It's time to go home. It's time the kids went to bed.*

would rather/sooner do ... than do ...; would/(would) prefer to do ... rather than do ...; Would you rather do ...? <u>BUT</u>: would rather <u>sy</u> + *Past Tense/Past Perfect*

➢ *I'd rather wait till tomorrow than do it now. I'd rather not do it now. I'd prefer to buy a computer rather than spend the money on clothes. Would you rather stay home or go to the cinema? I'd rather you didn't say a word. (present) I'd rather you hadn't said a word.* (past)

had better do ... <u>BUT</u>: It would be better to do ...

➢ *You'd better start at once. You'd better not say anything. It would be better to talk to him before we do anything.*

to be about to ... = to be on the point of ..., to be going to ...

➢ *We were about to leave when the phone rang and he told us the performance had been cancelled.*

to make sy do sg (to be made <u>to</u> do sg!); to have sy do sg; to get sy to do sg <u>BUT</u>: to have/get sg done

➢ *They can't possibly make us go if we don't want to. These stories always make me cry. What makes you think so? We were made to pay 200 pounds on the spot. I must have someone type this letter as soon as possible. It's never been easy to get him to study. You should have your blood pressure tested. I had my car serviced last week. We are having our flat redecorated at the moment.*

to be said, thought, considered, believed, known, reported, alleged, supposed

➢ *He is said to be one of the richest people in the country. He is said to have won a lot of money. She is alleged to have helped the criminals. You are supposed to remember your teacher's name.*

infinitive of purpose:

➢ *I phoned her (in order) to tell her about the news. I wrote the number down so as to remember/not to forget it. BUT: I left quite early so that I would not miss the train.* (negative) *I bought a bike so that I could cycle to school.* (auxiliary) *I locked the door so that nobody would disturb us.* (another person)

to be to ... = a) a rule/order [must], b) a plan, arrangements for the future *[úgy van, hogy; az a szándéka, hogy; a tervek szerint]*, c) should do sg, d) if, by any chance, sy did sg.

➢ *You are to stay here till I return. Ann and Peter are to be married in May. We were to have gone to the cinema last night but I didn't feel very well, and we stayed home. (something that had been planned did not actually happen) If you are to get into university, you should start working immediately. What am I to do now? If I were to marry her, what would you say?*

let sy do sg, let's do

➢ *I wonder why they let the kids stay up so late. Let's start now. Let me try it.*

too hot (for sy) to ... ; (not) hot enough (for sy) to ...

➢ *You're too young to understand these things. He is too old for me to marry. This tea is too hot for me to drink. The grass was too wet to sit on. He is not rich enough for me to marry. You're old enough to travel alone.*

to take ten minutes **(for sy) to ..., to cost** ten thousand **(for sy) to ...**

➢ *How long did it take for you to translate this text? It would cost a fortune to repair this car.*

where/how/what/when/which to ... <u>BUT</u>: why sy should ...

➢ *I had no idea how to start the whole thing. I showed her where to park the car. They wondered why they should pay so much.*

wonder/want to know/decide/remember/think whether to ...

➢ *I wondered whether to write or phone. He couldn't remember whether to turn left or right. I can't decide whether or not to go to the party.*

noun + the Infinitive:

➢ *some letters to write, someone to talk to, some books to read, plenty to do, someone to play with, etc.*

to be so foolish/so kind as to ...

➢ *I was so foolish as to tell him my address. Would you be so kind as to shut up?*

to do everything/anything/nothing but/except ...

➢ *He does nothing but complain. I couldn't do anything but apologise. My dog does everything but speak.*

to do one's best to ... ; to do what one can to ...

➢ *The team will do their best to win the Cup Final. I hope you'll do what you can to pass the exam.*

the first/second/last/only to ...

➢ *He is always the first to arrive and the last to leave. She is the only person to have survived the accident.*

the first/only/best thing sy does/can do ...

➢ *The only/best thing we can do is (to) phone him. The first thing I do in the morning is (to) drink a cup of tea.*

the Infinitive as subject (with set phrases):

➢ *To be or not to be, that is the question. To err is human. To lean out of the window is dangerous.*

introductory phrases:

➢ *to be frank, to tell you the truth, to be honest, to cut a long story short, to be fair, etc.*

special phrases:

➢ *I've <u>make up my mind</u> to continue my studies after leaving school. We <u>set out</u> to buy a nice pair of shoes for the occasion. He was very helpful, he even <u>took the trouble</u> to see me off to the airport. It was <u>a relief</u> to know that I'd passed the exam. <u>It's (no) fun</u> to be sitting here doing nothing when the others are working so hard.*

LESSON 2

VOCABULARY
survival kit
checkpoint

a **Check the fill-in-the-blank homework task with the rest of the class.**

b **What are the "opposites" of the following words and phrases?**

- headlight
- driver's seat
- to release the handbrake
- to pull over
- to slow down
- to get on
- to pay the fare
- single ticket
- to miss the bus
- to land
- arrival

c **What are the corresponding words and phrases with a similar meaning?**

lorry *[BrE]*	→	**t**..... *[AmE]*
to indicate	→	**to s**.....
gas *[AmE]*	→	**p**..... *[BrE]*
to stop	→	**to p**... ..
motorway *[BrE]*	→	**f**...... *[AmE]*
toll road	→	**t**....... *[AmE]*
underground *[BrE]*	→	**s**..... *[AmE]*
journey	→	**r**... *[AmE]*
holiday	→	**v**....... *[AmE]*
travel bureau	→	**travel a**.....
to stay somewhere	→	**to p**.. .. **somewhere**
to pitch a tent	→	**to p**.. .. **a tent**

d Complete the definitions.

- A .... is a metal object that is fastened to the wheel of an illegally parked car.
- .... luggage is bags or cases that weigh more than the legal limit that you are allowed to take on a plane.
- A .... is a private house where people can pay to stay and have meals.
- If you ...., you travel by asking the drivers of passing cars for free rides by putting your hand out with your thumb raised.
- A .... is some kind of a document which shows that you are allowed to travel on something without paying (on the spot).

GRAMMAR FOCUS

translation into English

The Infinitive

Translate the following sentences into English, discussing each section with the rest of the class as you progress.

1 Egyszerűen nem engedhetem meg magamnak, hogy kocsival járjak dolgozni. Arra sem vették a fáradságot, hogy válaszoljanak a levelemre. Az fel sem merült benned, hogy hozzám fordulj? *(it; to turn to)* Legyen szíves megmutatni nekem, hogy hogyan kell kiejteni ezt a szót helyesen. Emlékeztettem, hogy adja fel a levelet, amint lehetséges. Azt állítja a kormány, hogy mindent megtett az életszínvonal romlásának megállításáért. *(decline in)* Ha a helyzet nem javul hamarosan, a kormány kénytelen lesz megemelni az adókat. *(to improve; to raise)*

....

....

....

....

....

....

2 Veszélyes dolog sok készpénzt magunknál tartani. Olyan izgalmas volt részt venni egy ilyen fontos eseményen. *(to take part in)* Nem volt valami szép tőled, hogy megetted az összes csokit. Ezek a döntések még valószínűleg sok problémát fognak okozni. Mázlid van, hogy ilyen aranyos férjed van. Már alig várom, hogy bebizonyítsam nekik, hogy meg tudok birkózni a feladattal. *(to prove to sy)*

....

....

....

....

....

....

❸ Az, hogy a kormánynak nem sikerült megállítani az inflációt, döntőnek bizonyulhat a választásokon. *(failure; decisive; at the elections)* A sztrájk tűnik a legegyszerűbb módnak arra, hogy megoldjuk ezt a problémát. Mivel mindkét nagyapám tanár volt, a szüleim nem nagyon örültek annak a törekvésemnek, hogy tanár legyek.

....

....

....

....

....

❹ Ideje, hogy a cég vezetése tegyen valamit a problémák megoldása érdekében. *(management)* Jobb szeretném, ha nem innál többet. Inkább fizetnék, mintsem hogy szívességet kérjek tőle. Jobb lesz, ha nem szólsz neki erről az egészről egy szót sem. Mindenki üljön le, a busz mindjárt indul. Már éppen alá akartam írni a szerződést, amikor eszembe jutott, hogy jobb lesz, ha még egyszer ellenőrzöm az adatokat; ez egy nagyon bölcs cselekedetnek bizonyult. *(contract; to remember; clever/wise)*

....

....

....

....

....

❺ Ez a dal mindig a gyerekkoromra emlékeztet. Ezer forintot fizettettek velünk ezért a vacakért. *(rubbish)* Muszáj lesz lefordíttatni ezt a levelet, a hatóságok csak hivatalos fordítást fogadnak el. *(authorities)* Azt tartják róla, hogy ő az „agy" az egész akció mögött. *(operation)* Beszereltettem egy riasztót a kocsimba, hogy az autótolvajoknak egy kicsit nehezebb legyen az életük. *(to put; car alarm; car thieves)*

....

....

....

....

....

❻ Úgy van/Úgy néz ki, hogy tízre befejezzük az egész munkát. Hagyd, hadd (t)egyenek amit akarnak. Ez a vers túl elvont ahhoz,hogy megértsem. *(abstract)* Nem tudtam, hogy válaszoljak-e a kérdésre, vagy sem. Voltam olyan hülye, hogy aláírtam a szerződést anélkül, hogy rendesen elolvastam volna. *(properly)* Ígérem, hogy minden tőlem telhetőt megteszek, hogy megbuktassalak édes fiam. Ez a gyerek mást sem csinál egész nap csak eszik.

....

....

....

....

....

7 Szegényt meggyilkolták; én vagyok az utolsó ember, aki élve látta. Nagy megkönnyebbülés volt látni, hogy senki nem sérült meg. Klassz dolog horror regényeket olvasni, olyan megnyugtatóak. *(soothing)*

....

....

....

....

LISTENING

Travel experiences

Excerpts from interviews with travellers

a Read the question and try to answer it when you have listened to the recording once. Discuss your answer with your partner.

- What's special about the people the recording is about?

b Answer the following questions as you listen to the tape for the second time. Discuss your answers with the rest of the class.

- How do most people choose their vacations according to the announcer?
- What common features of cities does the man mention? (He mentions 3 such features.)
- What particular features does he mention in connection with the three places he names?
- What are the woman's impressions of Dublin?
- What kind of a landscape was described to the man in Corsica?
- What sort of things does the man say are the lasting memories of his travel?

HOMEWORK

TRANSLATION

English into Hungarian

Use a dictionary to translate the following article into Hungarian.

Travel Guide to the Moon

Hardly anything ever happens on the moon. It is as if time had stopped — just dust, pits, craters and hills frozen into a kind of cosmic still-life.

You won't appreciate all this when you first arrive. There will be all the hustle of getting into your space suit for the trip from the spaceport to the astrotel. Probably the first thing you will want to see is the earth hanging in the jet-dark sky. It will be a sight to remember all your life. The earth will dominate the sky, looking nearly four times bigger than the moon does from home, and much brighter. Do remember to pick the right week for your trip. If you want to see a 'full earth', it will be the middle of the night on the moon, which lasts $13\frac{1}{2}$ earth days and is bitterly cold.

A word about the climate. Some people planning a moon holiday worry: With noon temperatures reaching 105° Centigrade on the equator, dropping to –168° at midnight, surely it is a place fit only for mad dogs and Eskimos? Well, it is not as bad as it seems. There's no air or wind to make contact with — and it is this that makes us too hot or too cold on earth. The only problem is to insulate your feet from the intense heat or cold of the surface, but your space suit will see to that.

As for where to go, don't on any account be fobbed off by one of those bargain price trips to the back of the moon. You won't see the earth at all. Among the sightseeing musts, there is the site of the first landing in Apollo 11. By it is the famous First Footprint. But regrettably, like most relics, it is not genuine. Neil Armstrong's first footprint was erased by his and Edwin Aldrin's boots long before they took off (the print actually belongs to an engineer from Milwaukee).

Take a Ticket to the Moon, by Gerald Leach, Observer Colour Magazine

LESSON 3

TRANSLATION
English into Hungarian
checkpoint

Travel Guide to the Moon

a What kind of translations have the different people in the class come up with for the following words and phrases in the context of the passage?

- frozen into a kind of cosmic still-life
- a place fit only for mad dogs and Eskimos
- your space suit will see to that
- don't on any account be fobbed off
- among the sightseeing musts
- by it
- long before they took off
- the print actually belongs to an engineer

b Compare and discuss the possible translations for each and every sentence with the whole class.

c Choose three new words or phrases from the text that you think are worth remembering.

READING & VOCABULARY

article

a Read through the article and answer the following question without using a dictionary. When you have finished, discuss your answer in pairs.

- What's Hope Governali's problem?

Subway? No way!

By Rose Kim
STAFF WRITER

Though 13-year-old Hope Governali was born and raised in New York City, she says she never rode a subway train until her first day of high school this year.

The results were disastrous.

"She went crazy," said her mother, Victoria Govarnali, who accompanied the Woodhaven teen on the A train to Manhattan Sept. 9. "She couldn't take it. She turned white as a ghost. She broke out in a rash."

Hope's unexpected reaction — which was duplicated when they tried the J train the following week — was a fright to mother and daughter alike. Asked to describe her fear of the subway, Hope said in a tremulous voice: "I get really nervous. My stomach starts to hurt and I feel like I'm going to get lost."

Is it transitphobia?

There is no specific term for a fear of the subway, but city psychologists said it's not unusual for individuals to develop phobias.

In fact, 11 percent of the population develops a panic attack or phobia at some point in life, said Dr. Carol Lindemann, director of the New York Psychological Center.

"There's a psychological component — a feeling of terror, or a feeling that you're going to die, or that you will suffer or lose control, or that something terrible is happening," Lindemann said.

Lindemann said people could suffer from a specific phobia when entering a subway. But symptoms like Hope Governali's could also result from claustrophobia or travel phobia and could be influenced by hormonal changes specific to her age or stress from starting at a new school.

"For some people, the subway may seem frightening because it's a closed space, or a closed space with a lot of people, or people who are different from their own culture or background," said Dr. Steven Tuber, a professor of psychology at the City University of New York.

The treatment for phobic patients can also vary, Tuber said. "They could simply avoid what upsets them. Others will say they want to try, but attempt it in a non-rush-hour time." They could also undergo behavioral therapy, he said.

New York Newsday

b Now try and find the words and phrases for the following definitions in the text, and make guesses about the possible derivatives. When you have finished, discuss them with the rest of the class.

- a feeling of extreme fear ⇒ the use of violence to obtain political demands ⇒ someone who uses violence to obtain such demands ⇒ to make someone very afraid ⇒ to be terribly afraid ⇒ making people extremely afraid
- making you feel afraid or nervous ⇒ to make someone feel afraid or nervous ⇒ feeling afraid ⇒ such a feeling
- to go somewhere with someone (so that they should not be alone)
- an unusually strong dislike or hatred of something ⇒ suffering from a particular ~
- to go into a place
- to try to do something difficult ⇒ the act of trying to do sg difficult
- a phrase used to say that you will definitely not do something
- exact, detailed; limited to or characterictic of one particular thing
- very bad, ending in complete failure ⇒ a sudden event tha causes serious damage
- unable to find your way or not knowing where you are ⇒ a phrase used to tell someone rather rudely to go away
- the spirit of a dead person
- equally
- a word or expression that has a particular meaning, especially in a scientific subject
- to be different in a group of similar things
- to accept something unpleasant without becoming upset
- the act of taking something or someone from one place to another
- shaking slightly because someone is nervous or afraid
- repeated

- to happen as a consequence of something

....

- to be unable to do what you want any longer

....

- a strong fear of being in a small closed space

....

c Now read the following questions and answer them in writing after reading the article again. When you have finished, discuss the answers with the rest of the class.

What are the symptoms of transitphobia according to Hope and her mother?

....

....

....

How common are phobias among the population?

....

....

....

What are the psychological symptoms of phobias according to the psychologist?

....

....

....

What factors does the psychologist mention that could have resulted in Hope's symptoms?

....

....

....

What does Dr. Tuber say about the possible causes of transitphobia?

....

....

....

What different treatments does Dr. Tuber recommmend to fight off the symptoms?

....

....

....

HOMEWORK

VOCABULARY

article

study tasks

Subway? No way!

a Read the article again, and memorise any vocabulary items that are new to you. When you have finished, use the words in the box to fill in the gaps in the passage below.

I'm desperate. I don't think I can .... it much longer. Something terrible is happening to me, and it is making my life more and more difficult with each passing day.

I will .... to describe the situation in a few words; perhaps that'll make it a bit easier for you to understand my state of mind.

It all began a few months ago when I noticed that whenever I got on a bus, a tram, or the underground in Budapest, I turned white as a ...., and my stomach got upset. Then my voice would become ...., I would begin to gasp for air, and eventually I would get off the bus in .... for fear of choking to death.

At first I had no idea what the cause of all these .... symptoms might be, in fact, I thought it was some kind of a .... But one day my reactions were .... when I .... a shop and slowly it began to dawn on me what the real cause might be.

As it's turned out, the symptoms are caused by a .... cheap perfume creation called Hot Nights, which has a particularly aggressive, sickening, sweet smell, and which, to my despair, is becoming more and more popular with certain ladies.

The most .... effect of all this is that I simply can't use public transport at all any more. I haven't got a car, and I can't afford taxis, which means I have to walk it. I really like walking, but no .... can I possibly walk 25 kilometers a day. I simply don't know what to do.

Could I possibly ask everybody who is reading this to either kindly refrain from wearing this perfume or at least wear it in moderation. Please remember: you could save a life!

way
ghost
to take
to enter
phobia
tremulous
specific
frightening
to attempt
terror
disastrous
duplicated

b Prepare to summarise the article about "transitphobia" in a few sentences.

WRITING
letter

The number of motor cars has multiplied more than fifteen times over in the past thirty years in Hungary. Today there are about two million motor vehicles on the road, and about one quarter of these can be found in the capital. To make things worse, the majority of these vehicles are rather out of date. The result: traffic has become unbearably slow, you can hardly breathe any longer, and buildings are slowly being eaten away by the fumes from the traffic in most city centres.

Use (whatever you want from) the information above and the guidelines below to write an open letter to persuade all motorists to leave the car at home and use public transport so that the harmful effects could be reduced.

- What is the present situation like?
- What is the main cause of all this?
- What's the purpose of your letter?
- What can motorists do to improve the situation?
- What are the disadvantages of using a car for the individual? *(expensive, nerve-racking, dangerous, parking problems, etc.)*
- What are the personal advantages of public transport? *(cheaper, can be faster, you can read, you can see people, etc.)*
- What changes could take place if motorists followed your advice?

☞ When you have finished, don't forget to check your work for grammatical mistakes.

LESSON 4

VOCABULARY
article
checkpoint

a Compare your solutions to the fill-in-the-gap homework task with the rest of the class.

b Discuss with the rest of the class what you think the English would be for the following Hungarian sentences.

- Egy iszonyatos gyerekkori élmény egész életen át elkísérheti az embert.

....

....

- Semmiképpen nem fogom kifizetni ezt a büntetést.

....

....

- A teszt eredménye mind a tanárra, mind a diákokra nézve katasztrofális volt.

....

....

- A problémáim többsége abból (a tényből) fakad, hogy alacsony a fizetésem.

....

....

- Az étkezési szokások családról családra változnak.

....

....

- Részletes információra lenne szükségem egy adott típusról. (!)

....

....

- Akárhányszor kíséreltem meg meggyőzni őket, sohasem sikerült.

....

....

c Working in pairs, give a brief summary of the article we read last lesson.

GRAMMAR FOCUS
mini test

The Infinitive

Do the following test, and check it with the rest of the class.

1. Fortunately, our maths teacher agreed ... the test for a while.
A postpone
B to postpone
C with postponing
D to have postponed

2. The travelling public are requested ... any luggage unattended.
A to leave
B not leave
C to not leave
D not to leave

3. I would never ever let my daughter ... out with a guy like myself.
A to go
B to be going
C go
D to have gone

4. It's high time the police ... firm action to deal with car thives.
A took
B to take
C take
D to be taking

5. We ... anything until we get official permission.
A would better not do
B had better not to do
C had better not do
D had better to not do

6. It's quite unlikely that we can ... with us if it is not in their interest.
A make them cooperate
B get them cooperate
C have them cooperated
D make them to cooperate

7. Naomi Campbell is reported ... to hospital with symptoms of an overdose of drugs.
A that she has been taken
B to be taken
C to have been taken
D to have taken

8. I'd locked my bike up in the cellar ... stolen.
A not to get it
B so that it wouldn't get
C to not get it
D so that not to get it

9. If you ... this scholarship, you will need references from your teachers.
A to win
B wanted to win
C are to win
D are about to

10. I've just noticed that my passport has expired; I must ... as soon as possible.
A have it renewed
B make it renew
C get it to renew
D have it renew

SPEAKING
discussion

a **Have you ever taken part in/done/experienced the following things? Tell your partner about the details.**

Have you ever ...

- been caught by a ticket inspector while dodging the bus/tram fare or when you'd left your pass at home?
- travelled by plane?
- been involved in an accident?
- seen an accident?
- taken part in a package tour?
- been on a camping holiday?
- stayed at a real luxury hotel?

b **In groups of four, compare the pros and cons of the following pairs.**

	PROS	CONS
• coaches — trains	....	....
	....	....
	....	....
• having a car — not having a car	....	....
	....	....
	....	....
• package tours — camping holidays	....	....
	....	....
	....	....
• buses — trams	....	....
	....	....
	....	....
• automatic cars — traditional cars	....	....
	....	....
	....	....
• a holiday by the sea — a tour	....	....
	....	....
	....	....
	....	....

c Suppose the two of you had to explain to a foreigner how exactly the following things are done in Hungary. Make a list of the things you would say.

buying bus tickets ....

....

validating bus and underground tickets ....

....

expressing a wish to get off the bus ....

....

d Study the following notices (all found in metro stations and on buses and trams in Budapest), and help the poor Transport Authority (BKV) by correcting the mistakes (marked with the correction symbols in the text).

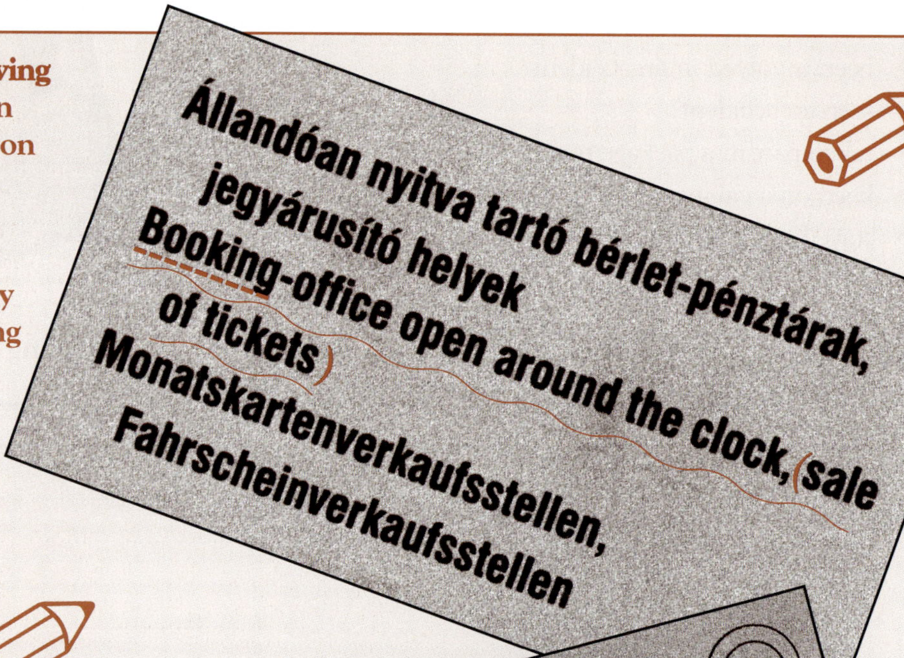

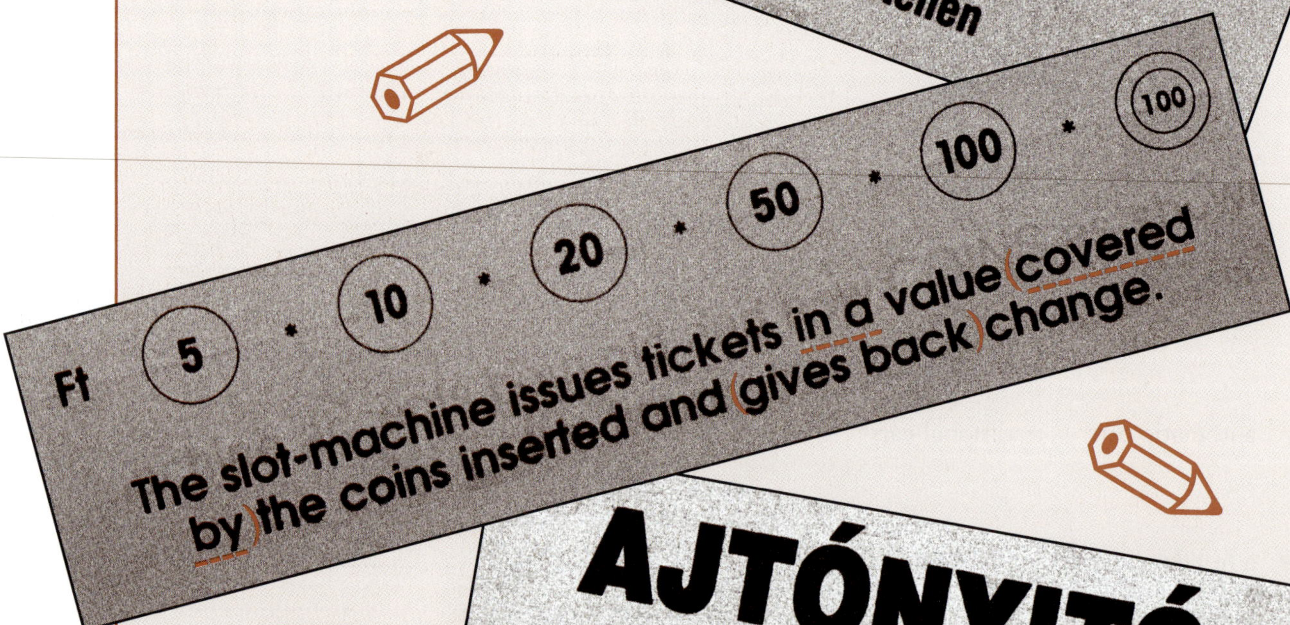

CHILDREN may travel free up to the age of six, above that age they can travel with a validated ticket or with a full price pass.

Attention! Passengers traveling without a valid ticket are to pay a fine.

You may find further information on the underground tickets and passes at the cashier's

We wish a pleasant journey !
Budapest Transport Limited

Information

Passengers who travel on a short distance or only change once on the underground can make use of the metro and the Millennium underground with a discount ticket **from July 1, 1996.** Depending on the type of their trip, passengers can choose from three types of tickets in addition to the single ticket which can further be used:

New types of metro tickets can be purchased in every ticket and pass selling office.

With these discount priced tickets we wish to reduce travel costs of passengers who do not possess season passes (or visitors of Budapest)

ESTE 8 UTÁN LESZÁLLÁSHOZ FÁRADJON AZ ELSŐ AJTÓHOZ

AFTER 8PM PLEASE USE FOR ALIGHTING THE FRONT DOOR

NACH 20 UHR STEIGEN SIE BITTE BEI DER VORDERTÜR AUS!

You can stay only with validated purchased ticket (in advance) or valid pass within the area of metro station behind the painted line. (Thank you for your attention.)

HOMEWORK

VOCABULARY survival kit preview

Read through the new vocabulary list on page 297-298, and consult a dictionary if you come across something that is unfamiliar or unclear to you.

EXAM TIPS

Time management

☞ The written exam

- There are only 30 minutes for the multiple choice test (and this is the only component of the written exam where the use of dictionaries is *not* allowed). Obviously, there's not much time to waste here.
- There are 3 hours for the rest of the written exam, and it is up to you in what order you do or how much time you want to devote to the different tasks.
- As for the order, perhaps the best policy is to get the tasks that you are more confident about over with, and leave yourself as much time as possible for the 'toughest' task.
- Normally there is not enough time to write a draft *and* a nice final version of anything at the exam. Make sure your handwriting in the first draft is reasonably neat and legible.
- Remember that the key factor in time management is dictionary use; on the one hand, it means *using the dictionary as little as possible*, and on the other hand it means *experience and skill in using it*.

☞ The oral exam

- There is no preparation time allowed here, but you will be given enough time to study the picture(s) and read through the role play task before starting. There is no need to hurry, but you shouldn't play for time either; read the task, spend 15–25 seconds thinking about the main points, and go right ahead.

UNIT 12 The world we live in

LESSON 1

VOCABULARY survival kit

Crime

Breaking the law: to commit a crime/an offence, a traffic offence, to be against the law/illegal, criminal, (young/juvenile) offender, culprit, gangster, thug, mafia

Theft & robbery: to steal/lift/pinch, car theft, thief, to rob (of), armed robbery, robber, to burgle, burglary, burglar, to break in, break-in, housebreaker, to hold up, holdup, stickup, mugging, mugger, shoplifting, shoplifter

Cheating: to deceive/cheat/trick sy, to con/swindle sy out of sg, conman/swindler, to be taken in, deception/fraud/con/swindle, to embezzle, to counterfeit/forge/fake, forgery, counterfeit /forged/ fake, to evade tax, tax evasion, to bribe sy, bribery, racketeering, drug abuse\trafficking\ dealer, prostitution, to extort, to blackmail, to libel, to smuggle

Violent crimes: to hijack, hijacking/hijack, hijacker, to kidnap/abduct, kidnapping/kidnap, kidnapper, terrorist, to assault, to attack, attacker, violence, to rape, rape, rapist, arson, arsonist, to kill, to murder, to assassinate, to eliminate, to liquidate, to slaughter, to do sy in, to stab, to poison, to shoot, to run over, to strangle, murderer, murderess, assassin, murder, manslaughter

Law enforcement:

The police: to investigate, investigation/inquiry/ inquest, to track down, detective, to (make an) arrest

The court: lawsuit, to sue, to charge sy with ..., to press charges against sy, case, to prosecute, judge, magistrate, jury, prosecution, lawyer, trial, hearing, defendant/the accused, plaintiff, witness, to testify/give evidence, to confess, to plead guilty

Punishment: to find sy guilty (of), to convict, to sentence sy to life\death\a term, capital punishment/ death penalty, to deter, deterrent, to acquit, to drop a case/charges, to appeal, the Criminal Code

The environment

The natural environment: the state of the environment, environmental protection, environmental hazard, (air\water\noise) pollution, waste dumping, landfill, to dispose of, disposal of hazardous waste, bottle bank, radioactive waste, (poisonous) emissions, car exhaust fumes, unleaded petrol, ozone layer, to recycle, recycling, environmentally (un)-friendly, global problems, green issues, environmentalist, ecological group, animal rights activist

Disasters: plane-crash, collision, derailment, fire/blaze, gas-leak, a broken water-main, explosion/blast, nuclear power station, industrial\ ecological disaster, destruction, volcanic eruption, earthquake, hurricane, famine

Social problems

Poverty: wealth, working\middle\upper class, the wage spectrum, living standards, inflation, price hikes, to be below the poverty line, social benefit, social inequality, the economic situation, homelessness, unemployment, invalidity, loneliness, alcoholism, an alcoholic, drug addiction, a drug addict , depression

Discrimination: the women's lib movement, women's libbers\rights, feminist, sexism, male chauvinism, to discriminate against, gender roles, division of labour, ethnic minorities\ problems, refugees

Politics

political system, (to win\lose the) election, to vote, party, (Smallholders\Socialist\Communist\ Labour\Conservative\Green Party, Christian\ Liberal\Young Democrats), left\right-wing, politicians, policy, government, Prime Minister, the President, Member of Parliament (MP), (Trade) Union, corruption, scandal, inefficiency

Religion

the church, denomination, sect, cult, religious, to believe in, faith, God, to go to church, service, mass, the Bible, to pray, prayer, priest, minister, the Pope, Roman Catholic, Protestant/Calvinist, Anglican, Christian, Jewish, Muslim/Moslem, Buddhist, Hindu, atheist, non-believer, religious education/RE

SPEAKING
conversation

Use the vocabulary list and the guidelines to talk to your partner about the following issues.

1. **Have you, or an acquaintance of yours ever been the victim of crime?** ➜ What exactly happened? ➜ What did you do? ➜ What sort of an ending does the story have?
2. **Do you feel threatened with crime in any way?** ➜ Do you ever have any fears in public places? Have you taken/Do you usually take any precautions against crime?
3. **Can you think of any major crimes that have happened recently?** ➜ What happened? Is the crime explicable in any way? What do you know about the police investigation? ➜ What sentence do you think the offender(s) would deserve?
4. **In what ways can you experience the pollution of the environment at first hand?** ➜ Air pollution? ➜ Water pollution? Noise pollution?
5. **Are there any social problems that affect you or your close environment? Do you think there are any social problems that are quite unlikely to ever affect you personally?** ➜ Unemployment? ➜ Invalidity (the state of being too ill to work)? ➜ Poverty? ➜ Homelessness? ➜ Loneliness?
6. **What do you think would be the results of the general election in Hungary if the event were held next Sunday?**

A

B

SPEAKING pictures

C

D

a **Discuss with the class what vocabulary you need to describe the pictures.**

	Verbs:	Nouns:	Adjectives:
A			
B			
C			
D			

b **Agree with three partners which one of you has picture A, B, C, and D, and take turns to describe what you can see in them, make guesses about the situation, and tell each other about the thoughts, feelings, memories, etc. they evoke in you.**

c **Take turns to say a few words about the subject of your pictures in general, viewing the contents from a wider – national or even global – perspective. The following questions might help you to come up with some ideas:**

- How widespread and/or important is the situation or phenomenon depicted in the picture? Is it characteristic of a particular area/social group/etc.?
- Do you think there's anything the individual should/could do about the problem?
- Is there anything that could/should be/have been done about the issue on a national/global level? (Apart from everybody's personal responsibility.)

You may find the following phrases useful here: This is a rather controversial issue/question/problem/subject, and ... ➾ This is one of the ... issues of our times, and ... ➾ This issue has been hotly debated for some time, and ... ➾ There has been a lot of (heated/fierce/intense) public debate on these issues, and ... ➾ The issue of ... has now become the focus of national/worldwide media attention, and ... ➾ ... has focussed public attention on ... ➾ It is very unfortunate/sad that ... ➾ Unless we/the government/etc. do something about this problem, ... will ... ➾ There are a number of things we could do about this problem ... ➾ The only thing we can do is to ... ➾ The only way out of this situation seems to be ...-ing ... ➾ The only solution to this problem seems to be ...-ing ... ➾ We are left with no choice, but to ... ➾ ... before it's too late. ➾ Generally speaking, ...

FUNCTIONS
role-play

a **Read both role-cards and agree with your partner who's A and who's B.**

A Ön civilruhás áruházi detektív egy angol város szupermarketjében. Feltűnik önnek egy nő/férfi, aki céltalanul sétálgat, de nem vesz semmit. Egyszer csak úgy látja, hogy az illető valamit a zsebébe tesz. Menjen oda hozzá, és ...

- közölje, hogy ön az áruházi detektív, és udvariasan kérje meg az illetőt, hogy kövesse önt az irodába.
- teljesítse a kérést, és mutassa meg az igazolványát.
- kérdezze meg, hogy az illetőnek mi a neve, honnan való, mit csinál Angliában, hol lakik, és mi dolga a szupermarketben.
- mondja el, hogy mit látott.
- kérje meg az illetőt, hogy bizonyítsa be, hogy igazat mond.
- nézzen meg mindent, és kérdezzen rá a bontatlan doboz cigaretta eredetére.
- vizsgálja meg a számlát, majd kérjen elnézést a zaklatásért. Magyarázza meg, hogy miért van szükség az ilyen vizsgálatokra. Kérje meg az illetőt, hogy fogadjon el egy üveg pezsgőt engesztelő ajándékként.

B Ön egy magyar turista, és egy angol város egyik szupermarketjében nézelődik, amikor váratlanul önhöz lép egy ember ...

- Kérje meg, hogy igazolja magát, majd teljesítse az illető kérését.
- Kérdezze meg, hogy mit óhajt.
- Adja meg a kért adatokat.
- Felháborodva tiltakozzon a gyanúsítás ellen.
- Ajánlja fel, hogy megmutatja, mi van a táskájában és a zsebeiben.
- Mondja meg, hogy a kérdéses árut egy másik boltban vette, és ezt számlával is tudja igazolni.
- Kis keresgélés után mutassa meg a számlát.
- Mondja azt, hogy nem történt semmi, de az ajánlatot utasítsa vissza.

b Try and agree with the rest of your class what phrases you could use in this situation.

c Rehearse the situation in pairs.

HOMEWORK

VOCABULARY survival kit

study task

Study the word list on page 297-298, and memorise the words and phrases. When you have finished, put the following words in their correct places in the passage below to check your knowledge. (You might try and do the task without using the box.)

environment, religious, political, banks, rape, Lib, ozone, denomination, noise, attacked, services, crimes, unleaded, pollution, politics, believe, mugging, offences, recycled, violent, politicians, burgled, discriminated, church, Member of Parliament, party, stolen, government, attackers

Ms Britain

While only 12 per cent of the British population regularly attend religious ...., nearly three-quarters say they .... in God. Women remain the main supporters of the .... with almost one in six belonging to a .... or some kind of a .... group in their neighbourhood.

The British are not particularly interested in their ....; more than half of them do not know the name of their local ...., and a high proportion do not even know the names of the .... ministers or .... leaders. Only 3 per cent of British women belong to .... parties and about 20 per cent say they have no interest in ....

Despite the efforts of the Women's .... Movement, British women are still .... against in the world of labour, they are paid less than men on average: 33 per cent of women earn under £190 a week, compared with 13 per cent of men; 75 per cent of men earn £230 a week compared with 50 per cent of women.

Women fear crimes against their homes more than being .... Almost a third of women worry that their homes will be ...., making this the most feared crime. Almost 20 per cent felt very, or fairly, unsafe when they were at home alone at night compared with 4 per cent of men. Fear of .... afflicts younger women most. Almost 40 per cent of women aged 16 to 29 fear rape. Older women are less worried about most ...., but more scared of being mugged. A third of women over 60 worry about .... Almost 90 per cent of women who suffer .... crime know their ...., if only by sight. Men worry less about crime. Their greatest fear is that their cars will be ....

Street Crime in London

In 1994 in London 33,000 street crimes were reported out of 837,000 crimes. That's about 4 per cent. Fraud and forgery accounted for as many .... and much more money, and five times more car crime and burglaries were reported, than muggings.

Greener Grass of Home

Concern about the .... is growing but more motorists still use leaded petrol than .... However, more than two-thirds of people claim they now use ....-friendly aerosols; bottle .... increased ten-fold in the Eighties; and the amount of glass .... doubled between 1984 and 1989. Public anxiety about .... is also rising. One-third of complaints in the mid-Eighties were about barking dogs and another third about loud music.

One in three cases of water .... is caused by industry, and 11 per cent by farms.

GRAMMAR FOCUS
p r e v i e w
Gerund or Infinitive

Some verbs can either take the Gerund or the Infinitive.

1. With certain verbs there's no difference in the meaning at all:

to begin, to start, to continue, to have the opportunity/chance of ...ing/to ...

➢ *I started playing/to play the piano when I was five. I didn't have the chance to talk/of talking to her yesterday.*

2. With certain verbs there may be a slight difference in the meaning:

to love, to hate, to prefer

can be used with both, but the *Infinitive* is used when they stand with *would*, or you refer to a particular situation.

➢ *I love to lie/lying in the sun. I hate writing/to write letters. I prefer taking/to take sugar in my tea. I'd love to/hate to/prefer to go home now.*

to like

The *Gerund* is used when we mean *'to enjoy doing'* (however, in American English, the *Infinitive* is also possible here), and the *Infinitive* is used with would and when the meaning is *'to think it is the right thing to do'*, *'to prefer to'*, *'to be in the habit of'*.

➢ *I like driving fast cars. (US: I like to drive fast cars.) I like to get up in time, you know I hate hurrying/ to hurry.*

3. With certain verbs the meaning will be completely different:

to stop

+ *-ing* = to end an activity
 ➢ *Will you please stop smiling?*
+ *to do* = to have a break in order to do sg
 ➢ *Let's stop to have a little rest*

to remember

+ *-ing* = to remember a past event
 ➢ *I can still remember writing down the first sentence of this book.*
+ *ing* = to remember sg you have to do
 ➢ *Did you remember to switch off the light?*

to forget

+ *-ing* = to forget a past event
 ➢ *I'll never forget meeting you for the first time.*
+ *to do* = to forget what you have to do
 ➢ *Don't forget to switch off the light.*

to go on

+ *-ing* = to continue an activity
 ➢ *Just go on reading.*
+ *to do* = to stop an activity and start a new one
 ➢ *He did the test and then went on to do the translation.*

to regret

+ *-ing* = to be sorry for a past event
 ➢ *I don't regret buying this car.*
+ to do = to be sorry for what you're going to say
 ➢ *I regret to tell you this, but I just crashed the car.*

to try

+ *-ing* = to experiment with another 'technique', to try sg new/different to see if it works
 ➢ *I even tried adding some sugar, but it is still not the right taste.*
+ *to do* = to make an attempt, to see whether you can do sg
 ➢ *He tried to fool me, but I wasn't born yesterday.*

to mean

+ by + *-ing* = to try to say sg, to hint at sg
 ➢ *What do you mean by getting up early? 6 o'clock?*
+ *to do* = to do sg on purpose/deliberately
 ➢ *I didn't mean to hurt you.*

to be sorry

+ for + *-ing* = + *that*-clause = + *to have done* = to apologise for a past event
 ➢ *I'm sorry for giving/that I gave/to have given you so much work with those letters.*
+ *to do* = to apologise for sg you are doing, or sg you are going to do
 ➢ *Sorry to disturb you, …*

to propose

(+ *-ing* = to intend, to suggest *[quite rare]*
 ➢ *How do they propose paying us for this job, I wonder? The boss proposed employing another secretary.*)
+ *to do* = to intend
 ➢ *How do they propose to pay us for this job, I wonder?*
+ *that sy should* clause = to suggest
 ➢ *I proposed that they should get married as soon as possible.*

4. With certain verbs there's a grammatical reason for using the *Gerund* or the *Infinitive*:

to allow, to advise, to forbid, to permit, to recommend, to encourage

We use the *Gerund* when we say who the verb refers to, but we use the *Infinitive* when there's no personal object.
 ➢ *We don't allow smoking in this school. We don't allow students to smoke in this school.*

to suggest

If the suggestion also refers to the person who is making the suggestion, the *Gerund* is normally used. If it does not, the *(that) sy (should)* structure is used.
 ➢ *I suggest going to the cinema. I suggest (that) you (should) go to the cinema.*

to see, to hear, to watch, to feel

These verbs take the *Infinitive without to* if we observe a whole action (however, after passive forms of *see* and *hear*, *to* is used with the Infinitive), and take the *Gerund* if we just observe a part of the action.
 ➢ *I saw him copy off his neighbour.* (I don't just think he did that, I saw it.) *He was seen to copy off his neighbour. I saw him copying off his neighbour.* (When I looked at him, he was doing that.)

The Participle

1. The **Present Participle** has the same form as the *Gerund*, but its function in the sentence is quite different; in addition to a number of other uses, it can be an adjective or it can introduce a clause.

a) The Present Participle as an adjective

If it a single word, the *Present Participle* usually comes before the noun (a kind of a standard characteristic), but when it has a compliment of its own, the phrase stands after the noun. (the action is more important)

➢ *a smiling face, a worrying problem, the rising prices, The guy sitting next to my wife is my boss. There was a big limousine waiting for us at the gate. Most of the people participating were black.*

b) The Present Participle introducing a clause
We can use the Present Participle ...

for one of two actions when they happen at the same time

➢ *She was standing at the window looking at the traffic down in the street.*

when one action happens during another

➢ *They had an accident (when/while) coming home from the disco.*

when one action happens before another one (We can use the *Present* if the second action happens immediately after the first; otherwise the *Perfect* is used.)

➢ *Having graduated from university, I started working at a secondary school. (After) finishing the test, I started to do the translation. Looking into the rear-view mirror, he pulled out and overtook the lorry in front of us.*

to give an explanation of why sg happened

➢ *Being a teacher, I simply can't afford to buy books. Not knowing she was married, I asked her to go out on a date with me. Having drunk the glasses of whisky, I decided to leave the car outside the restaurant and take a taxi.*

2. The **Past Participle** is the third form of the verb *(done)*. It has a passive meaning, and, besides a number of other uses, it can be used **as an adjective and to introduce a clause.**

a) Quite like the *Present Participle*, the *Past Participle* usually comes before the noun if it is a single word, but when it has a compliment of its own, the phrase stands after the noun.

➢ *stolen cars, a disputed issue, 80 per cent of all cars stolen in Hungary are never found. There was a parking ticket stuck behind the windscreen wiper. The majority of the people questioned objected to the idea.*

b) We can use the Past Participle ...

for one of two actions when they happen at the same time

➢ *Asked to describe her feelings, she said: "I'm absolutely devastated." Given the chance, I like to swim every morning. He entered the studio accompanied by four beautiful girls. Richard Wagner did his best work while dressed in flamboyant costumes.*

to give an explanation of why sg happened

➢ *Deeply hurt, she just went red and left the room.*

to shorten if clauses

➢ *If asked, I will say no to the proposal. If rejected, I would do it on my own.*

☞ **If the subject of the Participle and the main clause is different, the subject of the Participle comes immediately before it.**

➢ *The traffic being very heavy, we decided to go on foot.*

LESSON 2

VOCABULARY survival kit checkpoint

a **Check the fill-in-the-blank homework task with the rest of the class.**

b **Explain what the following people do to deserve their names.**

- criminals
- shoplifters
- forgers
- blackmailers
- assassins
- arsonists
- hijackers
- judges
- lawyers
- the jury
- prosecutors
- witnesses
- environmentalists
- women's libbers
- male chauvinists
- animal rights activists
- Members of Parliament
- the Pope

c **What are the corresponding words and phrases with a similar meaning?**

a crime	→	**an o**.....
to steal	→	**to p**....
holdup	→	**s**......
to cheat	→	**to d**......
conman	→	**s**.......
to abduct	→	**to k**.....
to murder	→	**to a**.........
inquiry	→	**i**..........
the accused	→	**d**........
judge	→	**m**..........
to find guilty	→	**to c**......
death penalty	→	**c**...... ....
non-believer	→	**a**......
minister	→	**p**.....

d **Use the words in the box to fill in the gaps in the newspaper article.**

charged, deception, swindling, investigators, false, prosecutor, suspicious, honest

Case closed

London, England – "If he is an .... traveller, he must be a very unfortunate one indeed" said a .... after a man was .... with .... $150,000 from airline insurance companies. Alak Krishnan, 43, says he lost at least one suitcase every time he flew abroad for two years, and on one trip from London to India he insured his baggage with various companies and used .... addresses. Three of his suitcases "went missing" on that trip and insurance .... became ...., but Mr Krishnan has denied .... charges despite claiming the loss of 36 suits, 86 shirts, 57 pairs of trousers, 10 leather jackets, seven pairs of binoculars and dozens of cameras, camcorders and laptop computers.

e **Complete the definitions.**

- A very rough and violent person (usually a criminal) is a ....
- .... steal money from their employers by falsifying accounts.
- Something that makes people less likely to commit something bad is a ....
- If a defendant is .... of a crime, the court decides that they are not guilty of it.
- People who live in .... are very poor.
- People who have been forced to leave their country are ....
- A .... is a religious group that is part of a larger religious organisation.
- A .... is an accident when a train goes off the railway line.
- An .... is a sudden shaking of the surface of our planet that often causes a lot of damage.

GRAMMAR FOCUS

translation into English

Gerund or Infinitive?, the Participles

Translate the following sentences into English, discussing each section with the rest of the class as you progress.

❶ Vigyél egy esernyőt, hátha elkezd esni. *(in case)* Szeretek egy kis pénzt magamnál tartani, hátha látok valami érdekeset a városban. *(in town)* A barátaim azt mondják, hogy nem vagyok normális; szeretek szótárakat olvasni. *(to be in sy's right mind/out of sy's mind)* Szeretnék valamit tisztázni; én nős vagyok, és van két gyerekem. *(to make sg clear)* Utálok korán kelni.

❷ Hazafelé megálltunk, hogy vegyünk valami ennivalót. *(on the way home)* Hagyd abba a panaszkodást, és kezdj el dolgozni. Ne felejtsd el átolvasni a fordítást mielőtt beadod. *(to read through; to hand sg in)* Tisztán emlékszem, hogy azt mondtam neki, hogy a határidő szerda. *(deadline)* Mindig csak rád gondolok; valahányszor megpróbálok elaludni, az arcodat látom, és annyi. *(whenever/every time; that's that)* Nem tudom, mit tegyek, már próbáltam altatót is szedni, de nem használt. Bocsánat, nem akartam beleszólni, de egyszerűen nem tudtam megállni. *(to interfere; can't help it)* Bocs, hogy beleszólok, de azt hiszem nincs igazad.

❸ Az új KRESZ nem engedi meg a mobiltelefon használatát vezetés közben. *(Highway Code; mobile phone)* Soha nem engedném, hogy a gyerekeim ilyen helyekre járjanak. Azt javaslom, hogy menjünk oda együtt, így nem lesz olyan kínos. Azt javasoltam a tanítványaimnak, hogy ismételjék át a nyelvtant vizsga előtt. *(to review)* Legalább négy ember látta, hogy megütötte a gyereket. Láttuk, hogy a Trabant megpróbálja megelőzni a Volvot, de semmi esélye nem volt.

....

....

....

❹ Az ágyában feküdt, és nagyon gyengének és elesettnek látszott. *(helpless)* Miután befejeztem a mosogatást, nekiláttam a takarításnak. *(to set about)* Megérkezvén a repülőtérre, azonnal felhívtam a barátomat telefonon. Mivel elfogyott a whisky, be kellett érnünk sörrel. *(to run out [of]; to make do with)* Mivel még csak 5 éves, a nyelvtanulás számára semmilyen erőfeszítést nem jelent. *(to require some effort from sy)* Mivel az idő nagyon meleg volt, rövidnadrágot vettem. A legtöbb diák, aki a tanfolyamra járt tizenéves volt. Az az aranyos hölgy, aki a kép jobb szélén ül, az anyósom.

....

....

....

....

....

....

....

❺ Amikor megkérdezték tőle, hogy akar-e valamit hozzátenni, csak annyit mondott, hogy “nem”. Bob Dylan legtöbb 60-as években írt dala sláger lett. A felmérés, amelyet Európa hat országában végeztek, érdekes dolgokra derített fényt.

....

....

....

L I S T E N I N G

Criminal elements

Interview with a police officer

a Read the question, and try to answer it after you have listened to the recording once. Discuss your answer with your partner.

- What does the police officer say the typical criminal is like today?

b Answer the following questions as you listen to the tape for the second time. Discuss your answers with the rest of the class.

- What does the officer say about violence?
- What was particularly unusual about the crime the officer talks about?
- What information does the officer give about the place where the man commited the crime?

- When did it all happen?
- Who were the victims?
- What did the offender do in the bedroom?
- What did he do in the kitchen?
- What was it that woke the occupants of the flat eventually?
- What happened then?
- Why was it relatively easy for the police to catch the man?
- What sort of punishment is the offender likely to get according to the officer?

HOMEWORK

TRANSLATION

English into Hungarian

Use a dictionary to translate the following article into Hungarian.

FORGET YOUR MANNERS IF YOU'RE GETTING MUGGED

On Oct. 7, I was about to board a nearly empty car on the yellow line at Hősök tere when a young man in a jogging suit pointed in the direction I was going and asked simply, "Oktogon?" I tellingly answered in an English/Hungarian mixture and boarded the car, closely followed by my questioner. I immediately found myself in a rush-hour vise, surrounded by approximately six young people, including at least one woman. But over their shoulders, I could see that the rest of the car was wide open. I tried to move toward the open space, but they were passively unyielding.

I placed my hand on my wallet pocket and tightened my grip on the bag I was carrying. Fortunately, the train doors were still open, and only one gang member stood between me and the empty platform. So I pushed out onto the platform and safety. Instead of leaving the station, I defiantly (and perhaps foolishly) stepped back into the car through the adjacent door, which was still open. The frustrated gang was still bunched together at the other end of the car. Their prey gone, they walked out the still open door, and the train finally left the station.

So be wary on the yellow line. Study the people waiting to board and suspect any predominantly male group from 18 to 28 years of age. Be particularly careful if one engages you in conversation. Hungarians are very courteous, so if you find yourself being squeezed, you are in trouble. If you can't extricate yourself from the situation, you might yell. If you remain polite, you are probably going to be robbed.

Kenneth Janda

Letter to the Editor, The Budapest Sun

LESSON 3

TRANSLATION
English into Hungarian
checkpoint

Forget Your Manners If You Are Getting Mugged

a **What kind of translations have the different people in the class come up with for the following words and phrases in the context of the passage?**

- forget your manners
- I tellingly answered in an English/Hungarian mixture
- closely followed by my questioner
- I immediately found myself in a rush hour vise
- they were passively unyielding
- they prey gone
- if one engages you in conversation
- if you find yourself being squeezed

b **Compare and discuss the possible translations for each and every sentence with the whole class.**

c **Choose three new words or phrases from the text that you think are worth remembering.**

READING & VOCABULARY
a r t i c l e

a **You are going to read an article about a survey into the opinions of young western European people. Before reading the article, make guesses to tick (✓) one box for each of the following findings. When you have finished, compare your guesses in pairs before reading the article to check your guesses.**

THE COUNTRY OR ITS PEOPLE	Germany	Italy	Britain	France	Holland	Spain	Sweden
consider environmental issues as important							
has the prettiest women							
has the most handsome men							
has the most exciting night life							
has the best TV programmes and rock concerts							
are serious people							
have the best sense of humour							
are most tolerant of extra marital affairs							
are the least worried about anything							
has the best public health service							
accept hitting children as a method of education							

A youthful image of Europe

An MTV survey, carried out by American research company "Yankelovich Partners Inc.", has revealed that Europe's best looking men *and* women are Italian. The Germans may have their supermark, the Dutch their green politics, and the British their sense of humour, but as far as good looks and charm are concerned they are left standing.

The survey questioned over 3,000 people from nine European countries. The subjects, aged between 16 to 34, were interviewed on a range of topics, among them social politics, lifestyle, and prospects for the future.

Young Italians are the keenest on further European integration: nearly 90% are in favour of a United States of Europe, while the average for most other nationalities was 65%. The British and the Swedish were the least in favour.

The Germans are seen by their peers as more sensitive to problems of the environment, and Germany appears also to be the country where extra-marital affairs are most tolerated.

The Dutch are defined as "serious people" and the Swedish come first for their public health service. They are also rated as being "impulsive". The Spanish nightlife gets a special mention as do its beautiful women.

The British win a price for the best TV programs and rock concerts and are considered a somewhat "laid back" race. They are alone, however, in supporting smacks and slaps as part of a healthy method of education.

The survey also revealed that a good part of the younger generation spends seven hours a day watching TV and listening to the radio or their favourite music. Only 38% read a daily newspaper – but 68% regularly buy a weekly magazine of some sort.

The nightmare of AIDS is first among the worries of this age-group, followed by unemployment and environmental problems. 57% think that their future looks bright, but a large proportion predict a hard life for babies being born today. The majority of young Europeans say they have a strong desire to work, and want jobs which satisfy rather than pay well. 63% want to study or work in another country in Europe.

Overall, Europe's youth is considered to have a sense of responsibility and social conscience: large numbers talk about wanting equal rights for ethnic and religious minorities; an average of 78% recognize a woman's right to abortion, and 95% say a fundamental value is being able to rely on friends.

The questions now being asked are the following: Is Europe's youth just young and naively idealistic? Or will its values remain as laudable as it gets older and moves into positions of power? There's plenty that could be changed in Europe: let's hope our youth has the guts and skills to do it.

Europa Times

b Now try and find the words and phrases for the following definitions in the text, and make guesses about the possible derivatives. When you have finished, discuss them with the rest of the class.

hits made with the palm of the hand in order to punish kids ⇒ to hit a kid ~ ⇒ the practice of ~

....

hits made with the palm of the hand ⇒ to hit sy ~

....

a part of a larger amount or number

....

to say that an event or action will happen, or that it will happen in a particular way ⇒ the act of saying what you think is going to happen, or something you say is going to happen

....

specialised in finding information about a particular subject ⇒ the activity of ~ ⇒ people whose job is to ~

....

something horrible that you fear might happen in the future

....

to be able to understand other people's feelings ⇒ the ability to ~

....

to describe sg correctly and thorougly ⇒ a sentence that says exactly what sg means

....

to trust sy or sg always to act, behave or happen in the way that you want them to

....

the chances of being successful in your career

....

on the whole, generally speaking

....

basic, essential, very important

....

a number of different things of the same general type

....

to be considered to have a particular quality or value ⇒ top quality

....

to be brave enough to do sg

....

a people or a nation

....

to accept and admit (that sy has the right to do sg)

....

deserving praise and appreciation

....

tending to do things suddenly without thinking about them carefully first

....

a moral sense of what our society should be like

....

to be by far worse than sy else

....

calm, relaxed, not worried about anything

....

someone of the same age, social class, etc. as you

....

c Now read the following questions, and answer them in writing after reading the article again. When you have finished, discuss the answers with the rest of the class.

What's the survey all about?

....

What's the subjects' attitude to the European integration?

....

What did the survey reveal about the subjects' habits concerning watching TV?

....

What are they most afraid of?

....

What do they think about the future?

....

What's their attitude to work?

....

What do they think about social issues?

....

What sort of doubts does the article raise about Europe's youth?

....

HOMEWORK

VOCABULARY

article

study tasks

A Youthful Image of Europe

a Read the article again, and memorise any vocabulary items that are new to you. When you have finished, use the words in the box to fill in the gaps in the passage below. Change the form of the words if necessary.

tolerant
laid back
smacking
to rate
to satisfy
minorities
image
impulsive
to rely
value
laudably
overall

"What are Hungarians like?" Being a British expatriate, this is one of the questions I am most frequently asked by my fellow countrymen and Hungarians alike.

Having lived in this country for the past six years of my life, I think by now I have quite a clear .... of the characteristic features, ..., desires and fears of Hungarians. You will not be surprised that these do not greatly differ from those of the nations of the European Union, but, still, there are some marked differences in the finer points.

First and foremost, I'm sure Hungarian women .... as one of the most .... women in Europe, and I don't just mean good looks; they are also a lot more friendly and open than their Western European counterparts. On the other hand, however, I'm not so sure about the men, and not just because I'm a man myself and I'm less .... to this, but also because I think they either tend to neglect their appearance, or, quite on the contrary, overdo it with all those conspicuous clothes, jewellery, and perfume.

Hungarians have a strong .... to work, but they want jobs that pay well rather than .... As for social ...., in theory they .... support equal rights for ethnic and religious ...., but when it comes to particular groups like the gypsies, or Jehovah's Witnesses, they seem to be much less .... Most of them .... a woman's right to abortion, but the vast majority are in favour of the death sentence. They are fairly tolerant to extra-marital ...., unless it's their partner who is involved in one. In such cases their normally .... attitude may change into rather

.... behaviour. At the same time, however, they are strongly against .... at school. They work a lot and they spend most of their limited spare time watching TV. Very few of them read quality newspapers, and it seems as if women read more than men; women's magazines are extremely popular.

The .... of poverty is first among the worries of Hungarians, followed by unemployment and loneliness. A large .... are disillusioned and rather pessimistic about the country's .... for the future, but, on the other hand, they are firmly convinced that Hungarians are an extremely talented race. I'd say that Hungarians are a bit introverted and preoccupied with their own problems and they prefer to .... on themselves. They do not seem to really believe that they could have an influence on the world around them, and, as a result, they are not particularly interested in general social issues and community affairs.

........................, I think Hungarians are quite like any Western European nation, except that they are less confident, and that they have to put a lot more effort into making a decent living.

prospects
attractive
affair
proportion
consciousness
sensitive
desire
to recognise
nightmare

b Prepare to summarise the article about the survey in a few sentences.

WRITING
composition

Follow the guidelines below to write down your thoughts about the growing crime rate in Hungary in 17–20 lines. Pay special attention to the integrity of your composition making sure there is always a link between the different parts of your writing.

1. Írja le, hogy ön szerint mennyire súlyos a helyzet.
2. Említsen meg egy-két bűncselekmény-fajtát, amelyek különösen elterjedtek (autólopás, lakásbetörés, utcai rablás, csalás stb.).
3. Írja le, hogy önt hogyan érinti ez a helyzet (írjon le példaként egy konkrét esetet, ha a környezetében történt valamilyen bűncselekmény, vagy írja le, hogy ön fél-e valamitől).
4. Soroljon fel néhány okot, amelyek a jelenlegi állapotok kialakulásához vezethettek (az életszínvonal romlása, társadalmi különbségek, nagyobb egyéni szabadság, a rendőrség tehetetlensége, pénzhiány, erkölcsi válság stb.).
5. Mondja el, hogy ön szerint mit lehetne/kellene tenni, hogy a helyzet javuljon (a szegénység és az egyenlőtlenségek csökkentése, több pénz a bűnüldözésre stb.).

☞ When you have finished, don't forget to check your work for grammatical mistakes.

LESSON 4

VOCABULARY
article
checkpoint

A Youthful Image of Europe

a Compare your solutions to the fill-in-the-gap homework task with the rest of the class.

b Discuss with the rest of the class what you think the English would be for the following Hungarian sentences.

Rossz modora ellenére valójában ő egy nagyon érzékeny ember.

....

Senki sem tudta volna tíz évvel ezelőtt megjósolni, hogy mi fog történni ebben az országban a kilencvenes évekven.

....

....

Alapvető különbség van a vágyaim és a realitások között.

....

Ezek az új lemezboltok rendkívül széles kínálatot nyújtanak rockzenei CD-kből, de sajnos nevetségesen drágák.

....

....

Csodálom, hogy olyan nyugis vagy; azt hiszem én sohasem fogok megszabadulni a lobbanékonyságomtól.

....

....

Magyarországot a legelső olyan közép-európai országok közé sorolják, amelyek az Európai Unió tagjaivá válhatnak.

....

....

Saját magát átlagosnak tartja, de legtöbb társa az osztály szóvivőjeként ismeri el.

....

c Working in pairs, give a brief summary of the article we read last lesson.

GRAMMAR FOCUS
m i n i t e s t

Gerund or Infinitive?, the Participles

Do the following test, and check it with the rest of the class.

1. I shall never forget ... the first item of my collection.
A to buy **C** to be buying
B to have bought **D** buying

2. Did you remember ... your address in the top right-hand corner of the letter?
A to write **C** to have written
B having written **D** writing

3. Although I'd told him to get lost, he just went on ... indecent proposals.
A to making **C** making
B to make **D** having made

4. If you can't find a word in the Országh dictionary, ... a good monolingual dictionary.
A try to use **C** try using
B you'd better to use **D** you'd rather use

5. All his colleagues encouraged ... for the post of headmaster.
A him to apply **C** him applying
B to apply **D** applying

6. At least three independent witnesses saw the guy ... the scene of the crime.
A to leave **C** to have left
B leave **D** left

7. The majority of the ... for admission to this college want to be businessmen.
A applying students **C** students applying
B students applied **D** applied students

8. ... in a situation like this before, I knew I had better not say a word.
A I had been **C** I being
B Been **D** Having been

9. ... out of order again, we had no choice but walk it.
A Being **C** Having been
B The lift being **D** Being the lift

10. She was lovely as usual with her blond hair ... back in a pony tail.
A tied **C** tying
B being tied **D** having tied

SPEAKING
discussion

a Read the following short articles, and, in small groups, try to agree on the punishment (replaced with dots in the articles) you think the offenders would deserve for doing the things they did. When you have finished, compare your judgement with the original verdicts (see footnotes).

Yazd, Iran – An uncompromising judge ordered a convicted burglar ....**2** . Nikun Thakur, 36, admitted the crime and accepted the punishment because he wanted to keep his job as a basket salesman.

(WWN)

Barcelona, Spain – 46-year old Manolo Ramos may face ....**1** after paying children to chew gum and spit it out on the pavement outside his competitor's restaurant. For months, say police, Ramos had bribed kids to spit their gum outside the Happy Duck Restaurant, two doors along from his own restaurant.

(*Periodico Extramadura*)

New York – A Brooklyn man was convicted yesterday by a Queens jury for his role in a stickup of a Roy Rogers fast-food restaurant that left a former U.S. Marine paralyzed when he was shot while trying to stop the robbery, authorities said.

Willie (Supreme) Brown, 27, of 480 Amboy St., was convicted of attempted murder, robbery, burglary and assault and faces ....**3** when he is sentenced on Oct. 18, said Queens District Attorney Richard Black.

Black was arrested in November, 1995, based on information received by detectives, authorities said. Brown's accomplice remains at large, authorities said.

(*Reuters*)

1 ... two months in jail and a US$1,500 fine ...

2 ... to walk on his knees for the next 14 months. If he is seen to be standing, he faces 8 years in prison ...

3 ... faces up to 25 years in prison ...

b What's your opinion about the following statements? Think of some reasons to support your view and then compare your ideas with your partner's.

1. "Unemployed people only have themselves to blame for their problems; if someone really wants to find a job in this country, they will."

2. "The Women's Lib Movement has quite a lot left to do in Hungary, too."
3. "Religious education should be compulsory in all schools."
4. "There's not much the ordinary citizen can do for the protection of the environment."
5. "Political parties claim to be giving priority to the interest of our country. Unfortunately, however, they never seem to take my interests into account. Apparently my interests do not seem to coincide with the interests of my homeland."

c In groups of three or four, collect arguments both for and against the institution of capital punishment, and then compare your lists with the rest of the class. When you have finished, come to a class decision by voting on the issue.

HOMEWORK

EXAM TIPS

Exam manners

☞ You are certainly not assessed on the basis of your manners at the exam, but ... good manners are just as important here as anywhere else – particularly if you are not outstandingly good at English.

Interestingly enough, examiners like clever, modest, friendly and well-behaved candidates, who look them in the eye. For some reason, very few of them like ...

- aggressive, self-important, pompous, loud-mouthed candidates who think they can fool them, or
- painfully shy, oversensitive, unwilling ones who take the exam as an insult.

There are, of course, no written rules that say how you should be dressed at an exam like this (the oral exam, of course), but the unwritten rules might be important, if only to create a favourable impression (or an unfavourable one, for that matter). Examiners are only human (believe or not), and they might subconsciously be influenced by what they see. Just to be on the safe side, you'd better avoid ...

- clothes and accessories that divide the public anyway (very short skirts, nose-rings, etc.).
- very informal clothes (shorts, vests, gym-shoes, etc.).
- far too formal clothes (after all, it's not a wedding).
- very conspicuous or expensive things.

In other words, you should not be dressed to kill, but your outfit should somehow reflect that the exam is a somewhat special occasion, and you consider it as important.

Just forget chewing gum, mobile phones, mascots, food and drink, and very strong perfumes at the oral exam.

Do not forget that you are supposed to speak English all through the exam.

REVISION Test 3

A

Do the following multiple choice test, and when you have finished, discuss it with the rest of the class.

1. The family ... live next door to us have four large dogs ... bark all day.
- **A** what // who
- **B** which // what
- **C** that // that
- **D** who // —

2. Women have a wonderful sense of right and wrong, but ... sense of right and left.
- **A** little
- **B** a few
- **C** a little
- **D** few

3. My other neighbour has a son ... practises the trumpet every afternoon ... is pretty nerve-racking.
- **A**, who // , which
- **B** that // what
- **C** who // what
- **D** which // that

4. You'll have to go now, ... you'll miss the bus.
- **A** else
- **B** otherwise
- **C** however
- **D** because

5. He did his best ... as convincing as possible, but it was obvious that he wasn't used ... to such an unsympathetic audience.
- **A** sounding // speak
- **B** sound // to speak
- **C** to sounding // speaking
- **D** to sound // to speaking

6. Needless to say, he forgot about the whole thing ... we expected.
- **A** as just
- **B** exactly
- **C** just as
- **D** just

7. He claims ... the money back in January, but he is unable ... a receipt ... that he really did so.
- **A** to pay // to produce // proving
- **B** to have paid // to produce // to prove
- **C** that he paid // producing // to prove
- **D** he paid // to produce // to have proved

8. We were left with no choice but wait there ... the performance was over.
A during
B while
C as long as
D until

9. They are highly unlikely ... all about the party; they may just be having difficulty ... the address.
A to forget // to find
B to have forgotten // to find
C to have forgotten // finding
D to forget // in finding

10. We must pay the full price, ... ?
A don't we
B mustn't we
C needn't we
D aren't we

11. There's nothing that could ... the windows; I'd sooner ..., even if I had to pay a lot of money.
A make me clean // have it done
B have me cleaned // get someone to do it
C make me to clean // have it do
D get me clean // make someone do it

12. I am a very clever little boy, ...?
A aren't I
B don't I?
C isn't I?
D amn't I?

13. "Don't you think that that guy ... the blue baseball cap is behaving rather suspiciously?" "Yeah, I saw him … something in his pocket a minute ago."
A wearing // to put
B is wearing // putting
C wearing // put
D who is wearing // to have put

14. We talked very ... : you know long distance calls are extremely expensive.
A short time
B briefly
C shortly
D hardly

15. "It's pretty late, we ... home now." "Oh, come on, the party's in full swing, I'm enjoying myself, so I ... , if you don't mind."
A had better go // would rather not go
B would better go // would rather we didn't go
C had better to go // had rather not go
D better go // rather wouldn't go

16. ... going to English evening classes twice a week I also take driving lessons every morning.
A Beside
B Plus
C Not only
D Besides

17. "Do you mind if I ... your car tonight?" "Not at all, it's all yours, but remember that both the oil and the tyres need ... ."
A borrowed // to check
B borrow // checking
C borrowing // to check
D am borrowing // checked

18. "How many 'ones' have you got this term?" " ..."
A Any.
B None.
C No.
D No one.

19. He made it clear that he objected ... so much money on such things; I really don't think ... him again.

A to spending // there's any point in asking
B spending // there's any use asking
C to spend // it's any point asking
D to spend // it's worth to ask

20. You know my brother is quite different, he's more ... my father.

A as
B so
C like
D than

21. This new English teacher is so funny that everything ... he does makes the whole class ... .

A that // to laugh
B what // laugh
C — // laugh
D what // laughing

22. What's the trouble with you? You look almost ... drunk.

A as if you were
B like you are
C although you are
D as though

23. Peter suggested ... my car ... in that garage because their prices are the highest in town.

A me not to have // to service
B that I shouldn't have // serviced
C not having // servicing
D me not having // service

24. ... understands what's going on in this country.

A Not anybody
B Hardly somebody
C Hardly anybody
D Hardly nobody

25. It was in England ... we first met. I was feeling lonely and I was so glad ... someone ... .

A that // to have // to talk to
B where // that I had // to talk
C when // to have // talking
D where // having // to talk to

26. Alice doesn't live here ...

A more.
B longer.
C no longer.
D any more

27. This is the best restaurant ... I've heard of in Budapest; it is not only said ... elegant, but reasonably cheap, too.

A what // that it's
B which // to be
C — // being
D that // to be

28. I've been in bed with the flu ...

A for the last week.
B last week.
C on the last week.
D during last week

29. As I can't afford ... my thesis ... , I'll try ... my girlfriend ... it for me.

A to get // to be typed // having // typed
B to have // typed // to get // to type
C having // typed // and get // type
D to get // to type // to make // to type

30. Nobody phoned while I was away, ...

A did it?
B did anyone?
C did they?
D did he?

31. Even though it was obvious that he didn't particularly enjoy ... like this, he just kept ... .

A to be questioned // on smiling
B to be questioning // to smiling
C being questioned // smiling
D questioning // on to smile

32. Somebody has helped you do the homework, ...

A hasn't they?
B hasn't anybody?
C haven't they
D hasn't it?

33. She is an ardent animal rights activist; she refuses ... anything ... fur.

A wearing // that is made of
B to wear // made of
C to be wearing // was made of
D to be worn // being made of

34. When he puts on his glasses he looks ... intelligent.

A almost
B hardly
C nearly
D enough

35. It's no use ... with her; there's no way we can prevent her ... this selfish pig.

A arguing // marrying
B to argue // from getting married to
C arguing // from marry
D argue // to marry

36. Could you explain ... how to fill in this form, please?

A me
B to me
C for me
D me that

37. Needless to say, he's forgotten ... the fiver ... I lent him two weeks ago. That's the last time I lend him any money!

A repaying // —
B to have repaid // what
C about repaying // when
D to repay // that

38. Just wait and see; I'll be the prime minister of this country ...

A once
B lately
C one day
D the other day

39. As we didn't feel like ... a test, our teacher finally agreed ... it until next week.

A doing // to postpone
B to do // to delay
C do // that we postpone
D doing // to delaying

40. Only the insane take ... quite seriously.

A themself
B itself
C oneself
D themselves

B

Read the definitions and supply the appropriate words or phrases.

1. A .... is a piece of paper showing that you have received money or goods from someone.

2. A .... is a box made of cardboard in which drink is sold.

3. .... food is food produced or grown without using artificial chemicals.

4. The tax added to the price of goods and services is called ....

5. If you pay for something in .... you pay small sums of money over a period of time until you have paid the full price of the item.

6. The quick spread of an infectious disease in a particular area is called an ....

7. Your .... are the top part of your leg, between your knees and hips.

8. A .... is a lot of spots that appear on your skin when you have certain illnesses or are allergic to something.

9. If you are .... to something (harmful), you are unable to stop taking it, or you like it so much that you do not want to stop doing or having it.

10. A .... is a medicine or drug used to make someone calm or sleepy.

11. If you .... a problem or difficulty, you find a satisfactory way of dealing with it.

12. The .... of a car is a covered space at the back or front of the car, in which you carry such things as luggage, shopping, etc.

13. The two or three parallel parts of a main road which are divided by painted lines, which tell drivers where to drive, are called ....

14. The .... is the set of official rules and laws about driving and using roads.

15. A .... is the station or stop at the end of a bus/tram service or a railway line.

16. A .... is a place a lot of people go to for a holiday.

17. An .... is an illegal action or a crime, especially one that breaks a particular law and requires a particular punishment.

18. .... is stealing from a shop by hiding things in your bag or in your clothes.

19. .... is the process of making air, water, etc. dangerously dirty and not suitable for people to use.

20. .... is the state of being extremely poor.

C

Translate the following text into English. (Use a dictionary if necessary.)

✓ Nincs kedvem tévét nézni. Menjünk el valahova, jó?

....

✓ Jó. Mit szólnál, ha megnéznénk *Az angol beteg* című filmet? Biztosan érdemes megnézni, azt mondják kapott egy csomó Oscar-díjat. Már minden barátunk látta, ideje lenne, hogy mi is megnézzük.

....

....

✓ Nem, ma inkább nem mennék moziba. Elegem van már az ülésből, jobb szeretnék valamilyen testmozgást végezni.

....

....

✓ Rendben. Például jó lenne teniszezni egyet, nem? Imádok teniszezni.

....

✓ Hát, ha teniszezni akarunk, akkor pályát kell bérelnünk.

....

✓ Azt hiszem, itt lehet pályát bérelni.

....

✓ Nem, jobb lesz ha nem bérelünk mi itt semmit. Legalább 4000 forintba kerülne egy pályát egy órára kibérelni. Egész egyszerűen nem engedhetjük meg magunknak, hogy ennyit fizessünk, de őszintén szólva nincs is értelme ennyit fizetni egy óra játékért. Különben is túl meleg van teniszezni.

....

....

....

✓ Hát akkor menjünk úszni!

....

✓ Ez a legjobb ötlet, amit ma hallottam! Gyerünk!

....

MOCK Exam

"A" THE ORAL EXAM

Maximális pontszám: 70 (55+15)

Értékelés:*

*Mindhárom szóbeli feladat pontozása három szempont alapján történik: **0**-tól **5** pontig értékelik a produkció a) kommunikatív értékét, b) a szókincset és a c) nyelvhelyességet. A feladatonként maximum **15** ponton kívül az egész szóbeli produkció alapján maximum **5–5** pontot adnak a kiejtésre és a beszédértésre. Így a szóbeli vizsgán összesen **55** pont érhető el, amelyhez később hozzáadják a magnós beszédértés pontszámait (maximum **15**). A komplett „A" típusú vizsgán így a maximálisan elérhető pontszám **70**.*

1. FELADAT

irányított interjú

(kötetlen párbeszéd)

Examiner: I can see in your ID-card that you live in Avar utca. Where exactly is it?
Applicant: ...
Examiner: I see. And what's the neighbourhood like?
Applicant: ...
Examiner: That doesn't sound very bad, does it? And how about the block itself? Or is it a house?
Applicant: ...
Examiner: Suppose you wanted to sell the place, what do you think would be the features you would emphasise in an advertisement?
Applicant: ...
Examiner: And is there anything you'd prefer to keep quiet about?
Applicant: ...
Examiner: I see. And how satisfied are you with the public transport services there?
Applicant: ...
Examiner: Let's take a very concrete example. How did you come here, for instance?
Applicant: ...
Examiner: So the whole journey took about 40 minutes. Supposing you were in a hurry, say you had overslept, or something like that, do you think there would be any way to cover this distance any faster?
Applicant: ...
Examiner: Well, these are the little beauties of city life, aren't they? But, for all its disadvantages and inconveniences, would you be ready to trade it, exchange it for living in a small village, for example?
Applicant: ...
Examiner: Well, that's quite understandable. There's a price to pay for anything, isn't there? Anyway, thank you very much.

---

*Az értékelési szempontok forrásai: Fekete hajnal – Dr. Fonyódi jenő (szerk.): Írásbeli dolgozatok. Javítás és értékelés az állami nyelvvizsgán. Angol „B" vizsga. (ITK) című kiadvány (é. n.), valamint az ITK Tájékoztató és Jelentkezési Lap.

2. FELADAT

önálló témakifejtés kép(ek) alapján

Válasszon ki <u>egyet</u> a két feladatból (A vagy B), írja le, hogy mit lát, majd önállóan fejtse ki véleményét a látottakról.

A

1 2 3

1 2 3 4

B

3. FELADAT

szituációs párbeszéd

Ön Angliában van, és pénzt szeretne váltani. A pénztáros gyanakodva nézegeti a 10 000 forintos bankjegyet, és először nem akarja beváltani.

- Tiltakozzon, hogy ez egy teljesen legális fizetőeszköz Magyarországon. (*Ez az egyik legújabb magyar bankjegy, csak 1997 júniusában bocsátották ki.*)
- Javasolja, hogy a pénztáros valahogy ellenőrizze, hogy létezik-e ilyen magyar bankjegy. (*Nézze meg valamilyen brosúrában vagy telefonáljon a Bank of England-be.*)
- Miután tisztázódott a félreértés, a pénztáros érdeklődésére mondja el, hogy mit ábrázol a bankjegy. (*A pénz egyik oldalán Szent István, első [államalapító] királyunk látható, a másik oldalon pedig az esztergomi Bazilika, a katolikus egyházi központ.*)
- Panaszolja el, hogy a nagy címlet ellenére a pénz nem túl sokat ér. (*Magyarországon magas az infláció, és tízezer forint már csak akkor nagy pénz, ha meg kell keresni. Például ezért a kis darab papírért több mint egy hetet kell dolgoznia, és mindössze 30 fontot ér az egész. Jövőre viszont már 25 fontot sem fog érni.*)
- Köszönje meg a pénztáros segítségét, és búcsúzzon el.

4. FELADAT

beszédértés

gépi hang alapján

Maximális pontszám: 15

Hallgassa meg a következő felvételt egyszer, majd olvassa el a kérdéseket. Két további meghallgatás után válaszoljon a kérdésekre magyarul.

Lost and found

Interview with Mr Brian Simmons, head of the lost property department of Albion Airways.

1. Naponta hány utas veszít el valamit az Albion Airways járatain, és melyek a legtipikusabb talált tárgyak? (*1 pont*)
2. Milyen példákat hoz az interjúalany arra a megállapítására, hogy a repülőgépeken az elmúlt 20 évben talált tárgyak jellegének változása jól tökrözi a technika fejlődését? (*2 pont*)
3. Milyen példákat említ a különlegesebb talált tárgyakkal kapcsolatosan? (*1 pont*)
4. Miért fordul az elő időnként, hogy értékes tárgyakat tartalmazó táskákért nem jelentkeznek a tulajdonosok? (*3 pont*)
5. Milyen érdekes példákkal illusztrálja, hogy milyen sikeresen működik a talált tárgyak osztálya? (*4 pont*)
6. Mi történik azokkal a talált tárgyakkal, amelyek tulajdonosát nem sikerül megtalálni? (*4 pont*)

Az egész „A" típusú vizsga értékelése

A sikeres vizsgához az elérhető maximális pontszám (70) 60%-át kell elérni, azaz **legalább 42 pontot.**

"B" THE WRITTEN EXAM

Maximális pontszám:

100 (15+25+15+25+20)

1. FELADAT

feleletválasztós teszt

Maximális pontszám: 15

Válassza ki a helyes megoldást!

1. What can you expect of a day ... begins with getting up in the morning?

A what **C** that
B — **D** it

2. "Why are you switching on the TV?" "I ... the football match."

A am watching **C** will watch
B will be watching **D** am going to watch

3. There's been a lot of heated debate on this issue recently, ...?

A isn't it **C** hasn't there
B hasn't it **D** isn't there

4. There's something wrong with this plant. I've even tried ... it some fertiliser, but it's still in very bad shape.

A giving **C** give
B and give **D** to give

5. If I ... any further information, I ... it on to you immediately.

A receive // will pass **C** receive // would pass
B will receive // will pass **D** receive // would have passed

6. All animals are equal, but some are ... others.

A equaller as **C** equaller than
B more equal than **D** more equal like

7. My wife suggested ... to the cinema.

A the kids to go **C** going
B that the kids going **D** that the kids should have go

8. "I love Brazilian soap operas." "..."
A I, too.
B So I do.
C So do I.
D I do so.

9. So you're back. How was your ... ?
A travel
B journey
C way
D travelling

10. This is the coldest autumn in years. We ... heat the flat since the end of September.
A must
B have to
C had to
D have had to

11. Unless you ... being rude to her, she'll leave you in no time.
A stop
B won't stop
C will stop
D don't stop

12. Arizona is famous ... its mountains and deserts.
A about
B from
C for
D with

13. ... was at 4.30 am. ... my mother woke me up this morning.
A It // that
B It // when
C That // when
D There // then

14. ... is a sexually transmitted disease and there is a 100% mortality rate.
A The life
B Life
C A life
D One life

15. I ... a proper summer holiday since I ... up my business five years ago.
A didn't have // set
B haven't had // set
C haven't had // have set
D didn't have // have set

16. If only I ... handle girls as well as you!
A should
B would
C could
D might

17. You are supposed to arrive at the airport at least an hour before your flight takes ...
A up
B away
C off
D out

18. I ... my parents to lend me the Trabant for my trip in the country.
A convinced
B suggested
C proposed
D persuaded

19. The tickets cost a fortune, and, on top of everything else, we ... most of the time.
A were boring
B were bored
C bored
D felt boring

20. An idea isn't responsible ... the people who believe in it.
A for
B with
C from
D to

21. Actually, the written test wasn't quite ... I'd thought.

A so easy that
B as easy than
C as easy as
D so easy than

22. ... the shortest distance between two people.

A The smile is
B A smile is
C The smiles are
D Smile is

23. ... yourself to death is the only socially acceptable form of suicide.

A To work
B The working
C Working
D Work

24. When Mozart was my age, he ... for two years.

A was died
B had been dead
C was dead
D had died

25. "Our telephone answering machine is ..., this is a person speaking."

A repairing
B repaired
C being repaired
D having repaired

26. The final results of the vote haven't been published yet, but at least 80 per cent of the voters ... for Hungary joining NATO.

A think to have voted
B is thought to vote
C thought to have voted
D are thought to have voted

27. There's nothing I hate more ... my homework on Sunday afternoon.

A like doing
B than to do
C than having to do
D than do

28. ... car theft is a very serious problem in Budapest; ... thieves steal a car every six minutes in the capital.

A The // the
B —// —
C The // —
D — // the

29. I simply don't believe you any longer. You ... lies.

A always are telling
B tell always
C are always telling
D are telling always

30. ... I sign my name on the dotted line here?

A Will
B Would
C Shall
D Won't

31. As soon as I ... home, I sat down to do my homework.

A get
B was getting
C have got
D got

32. This skirt is all right, but I'll have to find a nice blouse ...

A fitting it.
B to go with it.
C that suits it.
D for matching.

33. If all goes well, I ... this chapter of the book by the end of the week.
A have completed
B will have been completing
C complete
D will have completed

34. You ... have seen me with anybody in the park my dear; I wasn't even in town yesterday.
A can't
B mustn't
C mightn't
D oughtn't to

35. Is it any use ... even more money in this enterprise? It seems so hopeless.
A investing
B invest
C to invest
D in investing

36. My one regret in life ... I am not somebody else.
A is what
B is this
C is that
D that

37. ... have any difficulty, don't hesitate to ask for help immediately.
A If you would
B If you will
C Should you
D Would you

38. It wasn't clear how ... to solve these serious problems.
A the government intended
B did the government intend
C intended the government
D does the government intend

39. She offered to give me a lift, ... I gratefully accepted.
A that
B what
C which
D —

40. I'd rather you ... me lies. There's no truth whatsoever in your story. It's all lies!
A not to tell
B not telling
C didn't tell
D don't tell

41. Students in Bangladesh have to cheat ... any chance of passing their exams.
A for standing
B to stand
C so as they stand
D in order standing

42. Does your wife want to return to ... after having the baby?
A work
B job
C career
D occupation

43. I've been fined ... speeding three times this year.
A on
B because
C by
D for

44. Although my leg hurt terribly, I ... limp to the phone box and call for help.
A succeeded to
B could
C was able to
D manage to

45. Everything ... is any fun is either immoral, illegal or fattening.
A what
B which
C that
D —

46. ... young kids are mad about ... computer games.

A The most // the
B Most // —
C Most of // —
D The most of the // the

47. I wish I ... a better paid profession. I am sick and tired of this miserable salary.

A chose
B would have chosen
C had chosen
D have chosen

48. I was wondering if you could possibly ... me a favour.

A make
B do
C give
D take

49. I do apologise ... you, especially on a Sunday, but this is really urgent.

A for troubling
B to trouble
C troubling
D that I trouble

50. Today is the first day of the ... of your life.

A left
B remain
C leftover
D rest

Értékelés:

16–22	=	1	pont
23–29	=	3	pont
30–35	=	5	pont
36–38	=	7	pont
39–41	=	9	pont
42–44	=	11	pont
45–47	=	13	pont
48–50	=	15	pont

2. FELADAT

fordítás

magyarról angolra

Maximális pontszám: 25

1. – Valamit csinálnom kellene a hajammal, szörnyen nézek ki.
2. Már kipróbáltam legalább öt különböző frizurát, de mindegyik katasztrofálisnak bizonyult.
3. Bárcsak olyan klassz hajam lenne mint neked! Szerinted mit csináljak vele?
4. – Én a helyedben levágatnám, és befestetném szőkére.
5. – Azt nem bánnám, ha rövid hajam lenne, de a festetéstől egy kicsit félek.
6. Azt mondják, a festés ártalmas a hajnak.
7. De a fő probléma az, hogy a szüleim nagyon mérgesek lennének, ha meglátnák, hogy befestettem a hajam. A papám azt mondta, hogy kitagad, ha ilyesmit teszek.
8. – Á, az én papámnál a te papád sem lehet konzervatívabb.
9. Először biztosan mérges lenne, de amikor már megszokta, hogy az új frizurával lát, lehet, hogy tetszeni is fog neki.
10. – Lehet, hogy igazad van. Döntöttem: befestetem a hajam.

Értékelés:

Az egész szöveget 40 pontnak tekintik, majd a súlyosságtól függően 3, 2, illetve 1 pontot vonnak le minden egyes hibáért. A maradék pontszámot az alábbi táblázat szerint vizsgapontokká alakítják át.

1–2 = **1**	9–10 = **6**	17–18 = **11**	25–26 = **16**	33–34 = **21**
3 = **2**	11 = **7**	19 = **12**	27 = **17**	35 = **22**
4–5 = **3**	12–13 = **7**	20–21 = **13**	28–29 = **18**	36–37 = **23**
6–7 = **4**	14–15 = **7**	22–23 = **14**	30–31 = **19**	38–39 = **24**
8 = **5**	16 = **10**	24 = **15**	32 = **20**	40 = **25**

- Súlyosnak (3 pontosnak) számítanak a következő hibák: nem létező alakok használata, téves nyelvtani szerkezet miatti lényeges jelentéstorzulás, hibás nyelvtani szerkezet használata, értelmetlenséget okozó szóhasználat.
- 2 pontos hibának számítanak a szórendi hibák, kettős tagadás, a legtöbb igeidő tévesztés, téves módbeli segédige használat, Gerund/Infinitive tévesztés, névmások tévesztése, hibás melléknév fokozás, megszámlálhatósággal kapcsolatos hibák, szótévesztések.
- 1 pontos hibának számítanak a névelőhibák, a helytelen elöljáró használata, kisebb szóhasználati tévedések és a helyesírási hibák.
- Nem vonnak le pontot vesszőhasználati hiba miatt, kivéve vonatkozó mellékmondatok esetén.

3. FELADAT

irányított fogalmazás

Maximális pontszám: 15

Az alábbi két feladat közül az EGYIKET kell kidolgoznia.

I. téma

Írja le 17–20 sorban gondolatait a témáról úgy, hogy minden irányítási szempontra térjen ki. Fontos, hogy a fogalmazás egységes szöveget alkosson, ezért kérjük, hogy az egyes gondolatkörök közötti átmenetet biztosítsa. Ügyeljen arra, hogy ne lépje túl az előírt terjedelmet! Az angol levélforma jellemzőit tartsa be! (Dátum, megszólítás, üdvözlő forma, aláírás.)

Egy másik településen dolgozó, ideiglenesen Magyarországon állomásozó angol tanár barátja panaszkodik Önnek, hogy nehezen boldogul a magyar nyelvvel; a múltkor is *rántotthúst* szeretett volna enni egy étteremben, de véletlenül *rántottát* mondott, és persze azt is hozták, pedig szívből utálja a rántottát. Írjon válaszlevelet barátjának, amelyben:

1. Emlékeztesse, hogy még csak három hónapja van Magyarországon. (A nyelvtanulás időigényes dolog stb.)
2. Ajánlja figyelmébe a nemrég megjelent Let's Speak Hungarian című kiváló könyvet (angol nyelvű magyarázatokkal, kazettákkal).
3. Hívja fel a figyelmét, hogy ma már a legtöbb nyelviskola indít tanfolyamokat magyarul tanulók számára.
4. Javasolja, hogy minél többet járjon magyarul beszélő társaságba, és említse meg, hogy persze a legjobb megoldás egy magyar barátnő lenne.
5. Nyugtassa meg, hogy a magyar nagyon nehéz nyelv. (Még Ön is összekeveri néha a szezont a fazonnal/Gizikét a gőzekével stb.)

II. téma

Írjon fogalmazást 17–20 sorban az alábbi kérdésekről. Ön dönti el, hogy melyik kérdéseket fejti ki részletesebben, és melyekre ad rövidebb választ. Fontos, hogy a fogalmazás egységes szöveget alkosson, ezért kérjük, hogy az egyes gondolatkörök közötti átmenetet biztosítsa. Ügyeljen arra, hogy ne lépje túl az előírt terjedelmet!

Írja le, hogy mi a véleménye a kutyák, macskák és egyéb kedvenc állatok városi körülmények közötti tartásáról. Térjen ki a következő főbb gondolatokra:

1. Miért tartanak az emberek "kedvenceket"?
2. Milyen (tárgyi és személyi) feltételei vannak az állatok tartásának városi körülmények között?
3. Milyen állatok tartását tartja elfogadhatónak, illetve elfogadhatatlannak?
4. Mi az amire az állat-tulajdonosoknak vigyázni kell, hogy ne zavarják a környezetüket?
5. Van-e olyan a témával kapcsolatos kérdés, amelyet hatóságilag kellene szabályozni?

Értékelés:

A fogalmazás pontozásánál három szempontot vesznek figyelembe, és ezeket egyenként 0-tól 5 pontig értékelik a következő szempontok szerint:

Tartalom:

a) az irányítási szempontokat logikusan kifejtő, világos, könnyen érthető gondolatok
b) az egyes részek közötti gördülékeny átmenet biztosítása
c) a formai sajátosságok betartása (levélíráskor cím, dátum, megszólítás, üdvözlő és búcsúzó formulák stb.)
d) stílus (hivatalos vagy közvetlen, a levél típusától és a fogalmazás tartalmától függően)
e) elrendezés, tagolás, bekezdések
f) a terjedelem betartása (inkább kissé hosszabb legyen, mint rövidebb)

Kifejezésmód:

a) szövegbe illő, változatos szókincs
b) szövegbe illő, változatos nyelvtani, mondattani szerkezetek
c) kifejezések használata
d) gördülékeny stílus

Nyelvhelyesség:

a) a nyelvtan helyes használata
b) a helyesírás, az írásjelek megfelelő használata

4. FELADAT
Fordítás
angolról magyarra

Maximális pontszám: 25

Somebody's got to win

Everybody loves the idea of winning, whether it's a fairground shooting gallery or the London Marathon. But while we can't all enter races or win the first prize in Mastermind*, anyone can enter consumer competitions. There is an estimated £4,000,000 worth of prizes to be won in Britain at any one time, and more and more people are aiming to get something for nothing. Entries to competitions have never been higher – a Best holiday competition back in January attracted 40,000 entries. But, as competitors keep telling themselves – somebody's got to win.

While the rest of us win the odd grocery voucher, there is a growing bunch of people who are picking up houses, holidays, cars and cash. They are a dedicated band – some even giving up their jobs to indulge their will to win.

Rita Smallburn first got the competition bug when she was off work from her teaching job with flu. Just to kill time, she entered a magazine competition and won a cassette player. Encouraged, she decided to "try gathering a few luxuries of life." And, says a delighted Rita, "It escalated far beyond what I expected."

Rita, now 60, gave up her job 10 years ago to concentrate on competing. In her most successful year her prize-winnings added up to £80,000. She once won a new house, lived in it for 18 months and sold it at double the price. Her other prizes include 34 holidays, four cars, three washing machines, eight televisions, four videos and six microwave ovens.

A week's football coaching featured among her more unusual prizes – and, laughs Rita, "a hair-do for my husband, who is completely bald!"

Best

* A quiz game, which is something like "Mindent vagy semmit" on Hungarian TV.

Értékelés:

- Az egyáltalán nem fordított részekért soronként 4 pontot vonnak le.
- 3, 2, illetve 1 pontot vonnak le a következő hibák előfordulása esetén:

  –3 pont súlyos hibáknál, azaz ha a megfogalmazás magyarul teljesen értelmetlen vagy képtelen, vagy ha a hiba a szövegrészben közölt információt alapvetően megváltoztatja

  –2 pont komoly félreértéseknél, azaz ha a hiba a szövegrész jelentését lényegesen módosítja, de a közölt információ lényegét nem érinti (ez legtöbbször egy szó vagy rövidebb szerkezet félreértéséből származik)

  –1 pont kisebb hibáknál, azaz rossz szóválasztás (szinoníma), kimaradó, nem lényeges szó, adat, illetve durva stilisztikai hiba esetén

5. FELADAT

szövegértés

Maximális pontszám: 20

Olvassa el figyelmesen az alábbi szöveget, majd annak alapján válaszoljon magyarul a kérdésekre! A válasz gyakran összetett, vagyis megfogalmazásához a szöveg különböző részeiből szerzett információ szükséges.

A new report tells us who in Europe is most tolerant — and most intolerant — of whom

NOT SO EASY TO LOVE THY NEIGHBOUR

Martin Rosenbaum reports

The best way to find out about what people really feel about members of unpopular or minority groups is to ask: would you live next door to one of them? This question was put to nearly 20,000 people in 14 European countries by the European Value Systems Study Group, a network of academics across the continent who research the underlying beliefs and values of different nationalities. The survey itemised 11 kinds of potential neighbour and asked participants to indicate those they did not want to live next to. The result revealed national differences as well as common fears and prejudices across Europe.

According to the group, Europeans object to neighbours whom they are afraid may cause trouble more than to those who are simply different in some way. The most unpopular neighbours across the continent are drug addicts — 60 per cent of Europeans do not want them next door. Forty seven per cent reject heavy drinkers and 36 per cent people with a criminal record.

By comparison, only ten per cent say that they do not want people of a different race in the next house.

The survey shows that, overall, the most easy-going nation by far is Denmark. The other Scandinavian countries — Sweden, Norway and Iceland — also live up to the region's reputation for tolerance. But the second most tolerant nation is actually France. In other research this was found to be Europe's outpost of civic immorality. The French were the happiest to buy stolen goods, cheat on claiming State benefits and drive off after accidentally colliding with a parked car.

(to be continued on page 342)

NOT SO EASY TO LOVE THY NEIGHBOUR

The least tolerant nation is Portugal: 50 per cent object to living next door to homosexuals, 47 per cent to emotionally unstable people and 19 per cent to religious minorities. The greatest hostility to neighbours suffering from Aids comes from the traditionally Catholic countries of Italy, Spain and Ireland, as well as Portugal. But in other respects Spain and Ireland are quite relaxed — for example, to heavy drinkers and people with large families.

Across Europe the most important demographic factor associated with intolerance of neighbourhood is age. Older people in different countries are consistently more fussy about who they live next door to. Older people often represent a settled traditional lifestyle and can resent what they see as invasion of different lifestyles. But they also spend more time in their houses — younger people go out to work and entertainment — so their personal space is more important to them.

By contrast there is only a small gender gap. Women are slightly more likely to reject potentially difficult neighbours such as heavy drinkers, men those who are simply different — religious minorities, for example.

But there is one other factor which correlates with intolerance — right-wing views. People who place themselves on the far Right are even more likely to object to having other right-wing political extremists next door than are people on the far Left. As researchers say: "They may just be very intolerant people."

The European

1. Kik végezték a felmérést, mi célból és milyen körben?
2. Sorolja fel a tizenegy "mássági"csoportot, amelyről a felmérés készült.
3. Általánosságban véve mely csoportok mellett nem szeretnének lakni az európaiak?
4. Mit állít a cikk a franciákkal kapcsolatban egy másik vizsgálat alapján?
5. Milyen demográfiai tényező játssza a legfontosabb szerepet a mássághoz való viszonyban, és miért van ez így?
6. Mi a különbség a nők és a férfiak szomszédokkal kapcsolatos előítéletei között?
7. Kik tiltakoznak leginkább a szélsőjobboldali nézeteket valló szomszédok ellen, és mi lehet ennek az oka a kutatók szerint?

Értékelés:

Kérdés-elemenként (az egyes információrészletek 1-1 pontot érnek) lehet elérni a kérdésre maximálisan adható pontszámot. Levonás akkor történik, ha a válaszban olyan félreértés van, amely a cikk lényegét érinti.

A komplett „B" típusú vizsgán elérhető maximális pontszám így **100** pont.

Az egész „B" típusú vizsga értékelése

A sikeres vizsgához az elérhető maximális pontszám (100) 60%-át kell elérni, azaz **legalább 60 pontot.**

A „C" típusú vizsga

A „C" típusú vizsga egy-egy önmagában sikeres „A" és „B" vizsgából tevődik össze. A két részvizsga külön-külön is letehető, de a „C" típusú vizsgaként való elfogadáshoz a két vizsga időpontja között legfeljebb két naptári év különbség lehet. A különböző szintű vizsgákon csak az adott szintnek megfelelő nyelvvizsgát lehet megszerezni (tehát például egy gyengébb felsőfokú nem értékelhető közép- vagy alapfokúként). Különböző szintű „A" és „B" típusú vizsgák esetén csak az alacsonyabb szintű „C" típusú vizsga kapható meg.

FIRST AID KIT 1 Letter writing

1. PERSONAL letters

The lay-out of the letter

- Write your address *in the top right-hand corner* of the page.
- The date comes immediately *below the address* (still on the right-hand side).
- Place the opening greeting *on the left-hand side* (and not in the middle) of the sheet, a bit *lower down* than the date.
- Start the first line of each pragraph with a small indentation.
- Write the closing greeting either *on the left-* or *right-hand side* of the sheet (or you may even put it in the middle) on a separate line.
- Sign the letter *below the closing greeting*.

The heading

- *The address:*
  Write your address in the Hungarian way using *utca, tér,* etc.; remember that your partner will copy it from here to address the envelope when replying to your letter. Do *not* write your name here.

Avar utca 9.
Budapest,
1123
Hungary

- *The date:*
  There are lots of different ways of writing the date, but the most suitable form for letters seems to be this one:

24 December 1998

Note that there are *no* abbreviations (Dec.), full stops (.), or commas (,).

The opening greeting (salutation)

Use first names with friends. When writing a friendly letter to persons with whom you are not on first-name terms, you should address them as Dear Mr/Ms/Mrs/Miss So-and-so. You may put a comma at the end of the salutation (optional), but nothing else is suitable. Do not use first names and family names together, and *never* end a salutation with an exclamation mark *(!)*.

(My) dear Judy(,)
Dear Mr Jones(,)

Some useful phrases

The first few lines

- *Thanks:*
  Thank you so much for answering my letter so quickly.
  Thank you / Thanks very much for your letter.
  What a surprise it was to get a letter from you after all this time!
  How nice it was to hear from you again / at last.
  I had given you up for lost but this morning ...
  I was glad / It was nice to hear from you (again).
  How lovely to receive your last letter.
  Lovely to hear from you.
  Your letter was waiting for me when I came home and I was delighted to hear ...
- *Sorry:*
  I must apologise for not writing to you for so long but I have ...
  I am sorry it has taken me so long to reply to your last letter but ...
- *The reason for writing:*
  I am writing to you by return post and ...
  I have just this moment received your letter and am writing at once because ...
  I am very pleased to hear that ...
  I am writing to you for some advice ...
  You asked me about the ...
  In your last letter you asked me to write you about ...
  Thank you for your letter full of so many questions about how ... You seem to be really interested in the way things go over here.
  Now I'll try to summarise the most important things in a few sentences.
  Whatever has become of you?

Before saying goodbye

- *That's all:*
  Well, that seems to be all my news now.
  That's all for now.
  No more news for the moment. Write soon and let me know about what's going on around you these days.
- *Write soon:*
  (I shall be / I am) Looking forward to hearing from you soon.
  I hope to have a letter from you before long.
  Hope to hear from you soon.
  Write soon!
  Well, I hope I have remembered everything, but if I haven't, please write again and ask any questions you've got.
  I would very much like to hear your opinion about ...
  Please let me know what you think about ....
  Do write soon and let me know how you are getting on.
  Just feel free to ask me about anything you want to hear more about.
  Thank you again for your letter.

Closing the letter

- *Almost finished:*
  Hope all goes well with you.
  I hope everybody is all right in your family.
  My very best to you and your parents.
  My sister sends her regards.
- *Friendly, but formal:*
  All the best,
  (With kind/best/warm) Regards,

(With very) Best wishes, With every good wish,

- *Neutral:*

  Yours, Yours ever,

  Yours sincerely, Sincerely yours,

- *Loving:*

  Yours affectionately,

  Your loving niece,

  Love,

  (With) Lots of love,

  X X X

  P.S., P.P.S.

2. FORMAL letters

The lay-out of the letter

The heading

- The main difference between personal and formal letters is that in the case of the latter the recipient's name (or position, or both) and address also appear, normally above the opening greeting, on the left-hand side of the sheet.

  Mr Basil Fawlty/The Manager
  Fawlty Towers
  10 Salisbury Road
  Finsbury Park
  London, N.4
  Great Britain

- If there is a printed letter head, it contains all the necessary information for a reply, so there's no need to write our address separately. In this case normally *everything* is placed on the left-hand side of the sheet (including the date and the signature).

The salutation and the closing greeting

- If you know the recipient's name, use *Mr/Ms/Mrs/Miss* and the family name. In this case, the closing greeting should be *Yours sincerely*.
- If you don't know the person's name, use *Dear Sir, Dear Sirs* (when writing to a firm), or *Dear Madam*, but in this case the closing greeting will be *Yours faithfully*.

Some useful phrases

The first few lines

- *Thanks:*

  Thank you for you letter of November 10th.

  Many thanks for your letter of November 10th, in which ...

  It was a great pleasure to receive your letter of 10 November.

- *Asking for information:*

  Please kindly inform me about the possibilities for ...

I would like to get/Please send me/I would be very grateful if you would send me some information about ... \full details of ...

- *Replying to inquires:*

In your letter of November 10 you inquire about ...

In reply to your inquiry of Nov. 10th, ...

Regarding/In connection with your recent inquiry about ...

Referring to/I read your letter \advertisement in last Tuesday's issue of Kiskegyed, ...

- *Making a complaint:*

I am writing to you to make/lodge a complaint about ...

I am writing to you in connection with ...

Closing the letter

I sincerely hope you will be able to help me in this matter.

I do hope I am not putting you to too much trouble.

I thank you in advance for your reply \kind help \consideration \arrangements.

Should you need/require any further information, please ...

I enclose my CV \a brochure \a cheque for £ 10 to cover costs \the application form.

I am looking forward to/I look forward to hearing from you soon.

I would greatly appreciate an early reply.

American letters

- There is a colon (:) after the salutation *(Dear Mr. Smith:)*, or, in informal letters, a comma (,).
- The Americans have *Gentlemen* instead of *Dear Sirs*, and *Sincerely*, *Yours sincerely*, *Sincerely yours* or *Yours truly* is used instead of *Yours faithfully*.
- Americans have a full stop after *Mr.*, *Mrs.*, *Dr.*, etc.

FIRST AID KIT 2
Functions

A. SITUATIONS

1. Asking for information
2. Saying you are sure
3. Saying you don't know
4. Saying you are not sure
5. Asking for advice & giving advice
6. Asking for opinion & giving your opinion
7. Agreeing
8. Saying you partly agree & polite disagreement
9. Disagreeing
10. Making suggestions, accepting & rejecting suggestions
11. Introducing yourself
12. Introducing someone
13. Greeting someone & saying how you are
14. Saying goodbye
15. Thanking
16. Apologising & accepting an apology
17. Complaining
18. Saying someone must do something
19. Saying someone need not do something
20. Asking for permission, granting permission, & refusing permission
21. Making a request, granting a request, & refusing a request
22. Giving
23. Offering
24. Inviting
25. Accepting an offer or invitation, & refusing an offer or invitation
26. Good wishes
27. Persuading
28. Threatening
29. Asking if someone can do something, & saying you can/can't do something

B. ATTITUDES

1. Expressing surprise
2. Expressing excitement
3. Expressing boredom
4. Expressing worry/fear & giving reassurance
5. Saying you are not satisfied/Expressing anger
6. Expressing relief
7. Saying you are disappointed
8. Praising, & accepting praise
9. Complimenting someone on their appearance
10. Criticism
11. Expressing sympathy/Consolation
12. Saying what you prefer

C. INTERACTION

1. Asking someone to say something again
2. Saying something in another way
3. Checking that someone has understood you
4. Giving an example
5. Taking up a point
6. Hesitating
7. Changing the subject
8. Summing up

N stands for *neutral* or *general*, I for *informal*, and F for *formal* in the tables.

A SITUATIONS

1. Asking for information

N	Excuse me, ...// Can you help me? // Sorry to trouble you, but ... ... I'd like to know ..., please. ... I'd like to inquire about ..., please. ... can/could you tell me ..., please? ... do you happen to know ..., please? ... I wonder if you could tell me ..., please? I hope you don't mind my asking ... // Excuse my asking ... // Forgive me for asking, but ...? And there's another thing I'd like to know ... // And how about ...?
I	Have you (got) any idea if/about ...?
F	Excuse me, can/could you give me any information on/about ..., please?

2. Saying you are sure

N	Oh yes, I'm quite/absolutely sure/certain (...). I've/There's no doubt (about/that ...).
I	Sure. Absolutely certain/positive.
F	There can't be any doubt (about/that ...). I'm quite convinced (that/of ...).

3. Saying you don't know

N	I'm sorry/afraid I really don't know (anything/very much about ...). I'm afraid I can't help you//I've no idea.
I	Sorry, I don't know//I haven't got a clue. (Well, I have) no idea. // I haven't got the faintest idea. Don't ask me. I wish I knew.
F	I'm sorry to say I know very little about // don't know very much about ... I must/have to admit that I don't know very much about ...

4. Saying you are not sure

N	Sorry/I'm afraid, I'm not really/quite sure (about ...). It's hard to say/tell ... I don't think ...
I	I can't/couldn't say for certain/sure. I'm not/I wouldn't be too sure (about ...).
F	I'm not at all convinced of/about/that ...).

5. Asking for advice & giving advice

N	I'd like some/your advice on/about ... Can/Could you give me some advice on/about...? What would you advise me to do? Do you think I should ...? What do you think I should do? What should/shall I do?	I advise you to ... If I were you, I'd ... The way I see it, you should ... If you follow my advice, you'll ... Take my advice, and ...
I	What would you do if you were in my shoes/ if you were me/in my place? Reckon I should ...?	You'd better ... You (really) should/ought to ..., you know.
F	Could I ask for your advice on ...? I would appreciate your/some advice on/about...? What would you recommend?	I know it's none of my business, but I think you should/shouldn't ...

6. Asking for opinion & giving your opinion

N	What/How do you feel about ...? What/How do you think of/about ...? What's your opinion of ...?	I think/believe/feel/guess/reckon ... In my opinion/view ... As far as I'm concerned ... From my point of view ... It seems to me that ...
I	How do you see ...? What are your views on/thoughts about ...?	I'd say ... // If you ask me ... To my mind ... // The way I see it ...
F	Could you tell me how you feel/think about ...?	It's my opinion/view that ... I'm convinced that ...

7. Agreeing

N	I (absolutely/entirely/quite) agree. Oh, absolutely/exactly/definitely. I couldn't agree more.
I	Yes!/Yeah!/Right! // That's it (exactly)! You're right. True enough. // How true.
F	That's exactly my opinion/view. I'm of exactly the same opinion.

8. Saying you partly agree & polite disagreement

N	I see your point/what you mean, but ... Yes, perhaps you have a point there, but ... There's a lot in what you say, but ... That's one way of looking at it, but ... I agree with much/most of what you say, but ... Yes, but on the other hand/don't you think/we shouldn't forget ...
I	OK/Yes, Could be, but ... I can see that, but ...
F	There's some/a lot of truth in what you say, but ... I agree on the whole, but ... I wouldn't go as far as (to say) that.

9. Disagreeing

N	I'm afraid I disagree/don't agree/can't agree (with ...). I think that's nonsense. That's not the way I see ... // Do you really think ...? Actually/In fact, I think ....
I	Oh, surely not! // I don't see why. // Oh, come off it! Rubbish!//Nonsense!/No way!//Never! You must be joking. // You can't be serious.
F	I'm afraid I can't accept ... // I entirely disagree (with ...). I see things rather differently (myself).

10. Making suggestions, accepting & rejecting suggestions

N	We could/might ... Shall we ...?	Yes, let's do that. Yes, all right. That's a good idea.	No, let's not (do that). I'd rather not. No, I don't think that's a (very) good idea.
I	Let's ..., shall we? Why don't we ...? How/What about ...? Why not (do) ...? Do you think it would be an idea to ...?		
F	May/Might I suggest that ...? I'd like to suggest/propose ... // I'd like to suggest/propose ...		

11. Introducing yourself

N	How do you do? My name's Peter. Hello. I'm Peter. I don't think we've met before. My name's Peter.	How do you do? I'm Linda Graham. Hello. My name's Linda. No, we haven't actually. // No, I don't think we have. My name's Linda.
I	Hi! I'm Peter. Hello! I'm Peter.	Hello! I'm Linda. Nice/Good to see you, Peter.
F	May I/Let me/Allow me to introduce myself: Peter Frampton.	How do you do? Pleased to meet you.

12. Introducing someone

N	Paul Simon. This is Paul Simon. I'd like you to meet Paul Simon.	How do you do? Pleased to meet you.	How do you do?
I	Peter, meet Paul. Peter, I'd like you to meet Paul. Have you met Paul? Paul - Peter, Peter -Paul	Hi/Hello, Peter. Good/Nice to meet you.	Hi/Hello, Paul.
F	I'd like to/Let me/Allow me to introduce Mr Anthony Blair.	How do you do? Pleased to meet you, Mr Blair.	How do you do?

13. Greeting someone & saying how you are

N	(Good) Morning/Afternoon/Evening. Hello, Peter/Mr Jones. How are you?	(Good) Morning/Afternoon/Evening. Hello, Linda/Mr Holmes. How are you? Fine thanks. And you? Very well thank you.
I	Hello, Peter. Hello there, Peter. Hi, Peter. Long time no see. // Good to see you again! How's life? How are you keeping? // How are things with you? // How goes it with you? // How's things?	Hello/Hi, Linda. Hello! It's good to see you! Can't complain. // Mustn't grumble. // Not too bad. Quite well. // So-so. // OK. // Surviving. // Still alive, thanks.
F	Good morning/afternoon/evening. Hello! How are you?	Good morning/afternoon/evening. Hello, Linda/Mr Holmes. How are you? Fine thanks. And you? // Very well thank you.

14. Saying goodbye

N	I'm afraid I really must go now. // Excuse me a moment/minute. // I'll be back in a minute. Good bye (then). // Good night.
I	Well, I must be off now. // I'll be right back. // Hang on a second/moment/minute. Bye (for now)! // Cheers! // Cheerio! // Take care. See you soon/later/on Friday! // I'll be seeing you!
F	I'm afraid I must leave you now. // Will you excuse me for a moment, please? // I'm very glad to have met you.

15. Thanking

N	Thank you (very much [indeed]). // Many thanks. // Thank you very much for ...-ing ...	Not at all. // It's a pleasure. // My pleasure. // Don't mention it.
I	Thanks! // Thanks a lot/a million. // Cheers! // Great!	That's OK/all right. // Any time.
F	That's very kind of you. // I do appreciate ... // I'm very grateful to you for ...	I'm glad to have been of some help.

16. Apologising & accepting an apology

N	I'm very/so/terribly/awfully sorry (for/about ...). // I really am very sorry. // It was entirely my fault.	That's (quite) all right. It really doesn't matter.
I	Sorry (for/about ...). // How silly/stupid of me. // Oh, my fault.	That's OK. // Forget it.
F	I do/must apologise (for/about ...). // Please accept my apologies (for ...). // Please forgive me (for ...).	It's/That's perfectly all right.

17. Complaining

N	I'm sorry to say this but ... is most unsatisfactory//just isn't good enough. I'd like to/want to complain/make a complaint about ... Would you mind not ... // Would you please not ...
I	Look! I'm fed up with ... // I've had enough of ... I wish you wouldn't/would ...
F	I'm not at all satisfied with ... I wish to make a complaint about ...

18. Saying someone must do something

N	I think/I'm afraid you should/ought to/have to/must ... I think/I'm afraid you're supposed to/you'll have to ...
I	I'm afraid you've got to ...
F	I'm afraid you're obliged to ...

19. Saying someone need not do something

N	You needn't/don't need to/don't have to ... // It isn't/won't be necessary (to ...) There's no need (to ...) // There's no reason why you should (...)
I	It's up to you. // You haven't got to ... I can't see why you should (...)
F	You are not obliged to (...)

20. Asking for permission, granting permission, & refusing permission

N	Can/May/Could I ...?	Yes, certainly/of course.	No, I'm afraid not.
	Is it all right if I ... Would it be possible to ...? Do you mind if I ...?	That's fine/all right. By all means. Not at all./Of course not.	I'm sorry. I'd rather you didn't. I'm afraid it's/that's not possible. I'm afraid it's out of the question.
I	Mind if I ...? OK/All right if I ...? Any chance of ...-ing ...?	Sure. // Go ahead. // Why not? That's OK/fine/all right. Feel free to ...	Sorry, that's not on. No way.
F	I wonder if I could ...? Do you have any objection if I ...?	That seems to be perfectly/quite acceptable.	I'm afraid no one is allowed/permitted to ...

21. Making a request, granting a request, & refusing a request

N	Excuse me // Sorry to trouble you, but ...	Yes, of course/certainly.	I'd prefer not to. By all means.
	Could/would/Will you ... please? Do you think you could ..., please?	I'd be happy to. It'd be a pleasure.	I'm afraid not.
	Do/Would you mind ..., please?	No, of course not.	I'm sorry, I can't/it's not possible. I'd rather not, actually.
I	Can I ask a favour of you? You couldn't ..., could you? Any chance of ...? Do me a favour and ..., please.	Sure./OK. Right you are. No problem.	Sorry, I'm not too keen on ... I don't really fancy ... Not likely! // No way!
F	I wonder if you'd mind ...-ing ...?	Not at all.	Well, to be honest, I don't think ... I'm sorry to say it's quite impossible.
	Could you possibly ...? Do you think it would be possible to ...? Would you be so kind as to ...? I wonder if you could do me a favour.	By all means.	

22. Giving

N	Here's a/the/your ... // This is for you. Can I/I'd like to give you ... Here/There you are.
I	Here.
F	Please accept ... // Allow me to present you with ...

23. Offering

N	Would you like ... // Can I offer you ...? What can I get you? // Won't you have ...?
I	Like a/some ...? // Have a/some ..? What'll you have?
F	Could I/I wonder if I can get you ...? // Do have a/some ... May I offer you a/some ...?

24. Inviting

N	Would you like ...? // You will ..., won't you?
I	How/What about ...(-ing)? // Do you fancy ...(-ing)? Why don't you ...? // Like to ...?
F	I wonder if you'd like to ... // I should be very pleased if you could ... May I invite you to ...?

25. Accepting an offer or invitation, & refusing an offer or invitation

N	Thank you very much. // Yes, please! That sounds/would be very nice. That's very kind of you.	No, thank you (very much). Well, that's very kind of you, but ...
I	Great! // Lovely! // Cheers! // You bet!	I wish I could, but ... Thanks all the same/anyway, but ...
F	Thank you so much. // You are most kind.	I'm afraid it won't be possible, but thank you very much anyway.

26. Good wishes

N	All the (very) best! // The (very) best of luck (in/with ...)! // Every success in/with ...! I hope you have a good time/pleasant holiday/good journey. (A) merry Christmas (to you)! // A merry Christmas and a happy New Year! // Happy birthday! Many happy returns (of the day)! // Happy Easter! ➜ Thank you. // And the same to you too! // You too!
I	Good luck (in/with ...)! // Hope things go well/all right with ... Enjoy yourself/yourselves! // Have a nice/good time/journey ... // Have fun!
F	I (would like to) wish you success in/with ...

27. Persuading

N	I really think you should ... // Won't you ...? // Are you really sure you won't/can't/wouldn't ...?
I	Go on!/Come on!//Please! // Just this once! // Just for me!
F	How can I persuade you to ...? // Can/Can't/Couldn't/Could I persuade you to ...?

28. Threatening

N	If you do that again, I'll (have to) ... // I wouldn't do that, if I were you, (or ...) // Unless/If ... I'll ...
I	Do that again and I'll ... // Don't ... or I'll ... // Don't you dare! // Just you try!
F	You'd be very unwise (not) to ... // I (must) warn you that ...

29. Asking if someone can do something & saying you can/can't do something

N	Can you ...? Do you know how to ...? Do you think you can/could ...? Do you have any experience of ...? Do you feel capable of ...?	I can ... // I know how to ... // Sure // I might be able to ... // I feel capable of ... // I'm able to ... I'm not sure I'm capable of ... I don't feel I could ... I must admit I'm no good/hopeless at ... I have no experience of ... I'm afraid I couldn't cope with ...

B ATTITUDES

1. Expressing surprise

N	Really? That's very surprising. // What a surprise! That's extraordinary/amazing/unbelievable!
I	What?//No! // I don't believe it! // Well, I never! Fantastic! // Crazy! // Good heavens! // My goodness! You're kidding/joking! // You must be kidding/joking! Are you serious? // Good Lord! I don't believe it!
F	I find it extraordinary/incredible/very surprising.

2. Expressing excitement

N	How/That's exciting/thrilling/sensational!
I	Wow! [waʊ] Great!/Fantastic!
F	This is most exciting. // I'm very enthusiastic about .../excited by ...

3. Expressing boredom

N	How boring/dull! That isn't/I don't think that's very interesting/exciting.
I	That bores me stiff. // That's a waste of time. So what?
F	Well, to be honest, I find ... rather uninteresting. Well, I'm not particularly interested in ...

4. Expressing worry/fear & giving reassurance

N	I'm very worried about ... I'm really terrified/frightened/afraid of ... I find ... very worrying/upsetting.	You really needn't worry/get upset about ... There's no need to worry/to get upset about ... There's nothing to worry about. Everything will be/turn out to be fine/all right.
I	I'm scared stiff that/of ... I'm worried sick by/about ...	There, there // Cheer up! // Don't worry. Come on! It's not as bad as all that. No need to get worked up about ...
F	I'm extremely concerned/anxious about ...	There's no reason to be worried about ...

5. Saying you are not satisfied/Expressing anger

N	Oh no/dear! What a nuisance! // How annoying/irritating!
I	Oh damn/blast/(bloody) hell! But that's impossible/ridiculous! I can't stand ... // I'm fed up with ... // ... (really) makes me mad. I was such a fool/idiot ... // How stupid of me to have ... ..., which was a silly thing to do.
F	This is most unsatisfactory. I'm extremely/most unhappy about ... I object to ...

6. Expressing relief

N	That's/What a relief! // Thank goodness (for that)!
I	Phew! [fju:] // Thank goodness (for that)! Boy, I'm glad about ...! // Thank God for ...
F	That's/It's a great relief. I'm very glad to hear (about) ...

7. Saying you are disappointed

N	Oh, I am disappointed. That's/What a (great) pity/shame/disappointment.
I	Oh, no. Just my/our luck. That's a real letdown.
F	... comes as a great disappointment.

8. Praising/Congratulating, & accepting praise/congratulation

N	What a good/great/wonderful ...! Congratulations (on ...) Well done!	Thanks. Really? Thank you.
I	What a terrific/fantastic ... (You were) great/fantastic!	(It's) (very) nice of you to say so. I'm glad you like/liked/enjoyed it.
F	I'm very impressed with your ... Let me/May I/I must congratulate you on ...	Thank you very much for saying so. Oh, I wouldn't say that.

9. Complimenting someone on their appearance

N	What a nice/smart ... (you are wearing.) // That's a nice/smart ... // You look/you are looking very nice/smart. ... looks very smart. // ... suits you very well.
I	You're looking good! // You look great/fantastic! // I like/love your ... // Wow! [waʊ] // Cor! [kɔː] // What a super/terrific/smashing/lovely/fantastic ...
F	May I say how elegant/charming you look?

10. Criticism

N	What a terrible/dreadful ...! // What a disappointment! // You were awful/terrible.
I	(You) (stupid) idiot/fool! // Rubbish!
F	(I'm afraid) I'm disappointed (in you/by your ...).

11. Expressing sympathy/Consolation

N	What a pity/shame (you couldn't/didn't ...). (What) bad luck! // How awful! I'm very sorry to hear that.
I	Never mind. // Don't worry about that. // There'll be plenty of other opportunities. // Poor (old) you/Peter. // I know how it feels. // Cheer up!
F	I do sympathise (with you).

12. Saying what you prefer

N	(On the whole // As far as I'm concerned) I like/enjoy ... more/better (than ...). // I'd rather/prefer ...
I	If it was up to me, I'd ... // I'd/I'll go for/plump for ...
F	I'd prefer ...

C INTERACTION

1. Asking someone to say something again

N	Pardon? // Sorry? // What did you say? I'm sorry, I didn't (quite) catch/hear that. I'm sorry, what did you say? // I'm sorry, what was that name? Would/Could you repeat what you said/that name, please?
I	Who?/Where?/When?/What? Sorry, I didn't get that. What was that again?
F	I beg your pardon? I'm sorry, would you mind repeating that, please?

2. Saying something in another way

N	Let me/To put it another way, ... In other words, ... What I mean is/meant was ... That is to say ...
I	What I'm trying to say is .. What I mean is ...
F	Let me just rephrase that: ...

3. Checking that someone has understood you

N	Do you see/know what I mean? I hope that's clear/that makes sense. ..., if you see/know what I mean.
I	Do you see? // Right? // OK? // Get it? Got it? // Are you with me?
F	Do I make/Am I making/have I made myself clear? ..., if you follow/understand me.

4. Giving an example

N	(Take ...,)... for example/for instance.
I	Take ...
F	Let me give you/take an example:... . // To illustrate this point/what I mean ...

5. Taking up a point

N	That reminds me of ... Talking of ... It's interesting that you should say that, because ... To go back to what you were saying about ... // Sorry to interrupt, but ...
I	Funny/strange you should say that. // Sorry to butt in, but ...
F	If I may go back to what ...

6. Hesitating

N	Let me see, ... // let me think... // you see/know, ... How shall I put it ...? ... // sort of ... // Well, ...
I	It's on the tip of my tongue. // I've nearly got it. Hang on a sec/mo ... // Just a sec(ond) ...
F	Let me think about that for a moment.

7. Changing the subject

N	By the way ... // Incidentally ... // Before I forget, ...

8. Summing up

N	So what it boils down to is. ... // So what it comes down to is, ... // The point I'm trying to make is, ...
I	To put it in a nutshell, ... // Let me just recap ['ri:kæp] what's been said so far.
F	In short, ... // In a word, ... // Briefly, ... // To sum up, ... // To summarise, ...

FIRST AID KIT 3

Link words/fillers

ENGLISH–HUNGARIAN

about	körülbelül
according to	1. szerint 2. valaminek megfelelően
accordingly	1. ennek megfelelően 2. következésképpen
actually	1. tulajdonképpen 2. valójában; ténylegesen
admittedly	kétségkívül; kétségtelenül
after all	hát hiszen; végül is; elvégre; különben is
against all appearances	a látszat ellenére
all in all	mindent összevetve
all the same	mindennek ellenére; mégis
all things considered	mindent egybevéve
almost	majdnem
although	bár; habár
and so forth	és így tovább
and so on	és így tovább
and stuff like that	és hasonló dolgok/duma
and the like	és hasonló dolgok
and things like that	és hasonló dolgok; meg ilyenek
another problem is that …	a/egy másik gond az, hogy …
and what have you	vagy amit akarsz; vagy mit tudom én
anyhow	1. mindenesetre; legalábbis 2. na mindegy; szóval
anyway	1. mindenesetre; azért mégis 2. szóval 3. különben
apart from	eltekintve valamitől; valamin/valakin kívül
approximately	körülbelül; megközelítőleg
as a consequence	ennek eredményeképpen/következtében
as a matter of fact	tulajdonképpen; valójában; igazából

as a result	ennek eredményeképpen/következtében; e miatt
as far as … is concerned	ami … -t illeti
as far as I can judge	amennyire meg tudom ítélni
as far as I know	amennyire én tudom; ha jól tudom
as for	…-t illetően; ami a …-t illeti
as I mentioned	mint említettem
as I said	mint mondottam
as I see it	véleményem szerint; szerintem
as I understand	információim szerint; legjobb tudomásom szerint
as if	mintha
as it is	1. a dolgok jelenlegi állása szerint 2. már így is
as it seems	úgy tűnik/látszik, a jelek szerint
as it turned out	mint kiderült
as it were	úgymond; úgyszólván; mintegy; "kvázi"
as regards	ami … -t illeti
as the saying goes	ahogy a mondás tartja
as though	mintha
as to …	… vonatkozásában; … tekintetében
as yet	ezidáig; mostanáig
at any rate	mindenesetre; legalább(is)
at first	kezdetben; eleinte; először
at last/at long last	végre (valahára)
at least	legalább(is)
at most	legfeljebb
at the beginning of	valaminek a kezdetén
basically	alapvetően; alapjában véve
because of this	emiatt; ezért
believe it or not	akár hiszed, akár nem
besides	azon/ezenkívül; mi több; egyébként
briefly	röviden (összefoglalva)
but	de; kivéve
by and large	nagyjából; egészében véve
by no means	semmi esetre sem
by the way	apropó; erről jut eszembe
certainly	persze; feltétlenül, tényleg; az biztos, hogy
come to that	1. erről jut eszembe 2. ha már erről van szó
come to think of it	1. erről jut eszembe 2. ha már erről van szó
consequently	ennek eredményeképpen/következtében
contrary to popular belief	a közhiedelemmel ellentétben
despite	ellenére
due to	miatt; köszönhetően
e.g.	például
et cetera	és így tovább
especially	különösen
etc.	satöbbi

even if	még akkor is; még ha
even so	mégis; ennek ellenére
eventually	végül (aztán)
except (for)/with the exception of	kivéve
finally	(és) végül
first and foremost	mindenekelőtt
first of all	mindenekelőtt; először is
firstly	először (is)
for all I know	amennyire tudom
for example	például
for instance	például
for one thing	hogy mást ne mondjak; csak egy okot említsek
for some reason	valamilyen oknál fogva
for that matter	ha már erről van szó; ami azt illeti
for that reason	ez okból; emiatt
frankly	őszintén (szólva)
from this aspect; from all/other aspects	ebből a szempontból; minden/egyéb ~
furthermore	(sőt) mi több; ezenkívül; ráadásul
generally speaking	általánosságban véve
God only knows	(ezt csak) Isten tudja; nem lehet tudni
hardly	alig
hence	ennélfogva; ezért
honestly	őszintén (szólva)
how shall I put it	hogy is mondjam; hogy is fogalmazzak
however	azonban; mégis; mindamellett
however strange it (may) sound(s)	bármilyen furcsán is hangzik
I'd go further than that	sőt, továbbmennék; sőt mi több
I'm convinced that …	meg vagyok győződve, hogy …
I'm of the opinion that	azon a véleményen vagyok, hogy
I believe	azt hiszem; úgy gondolom
I guess	azt hiszem; úgy gondolom
I have no doubt in my mind that …	semmi kétségem afelől, hogy …
I mean	úgy értem
I must/have to admit	be kell vallanom; el/be kell ismernem
I reckon	úgy vélem; úgy gondolom
I suppose	1. azt hiszem; úgy gondolom 2. feltételezem
I think	azt hiszem; úgy gondolom
I've got it	megvan!; rájöttem!; eszembe jutott!
i.e.	azaz
if	ha
if anything	ha egyáltalán valami
if I'm not mistaken	ha nem tévedek
if it comes to that	ha erre kerül(ne) a sor
if you ask me	ha kíváncsi a véleményemre; szerintem
if you like	ha úgy tetszik

if you see/know what I mean	ha érted mire gondolok
imagine, let's imagine	képzeld; képzeljük csak el
in (actual) fact	igazából; valójában
in addition to	...-n kívül; ...-n felül; ráadásul
in all likelihood	minden valószínűség szerint
in any case	mindenképpen
in brief	röviden (összefoglalva)
in case	hátha (valami történik); ha (netán) *[AmE]*
in case of	valami esetén
in every sense of the word	minden értelemben
in general	általánosságban (véve)
in my opinion	véleményem szerint
in one word	egyszóval; összefoglalva
in other words	más szóval
in practice	gyakorlatban
in some ways	bizonyos értelemben
in spite of	ellenére
in terms of	tekintetében; vonatkozásában
in that case	ebben az esetben
in the beginning	kezdetben; eleinte
in the end	végül (aztán)
in the event of	valami bekövetkezte esetén
in theory	elméletben; elméletileg
in the first place	először is; mindenekelőtt
incidentally	mellékesen; amúgy; apropó
incredible as it sounds	bármilyen hihetetlenül is hangzik
instead (of)	helyett
interestingly/curiously/oddly strangely enough	érdekes/furcsa módon
it goes without saying	mondani sem kell
it's as if	olyan mintha
it's not necessarily ...	nem feltétlenül ...
it's out of the question	ki van zárva; semmi esetre sem
it's quite (im)possible that	teljesen lehetetlen // nagyon is lehetséges, hogy ...
it's quite/(not) very likely that	nagyon valószínű, hogy ... // nem valószínű, hogy ...
it's the other way round	(pont) fordítva
it's true that	igaz, hogy ...
it's unlikely that	valószínűtlen, hogy ...
it depends (on)	attól függ
it goes without saying	mondani sem kell; mondanom sem kell
it varies	változó
just in case	mindenesetre; a biztonság kedvéért
just the same	mindennek ellenére; mégis
kind of	valamilyen; valamiféle
(and) **last**	és végül
last but not least	végül, de nem utolsósorban

let's say	mondjuk
let alone	hát még; pláne
like	mint
literally	a szó szoros értelmében; szó szerint
little wonder	nem csoda, hogy …
mind you	de ne feledd; de vigyázz; vigyázat
more or less	többé-kevésbé
moreover	mi több; sőt; ráadásul
(and) most important of all	(és) ami a legfontosabb
most probably	nagyon valószínű, hogy …
my opinion is that	az a véleményem, hogy …
namely	mégpedig; azaz; nevezetesen
naturally	természetesen
nearly	majdnem
needless to say	mondani sem kell
never mind	nem érdekes; ne izgasd magad; nem fontos
nevertheless	mindazonáltal; mégis; azonban
no chance	semmiképpen; semmi esetre sem; lehetetlen
no doubt	kétség kívül; nem vitás; vitán felül
no way	semmiképpen; semmi esetre sem; lehetetlen
no wonder	nem csoda, hogy …
none the less	mindazonáltal; mégis; azonban
not at all	egyáltalán nem
not in the least	legkevésbé sem; kicsit sem
not to mention	nem beszélve
now	nos; hát; szóval
obviously	nyilvánvalóan; világos, hogy
of course	persze; természetesen
on second thoughts	jobban átgondolva; mégis inkább
on the contrary	éppen ellenkezőleg
on the one hand	egyrészt; egyfelől
on the other hand	másrészt; másfelől
on the whole	egészében véve
on top of this	és még ráadásul; és ha ez nem lenne elég baj
one way or another	vagy így, vagy úgy; valamilyen módon
or else	mert különben; máskülönben
or rather	vagyis inkább; helyesebben; pontosabban
or so	vagy valami ilyesmi (jellegű)
or something like that	vagy valami hasonló (dolog)
or something to that effect	vagy valami hasonló értelmű dolog
otherwise	1. egyébként; máskülönben 2. mert különben
owing to	miatt
particularly	különösen; különösebben
partly	részben
practically	gyakorlatilag

preferably	inkább, ha mód van rá
provided	feltéve, hogy
providing	feltéve, hogy; ha
quite the contrary	éppen ellenkezőleg
really	igazán; tényleg; persze; nagyon
say	mondjuk
secondly	másodsorban
small wonder	nem csoda, hogy …
so	1. szóval; tehát; úgyhogy 2. így; ezért
so far	eddig; ezidáig; mostanáig
so it seems at least	legalábbis így tűnik
so much for	(na) ennyit a …
so to speak	hogy úgy mondjam
so what?	na és akkor mi van?
some say that	van aki azt mondja; egyesek szerint
somehow	1. valamilyen módon 2. bizonyos értelemben
somehow or other	vagy így, vagy úgy; valamilyen módon
sort of	valami féle; valamilyen; olyan …
still	mégis
strange/funny as it (may) sound(s)	bármilyen furcsán is hangzik
strictly speaking	szigorú értelemben véve
such	ilyen
such as	mint például
summarising	összefoglalva; hogy összefoglaljam
summing up	összefoglalva; hogy összefoglaljam
suppose/supposing/let's suppose	tételezzük fel
supposedly	feltehetőleg
sure enough	ahogy előre megmondtam
surely	bizonyosan; biztos
talking of	ha már …-ről van szó; ha már szóba került
thank God	hála Istennek
thanks to	köszönhetően
that's all	ennyi (az egész)
that's right	így van; helyes
that is	azaz
(oh,) that reminds me	erről jut eszembe
the thing is	arról van szó, hogy …
the other side of the coin is that	az érem másik oldala
the other way round	(pont) fordítva
then	aztán; aztán még; azonkívül
theoretically	elvileg; elméletileg
there's a chance that	van esélye, hogy; nem kizárt, hogy
therefore	ezért aztán; így aztán
this/that being so	mivel ez a helyzet; mivel ez így van
though	bár; habár

thus	így; ily módon; ennélfogva
to begin with	eleinte/kezdetben; először is
to a certain degree	bizonyos fokig
to a certain extent	bizonyos fokig
to be frank	őszintén szólva; hogy őszinte legyek
to be honest	őszintén szólva; hogy őszinte legyek
to be left with no choice but …	nincs más választás, mint …
to coin a phrase	hogy a közhellyel éljek
to cut a long story short	hogy rövidre fogjam a dolgot/szót
to make things worse	és ami még súlyosbítja a dolgokat
to my (great) relief/surprise	nagy megkönnyebbülésemre/meglepetésemre
to put it in a nutshell	dióhéjban, pár szóban
to recap what has been said so far	összefoglalva az eddig elhangzottakat
to say nothing of	nem beszélve a …
to say the least	hogy ennél rosszabbat már ne is mondjak
to start with	eleinte/kezdetben; először is
to sum up	összefoglalva; hogy összefoglaljam
to tell (you) the truth	az igazat megvallva; őszintén szólva
to the best of my knowledge	legjobb tudomásom szerint
under no circumstances	semmilyen körülmények között
(quite) understandably	érthető módon
undoubtedly	kétség kívül; kétségtelenül
unlike	nem úgy mint; szemben …-val
very well, but	jó, de; rendben van, de
we mustn't forget that	nem szabad elfelejtenünk, hogy …
well (now)	szóval; hát; tehát; na most
what's even worse	ami még rosszabb
what's more	mi több; sőt
What?	micsoda?
when it comes to	ha …-ra kerül a sor
whereas	míg
while	míg
who knows	ki tudja, talán
with regard to	vonatkozásában/tekintetében
yet	1. még 2. mégis
you have me there/you've got me there	na most megfogtál; erre nem tudok válaszolni
you know	tudod; szóval
You mean …?	azt akarod mondani, hogy …?; Úgy érted, hogy …?
you name it	és még egy csomó egyéb minden
you see	tudod; szóval

HUNGARIAN–ENGLISH

a biztonság kedvéért	just in case
a dolgok jelenlegi állása szerint	as it is
a jelek szerint	as it seems
a látszat ellenére	against all appearances
a közhiedelemmel ellentétben	contrary to popular belief
a szó szoros értelmében	literally; in the strict sense of the word
ahogy a mondás tartja	as the saying goes
akár hiszed, akár nem	believe it or not
alapjában véve/alapvetően	basically
általánosságban véve	generally speaking; in general
amennnyire meg tudom ítélni	as far as I can judge
amennyire tudom	as far as I know; to the best of my knowledge; for all I know
(és) ami a legfontosabb …	(and) most important of all, …
ami …-t illeti	as for …; as far as … is concerned, as regards
ami azt illeti	for that matter
amúgy	otherwise
apropó	by the way; incidentally
arról van szó, hogy …	the thing is that …
attól függ	it depends (on)
az a véleményem, hogy …	it is my opinion that …; as I see it
az biztos, hogy …	it is for sure that …; no doubt
az érem másik oldala	the other side of the coin
az igazat megvallva	to be frank/honest; to tell (you) the truth, honestly, frankly
azaz	that is; i.e.
azért mégis	still, in spite of this
azon a véleményen vagyok, hogy …	I'm of the opinion that …
azon/ezenkívül	besides; in addition to this; furthermore; moreover
azt akarod mondani, hogy …?	You mean …? Are you saying that …?
azt hiszem	I think/guess/reckon/believe
aztán/aztán még	then
bár	though; although; however
bármilyen furcsán is hangzik	strange/odd/curious as it (may) sound(s); however ~ it (may) sound(s)
bármilyen hihetetlenül is hangzik	incredible/unbelievable as it (may) sound(s)
be kell ismernem/be kell vallanom	I must/have to admit
bizonyos értelemben	in a way; somehow
bizonyos fokig	to a certain degree/extent
bizonyosan/biztosan	surely
de	but
de ne feledd	mind you; don't forget

de vigyázz	mind you
dióhéjban	in a nutshell
e miatt	
ebben az esetben	for this reason; that's why
egészében véve	in this case
egyáltalán nem	on the whole
egyébként	not at all
egyesek szerint	otherwise
egyfelől/egyrészt	some (people) say
egyszóval	on the one hand
eleinte	in one word
ellenére	in the beginning; at first; to begin/start with
elméletben	despite; in spite of
elméletileg	in theory
először/először is	theoretically
eltekintve valamitől	first; firstly; to begin/start with; in the first place
elvégre	apart from
elvileg	after all
emiatt	in theory/principle
ennek ellenére	because of this; as a result/consequence
ennek eredményeképpen/következtében	in spite of this; despite
ennek megfelelően	as a result/consequence; consequently
ennélfogva	accordingly
ennyi (az egész)	therefore; thus
(na) ennyit a …	that's all
éppen ellenkezőleg	so much for …
érdekes/furcsa módon	(quite) on the contrary
erre nem tudok válaszolni	in a funny/strange/odd way; interestingly enough
erről jut eszembe	you've got me there; you have me there
érthető módon	incidentally; by the way; (oh,) that reminds me
és hasonló dolgok	(quite) understandably
és így tovább	and things/stuff like that
és végül	and so on; and so forth
eszembe jutott!	(and) finally; (and) last
ez okból	I've got it!
ezenkívül	that's why; for this reason; because of this
ezért/ezért aztán	besides; in addition to this
ezidáig	that's why; for this reason; because of this
	so far; up to now; until now; as yet
feltehetően	supposedly
feltételezem	I suppose
feltéve, hogy	provided
…-n felül	in addition to …; on top of …; besides
(pont) fordítva	the other way round
gyakorlatilag	practically
ha	if; in case *(AmE)*; provided

ha …-ra kerül a sor	if it comes to …
ha egyáltalán valami	if anything
ha érted mire gondolok	if you know/see what I mean
ha jól tudom	if I'm not mistaken; as far as I know, to the best of my knowledge; for all I know
ha kíváncsi a véleményemre	if you ask me
ha már …-ről van szó/ha már erről van … szó/ha már szóba került	talking of …
ha úgy tetszik	if you like it
habár	though; although
hála Istennek	thank God
hát	well; now
hát hiszen	after all
hát még	let alone; not to mention
hátha (valami történik)	in case (it rains)
helyes	that's right
helyesebben	or rather; I should say
helyett	instead (of)
hogy a közhellyel éljek	to coin a phrase
hogy csak egy okot említsek	for one thing
hogy ennél rosszabbat már ne is mondjak	to say the least
hogy is mondjam/ hogy is fogalmazzak	how shall I put it
hogy mást ne mondjak	to say the least
hogy összefoglaljam	to sum up; summing up; summarising
hogy őszinte legyek	to be frank/honest; to tell (you) the truth; (quite) honestly/frankly
hogy rövidre fogjam a dolgot/szót	to cut a long story short
hogy úgy mondjam	as it were
igaz, hogy …	it's true that …, true enough
igazán/igazából	actually; really; as a matter of fact; in fact
így (aztán)	so; that way; therefore
így van	that's right
…-t illetően	as for; as regards; as far as … is concerned
ily módon	this way; so; therefore
információim szerint	as I understand; to the best of my knowledge
(ezt csak) Isten tudja	God only knows; who knows
jó, de …	well, but …
jobban átgondolva	on second thoughts
képzeld	(just) imagine; fancy (that)! (expressing surprise)
képzeljük csak el	let's imagine
kétségkívül/kétségtelenül	no doubt; undoubtedly
kezdetben	at first; in the beginning; to start/begin with
ki tudja, talán	who knows; you never know
ki van zárva	it's out of the question; no way; no chance
kicsit sem	not at all

kivéve	except (for); with the exception of; but (for)
...-n kívül	apart from
körülbelül	about; approximately
köszönhetően	thanks to; due to
következésképpen	as a consequence; consequently; therefore
különben	otherwise; or else
különben is/sem	anyway
kvázi	as it were
legalább	at least
legalábbis	at least; at any rate
legalábbis így tűnik	or so it seems (at least)
legfeljebb	at most; maximum
legjobb tudomásom szerint	as far as I know; to the best of my knowledge; for all I know; as I understand; if I'm not mistaken
legkevésbé sem	not in the least
lehetetlen	(it's quite) impossible
lehetőleg; ha mód van rá	preferably
majdnem	almost; nearly *(only with the idea of progress towards an end)*
már így is	as it is
más szóval	in other words; to put it in another way
másfelől (viszont)	on the other hand
máskülönben	otherwise; or else; from other aspects
másodsorban	second; secondly
másrészt (viszont)	on the other hand
még akkor is/ még ha	even if
meg ilyenek	and things/stuff like that
mégis	still; yet
még mindig	still
még nem	(not) yet; (not) as yet
mégpedig	namely
meg vagyok győződve	I'm convinced
megvan!	I've got it!
mellékesen	incidentally
mert különben	or else; otherwise
mi több	what's more
miatt	because of; due to; owing to
micsoda?	What?; What do you mean?
míg	while; whereas
mindamellett	besides
mindazonáltal	nevertheless
mindenekelőtt	first of all; first and foremost; in the first place
mindenesetre	at any rate
minden értelemben	in every sense of the word
mindenképpen	in any case
mindennek ellenére	in spite of all this; all the same; yet; still
mindent egybevéve/mindent összevetve	all in all; all things considered

mintegy	as it were *(úgymond)*; about/approximately *(with numbers)*
mint említettem	as I said; as I mentioned; as I was saying
mint kiderült	as it turned out
mint mondottam	as I said; as I was saying
mintha	as if; as though
mint például	such as; like
mivel ez a helyzet/mivel ez így van	this being the case
mondani sem kell/mondanom sem kell	needless to say; it goes without saying
mondjuk	say; let's say
mostanáig	so far; as yet; up to now; until now
na és akkor mi van?	so what?
na mindegy	anyway; anyhow
na most	well then; now
na most megfogtál	You've got me there; You have me there.
nagyjából	more or less; approximately; basically
nagy meglepetésemre/megkönnyebbülésemre	to my surprise/relief
nagyon is lehetséges, hogy .../nagyon valószínű, hogy ...	it's quite likely that ...; there's a good chance that ...; in all likelihood; it's quite probable that ...
nem beszélve a ...	not to mention; let alone
nem csoda, hogy ...	no/little/small wonder ...
nem feltétlenül ...	not necessarily
nem kizárt, hogy ...	it's not impossible that ...; there's a chance that ...
nem lehet tudni	you never know
nem szabad elfelejtenünk, hogy ...	we mustn't forget
nem valószínű, hogy ...	it's quite/pretty unlikely that ...
nem vitás	no doubt; undoubtedly
nevezetesen	namely
nincs más választás/nincs mit tenni , mint ...	to be left with no choice, but ...
nos	well; now
nyilvánvalóan	obviously; clearly
olyan mintha	it's as if/though
összefoglalva/összefoglalva az eddig ... elhangzottakat	to recap/summarise/sum up what has been said so far
őszintén (szólva)	frankly/honestly; to be frank/honest
pár szóban	in a few words; briefly
például	for example/instance; e.g.
persze	of course; certainly; obviously
pláne	especially; particularly *(különösen)*; let alone *(hát még)*
pontosabban	or rather
ráadásul	in addition to this ...; on top of this; what's more

rájöttem!	I've got it!
rendben van, de	all right, but; very well, but
részben	partly
(és ami még) rosszabb	and what's even worse; and, even worse that that
röviden (összefoglalva)	in brief; briefly; in short

satöbbi	et cetera; etc.; and so on
semmiképpen/semmi esetre sem	no way
semmi kétségem afelől, hogy …	I have no doubt in my mind that …
semmilyen körülmények között	under no circumstances (will I …)
sőt (mi több)	what's more; moreover; furthermore
sőt, továbbmennék	I'd go further than this/that
(és ami még csak) súlyosbítja a helyzetet	(and) to make things worse
(ebből a/minden/egyéb) szempontból	from this aspect/point of view; from all/other aspects

szerint	according to
szerintem	I think/believe; as I see it; in my opinion/view
szó szerint/a szó szoros értelmében	literally
szóval	so; anyway; anyhow; well; now

tehát	so; anyway; anyhow; well; now
tegyük fel, hogy …	suppose; supposing
… tekintetében	in terms of …; as to …; as regards …; as for …; as far as … is concerned
teljesen lehetetlen	that is out of the question; that's quite impossible
tényleg	really; certainly
ténylegesen	actually
természetesen	naturally; of course; certainly
tételezzük fel	suppose; let's suppose
többé-kevésbé	more or less
tudod	you know/see
tulajdonképpen	actually; in fact; as a matter of fact; really

úgy érted, hogy …?	You mean …? Are you saying …?
úgy értem	I mean …
úgy gondolom/vélem	I think/believe
úgy tűnik/látszik	as it seems
úgyhogy	so; therefore; thus
úgymond	as it were; kind of; sort of
úgyszólván	basically; practically; almost; literally

vagy amit akarsz	or/and what have you
vagy így, vagy úgy	one way or another
vagy mit tudom én	or/and what have you
vagy valami hasonló (dolog)	or something like that
vagy valami hasonló (értelmű dolog)	or something to that effect
vagy valami ilyesmi (jellegű)	or so
vagyis inkább	or rather
valahogy (bizonyos értelemben)	somehow; in some ways

valami bekövetkezte esetén	in the event (of war)
valami esetén	in case of (fire)
valamiféle/valamilyen	a/some sort/kind of
valamilyen oknál fogva	for some reason
valamin/valakin kívül	apart from
valaminek a kezdetén	at the beginning
valaminek megfelelően	according to
valójában	really; actually; in fact; in reality
valószínűtlen, hogy …	it's (quite/rather/pretty) unlikely that …
változó	it varies
van aki azt mondja	some (people) say
van esélye, hogy …	there's a chance/some likelihood that …
végre (valahára)	at last; at long last
végül (aztán)	eventually; in the end
végül is	after all
végül, de nem utolsósorban	last but not least
véleményem szerint	I think; as I see it; in my opinion
(de) vigyázat	mind you
világos, hogy …	it's (quite) obvious/clear that …
vitán felül	undoubtedly; no doubt
vonatkozásában	in terms of; as to; as regards; as far as … is concerned

FIRST AID KIT 4
Pronunciation dictionary

abandon [ə'bændən]
abdomen ['æbdəmən]
abduct [əb'dʌkt]
ability [ə'bɪlətɪ]
above [ə'bʌv]
abroad [ə'brɔ:d]
absent ['æbsənt]
absenteeism [,æbsn'ti:ɪzəm]
academy [ə'kædəmɪ]
accelerator [ək'seləreɪtə]
accept [ək'sept]
accessory [ək'sesərɪ]
accident ['æksɪdənt]
accommodation [ə,kɒmə'deɪʃn]
accompany [ə'kʌmpənɪ]
accountancy [ə'kaʊntənsɪ]
accountant [ə'kaʊntənt]
accusation [,ækjʊ'zeɪʃn]
accuse [ə'kju:z]
ache [eɪk]
acid ['æsɪd]
acquire [ə'kwaɪə]
acquit [ə'kwɪt]
action ['ækʃn]
active ['æktɪv]
activist ['æktɪvɪst]
activity [æk'tɪvətɪ]
actor ['æktə]
actress ['æktrɪs]
add [æd]
addict ['ædɪkt]
addicted [ə'dɪktɪd]
addition [ə'dɪʃn]
additional [ə'dɪʃənl]
adjacent [ə'dʒeɪsnt]
admiration [,ædmə'reɪʃn]
admire [əd'maɪə]
admirer [əd'maɪərə]
admission [əd'mɪʃn]
admit [əd'mɪt]
admittedly [əd'mɪtɪdlɪ]
adolescent [,ædə'lesnt]
ad [æd]
adult ['ædʌlt; also ə'dʌlt]
advance *BrE* [əd'vɑ:ns];
AmE [əd'væns]
advanced level [əd'vɑ:nst levl]
adventure [əd'ventʃə]
advertisement *BrE* [əd'vɜ:tɪsmənt];
AmE [,ædvər'taɪzmənt]
advertising ['ædvətaɪzɪŋ]
advice [əd'vaɪs]
aerobic [eə'rəʊbɪk]
aeroplane ['eərəpleɪn]
affair [ə'feə]
affect [ə'fekt]
afraid [ə'freɪd]
against [ə'genst]
age [eɪdʒ]
ageing ['eɪdʒɪŋ]
agency ['eɪdʒənsɪ]
agent ['eɪdʒənt]
agricultural [,ægrɪ'kʌltʃrəl]
agronomics [,ægrəʊ'nɒmɪks]
aid [eɪd]
AIDS [eɪdz]
air [eə]
airport ['eəpɔ:t]
alarm [ə'lɑ:m]
album ['ælbəm]
alcoholic [,ælkə'hɒlɪk]
alcoholism ['ælkəhɒlɪzəm]
alert [ə'lɜ:t]
A-level ['eɪ levl]
alike [ə'laɪk]
allergic [ə'lɜ:dʒɪk]
allergy ['ælədʒɪ]
allowance [ə'laʊəns]
almond ['ɑ:mənd]
almost ['ɔ:lməʊst]
amateur ['æmətə]
amber ['æmbə]
ambulance ['æmbjələns]
amenities [ə'mi:nətɪz]
amount [ə'maʊnt]
anchor ['æŋkə]
Anglican ['æŋglɪkən]
angling ['æŋglɪŋ]
ankle ['æŋkl]
annual ['ænjʊəl]
anorak ['ænəræk]
answer *BrE* ['ɑ:nsə]; *AmE* ['ænsə]
antibiotic [,æntɪbaɪ'ɒtɪk]
antiseptic [,æntɪ'septɪk]
apartment [ə'pɑ:tmənt]
appeal [ə'pi:l]
appear [ə'pɪə]
appearance [ə'pɪərəns]
appendix [ə'pendɪks]
appetite ['æpɪtaɪt]
appliance [ə'plaɪəns]
apply [ə'plaɪ]
appointment [ə'pɔɪntmənt]
appreciate [ə'pri:ʃɪeɪt]
appreciation [ə,pri:ʃɪ'eɪʃn]
approximately [ə'prɒksɪmətlɪ]
apricot ['eɪprɪkɒt]
aquarium [ə'kweərɪəm]
archery ['ɑ:tʃərɪ]
architect ['ɑ:kɪtekt]
area ['eərɪə]
argue ['ɑ:gju:]
argument ['ɑ:gjʊmənt]
arisen [ə'rɪzn]

armchair ['ɑ:mtʃeə]
armoury ['ɑ:mərɪ]
arrange [ə'reɪndʒ]
arrest [ə'rest]
arrow ['ærəʊ]
arson ['ɑ:sn]
artery ['ɑ:tərɪ]
article ['ɑ:tɪkl]
artificial [,ɑ:tɪ'fɪʃl]
artist ['ɑ:tɪst]
arts [ɑ:ts]
asleep [ə'sli:p]
assassin [ə'sæsɪn]
assassinate [ə'sæsɪneɪt]
assault [ə'sɔ:lt]
assignment [ə'saɪnmənt]
assistant [ə'sɪstənt]
atheist ['eɪθɪɪst]
athlete ['æθli:t]
athletics [æθ'letɪks]
atmospheric [,ætməs'ferɪk]
attack [ə'tæk]
attempt [ə'tempt]
attend [ə'tend]
attendant [ə'tendənt]
attraction [ə'trækʃn]
auction ['ɔ:kʃən]
auctioneer [,ɔ:kʃə'nɪə]
audience ['ɔ:dɪəns]
auditorium [,ɔ:dɪ'tɔ:rɪəm]
aunt *BrE* [ɑ:nt]; *AmE* [ænt]
author ['ɔ:θə]
autobiography [,ɔ:təbaɪ'ɒgrəfɪ]
automatic [,ɔ:tə'mætɪk]
autopsy ['ɔ:tɒpsɪ]
average ['ævərɪdʒ]
avoid [ə'vɔɪd]
award [ə'wɔ:d]
awful ['ɔ:fl]

baby ['beɪbɪ]
bachelor ['bætʃələ]
backbone ['bækbəʊn]
backpack ['bækpæk]
bacon ['beɪkən]
badminton ['bædmɪntn]
baggage ['bægɪdʒ]
bail [beɪl]
bait [beɪt]
baker's ['beɪkəz]
bake [beɪk]
balanced ['bælənst]
balcony ['bælkənɪ]
balding ['bɔ:ldɪŋ]
banana *BrE* [bə'nɑ:nə];
AmE [bə'nænə]
bandage ['bændɪdʒ]
bargain ['bɑ:gɪn]
baseball ['beɪsbɔ:l]
basic ['beɪsɪk]
basin [beɪsn]
basketball *BrE* ['bɑ:skɪtbɔ:l]
AmE ['bæskətbɔ:l]
bat [bæt]
bathing suit ['beɪðɪŋ su:t]
baths *BrE* [bɑ:ðz]; *AmE* [bæðz]
bathtub *BrE* ['bɑ:θtʌb];
AmE ['bæθtʌb]
beans [bi:nz]
beard [bɪəd]
beat [bi:t]
become [bɪ'kʌm]
beefsteak ['bi:fsteɪk]
beer [bɪə]
beetroot ['bi:tru:t]
believe [bɪ'li:v]
belong [bɪ'lɒŋ]
below [bɪ'ləʊ]
belly ['belɪ]
benefit ['benɪfɪt]
berth [bɜ:θ]
Bible ['baɪbl]
bike [baɪk]
bikini [bɪ'ki:nɪ]
billiards ['bɪljədz]
bills [bɪlz]
biology [baɪ'ɒlədʒɪ]
birdie ['bɜ:dɪ]
birthmark ['bɜ:θmɑ:k]
biscuit ['bɪskɪt]
bitterly ['bɪtəlɪ]
black [blæk]
blackmail ['blækmeɪl]
bladder ['blædə]
blame [bleɪm]
bland [blænd]
blast *BrE* [blɑ:st]; *AmE* [blæst]
blaze [bleɪz]
blazer ['bleɪzə]
blind [blaɪnd]
blister ['blɪstə]
blond [blɒnd]
blood [blʌd]
blouse [blaʊz]
boarding ['bɔ:dɪŋ]
boating ['bəʊtɪŋ]
bobsleighing ['bɒbsleɪɪŋ]
boil [bɔɪl]
boiling ['bɔɪlɪŋ]
bolt ['bəʊlt]
bone [bəʊn]
bonnet ['bɒnɪt]
bonus ['bəʊnəs]
boom [bu:m]
boot [bu:t]
border ['bɔ:də]
bottle [bɒtl]
bottom ['bɒtəm]
bow [baʊ]
bow tie [,bəʊ 'taɪ]
bowel ['baʊəl]
bowl [bəʊl]
bowling ['bəʊlɪŋ]
bowls [bəʊlz]
box [bɒks]
boxing ['bɒksɪŋ]
boyfriend ['bɔɪfrend]
bra [brɑ:]
brain [breɪn]
brake [breɪk]
brand [brænd]
brandy ['brændɪ]
brass *BrE* [brɑ:s]; *AmE* [bræs]
brave [breɪv]
breadcrumbs ['bredkrʌmz]
break [breɪk]
breakfast ['brekfəst]
breast [brest]
breathalyser ['breθəlaɪzə]
breath [breθ]
breathe [bri:ð]
breeze [bri:z]
bribery ['braɪbərɪ]
bride [braɪd]
bridegroom ['braɪdgru:m]
bridge [brɪdʒ]
bright [braɪt]
bring [brɪŋ]
broad [brɔ:d]
broadcast *BrE* ['brɔ:dkɑ:st];
AmE ['brɔ:dkæst]
broccoli ['brɒkəlɪ]
broken [brəʊkn]
broker ['brəʊkə]
bronze [brɒnz]
broom [bru:m]
brother ['brʌðə]
brown ['braʊn]
bruise [bru:z]
brush [brʌʃ]
brussels-sprouts [,brʌslz 'spraʊts]
buckle [bʌkl]
Buddhist ['bʊdɪst]
budget ['bʌdʒɪt]
buff [bʌf]
builder ['bɪldə]
bulky ['bʌlkɪ]
bumper ['bʌmpə]
bun [bʌn]
bunched ['bʌntʃt]
bungalow ['bʌŋgələʊ]
bungee jump ['bʌndʒi: dʒʌmp]
bureau ['bjʊərəʊ]
burglary ['bɜ:glərɪ]
burgle [bɜ:gl]
burn [bɜ:n]
business ['bɪznəs]
butcher's ['bʊtʃəz]
butter ['bʌtə]
butterfly ['bʌtəflaɪ]
buttocks ['bʌtəks]
button [bʌtn]
buy [baɪ]

cab [kæb]
cabbage ['kæbɪdʒ]
cabinet ['kæbɪnɪt]
cake [keɪk]
Calvinist ['kælvɪnɪst]
camisole ['kæmɪsəʊl]
camping ['kæmpɪŋ]
cancer ['kænsə]

candlestick ['kændlstɪk]
canoeing [kə'nu:ɪŋ]
cantaloupe ['kæntəlu:p]
canteen [kæn'ti:n]
capital ['kæpɪtl]
capped [kæpt]
caravanning ['kærəvænɪŋ]
caraway ['kærəweɪ]
cardboard ['kɑ:dbɔ:d]
cardigan ['kɑ:dɪgən]
cards [kɑ:dz]
care [keə]
career [kə'rɪə]
carefully ['keəflɪ]
carp [kɑ:p]
carpenter ['kɑ:pɪntə]
carpet ['kɑ:pɪt]
carriage ['kærɪdʒ]
carrot ['kærət]
carry ['kærɪ]
carton [kɑ:tn]
cartoon [kɑ:'tu:n]
case [keɪs]
cash [kæʃ]
cashier [kæ'ʃɪə]
cassette [kə'set]
cast *BrE* [kɑ:st]; *AmE* [kæst]
castle *BrE* ['kɑ:sl]; *AmE* [kæsl]
castor *BrE* ['kɑ:stə]; *AmE* ['kæstə]
casual ['kæʒʊəl]
casualty ['kæʒʊəltɪ]
catalogue ['kætəlɒg]
catering ['keɪtərɪŋ]
cathedral [kə'θi:drəl]
catwalk ['kætwɔ:k]
cauliflower ['kɒlɪflaʊə]
cause [kɔ:z]
cavity ['kævətɪ]
CD [,si:'di:]
CD player [,si:'di: pleɪə]
cease [si:s]
celebration [,selɪ'breɪʃn]
celery ['selərɪ]
cellar ['selə]
Celsius ['selsɪəs]
Centigrade ['sentɪgreɪd]
centre ['sentə]
cereal ['sɪərɪəl]
ceremony ['serɪmənɪ]
certificate [sɜ:'tɪfɪkət]
chain [tʃeɪn]
champagne [ʃæm'peɪn]
champion ['tʃæmpɪən]
championship ['tʃæmpɪənʃɪp]
change [tʃeɪndʒ]
changeability [,tʃeɪndʒə'bɪlətɪ]
changeable ['tʃeɪndʒəbl]
channel [tʃænl]
chap [tʃæp]
character ['kærəktə]
characteristic [,kærəktə'rɪstɪk]
charge ['tʃɑ:dʒ]
charwoman ['tʃɑ:wʊmən]
chat [tʃæt]
chauvinism ['ʃəʊvənɪzəm]
cheat [tʃi:t]
check [tʃek]
cheek [tʃi:k]
cheerful ['tʃɪəfl]
cheese [tʃi:z]
chemical ['kemɪkəl]
chemist's ['kemɪsts]
chemistry ['kemɪstrɪ]
cherish ['tʃerɪʃ]
cherry ['tʃerɪ]
chess [tʃes]
chest [tʃest]
chest of drawers [,tʃestə'drɔ:z]
chic [ʃi:k]
chicken [tʃɪkn]
chief [tʃi:f]
child minder ['tʃaɪld maɪndə]
childless ['tʃaɪldləs]
children ['tʃɪldrən]
chilly ['tʃɪlɪ]
chin [tʃɪn]
china ['tʃaɪnə]
chocolate ['tʃɒklət]
choice [tʃɔɪs]
choir [kwaɪə]
cholesterol [kə'lestərɒl]
chop [tʃɒp]
chores [tʃɔ:z]
Christian ['krɪstʃən]
chubby ['tʃʌbɪ]
church [tʃɜ:tʃ]
cinema ['sɪnəmə]
cinematographic [,sɪnəmətə'græfɪk]
cinnamon ['sɪnəmən]
circle [sɜ:kl]
Citadel ['sɪtədəl]
civil [sɪvl]
claim [kleɪm]
clamp [klæmp]
clap [klæp]
classical ['klæsɪkl]
claustrophobia [,klɔ:strə'fəʊbɪə]
clean [kli:n]
clear [klɪə]
clerk *BrE* [klɑ:k]; *AmE* [klɜ:rk]
climate ['klaɪmɪt]
clinic ['klɪnɪk]
cloakroom ['kləʊkru:m]
clog [klɒg]
close [kləʊs] *adj*
close [kləʊz] *v*
closet ['klɒzɪt]
clothed [kləʊðd]
clothes *BrE* [kləʊðz]; *AmE* [kləʊz]
clothing ['kləʊðɪŋ]
cloud [klaʊd]
clove [kləʊv]
club [klʌb]
clutch [klʌtʃ]
coach [kəʊtʃ]
coat [kəʊt]
cod [kɒd]
code [kəʊd]
coffee ['kɒfɪ]
cogwheel ['kɒgwi:l]
cohabit [kəʊ'hæbɪt]
cohabitation [,kəʊhæbɪ'teɪʃn]
coin [kɔɪn]
cold cuts ['kəʊld kʌts]
collagen ['kɒlədʒen]
collar ['kɒlə]
collect [kə'lekt]
collectable [kə'lektəbl]
collectible [kə'lektəbl]
college ['kɒlɪdʒ]
collision [kə'lɪʒn]
comb [kəʊm]
combat ['kɒmbæt]
comedy ['kɒmədɪ]
comfortable ['kʌmftəbl]
comforts ['kʌmfəts]
comic strip ['kɒmɪk strɪp]
commercial [kə'mɜ:ʃl]
commit [kə'mɪt]
communal ['kɒmjʊnl]
communist ['kɒmjʊnɪst]
community [kə'mju:nətɪ]
company ['kʌmpənɪ]
comparison [kəm'pærɪsn]
compartment [kəm'pɑ:tmənt]
compensation [,kɒmpen'seɪʃn]
competition [,kɒmpə'tɪʃn]
competitive [kəm'petətɪv]
competitor [kəm'petɪtə]
complete [kəm'pli:t]
complex ['kɒmpleks]
complexion [kəm'plekʃn]
comprehensive [,kɒmprɪ'hensɪv]
compulsory [kəm'pʌlsrɪ]
con man ['kɒn mæn]
concert ['kɒnsət]
condition [kən'dɪʃn]
condominium [,kɒndə'mɪnɪəm]
conductor [kən'dʌktə]
confectioner's [kən'fekʃnəz]
confess [kən'fes]
connection [kə'nekʃn]
conscience ['kɒnʃns]
conscientious [,kɒnʃɪ'enʃəs]
consciousness ['kɒnʃəsnəs]
consequence ['kɒnsɪkwəns]
consequent ['kɒnsɪkwənt]
conservative [kən'sɜ:vətɪv]
consider [kən'sɪdə]
constipation [,kɒnstɪ'peɪʃn]
consult [kən'sʌlt]
consumer [kən'sju:mə]
consumption [kən'sʌmpʃn]
contagious [kən'teɪdʒəs]
contain [kən'teɪn]
contempt [kən'tem(p)t]
content [kən'tent] *adj*
content ['kɒntent] *n*
contentedly [kən'tentɪdlɪ]
continue [kən'tɪnju:]
contraceptive [,kɒntrə'septɪv]
control [kən'trəʊl]

conveniences [kən'vi:nıənsız]
conversational [,kɒnvə'seıʃənl]
convert [kən'vɜ:t]
convict ['kɒnvıkt] *n*
convict [kən'vıkt] *v*
cook [kʊk]
cookbook ['kʊkbʊk]
cop [kɒp]
cope [kəʊp]
corduroy ['kɔ:dərɔı]
corn cob ['kɔ:n kɒb]
cornflakes ['kɔ:nfleıks]
correct [kə'rekt]
corruption [kə'rʌpʃn]
costume ['kɒstju:m]
cottage cheese [,kɒtıdʒ 'tʃi:z]
cotton ['kɒtən]
couch [kaʊtʃ]
cough [kɒf]
council ['kaʊnsl]
counter ['kaʊntə]
counterfeit ['kaʊntəfıt]
country ['kʌntrı]
countryside ['kʌntrısaıd]
county ['kaʊntı]
course [kɔ:s]
coursebook ['kɔ:sbʊk]
court [kɔ:t]
courteous ['kɜ:tıəs]
cousin [kʌzn]
cracker ['krækə]
cram [kræm]
crash [kræʃ]
crater ['kreıtə]
crawl [krɔ:l]
craze [kreız]
cream [kri:m]
créche [kreʃ] or [kreıʃ]
credit ['kredıt]
crew [kru:]
cricket ['krıkıt]
crime [kraım]
cross-country [,krɒs'kʌntrı]
crosswords ['krɒswɜ:dz]
crown [kraʊn]
cruise [kru:z]
cucumbers ['kju:kʌmbə]
cue [kju:]
cuff [kʌf]
cuisine [kwı'zi:n]
culprit ['kʌlprıt]
cult [kʌlt]
cup [kʌp]
cupboard ['kʌbəd]
cure [kjʊə]
curly ['kɜ:lı]
currant ['kʌrənt]
current ['kʌrənt]
curricular [kə'rıkjʊlə]
curriculum [kə'rıkjʊləm]
curriculum vitae [kə,rıkjʊləm 'vi:taı]
curtail [kɜ:'teıl]
curtain [kɜ:tn]
customer ['kʌstəmə]
customs ['kʌstəmz]
CV [,si:'vi:]
cycling ['saıklıŋ]

dairy ['deərı]
damage ['dæmıdʒ]
damp [dæmp]
dancer *BrE* [dɑ:nsə]; *AmE* [dænsər]
dangerous ['deındʒərəs]
Danube ['dænju:b]
dark [dɑ:k]
darts [dɑ:ts]
date [deıt]
day-nursery ['deı nɜ:sərı]
deaf [def]
deal [di:l]
dealer ['di:lə]
death [deθ]
decay [dı'keı]
decease [dı'si:s]
deceive [dı'si:v]
deception [dı'sepʃn]
decide [dı'saıd]
decision [dı'sıʒn]
declare [dı'kleə]
decorator ['dekəreıtə]
defeat [dı'fi:t]
defendant [dı'fendənt]
defender [dı'fendə]
defiantly [dı'faıəntlı]
deficiency [dı'fıʃnsı]
define [dı'faın]
definite ['defınət]
definitely ['defınətlı]
definition [,defı'nıʃn]
defunct [dı'fʌŋkt]
degree [dıg'ri:]
delighted [dı'laıtıd]
demand *BrE* [dı'mɑ:nd];
AmE [dı'mænd]
demonstrate ['demənstreıt]
demonstration [,demən'streıʃn]
denim ['denım]
denomination [dı,nɒmı'neıʃn]
deny [dı'naı]
department [dı'pɑ:tmənt]
departure [dı'pɑ:tʃə]
depict [dı'pıkt]
deposit [dı'pɒzıt]
depressed [dı'prest]
depression [,dı'preʃn]
deprive [dı'praıv]
derailment [dı'reılmənt]
describe [dı'skraıb]
description [dı'skrıpʃn]
deserve [dı'zɜ:v]
designer [dı'zaınə]
despair [dı'speə]
desperado *BrE* [,despə'rɑ:dəʊ];
AmE [,despə'reıdəʊ]
despite [dı'spaıt]
dessert [dı'zɜ:t]
destroy [dı'strɔı]
destruction [dı'strʌkʃn]
detail ['di:teıl]
detective [dı'tektıv]
deter [dı'tɜ:]
detergent [dı'tɜ:dʒənt]
determine [dı'tɜ:mın]
develop [dı'veləp]
device [dı'vaıs]
dew [dju:]
diagnosis [,daıəg'nəʊsıs]
diamond ['daıəmənd]
diarrhoea [,daıə'rıə]
die [daı]
diet ['daıət]
dietician [,daıə'tıʃn]
difference ['dıfrəns]
dining-room ['daınıŋru:m]
director [də'rektə]
disability [,dısə'bılətı]
disappear [,dısə'pıə]
disaster *BrE* [dı'zɑ:stə];
AmE [dı'zæstər]
disastrous *BrE* [dı'zɑ:strəs]
AmE [dı'zæstrəs]
discipline ['dısıplın]
discover [dıs'kʌvə]
discriminate [dı'skrımıneıt]
discrimination [dı,skrımı'neıʃn]
discus ['dıskəs]
discuss [dı'skʌs]
discussion [dı'skʌʃn]
disease [dı'zi:z]
dish ['dıʃ]
dishwasher ['dıʃwɒʃə]
dislike [dıs'laık]
dismiss [dıs'mıs]
disposal [dı'spəʊzl]
distance ['dıstəns]
distant ['dıstənt]
distinction [dıs'tıŋkʃn]
distinguish [dı'stıŋgwıʃ]
distraction [dı'strækʃn]
divine [dı'vaın]
diving ['daıvıŋ]
division [dı'vıʒn]
divorce [dı'vɔ:s]
divorced [dı'vɔ:st]
DIY [,di: aı 'waı]
dizzy ['dızı]
document ['dɒkjʊmənt]
documentary [,dɒkjʊ'mentrı]
dodge [dɒdʒ]
dole [dəʊl]
dominate ['dɒmıneıt]
dotted ['dɒtıd]
doubles ['dʌblz]
downhill [,daʊn'hıl]
downstairs [,daʊn'steəz]
downtown [,daʊn'taʊn]
doze [dəʊz]
drag [dræg]
drama ['drɑ:mə]
dramatic [drə'mætık]
dramatist ['dræmətıst]
drapes ['dreıps]

draw [drɔ:]
drenched ['drentʃt]
dressed [drest]
dressmaker ['dresmeɪkə]
drizzle [drɪzl]
drought [draʊt]
drugstore ['drʌgstɔ:]
dry [draɪ]
dub [dʌb]
duck [dʌk]
dull [dʌl]
dumb [dʌm]
dump [dʌmp]
dumplings ['dʌmplɪŋ]
dungarees [,dʌŋgə'ri:z]
duplicate ['dju:plɪkeɪt]
durable ['djʊərəbl]
dust [dʌst]
dustbin ['dʌstbɪn]
dustman ['dʌstmən]
duty ['dju:tɪ]
dye [daɪ]

eagle [i:gl]
ear [ɪə]
ear-ache ['ɪəreɪk]
earn [ɜ:n]
earthquake ['ɜ:θkweɪk]
ecological [,i:kə'lɒdʒɪkl]
economic [,i:kə'nɒmɪk]
economics [,i:kə'nɒmɪks]
economist [ɪ'kɒnəmɪst]
editorial [,edɪ'tɔ:rɪəl]
education [,edjʊ'keɪʃn]
educational [,edjʊ'keɪʃənl]
effect [ɪ'fekt]
effective [ɪ'fektɪv]
effectiveness [ɪ'fektɪvnəs]
efficiency [ɪ'fɪʃnsɪ]
efficient [ɪ'fɪʃnt]
effort ['efət]
Elastoplast [ɪ'læstəplɑ:st]
elbow ['elbəʊ]
elderly ['eldəlɪ]
election [ɪ'lekʃn]
electric [ɪ'lektrɪk]
electrical [ɪ'lektrɪkl]
electrician [ɪ,lek'trɪʃn]
elegant ['elɪgənt]
elephant ['elɪfənt]
eliminate [ɪ'lɪmɪneɪt]
Elizabeth [ɪ'lɪzəbəθ]
embezzle [ɪm'bezl]
embroider [ɪm'brɔɪdə]
emission [ɪ'mɪʃn]
employ [ɪm'plɔɪ]
employed [ɪm'plɔɪd]
employee [,emplɔɪ'i:]
employment [ɪm'plɔɪmənt]
empty ['emptɪ]
encrusted [ɪn'krʌstɪd]
energy ['enədʒɪ]
enforcement [ɪn'fɔ:smənt]
engage [ɪn'geɪdʒ]
engine ['endʒɪn]
engineer [,endʒɪ'nɪə]
enrol [ɪn'rəʊl]
enter ['entə]
enterprise ['entəpraɪz]
entertainment [,entə'teɪnmənt]
entrance ['entrəns]
entrepreneur [,ɒntrəprə'nɜ:]
entry ['entrɪ]
environment [ɪn'vaɪərənmənt]
environmentalist [ɪn,vaɪərən'mentəlɪst]
environmentally [ɪn,vaɪərən'mentəlɪ]
epidemic [,epɪ'demɪk]
equal ['i:kwəl]
equalise ['i:kwəlaɪz]
equality [ɪ'kwɒlətɪ]
equipment [ɪ'kwɪpmənt]
equivalent [ɪ'kwɪvələnt]
erase [ɪ'reɪz]
eruption [ɪ'rʌpʃn]
escalate ['eskəleɪt]
essential [ɪ'senʃl]
estate [ɪ'steɪt]
ethnic ['eθnɪk]
European [,jʊərə'pi:ən]
euthanasia [,ju:θə'neɪzɪə]
evade [ɪ'veɪd]
evaporate [ɪ'væpəreɪt]
evasion [ɪ'veɪʒn]
evening ['i:vnɪŋ]
event [ɪ'vent]
evict [ɪ'vɪkt]
eviction [ɪ'vɪkʃn]
evidence ['evɪdəns]
evil [i:vl]
ex [eks]
exact [ɪg'zækt]
exam [ɪg'zæm]
examination [ɪg,zæmɪ'neɪʃn]
examine [ɪg'zæmɪn]
exception [ɪk'sepʃn]
excess [ɪk'ses]
excursion *BrE* [ɪk'skɜ:ʃn];
AmE [ɪk'skɜ:rʒn]
executive [ɪg'zekjʊtɪv]
exercise ['eksəsaɪz]
exhausted [ɪg'zɔ:stɪd]
exist [ɪg'zɪst]
expel [ɪk'spel]
experience [ɪk'spɪərɪəns]
expire [ɪk'spaɪə]
explanation [,eksplə'neɪʃn]
explosion [ɪk'spləʊʒn]
expulsion [ɪk'spʌlʃn]
extort [ɪk'stɔ:t]
extra ['ekstrə]
extravaganza [ɪk,strævə'gænzə]
extreme [ɪk'stri:m]
extricate ['ekstrɪkeɪt]
eyebrow ['aɪbraʊ]
eyelash ['aɪlæʃ]

fête [feɪt]
fabric ['fæbrɪk]
face [feɪs]
facilitate [fə'sɪlɪteɪt]
facility [fə'sɪlətɪ]
factor ['fæktə]
factory ['fæktrɪ]
faculty ['fækltɪ]
Fahrenheit ['færənhaɪt]
fail [feɪl]
failure ['feɪljə]
fainting ['feɪntɪŋ]
fair [feə]
fairy tale ['feərɪ teɪl]
faith [feɪθ]
fake [feɪk]
family ['fæmlɪ]
famine ['fæmɪn]
famous ['feɪməs]
fan [fæn]
fancy ['fænsɪ]
fare [feə]
farmer ['fɑ:mə]
fashionable ['fæʃnəbl]
fastener *BrE*['fɑ:snə];
AmE ['fæsnər]
fat [fæt]
fatal [feɪtl]
faucet ['fɔ:sɪt]
favour ['feɪvə]
favourite ['feɪvrɪt]
feather ['feðə]
feature ['fi:tʃə]
fee [fi:]
feminist ['femɪnɪst]
fencing ['fensɪŋ]
fever ['fi:və]
fiancé masc *BrE* [fɪ'ɒnseɪ];
AmE [,fi:ɑ:n'seɪ]
fiancée fem *BrE* [fɪ'ɒnseɪ];
AmE [,fi:ɑ:n'seɪ]
fibre ['faɪbə]
fibrous ['faɪbrəs]
fiction ['fɪkʃn]
fiddle [fɪdl]
fighting ['faɪtɪŋ]
figs [fɪgz]
figure ['fɪgə]
final [faɪnl]
finance ['faɪnæns] *n*
finance [faɪ'næns] *v*
fine [faɪn]
finger ['fɪŋgə]
fire ['faɪə]
Fishermen's Bastion ['fɪʃəmenz
bæstɪən]
fishing ['fɪʃɪŋ]
fix [fɪks]
fixed [fɪkst]
fixtures ['fɪkstʃəz]
flake [fleɪk]
flamboyant [flæm'bɔɪənt]
flare [fleə]
flavoured ['fleɪvəd]
flesh [fleʃ]
flexible ['fleksəbl]

flexitime ['fleksɪtaɪm]
flight [flaɪt]
fling [flɪŋ]
flirt [flɜːt]
flood [flʌd]
florist's ['flɒrɪsts]
flour ['flaʊə]
flower ['flaʊə]
flu [fluː]
flung [flʌŋ]
fly [flaɪ]
foggy ['fɒgɪ]
foil [fɔɪl]
foodstuff ['fuːdstʌf]
football ['fʊtbɔːl]
forecast *BrE* ['fɔːkɑːst];
AmE ['fɔːkæst]
forefinger ['fɔːfɪŋgə]
forehead ['fɒrɪd also 'fɔːhed]
foreign ['fɒrən]
forestry ['fɒrɪstrɪ]
forgery ['fɔːdʒərɪ]
formal [fɔːml]
formality [,fɔː'mælətɪ]
fortunate ['fɔːtʃənət]
forward ['fɔːwəd]
foster ['fɒstə]
fought [fɔːt]
foul [faʊl]
fracture ['fræktʃə]
fraud [frɔːd]
free [friː]
freelance *BrE* ['friːlɑːns];
AmE ['friːlæns]
freestyle ['friːstaɪl]
freeze [friːz]
freshwater ['freʃwɔːtə]
fright [fraɪt]
frightening ['fraɪtnɪŋ]
fringe [frɪndʒ]
front [frʌnt]
frost [frɒst]
frozen ['frəʊzn]
fruit [fruːt]
frustration [frʌ'streɪʃn]
fry [fraɪ]
full [fʊl]
fume [fjuːm]
function ['fʌŋkʃn]
fundamental [,fʌndə'mentəl]
funds [fʌndz]
funny ['fʌnɪ]
fur [fɜː]
furnishings ['fɜːnɪʃɪŋz]
furniture ['fɜːnɪtʃə]
future ['fjuːtʃə]

gadget ['gædʒɪt]
gain [geɪn]
gale [geɪl]
gallery ['gælərɪ]
gambling ['gæmblɪŋ]
game [geɪm]
gangster ['gæŋstə]
garage *BrE* ['gærɑːʒ] or ['gærɪdʒ];
AmE [gə'rɑːʒ]
gardening ['gɑːdnɪŋ]
garlic ['gɑːlɪk]
garment ['gɑːment]
gas [gæs]
GCSE [,dʒiː siː es 'iː]
gear [gɪə]
gender ['dʒendə]
general ['dʒenrəl]
genes [dʒiːnz]
genitals ['dʒenɪtlz]
genius ['dʒiːnɪəs]
genre ['ʒɒnrə] or ['ʒɑːnrə]
genuine ['dʒenjʊɪn]
geographical [,dʒɪə'græfɪkl]
geography [dʒɪ'ɒgrəfɪ]
ghost [gəʊst]
gifted ['gɪftɪd]
girlfriend ['gɜːlfrend]
glamorous ['glæmərəs]
glasses ['glɑːsɪz]
gliding ['glaɪdɪŋ]
global ['gləʊbl]
gloves [glʌvz]
goalkeeper ['gəʊlkiːpə]
goalpost ['gəʊlpəʊst]
god [gɒd]
golf [gɒlf]
goose [guːs]
goulash ['guːlæʃ]
government ['gʌvənmənt]
governor ['gʌvənə]
gown [gaʊn]
graceful ['greɪsfl]
grade [greɪd]
graduate ['grædʒʊət] *n*
graduate ['grædʒʊeɪt] *v*
grammar ['græmə]
grandparent ['grændpeərənt]
grant [grɑːnt]
granulate ['grænjʊleɪt]
grape [greɪp]
greenbelt ['griːnbelt]
grey [greɪ]
gripe [graɪp]
grocer's ['grəʊsəz]
grocery ['grəʊsərɪ]
gross [grəʊs]
grown-up ['grəʊnʌp]
guard [gɑːd]
guest [gest]
guidance ['gaɪdəns]
guide [gaɪd]
guilty ['gɪltɪ]
gum [gʌm]
guru ['gʊruː]
gut [gʌt]
gym [dʒɪm]
gymnasium [dʒɪm'neɪzɪəm]
gymnastics [dʒɪm'næstɪks]

haberdasher's ['hæbədæʃəz]
hail [heɪl]
hairdresser ['heədresə]
hall [hɔːl]
ham [hæm]
hammer ['hæmə]
handball ['hændbɔːl]
handicapped ['hændɪkæpt]
handsome ['hænsəm]
handy ['hændɪ]
hang-gliding ['hæŋglaɪdɪŋ]
hardware ['hɑːdweə]
hardworking [,hɑːd'wɜːkɪŋ]
harmful ['hɑːmfl]
hatred ['heɪtrɪd]
haunt [hɔːnt]
hazard ['hæzəd]
hazardous ['hæzədəs]
haze [heɪz]
head [hed]
header ['hedə]
headline ['hedlaɪn]
heal [hiːl]
healthy ['helθɪ]
hearing ['hɪərɪŋ]
heart [hɑːt]
heartburn ['hɑːtbɜːn]
heatwave ['hiːtweɪv]
heavy ['hevɪ]
heel [hiːl]
height ['haɪt]
henpecked ['henpekt]
hero ['hɪərəʊ]
heroine ['herəʊɪn]
hiccup ['hɪkʌp]
high [haɪ]
highlight ['haɪlaɪt]
highway ['haɪweɪ]
hijack ['haɪdʒæk]
hike [haɪk]
hiking ['haɪkɪŋ]
Hindu [,hɪn'duː]
hire ['haɪə]
historical [hɪ'stɒrɪkl]
history ['hɪstrɪ]
hitch-hiking ['hɪtʃhaɪkɪŋ]
homelessness ['həʊmlɪsnəs]
honeymoon ['hʌnɪmuːn]
honour ['ɒnə]
hood [hʊd]
hook [hʊk]
hoover ['huːvə]
hopeless ['həʊpləs]
horn [hɔːn]
horrendous [hɒ'rendəs]
horror ['hɒrə]
horse [hɔːs]
horticulture ['hɔːtɪkʌltʃə]
hostel [hɒstl]
hotel [həʊ'tel]
household ['haʊshəʊld]
hubby ['hʌbɪ]
humanities [hjuː'mænətɪz]
humid ['hjuːmɪd]
humidity [hjuː'mɪdətɪ]
humorous ['hjuːmərəs]

hurdles [hɜːdlz]
hurt [hɜːt]
hypermarket ['haɪpəmɑːkɪt]
hypochondriac [ˌhaɪpə'kɒndrɪək]

ice hockey ['aɪshɒkɪ]
ignition [ɪg'nɪʃn]
illegal [ɪ'liːgl]
illness ['ɪlnɪs]
immaculate [ɪ'mækjʊlət]
immediately [ɪ'miːdɪətlɪ]
immigration [ˌɪmɪ'greɪʃn]
immodest [ɪ'mɒdɪst]
immune [ɪ'mjuːn]
immunise ['ɪmjʊnaɪz]
impact ['ɪmpækt]
implant *BrE* ['ɪmplɑːnt];
AmE ['ɪmplænt] *n*
imprisonment [ɪm'prɪznmənt]
improvements [ɪm'pruːvmənts]
impulsive [ɪm'pʌlsɪv]
inauguration [ɪˌnɔːgjə'reɪʃn]
include [ɪn'kluːd]
income ['ɪnkʌm]
increasing [ɪŋ'kriːsɪŋ]
incurable [ɪn'kjʊərəbl]
indicate ['ɪndɪkeɪt]
indigestion [ˌɪndɪ'dʒestʃən]
individual [ˌɪndɪ'vɪdʒʊəl]
indoor [ˌɪn'dɔː]
indulge [ɪn'dʌldʒ]
industrial [ɪn'dʌstrɪəl]
inequity [ɪ'nekwətɪ]
infection [ɪn'fekʃn]
infectious [ɪn'fekʃəs]
inflame [ɪn'fleɪm]
inflammation [ˌɪnflə'meɪʃn]
inflation [ɪn'fleɪʃn]
influence ['ɪnflʊəns]
informal [ɪn'fɔːml]
information [ˌɪnfə'meɪʃn]
ingredient [ɪn'griːdɪənt]
inhabitant [ɪn'hæbɪtənt]
injection [ɪn'dʒekʃn]
injure ['ɪndʒə]
in-laws ['ɪnlɔːz]
inner ['ɪnə]
innovative ['ɪnəʊveɪtɪv]
inquest ['ɪŋkwest]
inquiry *BrE* [ɪn'kwaɪərɪ];
AmE ['ɪŋkwərɪ]
insipid [ɪn'sɪpɪd]
insomnia [ɪn'sɒmnɪə]
inspector [ɪn'spektə]
inspiration [ˌɪnspɪ'reɪʃn]
install [ɪn'stɔːl]
instalment [ɪn'stɔːlmənt]
instant ['ɪnstənt]
instead [ɪn'sted]
instrument ['ɪnstrʊmənt]
insufficient [ˌɪnsə'fɪʃnt]
insulate ['ɪnsjʊleɪt]
insurance [ɪn'ʃʊərəns]
interest ['ɪntrəst]
interested ['ɪntrəstɪd]
interior [ɪn'tɪərɪə]
intermediate [ˌɪntə'miːdɪət]
international [ˌɪntə'næʃnəl]
interview ['ɪntəvjuː]
invalidity [ˌɪnvə'lɪdətɪ]
invasion [ɪn'veɪʒn]
investigation [ɪnˌvestɪ'geɪʃn]
iron ['aɪən]
irregular [ɪ'regjʊlə]
irreplaceable [ˌɪrɪ'pleɪsəbl]
issue ['ɪʃuː] or ['ɪsjuː]
item ['aɪtəm]

jacket ['dʒækɪt]
jail [dʒeɪl]
jam [dʒæm]
jar [dʒɑː]
javelin ['dʒævlɪn]
jaw [dʒɔː]
jazz [dʒæz]
jeans [dʒiːnz]
jersey ['dʒɜːzɪ]
jewel ['dʒuːəl]
Jewish ['dʒuːɪʃ]
job [dʒɒb]
jogging ['dʒɒgɪŋ]
join [dʒɔɪn]
joiner ['dʒɔɪnə]
joint [dʒɔɪnt]
journal ['dʒɜːnl]
journalist ['dʒɜːnəlɪst]
journey ['dʒɜːnɪ]
judge [dʒʌdʒ]
judgement ['dʒʌdʒmənt]
judo ['dʒuːdəʊ]
juice [dʒuːs]
jumper ['dʒʌmpə]
jumpy ['dʒʌmpɪ]
jury ['dʒʊərɪ]
just [dʒʌst]
juvenile ['dʒuːvənaɪl]

karate [kə'rɑːtɪ]
keen [kiːn]
kidnap ['kɪdnæp]
kidney ['kɪdnɪ]
kid [kɪd]
kindergarten ['kɪndəgɑːtn]
kitchen ['kɪtʃən]
kitchenware ['kɪtʃənweə]
knee [niː]
knickers ['nɪkəz]
knitted ['nɪtɪd]
knitting ['nɪtɪŋ]
knock [nɒk]
knockout ['nɒkaʊt]

labour ['leɪbə]
lace [leɪs]
ladies' wear ['leɪdɪz weə]
lake ['leɪk]
lamb [læm]
lame [leɪm]
lane [leɪn]
language ['læŋgwɪdʒ]
larder ['lɑːdə]
late ['leɪt]
latest ['leɪtɪst]
lavatory *BrE* ['lævətrɪ];
AmE ['lævətɔːrɪ]
lawn [lɔːn]
lawsuit ['lɔːsuːt]
lawyer ['lɔːjə]
layer ['leɪə]
lazy ['leɪzɪ]
leading ['liːdɪŋ]
league [liːg]
leak [liːk]
leasing ['liːsɪŋ]
leather ['leðə]
lecture ['lektʃə]
leggings ['legɪŋz]
leisure *BrE* ['leʒə]; *AmE* ['liːʒər]
lemon ['lemən]
length [leŋθ]
lenient ['liːnɪənt]
lesson [lesn]
lettuce ['letɪs]
libber ['lɪbə]
libel [laɪbl]
liberal ['lɪbrəl]
librarian [laɪ'breərɪən]
licence ['laɪsəns]
lightning ['laɪtnɪŋ]
likely ['laɪklɪ]
limbs [lɪmz]
linen ['lɪnɪn]
liquid ['lɪkwɪd]
liquidate ['lɪkwɪdeɪt]
listener ['lɪsnə]
literature ['lɪtrətʃə]
live broadcast [ˌlaɪv 'brɔːdkɑːst]
liver ['lɪvə]
loaf [ləʊf]
loan [ləʊn]
lobster ['lɒbstə]
local [ləʊkl]
located [ləʊ'keɪtɪd]
lodgings ['lɒdʒɪŋz]
loneliness ['ləʊnlɪnəs]
long [lɒŋ]
long-sighted [ˌlɒŋ 'saɪtɪd]
loo [luː]
loose [luːs]
lorry ['lɒrɪ]
lose [luːz]
lottery ['lɒtərɪ]
lounge ['laʊndʒ]
lovely ['lʌvlɪ]
low [ləʊ]
lower ['ləʊə]
ludicrous ['luːdɪkrəs]
luggage ['lʌgɪdʒ]
lump [lʌmp]
lungs [lʌŋz]
luxurious [lʌg'zjʊərɪəs] or [ləg'ʒʊərɪəs]
luxury ['lʌkʃərɪ]

MA [,em 'eɪ]
machine [mə'ʃi:n]
made-to-measure [,meɪdtə'meʒə]
Mafia ['mæfɪə]
magazine [,mægə'zi:n]
magistrate ['mædʒɪstreɪt]
maiden ['meɪdn]
mail [meɪl]
main [meɪn]
maintain [meɪn'teɪn]
maintenance ['meɪntənəns]
major ['meɪdʒə]
male [meɪl]
mall [mɔ:l]
malnutrition [,mælnju:'trɪʃn]
manage ['mænɪdʒ]
manageable ['mænɪdʒəbl]
management ['mænɪdʒmənt]
manager ['mænɪdʒə]
manual ['mænjʊəl]
marathon ['mærəθn]
marble ['mɑ:bl]
Margaret ['mɑ:grɪt]
margarine [,mɑ:dʒə'ri:n]
marital status [,mærɪtl 'steɪtəs]
mark [mɑ:k]
market ['mɑ:kɪt]
marmalade ['mɑ:məleɪd]
marriage ['mærɪdʒ]
married ['mærɪd]
marrow ['mærəʊ]
marry ['mærɪ]
martial arts [,mɑ:ʃl'ɑ:ts]
mass media [,mæs 'mi:dɪə]
mast [mɑ:st]
master ['mɑ:stə]
mat [mæt]
match [mætʃ]
material [mə'tɪərɪəl]
maternity [mə'tɜ:nətɪ]
mathematics [,mæθə'mætɪks]
maths [mæθs]
Matthias [mə'θaɪəs]
maximum ['mæksɪməm]
mayonnaise [,meɪə'neɪz]
measles ['mi:zlz]
meat [mi:t]
mechanic [mɪ'kænɪk]
mechanical [mɪ'kænɪkəl]
medal [medl]
medical ['medɪkl]
medication [,medɪ'keɪʃn]
medicine ['medsn]
medium ['mi:dɪəm]
Member of Parliament
[,membərəv 'pɑ:ləmənt]
memoirs ['memwɑ:z]
menial ['mi:nɪəl]
mentally ['mentəlɪ]
menu ['menju:]
mere [mɪə]
merely ['mɪəlɪ]
message ['mesɪdʒ]
metal [metl]
method ['meθəd]
metropolis [mə'trɒpəlɪs]
microwavable [,maɪkrə'weɪvəbl]
middle-aged ['mɪdleɪdʒd]
mild [maɪld]
milk [mɪlk]
millenary [mɪ'lenərɪ]
or ['mɪlɪnərɪ]
mince [mɪns]
minor ['maɪnə]
minority [maɪ'nɒrətɪ]
mirror ['mɪrə]
misery ['mɪzərɪ]
mistress ['mɪstrɪs]
mittens ['mɪtnz]
mixture ['mɪkstʃə]
model ['mɒdl]
moderation [,mɒdə'reɪʃn]
modernise ['mɒdənaɪz]
modest ['mɒdɪst]
moist [mɔɪst]
momentary ['məʊməntrɪ]
momentum [mə'mentəm]
monthly ['mʌnθlɪ]
monument ['mɒnjʊmənt]
moon [mu:n]
mop [mɒp]
moral ['mɒrəl]
moralise ['mɒrəlaɪz]
mortgage ['mɔ:gɪdʒ]
Moslem *BrE* ['mʊzlɪm];
AmE ['mʌzləm]
motel [məʊ'tel]
motor ['məʊtə]
mountaineering [,maʊntɪ'nɪərɪŋ]
moustache *BrE* [mə'stɑ:ʃ];
AmE ['mʌstæʃ]
mouth [maʊθ]
movement ['mu:vmənt]
movie-goer ['mu:vɪgəʊə]
mow [məʊ]
MSc [,em es 'si:]
mud [mʌd]
mugger ['mʌgə]
muggy ['mʌgɪ]
mumps [mʌmps]
murder ['mɜ:də]
murderess ['mɜ:dərɪs]
muscle ['mʌsl]
museum [mju:'zi:əm]
mushroom ['mʌʃru:m]
musical ['mju:zɪkl]
musician [mju:'zɪʃn]
Muslim *BrE* ['mʊzlɪm];
AmE ['mʌzləm]
mustard ['mʌstəd]
mutton ['mʌtn]
myth [mɪθ]

nail [neɪl]
naked ['neɪkɪd]
nap [næp]
nape [neɪp]
napkin ['næpkɪn]
nasty *BrE* ['nɑ:stɪ]; *AmE* ['næstɪ]
national ['næʃnəl]
native ['neɪtɪv]
natural ['nætʃrəl]
naturist ['neɪtʃərɪst]
naturopath ['neɪtʃrəpæθ]
naturopathy [,neɪtʃə'rɒpəθɪ]
nearby ['nɪəbaɪ]
necessary ['nesəsrɪ]
neck [nek]
necklace ['neklɪs]
needle [ni:dl]
negotiation [nɪ,gəʊʃɪ'eɪʃn]
neighbourhood ['neɪbəhʊd]
nephew ['nefju:]
nerve [nɜ:v]
nervous ['nɜ:vəs]
nevertheless [,nevəðə'les]
news [nju:z]
nice [naɪs]
nickname ['nɪkneɪm]
niece [ni:s]
night shift ['naɪt ʃɪft]
nightmare ['naɪtmeə]
noise [nɔɪz]
non-native [,nɒn 'neɪtɪv]
noodles ['nu:dlz]
nose [nəʊz]
nostril ['nɒstrɪlz]
notice ['nəʊtɪs]
novel [nɒvl]
novelist ['nɒvəlɪst]
nuclear ['nju:klɪə]
nude *BrE* [nju:d]; *AmE* [nu:d]
number ['nʌmbə]
nurse [nɜ:s]
nursery ['nɜ:sərɪ]
nutmeg ['nʌtmeg]
nutrient ['nju:trɪənt]
nutrition [nju:'trɪʃn]
nutritionist [nju:'trɪʃənɪst]
nutritious [nju:'trɪʃəs]
nylon ['naɪlɒn]

oar [ɔ:]
object ['ɒbdʒɪkt]
obtain [əb'teɪn]
occupation [,ɒkjʊ'peɪʃn]
occupy ['ɒkjʊpaɪ]
offence [ə'fens]
offend [ə'fend]
officially [ə'fɪʃəlɪ]
oil [ɔɪl]
ointment ['ɔɪntmənt]
Olympic [ə'lɪmpɪk]
onion ['ʌnɪən]
open-necked [,əʊpən 'nekt]
opera ['ɒprə]
operate ['ɒpəreɪt]
operation [,ɒpə'reɪʃn]
operator ['ɒpəreɪtə]
operetta [,ɒpə'retə]
opportunity [,ɒpə'tju:nətɪ]
optician [ɒp'tɪʃn]

optional ['ɒpʃənl]
oral ['ɔːrəl]
orange ['ɒrɪndʒ]
orchestra ['ɔːkɪstrə]
ordinary *BrE* ['ɔːdənrɪ]; *AmE* ['ɔːrdənerɪ]
organ ['ɔːgən]
organic [ɔː'gænɪk]
organisation *BrE* [,ɔːgənaɪ'zeɪʃn]; *AmE* [,ɔːgənɪ'zeɪʃn]
ornament ['ɔːnəmənt]
outbreak ['aʊtbreɪk]
outdoor [,aʊt'dɔː]
outfit ['aʊtfɪt]
outgoings [,aʊt'gəʊɪŋz]
outing ['aʊtɪŋ]
outrageous [aʊt'reɪdʒəs]
outskirts ['aʊtskɜːts]
oval ['əʊvl]
oven [ʌvn]
overall [,əʊvər'ɔːl]
overcast *BrE* [,əʊvə'kɑːst]; *AmE* [,əʊvər'kæst]
overcoat ['əʊvəkəʊt]
overcrowded [,əʊvə'kraʊdɪd]
overlook [,əʊvə'lʊk]
oversleep [,əʊvə'sliːp]
overtime ['əʊvətaɪm]
ozone ['əʊzəʊn]

package ['pækɪdʒ]
packet ['pækɪt]
paddle [pædl]
painful ['peɪnfl]
painter ['peɪntə]
pale ['peɪl]
palm [pɑːm]
pancake ['pæŋkeɪk]
panties ['pæntɪz]
pantihose ['pæntɪhəʊz]
pantry ['pæntrɪ]
pants [pænts]
paperback ['peɪpəbæk]
paprika *BrE*['pæprɪkə]; *AmE* [pə'priːkə]
parachuting ['pærəʃuːtɪŋ]
para-gliding ['pærəglaɪdɪŋ]
parent ['peərənt]
parliament ['pɑːləmənt]
parsley ['pɑːslɪ]
parsnip ['pɑːsnɪp]
participant [pɑː'tɪsɪpənt]
particular [pə'tɪkjʊlə]
part-time [,pɑːt'taɪm]
party ['pɑːtɪ]
pass *BrE* [pɑːs]; *AmE* [pæs]
passage ['pæsɪdʒ]
passenger ['pæsɪndʒə]
passive ['pæsɪv]
passport *BrE* ['pɑːspɔːt]; *AmE* ['pæspɔːrt]
pasta *BrE* ['pæstə]; *AmE* ['pɑːstə]
pastime *BrE* ['pɑːstaɪm]; *AmE* ['pæstaɪm]
patient ['peɪʃənt]
patio ['pætɪəʊ]
patterned ['pætnd]
pavement ['peɪvmənt]
payment ['peɪmənt]
pay-rise ['peɪraɪz]
PE [,piː'iː]
peace [piːs]
peach [piːʧ]
peanut ['piːnʌt]
pear [peə]
peas [piːz]
pedestrian [pɪ'destrɪən]
peel [piːl]
peer [pɪə]
penalty ['penltɪ]
pension ['penʃən]
pensioner ['penʃənə]
pentathlon [pen'tæθlən]
people ['piːpl]
pepper ['pepə]
per cent [pə'sent]
percentage [pə'sentɪdʒ]
performance [pə'fɔːməns]
perks [pɜːks]
permanent ['pɜːmənənt]
personal ['pɜːsnl]
petrol ['petrəl]
PhD [,piː eɪʧ 'diː]
phenomenon [fə'nɒmɪnən]
philosophy [fə'lɒsəfɪ]
phobia ['fəʊbɪə]
phobic ['fəʊbɪk]
phone card ['fəʊn kɑːd]
photograph *BrE* ['fəʊtəʊgrɑːf]; *AmE* ['fəʊtəʊgræf]
photographer [fə'tɒgrəfə]
phrase [freɪz]
physical ['fɪzɪkl]
physically ['fɪzɪklɪ]
physician [fɪ'zɪʃn]
physics ['fɪzɪks]
pickled ['pɪkld]
picture ['pɪkʧə]
piece [piːs]
pike [paɪk]
pilot ['paɪlət]
pimple [pɪmpl]
pinch [pɪnʧ]
pineapple ['paɪnæpl]
ping-pong ['pɪŋpɒŋ]
piste [piːst]
pitch [pɪʧ]
placebo [plə'siːbəʊ]
plaid [plæd]
plain [pleɪn]
plaintiff ['pleɪntɪf]
plan [plæn]
plaque *BrE* [plɑːk]; *AmE* [plæk]
plaster *BrE* ['plɑːstə]; *AmE* ['plæstə]
plastic ['plæstɪk]
plate [pleɪt]
platform ['plætfɔːm]
playwright ['pleɪraɪt]
plead [pliːd]
pleated ['pliːtɪd]
plimsolls ['plɪmslz]
plot [plɒt]
plough [plaʊ]
plum [plʌm]
plumber ['plʌmə]
plump [plʌmp]
plunge [plʌndʒ]
pneumonia [njuː'məʊnɪə]
pocket ['pɒkɪt]
poem ['pəʊɪm]
poet ['pəʊɪt]
poetry ['pəʊɪtrɪ]
poison ['pɔɪzn]
poisonous ['pɔɪzənəs]
pole vault ['pəʊlvɔːlt]
police [pə'liːs]
policeman [pə'liːsmən]
policy ['pɒləsɪ]
polite [pə'laɪt]
politician [,pɒlɪ'tɪʃn]
politics ['pɒlətɪks]
pollution [pə'luːʃn]
ponytail ['pəʊniː teɪl]
pool [puːl]
poor [pʊə] or [pɔː]
Pope [pəʊp]
popular ['pɒpjʊlə]
population [,pɒpjʊ'leɪʃn]
pork [pɔːk]
position [pə'zɪʃn]
post [pəʊst]
poster ['pəʊstə]
postgraduate [,pəʊst'grædʒʊət]
postman ['pəʊstmən]
potato [pə'teɪtəʊ]
poultry ['pəʊltrɪ]
pour [pɔː]
poverty ['pɒvətɪ]
powder ['paʊdə]
power ['paʊə]
practice ['præktɪs]
practitioner [præk'tɪʃənə]
praise [preɪz]
pray [preɪ]
preach [priːʧ]
predict [prɪ'dɪkt]
prediction [prɪ'dɪkʃn]
predominant [prɪ'dɒmɪnənt]
prefer [prɪ'fɜː]
pregnancy ['pregnənsɪ]
pregnant ['pregnənt]
prepare [prɪ'peə]
prescribe [prɪ'skraɪb]
prescription [prɪ'skrɪpʃn]
preserve [prɪ'zɜːv]
preside [prɪ'zaɪd]
presidency ['prezɪdənsɪ]
president ['prezɪdənt]
presidential [,prezɪ'denʃl]
pressure ['preʃə]
pretty ['prɪtɪ]

prevent [prɪ'vent]
prevention [prɪ'venʃn]
prey [preɪ]
price [praɪs]
priest [pri:st]
primary ['praɪmərɪ]
Prime Minister [,praɪm 'mɪnɪstə]
prison [prɪzn]
private ['praɪvɪt]
privilege ['prɪvəlɪdʒ]
prize [praɪz]
processed [prəʊ'sest]
product ['prɒdʌkt]
production [prə'dʌkʃn]
profession [prə'feʃn]
professional [prə'feʃnl]
prolong [prəʊ'lɒŋ]
promot [prə'məʊt]
promotion [prə'məʊʃn]
proper ['prɒpə]
property ['prɒpətɪ]
proportion [prə'pɔ:ʃn]
prose [prəʊz]
prosecute ['prɒsɪkju:t]
prosecution [,prɒsɪ'kju:ʃn]
prospect ['prɒspekt] *n*
prospect [prə'spekt] *v*
prostitution [,prɒstɪ'tju:ʃn]
protection [prə'tekʃn]
Protestant ['prɒtɪstənt]
prove [pru:v]
provide [prə'vaɪd]
psychiatrist [saɪ'kaɪətrɪst]
psychologist [saɪ'kɒlədʒɪst]
public ['pʌblɪk]
publish ['pʌblɪʃ]
puke [pju:k]
pullover ['pʊləʊvə]
pulse [pʌlz]
punch [pʌntʃ]
punish ['pʌnɪʃ]
punishment ['pʌnɪʃmənt]
purchase ['pɜ:tʃəs]
purport ['pɜ:pət] *n*
purport [pə'pɔ:t] *v*
purpose ['pɜ:pəs]
pursuit [pə'sju:t]
pyjamas [pə'dʒɑ:məz]

qualifications [,kwɒlɪfɪ'keɪʃənz]
qualify ['kwɒlɪfaɪ]
quality ['kwɒlətɪ]
question ['kwestʃən]
quit [kwɪt]
quiz [kwɪz]

race [reɪs]
racing ['reɪsɪŋ]
racket ['rækɪt]
racketeering [,rækə'tɪərɪŋ]
radio ['reɪdɪəʊ]
radioactive [,reɪdɪəʊ'æktɪv]
radish ['rædɪʃ]
raindrop ['reɪndrɒp]
raise [reɪz]
range [reɪndʒ]
rape [reɪp]
rash [ræʃ]
raspberry ['rɑ:zbrɪ]
rated ['reɪtɪd]
rather *BrE* ['rɑ:ðə]; *AmE* ['ræðər]
ratings ['reɪtɪŋz]
raw [rɔ:]
RE [,ɑ:r'i:]
ready ['redɪ]
rear [rɪə]
reason ['ri:zn]
reasonable ['ri:zənəbl]
receipt [rɪ'si:t]
receive [rɪ'si:v]
reception [rɪ'sepʃn]
recline [rɪ'klaɪn]
recognise ['rekəgnaɪz]
record ['rekɔ:d]
record player ['rekɔ:d pleɪə]
recover [rɪ'kʌvə]
recovery [rɪ'kʌvərɪ]
recycle [,ri:'saɪkl]
reduce [rɪ'dju:s]
reduction [rɪ'dʌkʃn]
redundancy [rɪ'dʌndənsɪ]
redundant [rɪ'dʌndənt]
referee [,refə'ri:]
reference ['refərəns]
refugee [,refjʊ'dʒi:]
refuse ['refju:s] *n*
refuse [rɪ'fju:z] *v*
regrettably [rɪ'gretəblɪ]
regular ['regjʊlə]
rehearse [rɪ'hɜ:s]
reinforce [,ri:ɪn'fɔ:s]
reject [rɪ'dʒekt]
relation [rɪ'leɪʃn]
relative ['relətɪv]
relaxed [rɪ'lækst]
relay ['ri:leɪ] *n*
release [rɪ'li:s]
relic ['relɪk]
religion [rɪ'lɪdʒən]
religious [rɪ'lɪdʒəs]
rely [rɪ'laɪ]
renew [rɪ'nju:]
repair [rɪ'peə]
repeat [rɪ'pi:t]
replacement [rɪ'pleɪsmənt]
report [rɪ'pɔ:t]
require [rɪ'kwaɪə]
requirements [rɪ'kwaɪəmənts]
research [rɪ'sɜ:tʃ]
resemble [rɪ'zembl]
reservation [,rezə'veɪʃn]
reserve [rɪ'zɜ:v]
resolve [rɪ'zɒlv]
resort [rɪ'zɔ:t]
restaurant ['restərɒnt]
result [rɪ'zʌlt]
retire [rɪ'taɪə]
retirement [rɪ'taɪəmənt]
retrain [,ri:'treɪn]
return [rɪ'tɜ:n]
reveal [rɪ'vi:l]
revenge [rɪ'vendʒ]
reverse [rɪ'vɜ:s]
revival [rɪ'vaɪvl]
rheumatism ['ru:mətɪzm]
rice [raɪs]
ride [raɪd]
ridiculous [rɪ'dɪkjʊləs]
rifle [raɪfl]
right [raɪt]
ring [rɪŋ]
rink [rɪŋk]
riot ['raɪət]
riotous ['raɪətəs]
roast [rəʊst]
roasting ['rəʊstɪŋ]
robbery ['rɒbərɪ]
robe [rəʊb]
rod [rɒd]
roller-blading ['rəʊləbleɪdɪŋ]
roller-skating ['rəʊləskeɪtɪŋ]
Roman Catholic [,rəʊmən 'kæθlɪk]
romance [rəʊ'mæns]
rotten ['rɒtən]
round [raʊnd]
routine [ru:'ti:n]
roux [ru:]
rowing ['rəʊɪŋ]
Royal Palace [,rɔɪəl 'pælɪs]
rubber ['rʌbə]
rubbish ['rʌbɪʃ]
ruby ['ru:bɪ]
rucksack ['rʌksæk]
rudely ['ru:dlɪ]
rug [rʌg]
rugby ['rʌgbɪ]
rugger ['rʌgə]
rule [ru:l]
runny ['rʌnɪ]
rush [rʌʃ]

sabre ['seɪbə]
sack [sæk]
safety ['seɪftɪ]
sailing ['seɪlɪŋ]
salad ['sæləd]
salami [sə'lɑ:mɪ]
salary ['sælərɪ]
sale [seɪl]
salmon ['sæmən]
salt [sɔ:lt]
sandals ['sændlz]
satellite ['sætəlaɪt]
satin ['sætɪn]
satisfaction [sætɪs'fækʃn]
satisfactory [,sætɪs'fæktərɪ]
sausage ['sɒsɪdʒ]
saving ['seɪvɪŋ]
scapegoat ['skeɪpgəʊt]
scar [skɑ:]
scare [skeə]
scarecrow ['skeəkrəʊ]

scarf [skɑ:f]
scarlet ['skɑ:lət]
scarred [skɑ:d]
schedule *BrE* ['ʃedju:l];
AmE ['skedʒu:l]
school leaver [,sku:l 'li:ve]
science ['saɪəns]
scientific [,saɪən'tɪfɪk]
scientist ['saɪəntɪst]
sci-fi [,saɪ'faɪ]
scoop [sku:p]
scooter ['sku:tə]
scorching ['skɔ:tʃɪŋ]
score [skɔ:]
scrape [skreɪp]
screen [skri:n]
scrub [skrʌb]
scuba diving ['sku:bədaɪvɪŋ]
seamstress ['semstrɪs]
seat [si:t]
secondary ['sekəndrɪ]
secretary ['sekrətrɪ]
sect [sekt]
sector ['sektə]
security [sɪ'kjʊərətɪ]
sedative ['sedətɪv]
seek [si:k]
seize [si:z]
semester [sɪ'mestə]
semi-detached [,semɪ dɪ'tætʃt]
seminar ['semɪnɑ:]
sensational [sen'seɪʃənl]
sensitive ['sensətɪv]
sensitivity [,sensə'tɪvətɪ]
sentence ['sentəns]
separate ['sepəreɪt]
serial ['sɪərɪəl]
series ['sɪəri:z]
serious ['sɪərɪəs]
service ['sɜ:vɪs]
session ['seʃən]
settee [se'ti:]
settle [setl]
sew [səʊ]
sexism ['seksɪzəm]
shabbily ['ʃæbɪlɪ]
shag [ʃæg]
shake [ʃeɪk]
shame [ʃeɪm]
shame-facedly [ʃeɪm'feɪstlɪ]
shameful ['ʃeɪmfl]
shameless ['ʃeɪmləs]
shape [ʃeɪp]
share [ʃeə]
sharp [ʃɑ:p]
shave [ʃeɪv]
sherry [ʃerɪ]
shirt [ʃɜ:t]
shivery ['ʃɪvərɪ]
shoelace ['ʃu:leɪs]
shoot [ʃu:t]
shoplifting ['ʃɒplɪftɪŋ]
shortage ['ʃɔ:tɪdʒ]
shorts [ʃɔ:ts]
shot [ʃɒt]
shot put ['ʃɒtpʊt]
shoulder ['ʃəʊldə]
shower ['ʃaʊə]
shuttlecock ['ʃʌtlkɒk]
sickness ['sɪknɪs]
side [saɪd]
sigh [saɪ]
sights ['saɪts]
sign [saɪn]
signature ['sɪgnətʃə]
silicone ['sɪlɪkən]
silver ['sɪlvə]
simultaneous *BrE* [,sɪməl'teɪnɪəs];
AmE [,saɪməl'teɪnɪəs]
single [sɪŋgl]
sister ['sɪstə]
site [saɪt]
situated ['sɪtʃʊeɪtɪd]
situation [,sɪtʃʊ'eɪʃn]
sixth ['sɪksθ]
size [saɪz]
skateboarding ['skeɪtbɔ:dɪŋ]
skating ['skeɪtɪŋ]
skiing ['ski:ɪŋ]
skijump ['ski:dʒʌmp]
skilled [skɪld]
skimpy ['skɪmpɪ]
skinny ['skɪnɪ]
skip [skɪp]
skirt [skɜ:t]
skull [skʌl]
sky [skaɪ]
slacks [slæks]
slap [slæp]
slaughter ['slɔ:tə]
sledging ['sledʒɪŋ]
sleek [sli:k]
sleet [sli:t]
sleeveless ['sli:vləs]
slight [slaɪt]
slip of the tongue [,slɪpəvðə 'tʌŋ]
slippers ['slɪpəz]
slippery ['slɪpərɪ]
slush [slʌʃ]
smack [smæk]
smartly ['smɑ:tlɪ]
smog [smɒg]
sneak [sni:k]
sneakers ['sni:kəz]
sneeze [sni:z]
snooker ['snu:kə]
snooze [snu:z]
snowboarding ['snəʊbɔ:dɪŋ]
snub [snʌb]
soak [səʊk]
soap opera ['səʊp ɒprə]
soccer ['sɒkə]
social [səʊʃl]
Socialist ['səʊʃəlɪst]
society [sə'saɪətɪ]
socks [sɒks]
soda ['səʊdə]
sofa ['səʊfə]
soft [sɒft]
sole [səʊl]
solicitor [sə'lɪsɪtə]
solitary ['sɒlɪtrɪ]
soloist ['səʊləʊɪst]
solution [sə'lu:ʃn]
something ['sʌmθɪŋ]
son [sʌn]
sore [sɔ:]
sorrel ['sɒrəl]
sought [sɔ:t]
sound [saʊnd]
sour [saʊə]
souvenir [,su:və'nɪə]
spare time ['speə taɪm]
spark [spɑ:k]
sparkle [spɑ:kl]
sparkling ['spɑ:klɪŋ]
special ['speʃl]
specialise ['speʃəlaɪz]
specialist ['speʃəlɪst]
specific [spə'sɪfɪk]
spectator [spek'teɪtə]
speed boating ['spi:dbəʊtɪŋ]
spice [spaɪs]
spinach ['spɪnɪdʒ]
spine [spaɪn]
spirit ['spɪrɪt]
split [splɪt]
spokesman ['spəʊksmən]
sponge [spʌndʒ]
spouse ['spaʊs]
sprain [spreɪn]
sprint [sprɪnt]
square meter [,skweə 'mi:tə]
squash [skwɒʃ]
squatter [skwɒtə]
squeeze [skwi:z]
stab [stæb]
stable [steɪbl]
stadium ['steɪdɪəm]
staff [stɑ:f]
stage [steɪdʒ]
stainless ['steɪnləs]
stalls [stɔ:lz]
stammer ['stæmə]
stamp [stæmp]
stand [stænd]
standard ['stændəd]
starch [stɑ:tʃ]
starter ['stɑ:tə]
station ['steɪʃn]
stationer's ['steɪʃnəz]
statue ['stætʃu:]
steal [sti:l]
steel [sti:l]
steer [stɪə]
step father ['step fɑ:ðə]
step mother ['step mʌðə]
stereo ['sterɪəʊ]
stew [stju:]
sticky ['stɪkɪ]
stimulate ['stɪmjʊleɪt]
stockings ['stɒkɪŋz]

stomach ['stʌmək]
store [stɔ:]
storey ['stɔ:rı]
straight [streıt]
strain [streın]
strangle ['stræŋgl]
strap [stræp]
strapped [stræpt]
strawberry ['strɔ:brı]
stretcher ['stretʃə]
strict [strıkt]
striped ['straıpt]
stroke [strəʊk]
structure ['strʌktʃə]
stuck [stʌk]
study ['stʌdı]
stuffed [stʌft]
stupid *BrE* ['stju:pıd]; *AmE* ['stu:pıd]
sty [staı]
style [staıl]
subject ['sʌbdʒekt]
subscribe [səb'skraıb]
substance ['sʌbstəns]
subtitle ['sʌbtaıtl]
suburb ['sʌbɜ:b]
suburban [sə'bɜ:bən]
subway ['sʌbweı]
succeed [sək'si:d]
successful [sək'sesfl]
sudden ['sʌdn]
suddenly ['sʌdnlı]
sue *BrE* [sju:]; *AmE* [su:]
suffer ['sʌfə]
suffocate ['sʌfəkeıt]
sugar ['ʃʊgə]
suit [su:t]
suite [swi:t]
sultry ['sʌltrı]
summer ['sʌmə]
sunbathing ['sʌnbeıðıŋ]
suntan ['sʌntæn]
sunny ['sʌnı]
supermarket ['su:pəma:kıt]
supervise ['su:pəvaız]
supervision [,su:pə'vıʒn]
supervisor ['su:pəvaızə]
supply [sə'plaı]
support [sə'pɔ:t]
supporter [sə'pɔ:tə]
surface ['sɜ:fıs]
surfing ['sɜ:fıŋ]
surgeon ['sɜ:dʒən]
surgery ['sɜ:dʒərı]
surpass *BrE* [sə'pa:s]; *AmE* [sər'pæs]
surprise [sə'praız]
surrounding [sə'raʊndıŋ]
susceptible [sə'septıbl]
suspect ['sʌspekt] *n*
suspect [sə'spekt] *v*
suspicion [sə'spıʃn]
suspicious [sə'spıʃəs]
sweater ['swetə]
sweep [swi:p]
sweet [swi:t]
sweetener ['swi:tnə]
swell [swel]
swelter ['sweltə]
swimming ['swımıŋ]
swimsuit ['swımsu:t]
swindle [swındl]
switch [swıtʃ]
swollen ['swəʊlən]
swot [swɒt]
syllabus ['sıləbəs]
symptom ['sım(p)təm]
syndrome ['sındrəʊm]
synthetic [sın'θetık]
syringe [sı'rındʒ]
system ['sıstəm]

table tennis ['teıbltenıs]
tablet ['tæblıt]
tabloid ['tæblɔıd]
tag [tæg]
tailor ['teılə]
talented ['tæləntıd]
tan [tæn]
tape [teıp]
tartan ['ta:tn]
tax [tæks]
taxi driver ['tæksı draıvə]
team [ti:m]
technical ['teknıkl]
techno ['teknəʊ]
technology [tek'nɒlədʒı]
teenager ['ti:neıdʒə]
teeth [ti:θ]
telly ['telı]
temperate ['tempərət]
temperature ['temprətʃə]
temple ['templ]
temporary ['temprərı]
tenant ['tenənt]
tennis ['tenıs]
term [tɜ:m]
terminal ['tɜ:mınl]
terminus ['tɜ:mınəs]
terraced house ['terəst haʊs]
terrible ['terəbl]
terrify ['terıfaı]
terror ['terə]
terrorise ['terəraız]
terrorism ['terərızəm]
terrorist ['terərıst]
testify ['testıfaı]
textbook ['teks(t)bʊk]
thaw [θɔ:]
theatre ['θıətə]
theft [θeft]
therapy ['θerəpı]
thermometer [θə'mɒmıtə]
theses ['θi:si:z]
thesis ['θi:sıs]
thick [θık]
thief [θi:f]
thigh [θaı]
thin [θın]
thinning ['θınıŋ]
thoroughly ['θʌrəlı]
threatening ['θretənıŋ]
three-piece suite [,θri: pi:s 'swi:t]
thriller ['θrılə]
throat [θrəʊt]
through [θru:]
throw [θrəʊ]
thug [θʌg]
thumb [θʌm]
thunderstorm ['θʌndəstɔ:m]
tidy ['taıdı]
tie [taı]
tighten ['taıtn]
tights [taıts]
tile stove ['taıl stəʊv]
timetable ['taımteıbl]
tinned [tınd]
tissue ['tıʃu:]
title [taıtl]
tobacconist's [tə'bækənısts]
tobogganing [tə'bɒgənıŋ]
toddler ['tɒdlə]
toe [təʊ]
tongue [tʌŋ]
tonsils ['tɒnslz]
tooth [tu:θ]
toothache ['tu:θeık]
tough [tʌf]
tourism ['tʊərızm]
tourist ['tʊərıst]
tow [təʊ]
towards *BrE* [tə'wɔ:dz]; *AmE* [tɔ:rdz]
towel rack ['taʊəl ræk]
toy [tɔı]
trace [treıs]
track and field [,trækən'fi:ld]
track suit ['træksu:t]
trade ['treıd]
traffic ['træfık]
tragedy ['trædʒədı]
trainers ['treınəz]
tranquilliser ['træŋkwılaızə]
Transdanubia [,trænzdə'nu:bıə]
transit ['trænzıt]
transparent [træn'spærənt]
transport ['trænspɔ:t] *n*
transport [træns'pɔ:t] *v*
treat [tri:t]
treatment ['tri:tmənt]
tremulous ['tremjʊləs]
trendy ['trendı]
trial ['traıəl]
triple [trıpl]
trolley ['trɒlı]
trouble ['trʌbl]
trousers ['traʊzəz]
trout [traʊt]
truant ['tru:ənt]
trunk [trʌŋk]
trusty ['trʌstı]
T-shirt ['ti: ʃɜ:t]

tube [tju:b]
tuition [tjʊ'ɪʃn]
tummy ['tʌmɪ]
tunnel ['tʌnl]
turkey ['tɜ:kɪ]
turner ['tɜ:nə]
turnpike ['tɜ:npaɪk]
turn-ups ['tɜ:nʌps]
turtle ['tɜ:tl]
tuxedo [tʌk'si:dəʊ]
tweed [twi:d]
twenties ['twentɪz]
twin [twɪn]
type [taɪp]
tyre ['taɪə]

ugly ['ʌglɪ]
ulcer ['ʌlsə]
umpire ['ʌmpaɪə]
unbearable [ʌn'beərəbl]
uncle ['ʌŋkl]
unconscious [ʌn'kɒnʃəs]
undergraduate [,ʌndə'grædʒʊət]
underground ['ʌndəgraʊnd]
underpaid [,ʌndə'peɪd]
underwear ['ʌndəweə]
undies ['ʌndɪz]
undo [ʌn'du:]
undress [ʌn'dres]
unemployed [,ʌnɪm'plɔɪd]
unemployment [,ʌnɪm'plɔɪmənt]
unfair [,ʌn'feə]
unification [,ju:nɪfɪ'keɪʃn]
uniform ['ju:nɪfɔ:m]
union ['ju:nɪən]
universe ['ju:nɪvɜ:s]
university [,ju:nɪ'vɜ:sətɪ]
unleaded [,ʌn'ledɪd]
unmarried [,ʌn'mærɪd]
unpleasant [ʌn'pleznt]
unpredictable [,ʌnprɪ'dɪktəbl]
unreasonable [ʌn'ri:znəbl]
unrecognisable [ʌn'rekəgnaɪzəbl]
unskilled [,ʌn'skɪld]
unusually [ʌn'ju:ʒʊəlɪ]
unwilling [ʌn'wɪlɪŋ]
unyielding [,ʌn'ji:ldɪŋ]
upper ['ʌpə]
upset ['ʌpset] *n*
upset [ʌp'set] *v*
upstairs [,ʌp'steəz]
urban ['ɜ:bən]

vacancy ['veɪkənsɪ]
vacation [və'keɪʃn]
vacuum cleaner ['vækjʊəm kli:nə]
value ['vælju:]
van [væn]
vapour ['veɪpə]
variety [və'raɪətɪ]
vary ['veərɪ]
vase *BrE* [vɑ:z]; *AmE* [veɪs]
VAT [,vi:eɪ'ti:]
VCR [,vi:si:'ɑ:]
veal [vi:l]
veg [vedʒ]
vegan ['vi:gən]
vegetable ['vedʒtəbl]
vegetarian [,vedʒə'teərɪən]
veggie ['vedʒɪ]
vehicle ['vi:ɪkl]
vein [veɪn]
Velcro-fastener ['velkrəʊ fɑ:snə]
velvet ['velvɪt]
vessel ['vesl]
vest [vest]
vet [vet]
veterinarian [,vetərɪ'neərɪən]
veterinary ['vetrənərɪ]
victim ['vɪktɪm]
Viennese [,vi:ə'ni:z]
viewer ['vju:ə]
vinegar ['vɪnɪgə]
violence ['vaɪələns]
violent ['vaɪələnt]
virtually ['vɜ:tʃʊəlɪ]
virus ['vaɪrəs]
visa ['vi:zə]
vise [vaɪs]
vitamin *BrE* ['vɪtəmɪn];
AmE ['vaɪtəmɪn]
vocation [vəʊ'keɪʃn]
vocational [vəʊ'keɪʃənl]
voice [vɔɪs]
volcanic [vɒl'kænɪk]
volleyball ['vɒlɪbɔ:l]
volume ['vɒlju:m]
vomit ['vɒmɪt]
vote [vəʊt]
voucher ['vaʊtʃə]
vow [vaʊ]

wage [weɪdʒ]
waistcoat *BrE* ['weɪskəʊt];
AmE ['weskət]
waiter ['weɪtə]
waitress ['weɪtrɪs]
walkie-talkie [,wɔ:kɪ 'tɔ:kɪ]
wall-to-wall [,wɔ:ltə'wɔ:l]
wall-to-wall carpet [,wɔ:ltəwɔ:l'kɑ:pɪt]
wall units ['wɔ:l ju:nɪts]
walnut ['wɔ:lnʌt]
waltz [wɔ:ls]
ward [wɔ:d]
wardrobe ['wɔ:drəʊb]
warn [wɔ:n]
wart [wɔ:t]
waste [weɪst]
water ['wɔ:tə]
water polo ['wɔ:təpəʊləʊ]
watermelon ['wɔ:təmelən]
water-skiing ['wɔ:təski:ɪŋ]
wavy ['weɪvɪ]
way [weɪ]
weak [wi:k]
wealth [welθ]
weapon ['wepən]
wear [weə]
weather ['weðə]
wedding ['wedɪŋ]
weekday ['wi:kdeɪ]
weekly ['wi:klɪ]
weightlifting ['weɪtlɪftɪŋ]
well-built [,wel 'bɪlt]
wellies ['welɪz]
wellingtons ['welɪŋtənz]
wheel [wi:l]
whimsical ['wɪmzɪkl]
whipped [wɪpt]
whodunit [,hu:'dʌnɪt]
whole [həʊl]
whooping cough ['hu:pɪŋ kɒf]
wide [waɪd]
widow ['wɪdəʊ]
widower ['wɪdəʊə]
willing ['wɪlɪŋ]
windscreen ['wɪndskri:n]
windshield ['wɪndʃi:ld]
windsurfing ['wɪndsɜ:fɪŋ]
windy ['wɪndɪ]
wine [waɪn]
wing [wɪŋ]
winter ['wɪntə]
within [wɪð'ɪn]
witness ['wɪtnɪs]
womb [wu:m]
women ['wɪmɪn]
won [wʌn]
wool [wʊl]
woollen ['wʊlən]
workout ['wɜ:kaʊt]
world [wɜ:ld]
worry *BrE* ['wʌrɪ]; *AmE* ['wɜ:rɪ]
worthwhile [,wɜ:θ'waɪl]
wound [wu:nd]
wreck [rek]
wrestling ['restlɪŋ]
wrist [rɪst]
writer ['raɪtə]
written ['rɪtn]

X-ray *BrE* [,eks'reɪ];
AmE ['eksreɪ]

yachting ['jɒtɪŋ]
yellow ['jeləʊ]
yoghurt *BrE* ['jɒgət];
AmE ['jəʊgərt]
youth ['ju:θ]

zealot ['zelət]
zealous ['zeləs]
zero ['zɪərəʊ]
zip [zɪp]
zone [zəʊn]

ACKNOWLEDGEMENTS

The Publisher and the author would like to thank the following for their kind permission to use articles and extracts from copyright material:

(Recipe) (Untitled)© AP • *70,000 in Moon's Mass Wedding*© The Mail on Sunday • *A Brooklyn man ...*© Reuters • *A Life In The Day Of George Brumwell Jameson*© The Sunday Times • *A youthful image of Europe*© Europa Times • *All I Want for Christmas Is an Underwater Joy* Ride© New York Newsday • *Breaking and entertaining*© Europa Times • *Case Closed*© The Glasgow Mirror • *Cellars in the Sky*© Daily News • *Clean Getaway*© Guardian International • *Do the shuffle*© WWN • *English Weather* (from: *The Xenophobe's Guide to the English* by Antony Miall) published by Ravette Books Ltd.© Oval Projects Ltd. • *Forget your manners if you're getting mugged* (Letter to the Editor)© The Budapest Sun • *Genius at Work*© Woman's Day • *Great Food Myths*© Woman • *Health Advice You Can't Trust*© Woman's Day • *Homework Can Have Harmful Effects*© The Independent • *I Bought Myself a New Body*© Best • *It's a riot*© AFP • *Judge paddles his own canoe to court*© The Times • *Modest Mary*© Sunday Mirror • *New York strapped for cash*© The Daily Telegraph • *Not so easy to love thy neighbour*© The European • *Pig Tales*© USA Today • *Ratings drop*© The Times of India • *Scarecop*© Daily News • *Sticky Situation*© Periodico Extramadura • *Subway? No way!*© *New York Newsday* • *Swimsuit man must face trial*© The Times • *Take a Ticket to the Moon*© *Observer Colour Magazine* • *Talk show in the nude*© Daily News • *The Big Game* (from: *The Xenophobe's Guide to the Americans* by Stephanie Faul) published by Ravette Books Ltd.© Oval Projects Ltd. • *The Nude Mr Mop*© News Group Newspapers • *This dead parrot is difunto*© Guardian Weekly • *You can't blame it on the box*© The Times

The Publisher and the author would also like to thank the following for their permission to reproduce photographs:

London Smog© UPI/Corbis-Bettmann
On a commuter train to Stamford (by CARL MYDANS) © The Time Inc. Magazine Company

Every effort has been made to trace the owners of copyright materials in this book, but we should be pleased to hear from any copyright owner whom we have been unable to contact in order to rectify any errors or omissions.

A Kiadó és a szerző szeretne továbbá köszönetet mondani az alábbi fotósoknak, ill. fotó-jogtulajdonosoknak műveik felhasználásának engedélyezéséért:

DARABOS GYÖRGY (Lakáskultúra)
MAGYAR TÁVIRATI IRODA
POSTABANK
STEFFLER BALÁZS (Reform)
SZÉKELY PÉTER (Lakáskultúra)
SZIGETI TAMÁS (Magyar Hírlap)
TÖRÖK GYÖRGY

Akadémiai Kiadó Rt.
Budapest, 1998
A kiadásért felel: dr. Sós Péter János ügyvezető igazgató
Felelős szerkesztő: Vincze Katalin
DTP: graphoman
Borítóterv: Gyárfás Gábor, Prim-Art Design Stúdió
Kiadványszám: NY-N-7-008
Szerkesztő: Horváth Balázs
Műszaki szerkesztő: Neményi Ildikó
Nyomtatta: Regia Rex Nyomda Kft., Székesfehérvár (22/328-505)